Originally published as
YALE HISTORICAL PUBLICATIONS
MISCELLANY XXXVI

THE SECOND DUMA

A STUDY OF
THE SOCIAL-DEMOCRATIC PARTY
AND
THE RUSSIAN CONSTITUTIONAL
EXPERIMENT

BY

ALFRED LEVIN

SECOND EDITION

ARCHON BOOKS
HAMDEN, CONNECTICUT
1966

Library of Congress Catalog Card Number: 66-13342
Printed in The United States of America

TO
MY FATHER
AND
MY MOTHER

PREFACE

IN the broad sweep of events in Russia during the first two decades of the present century, from revolution to revolution, the Imperial Duma played a highly significant rôle. As in the contemporary German, Austrian, and Japanese constitutional experiments, the Russian parliament was not granted final political control, yet it ground out reforms of potentially far-reaching import. And although it was, except for the brief sessions of the First and Second Dumas, essentially unrepresentative, yet each element of the population might always count on at least a handful of spokesmen to express its views and needs. In the duma, clearest of all, there were mirrored the political, economic, and social developments of the inter-revolutionary period, the final decade of the Old Régime. And this period has been covered, as yet, only in a general manner. Through studies of the duma, then, in these momentous years I hope to present a panorama of the Russian scene beginning with rebellion, traversing a period of reform, plunging into war, and culminating in revolution and the end of the parliamentary experiment.

I have begun with a study of the Second Duma for it was here that the government inaugurated the domestic policies peculiar to the duma period. I feel, moreover, that the First Duma stands apart from the others as belonging to the chaotic, active, period of the Revolution of 1905. For there were in this body practically no pro-governmental forces, and even the mould of liberal thought was essentially revolutionary. But the First Duma represents the dawn of the Russian parliamentary era, and I hope to give it fuller treatment than it has received here where it is presented as a part of the background for this study, the Revolution of 1905.

Finally, I should like to note that although I have

endeavored to present an adequate view of all political elements represented, I have stressed the activity of the Social-Democrats as the most significant in the developments which marked the course of the Second Duma.

I wish to express here my appreciation for the kind attention given me by the staffs of the Yale University and the Columbia University Libraries, and by the personnel of the Slavonic Division of the New York Public Library. I would also like to thank Professor H. H. Fisher and the Hoover War Library for the use of the manuscript of the Gessen memoires, and the Library of the University of California for their aid in source and journalistic materials. To Mr. L. Swatikoff of Paris I am grateful for his highly useful bibliographical aid in Social-Democratic materials, and to Mr. I. V. Gessen, also resident in Paris, for biographical information. In the preparation of this work for publication I have received invaluable, detailed, technical and literary assistance and criticism from Professor Leonard W. Labaree of Yale University. And I wish gratefully to acknowledge the kindness of Professor Hajo Holborn of Yale in reading the manuscript of this work, and in offering sound, historical criticism. Finally, I feel myself deeply indebted to Professor George Vernadsky for guidance in the preparation of this study of the Second Duma both as a doctoral dissertation and in its present form. As a student and as a contemporary of this period he gave assistance of incalculable value in reconstructing the events and the mood of the times.

A. L.

New Haven, Connecticut
January 3, 1940

PREFACE TO SECOND EDITION

Interest in the Second Duma and the Russian world of the duma period has developed significantly in the last two decades. But it has not attracted a significant number of scholars with varying degrees of experience and maturity. It is understandable that the field has been largely skirted by Soviet scholarship. The few students that have appeared in the USSR have advanced little beyond the attitudes proffered in Lenin's editorial writings. At most they supply detailed corroborative materials from archives not readily accessible to the non-Soviet investigator. For students in the western world the impressive volume of materials to be sifted may prove an inhibiting factor: the bulky *Stenographic Reports* and the appended committee reports and statistical, financial, biographical, and legislative materials; memoirs and the issues of a wide range of newspapers and journals reflecting a rainbow of political hues.

Yet some areas obviously have a lively fascination for students of twentieth-century Russia. A number of specialists on Russian political currents and parties have emerged. American and British scholarship is attracted naturally to the liberal movements. There is also a developing appreciation of the capabilities and maturity of Octobrist leadership as it probed the possibilities of cooperating with the regime and sought energetically to restrain its autocratic-bureaucratic proclivities and brake its headlong plunge toward self-destruction. A clearer perspective of the stature of Peter Arkad'evich Stolypin is emerging. His far-reaching program for social "renovation" is being assessed in the light of his cultural limitations as a member of the elite to which the regime would entrust the formulation of policy, particularly after the experience of 1905-07. And the Russian political rightists have been identified with the forerunners of rabid nationalisms which dominated European politics in the years between the great wars.

There is, above all, a growing awareness that in the dumas the various elements of the population of the Russian Empire, though disproportionately represented, were able to express themselves critically and creatively, if they chose, on a number of major issues which continue to confront them (argicultural organization, industrialization, the position of the national minorities, religion and education).

On a more profound, perhaps more significant, plane students of the period are concerned with the viability of institutions of a representative order in a culture with a long statist tradition. For this tradition generally has been acceptable to Russian society as a positive factor in the development of the organization of the society and its protection.

There are relatively few changes in this edition of the *Second Duma*. Errata have been noted and corrected. Additional factual information and interpretation have been included in the text and appendices where possible. Bibliographical materials have been expanded to include the most significant works concerned directly or indirectly with the duma period. The organization and emphasis of the study have been retained as appropriate for the first of a series of monographs on the development, operation, and significance of the Imperial Dumas.

The author is grateful to the Research Foundation, Oklahoma State University, for the time and resources provided for the completion of this revision and to the staff of the Oklahoma State University Library for the resources and assistance they have been able to provide.

Alfred Levin

Stillwater, Oklahoma
September, 1965

An additional bibliographical note and additions and corrections to the text and footnotes appear beginning page 385.

CONTENTS

CONTENTS

THE SECOND DUMA

INTRODUCTION

THE Second Duma marks the end of the Revolution of 1905. It was the last offensive of the "liberation movement." But more important, it marks a change in the constitutional development of Russia that was to have far-reaching effects. For such was the course of events that on the behavior of the Second Duma hung the fate of representative government on a national scale; the great concession wrested from autocracy by the Revolution of 1905. The great masses of the population had yet to test parliamentary government as an instrument for reform before lending it their whole-hearted support. The enemies of the new order were powerful and influential. And its few, if resourceful, friends who saw in the national representative body Russia's only hope for attaining freedom and plenty, were keenly aware that the old order, jarred but still in control of the resources of power, would take back what it had given.

With the introduction of the principle of popular representation in legislative affairs, Russia broke away from a long political tradition of centralized autocracy. Although Russian autocracy appeared as an anachronism, and in the early years of the twentieth century was under a weak-willed ruler, it had been a vital, unifying, and strengthening force in the development of the Russian state. Arising in Moscow with the need for a centralized defense against the Asiatic hordes which swept unhindered over the steppe, and against the Poles in the West, the Rurik dynasty, and after it the Romanovs, consolidated their position, drove out all invaders, and extended the reaches of their empire from the Baltic to the Black Seas; from the plains of Prussia to the Sea of Japan.

Yet, never in their long and varied career did the tsars relinquish one iota of their dictatorial grasp on the legislative, executive, and judicial functions of the central government. On the eve of the Revolution of 1905 tsarism still clung to the dictum of Peter the Great. The tsar, said Peter, is "an autocratic monarch who is to give an account to no one on earth, but has power and authority to rule his states and lands as a Christian sovereign according to his own will and judgment." [1]

But to advise and aid him in ruling his vast empire the tsar appointed a number of councils. The Imperial Council, organized by Alexander I, [2] advised the throne in legislative and financial matters and even on foreign relations. Judicial affairs were administered by the Ruling Senate, which was the supreme court of the empire. [3] In executive affairs the crown was counseled and represented by the Council of Ministers each member of which was individually responsible to the tsar. Eleven in number, they directed the various kinds of territorial administration and foreign affairs of the state. They also included a ministry of the Orthodox Church, the Holy Synod. For Peter I had subordinated that church to the throne and made its administration a department of state. For purposes of territorial administration Russia was divided into forty-nine provinces, or *guberniia*, each province into districts, or *uiezdy*, and *uiezdy* into *volosti*, or cantons. Each province was placed under a governor, appointed by and responsible to the tsar, through the ministry of the interior. He was allowed to regulate all except judicial affairs, some financial matters, and those functions reserved to organs of local self-government. In all ordinary affairs he was guided by a huge body of instruc-

1. D. M. Wallace, *Russia*, p. 374.
2. This council was created in 1801, and reorganized on broader lines in 1810, 1880, and 1885.
3. This body, founded in 1710 by Peter I, was originally empowered to oversee all sections of the administration and to replace the tsar in his absence or in case of a minority. However, its activities were gradually restricted in 1864 to judicial matters.

tions in the form of imperial orders and ministerial circulars. Independent of the governor there were in each province local representatives of the various ministries, each with his own bureau.

To operate this huge machine Peter I created a bureaucracy which was later incorporated into the ministerial system. It was drawn chiefly from the nobility and the clergy. Fourteen grades, or *chini*, were established. Everyone began at the bottom regardless of social position, and, theoretically, promotion was achieved through personal merit. This system resulted in the creation of a separate social stratum of bureaucrats, or *chinovniki*. These regarded themselves as a vital part of the central government, and were inclined to feel that they were a class apart from the masses to whom the aims of the government were incomprehensible.

Local rural administration was in the hands of the *zemstva*. These were gradually introduced into thirty-four provinces after emancipation when the local gentry lost some of their former authority.[4] A *zemstvo* assembly for each *uiezd* was elected by the landed proprietors, peasant communes, and burghers. Each category represented an equal amount of land or land value, and the representatives of any one group might not exceed the combined total of the other two. The assembly was elected for three years but met only once annually under the presidency of the marshal of the *uiezd* nobility. Its decisions were executed and its affairs administered by a board consisting of a chairman and several assistants. The *uiezd* assembly elected a provincial *zemstvo* assembly which likewise met annually under the presidency of the provincial marshal of the nobility and appointed its executive board. For local and provincial needs these *zemstva* could draw up budgets; tax real estate and commercial-industrial establishments; care for roadbuilding, medical, and sanitary affairs, hospitalization, famine relief, and local edu-

4. *Polnoe sobranie zakonov rossiiskoi imperii, (sobranie vtoroe)*, XXXIX, no. 40,457. This will hereafter be cited as *Pol. sob. zak.*

cation. Since the *zemstva* were originally independent of the central administration the governor could only keep check on the legality of their transactions.

The hopes which the public held for these organizations were quickly dissipated as the old bureaucracy, jealous of its powers, moved to restrict their competence. Their right to tax industrial establishments was curtailed when the government began to foster industrialization. In 1890 the provincial governor was allowed greater control over their activities, thus limiting their freedom of expression and the publicity of their affairs. And, finally, their representation was changed to give a predominance to the landowners.[5] These restrictions, however, had little effect on the liberal tendencies of the *zemstva* and the suspicious administration forbade any attempts at unification or common activity.

For the government of cities and towns, the City Council or Duma, a creation of Catherine the Great, was reorganized. The municipal reform law of 1870 made the City Duma an elective body.[6] For this purpose the taxpayers were divided into three categories: the rich, paying the highest third, the middle class, and finally the small taxpayers. As each group had an equal number of councillors, the system of representation favored the wealthier elements. The City Dumas, too, suffered from an inadequate taxing privilege, and when interest in them had fallen off by 1892, the government rescinded their original autonomy and placed them directly under the central bureaucracy.[7]

In general, while constitutionalism made great gains in the latter part of the nineteenth century in Western Europe, the last two Romanovs were unyielding in their determination to perpetuate the autocratic system. But the inability of that system to solve the major political

5. *Pol. sob. zak.*, (*sobranie tretie*), X, no. 6,922.
6. *Pol. sob. zak.*, (*sobranie vtoroe*), XLV, no. 48,498.
7. *Pol. sob. zak.*, (*sobranie tretie*), XII, no. 8,707. Henceforth *sobranie tretie* (third edition) is referred to unless otherwise noted.

and social problems which confronted it increased the restlessness of a wide popular opposition. After the failure of the government's foreign policy discontent reached the breaking point.

The Revolution of 1905 was long in brewing, and was chiefly the result of basic social and political contradictions which were sharply defined at the turn of the century. Capitalism, industrial and commercial, enjoyed a phenomenal growth in the last decades of the nineteenth century. But the lumbering bureaucratic machine, dominated by a highly class-conscious coterie of noble landowners, was hardly adapted to the needs of a capitalistic economy. Then, while industrialization proceeded at a rapid rate, the basic branch of the national economy, agriculture, stagnated under the medieval communal system with its backward methods. At the same time the village population increased, and the size of individual holdings contracted. The village was barely able to feed itself, and its low standard of living hindered the development of a wide domestic market for manufactured products. Finally, with the growth of manufacturing, there arose the industrial proletariat, drawn from the peasantry, and badly exploited during these early years of the Russian industrial revolution. Its suffering was, moreover, intensified by the economic depression which engulfed Russia in the first few years of the twentieth century, and by high prices artificially maintained by monopolies and high tariffs.

Still another socio-political problem beset the government in the nineteenth century; that of the various national minorities within the empire. Most of these, including the Poles, Letts, Lithuanians, Ukrainians, Asiatic Turks, and Mongols, had been brought into the empire by conquest, and formed a considerable majority on their native heaths. Moreover, in Poland and the western and southern provinces, there were the Jews who had migrated chiefly from Germany in the thirteenth century to escape persecution during the crusading era. Each of these races had endured cultural and political restrictions since the accession of Alexander III, as the government supported a vigorous russification policy, and in the early years of the twentieth century the Jews had suffered severely from race riots, or *pogroms*. These had been partly instigated by local police in an effort to divert popular unrest into channels less dangerous for the administration.

Thus, since the great majority of the population was dissatisfied with the tsarist régime, the undesired and unsuccessful war with Japan crystallized the mounting wave of opposition sentiment. The masses knew little, and cared less, about Russia's penetration into Manchuria, and the Korean boundary concessions which caused the war. A clumsy move on the part of the administration would now precipitate an upheaval.

And the administration was not slow in exasperating public opinion. In August, 1904, the moderate Prince Sviatopolk-Mirskii became prime minister after the assassination of the reactionary Pleve. As a token of his liberalism Mirsky allowed the convocation of a *zemstvo* congress which called for civil liberties, land, and labor reforms, free public education, and above all, a representative, legislative assembly. Professional men now began to form unions all over Russia which reiterated these demands and the peasantry were organized into a peasants' union. The cry for reform was soon taken up by the workers. Of late the government had been organizing them along economic lines to divert them from political activities. And when these unions showed surprising strength in a series of strikes in St. Petersburg, their director, Father Gapon, decided to lead them to the Winter Palace where they might present their demands for the abolition of poverty, ignorance, and oppression, directly to the tsar. But when the processions took place on Sunday, January 9, 1905, they were halted and fired upon repeatedly by the gendarmerie. This was the spark which set fire to the collective indignation of the Russian public and ushered in the Revolution of 1905.

The government, frightened and confused, adopted a dual policy of repression and conciliation. Sviatopolk-Mirskii was replaced by the bureaucrat Bulygin, and the Moscow police chief, Trepov, was made dictator of St. Petersburg. On the other hand, a commission was created to draft labor legislation. "Bloody Sunday," however, had completely discredited the government unions, and the workers were prepared for more revolutionary suggestions. Dictatorial acts on the part of the government were met with terroristic acts by the revolutionaries which culminated in the assassination of the tsar's uncle, Grand Duke Sergius, governor-general of Moscow. The government was forced to retreat. The tsar promised that the "worthiest persons" would be summoned to share in the drafting of laws.

The government's prestige was lowered still further by the naval defeat at Tsushima on May 14–15. The liberals took advantage of the popular mood, assembled at Moscow on June 6, in a convention of *zemstvo* and municipal leaders, and sent a delegation to the tsar which was promised a representative assembly. The Imperial Manifesto of August 6,[8] contained what the tsar regarded as a fulfillment of this promise. The so-called Bulygin Duma which it created was an advisory body with power to discuss all laws, the budget, and the report of the state auditor. After its conclusions had been considered by the Imperial Council, they were to be forwarded to the tsar. Bills rejected by a two-thirds majority of both bodies were to be returned to the minister who introduced them for further revision.

The electoral law for the Bulygin Duma, promulgated on August 6, though modified later, set up the basic principles and machinery of the Russian electoral system.[9] The government did not intend that suffrage should be universal, that "untrustworthy elements" should be given

8. *Ibid.*, XXV, Part 2, no. 26,661. All dates are Old Style, i.e. 13 days behind the Western Calendar.
9. *Ibid.*, no. 26,662.

a vote. Therefore, it divided the population into favored categories, or curiae, and restricted the suffrage by means of property qualifications. Elections were to be multi-staged. For this there was ample precedent in the project presented by Speranskii to Alexander I [10] and in the elections of the provincial *zemstva*. And it is entirely probable that the experience of the latter led the administration to hope that the peasantry and lower middle class would elect conservative and substantial persons in the higher stages.

Most of the deputies to the duma were to be elected by a provincial assembly which, in turn, was to be chosen, directly or indirectly, by various curiae. First there was the landowners' curia which consisted of two subordinate categories. Large landowners with minimum property holdings of five thousand rubles voted directly for their electors to the provincial assemblies at *uiezd* electoral assemblies. Small land and property owners and clergy using church lands in the *uiezd* whose holdings were valued at no less than 1,500 rubles, elected their representatives to the *uiezd* assemblies at preliminary electoral meetings; one representative being elected for every 5,000 rubles in property represented.

Separated from the main body of *uiezd* voters there was a category of *uiezd*-city voters, including home owners and owners of real estate in these provincial cities worth at least 1,500 rubles, persons owning highly taxed commercial and industrial enterprises, and tenants paying high apartment taxes. For election purposes these towns were divided into electoral districts corresponding to police districts, each of which voted for electors to the provincial assembly.

The third great category was the peasantry holding commune land. These were given a vote in an attempt to win them over from the opposition. In the same category were the Cossacks of Astrakhan, Orenburg, and the Don.

10. See G. Vernadsky, *Political and Diplomatic History of Russia*, p. 285.

These voters had first to elect one representative from every ten householders to a *volost* assembly at which two delegates were elected to sit at *uiezd* assemblies. These bodies, in turn, voted for electors to the provincial assemblies at which the duma deputies were elected. In the latter instance the peasants first elected representatives from their own class, and then voted with the rest of the assembly for a number of deputies allotted to the province by law.

The remaining members of the duma were elected by city electoral assemblies in twenty-six large cities which were given the right to elect their own deputies to the duma. The suffrage requirements for this category were somewhat higher than those established for the *uiezd* towns. Like these, the larger cities were divided into districts which voted directly for electors to the city assemblies where duma members were chosen.

The administration of elections was carefully provided for. To regulate elections and hear complaints *uiezd* and provincial committees on electoral affairs were established and empowered to annul elections which they considered had been illegally held. They were to consist of representatives of the nobility, *zemstva*, and judicial officials. Appeal was provided from the *uiezd* to the provincial committees, and from the latter to the Ruling Senate. Registers of *uiezd*, landowner and city voters were to be kept by *zemstvo* and city boards. These were to be published six weeks before elections and a two-week period was established for submitting complaints concerning omissions, errors, etc. Results were to be published on the day following city and provincials elections. Complaints concerning their illegality were to be presented to the Ruling Senate which might annul them.

Obviously, the Bulygin system did not provide for universal suffrage. The small industrial and commercial element, the professional men, except those who could afford to pay high rents, the city proletariat, the small but growing number of agricultural proletariat, all "un-trustworthy" in the eyes of the government, were excluded from the suffrage.

The publication of the Manifesto of August 6, brought the first serious break in the solid ranks of the opposition. The conservatives and moderates were prepared to accept the Bulygin Duma. They would utilize it to win a real legislative assembly. The liberals and the revolutionary Socialists, on the other hand, violently opposed it, and urged that the duma be boycotted. In the Union of Unions, formed by Professor Miliukov of all of the professional unions, the leftist liberals gained the upper hand. Conse-quently, the more moderate Dr. Miliukov withdrew with the right wing of the "Union," and together with the left wing of the *zemstvo* leaders, he formed the Constitutional-Democratic or Kadet Party, which he dominated until its destruction in 1917.

But the government was unable to take immediate advantage of this divergence, for the popular movement increased in intensity and violence throughout the sum-mer. Aroused by the Social-Revolutionaries,[11] fierce rural disorders took place during the late fall and winter, and local self-governments were set up. A sporadic strike movement during the summer developed into a nation-wide stoppage in October. And the Soviet of Workers' and Peasants' Deputies, recently created by the Socialist parties and guided by the Social-Democrats [12] began to direct affairs.

In the face of this powerful popular movement, and under strong pressure from Witte (who had just con-cluded a peace with Japan) the tsar made several far-reaching decisions. The honorary post of chairman of the committee of ministers held by Witte since his retire-ment from the finance ministry in 1904, became that of the chairman of the council of ministers. Its incumbent was made responsible for the general state policy and

11. See the following chapter.
12. *Ibid.*

control over his colleagues. This was Russia's first modern cabinet. Then, on October 17, a manifesto was published guaranteeing inviolability of person, freedom of conscience, assembly, speech, and organization. It further promised universal suffrage, and pledged that no law would become effective without the approval of the duma, and that the duma would be empowered to watch the legality of the activities of governmental authorities.[13]

The new premier persistently adhered to the policy of widening the differences already apparent between opposition elements by winning popular support for some of his measures. From the alarmed reactionary court circles who opposed his every liberal measure, and from the revolutionaries who demanded nothing less than a constituent assembly to create a democratic republic, he could expect no quarter. But the wealthy merchant and manufacturer began to look to the government for protection after the October strikes and demands for social change. And the moderate nobility turned to the administration for aid as the peasant uprisings multiplied. They wanted, above all else, a return to normality. They were quite satisfied with the October Manifesto and soon organized the "Union of October 17" to maintain the *status quo* created by that document. Yet the moderates and liberals refused a bid by Witte to join his cabinet. They would not shoulder the responsibility for the repressive acts of the "reactionary" Durnovo, whom Witte insisted on retaining as minister of the interior. But the premier was not discouraged. On October 21, he sought the support of the peasantry by reducing redemption payments for the following year after which they were to be abolished entirely.[14] Moreover, purchase of land through the Peasant Land Bank was facilitated.[15] On the same date he decreed a partial amnesty.[16] On October 26, he returned to the Finns the

13. *Pol. sob. zak.*, XXV, no. 26,803; F. A. Golder, *Documents of Russian History*, pp. 627–628.
14. *Pol. sob. zak.*, XXV, no. 27,029.
15. See Chap. VIII on Agrarian Affairs.
16. *Pol. sob. zak.*, XXV, no. 26,835.

autonomy which they lost in 1899.[17] And he established
the ministry of trade and industry to look after the interests of the capitalists.[18]

After the repression of a mutiny at the Kronstadt naval
base and the failure of two strikes called by the Soviet at
the end of October, the government felt that the revolutionary spirit was ebbing, and it began to take the offensive. On December 3, the Soviet was arrested. Its remnants called a third strike but the St. Petersburg workers
responded weakly. In Moscow, however, open conflict
broke out on December 9, between a comparatively small
number of armed workers and the government. But after
some delay the uprising was mercilessly crushed on December 19. The administration now realized that despite
mutinous tendencies in some sections of the army and
navy, it might count on its armed forces to suppress open
rebellion. The whole affair was roundly condemned by
the liberals and moderates as a blunder and a threat to
the success of the entire liberation movement. Thus the
difference between the reformers and the revolutionaries
was now sharply accentuated; the former demanded a liberal, constitutional régime, the latter the complete overthrow of the monarchy and the creation of a democratic
republic. The forces of the opposition were now hopelessly
divided.

In the midst of the Moscow uprising, Witte made a
great bid for popular support by issuing an electoral law
for the duma on December 11.[19] Basically, this measure
supplemented the law of August 6, to make it conform to
the promises contained in the October Manifesto. Thus,
the machinery and general principles of the August law
were retained. The class character of the suffrage and
the many-staged elections remained as before. But the
new law widened the electoral basis to include the industrial workers, the lower middle class, the intellectuals in

17. *Ibid.*, no. 26,847.
18. *Ibid.*, no. 26,851.
19. *Ibid.*, no. 27,029.

the cities, and the smallest landowners. Accordingly, the law of December 11, contained four categories of voters: landowners, city voters, peasants and Cossacks, and the workers. There was now no minimum land qualification; all persons owning land or real estate, regardless of its value, were admitted to the category of landowners. For the smaller landholding categories preliminary elections were retained. In urban elections anyone might vote who for a period of one year owned a commercial or industrial establishment, paid a professional tax, rented an apartment, or received support or pensions for state service. The provisions for the peasant and Cossack curia remained unchanged.

The new law provided that the workers were to elect delegates who were, in turn, to choose representatives from factories and mills, mines, metal works, and railroads employing at least fifty male workers. Factories employing from fifty to one thousand male workers were to have one representative, but for larger establishments there was to be one representative for each one thousand workers. In this manner the representation of the larger, more militant factories was balanced by the vote of the smaller establishments. These representatives were, in turn, to choose from their midst electors to city or provincial assemblies (if the factory was in a provincial town). Although the inclusion of the proletariat was in itself an advance, the franchise in this category was far from complete. Types of enterprises not mentioned in the law such as bakeries, or produce factories, though they employed more than fifty workers, might not participate in the elections. Likewise, those who worked in establishments employing less than fifty male workers might not vote, and agricultural labor continued to be disfranchised.

In establishing the procedure of elections for workers the law required that city and provincial administrations publish registers of voters. Since they voted as a separate class it was only natural that workers' elections should take place in shops and factories. Like peasants and small

landowners they did not directly choose electors for the
city or provincial assemblies but first elected delegates
who assembled to vote for them behind closed doors. As
in the law of August 6, complaints were to be registered
with *uiezd* and provincial committees on electoral affairs
and, as before, these bodies might annul the elections at
any stage. In the provincial and city election assemblies,
workers' electors voted with those of other curiae for
members of the duma and the final results were to be communicated by the governor to the Ruling Senate.

The government, we have said, was now definitely on
the offensive. Having granted a parliamentary constitution there was an end to sweeping concessions and the
throne began to qualify what it had granted with all sorts
of restrictions. To combat revolutionary and agrarian
disorder various parts of the country were placed under
martial law of one form or another and civil liberties in
these areas were suspended. In the months which preceded
the convocation of the First Duma the government did its
utmost to make the legislative body as innocuous as possible. And it combined these restrictions in a new edition of
the Fundamental Laws, the constitution of the Russian
Empire, inspired by Witte and promulgated on April 23,
1906.[20]

Despite the creation of a popular, legislative body
which exercised legislative powers together with the
throne, the tsar was still called the "supreme autocratic
power" and his person was declared to be sacred and inviolable. He enjoyed the initiative in all legislative matters and he alone could initiate changes in the Fundamental Laws. His sanction was necessary for the validity
of all laws. He was given complete executive power, acting
directly in important matters, and indirectly, through
officials representing him, in subordinate matters. The
tsar was vested with complete control in foreign affairs;
he directed foreign policy, declared war, and made peace
and treaties with other powers. As commander-in-chief of

20. *Ibid.*, XXVI, no. 27,805.

the army and navy he controlled all of their activities
and organization, and declared localities to be in a state
of war or any other exceptional state. The tsar alone
administered the currency. He alone appointed and dismissed the cabinet. Control of the crown estates and appanage lands assigned to members of the imperial family
were his sole prerogative. Judicial power was exercised
in his name, while he could pardon, commute sentence,
and stop proceedings against any prisoner. His *ukazes*
(decrees) and orders were to be countersigned by the
chairman of the council of ministers, or the proper minister, to insure unified executive policy.

The rights and duties of citizens were clearly defined.
The entire population was liable to military service and
taxation. On the other hand, the people were granted
inviolability of domicile, freedom of movement and choice
of occupation, and freedom of assembly, speech, organization, and conscience. Finally, property was declared to
be inviolable, could be expropriated for state needs only,
and at an adequate compensation.

The legislative procedure was dealt with extensively.
To the great chagrin of all progressive and revolutionary
elements, the Fundamental Laws provided, besides the
elective duma, for an equally powerful upper house, the
exclusive Imperial Council. It was to be composed of a
number of members appointed by the tsar and an equal
number elected by various privileged institutions including the Orthodox Church, provincial *zemstva*, assemblies
of the nobility, universities, the Academy of Science, and
commercial councils. Both the duma and the Imperial
Council might examine the credentials of their members
and no one might serve simultaneously in both. These
bodies might amend or repeal existing laws (except the
Fundamental Laws) and enact new legislation, and they
might interpellate the government. Bills initiated in one
house had to be approved in the other, and if not adopted
by either were considered as rejected. But at the tsar's
order such bills might be introduced in either body during

the same session. Bills approved by both houses had to be submitted to the tsar by the president of the Imperial Council and, as we have observed, could not become law without the imperial signature. Bills vetoed by the tsar had to await the following session before they might again be introduced in either house.

Moreover, parts of the budget were declared to be "iron clad," that is, they were not subject to examination by the legislative bodies. These included sums earmarked for covering loans contracted by the government and other obligations of the empire, credits for the ministry of the imperial household and the imperial family. Extraordinary credits for wartime needs were placed under supreme control, as were loans covering such expenditures. All other expenditures, revenues, and loans were subject to the approval of the duma and the Imperial Council. Should the budget not be approved by the end of the fiscal year, the last budget legally approved would remain in force.

The full term of both the duma and the Imperial Council was to last for five years. Both were to be convoked annually by imperial decree and the tsar was to determine the duration of the annual session. And the duma and the elective part of the Imperial Council might be dissolved by an imperial decree which was to fix the date for the convention of the newly elected body.

Of the articles on legislation, one of the most significant, because of the frequency of its application, was the widely discussed "number eighty-seven." [21] It provided that if, during a recess of the duma, extraordinary circumstances required the adoption of a measure which should by law be presented to the duma and the Imperial Council, the ministers might present that measure directly to the tsar. But no changes in the Fundamental Laws, the organiza-

21. This article was not original with the Russian administration but was derived from Article 14 of the Austrian Constitution. See H. F. Wright, *The Constitutions of States at War*, p. 118. Compare Baron B. E. Nolde, *Ocherki russkago gosudarstvennago prava*, Chap. I.

tion of either legislative body, or laws regulating elections to them might be made on the basis of this article. The legal force of a measure issued under Article 87 ceased if it were not submitted by the proper ministry to the duma within two months after it convened, or if it were rejected by the duma or the Imperial Council.[22]

In the last part of the Fundamental Laws the council of ministers was required to direct and unify the actions of the individual ministers. The latter were forbidden to vote in the duma or in the Imperial Council. They were made directly responsible to the tsar and were to be answerable for all criminal offenses committed while discharging their duties. No "duma cabinet," representing and accountable to the popular representative body, was foreseen here, but a bureaucratic chief of staff responsible to the throne. Tsarism abided by its promise to yield some of its legislative powers but continued to reserve the formulation and execution of state policy for itself. Moreover, in creating an Imperial Council as a check to the activities of the popular representative body, and in curbing the competence of the latter, these Fundamental Laws sorely violated the spirit, if not the letter, of the October Manifesto; for that document mentioned only the duma as a representative, legislative body. Yet, representative government had now become an established factor in Russian political life. And if the power of the popular representative body was rigidly limited by the selective upper house and the tsar's will, leaders of the liberation movement felt that a great stride forward had been made. The future development of parliamentary government, they believed, depended entirely on its ability to demonstrate its value as an instrument for vital reform.

Having clipped the duma's wings, the government rendered itself independent of the people financially in April, 1906, by negotiating a loan of two billion francs with French banking circles. After Witte had rendered this service to the state, the tsar, long estranged from him as

22. *Pol. sob. zak.*, XXVI, no. 27,805.

a result of his concessions to the liberals, replaced him
with the undistinctive Goremykin. This ministry contained V. N. Kokovtsov, an able finance minister and
several powerful reactionaries such as Shcheglovitov,
minister of justice, and Schwanebach, state auditor. It
also included a new man, P. A. Stolypin, minister of the
interior, who as governor of Saratov was the only provincial governor able to control the population in the last
months of 1905, and to win the respect of his adversaries
while restraining extremists, both right and left.

The first electoral campaign resulted in a great victory
for the opposition in general and the Kadets in particular. Their campaign among the masses was well organized, and by political manoeuvring they managed to win
solid majorities in the city and provincial electoral assemblies. With many small racial groups which joined them
in the hope of winning autonomy they formed a bloc of
two hundred deputies ably led by Petrunkevich, Nabokov,
Rodichev, and others. Moreover, they were usually followed by the Trudoviki, ninety to one hundred strong.
This was the party of the peasant union which Aladin
had created and astutely led. The Social-Democrats entered the fray late in the campaign and only eighteen
of their number were elected. For the more radical wing
of the party, the Bolsheviki, chose to boycott the duma
as an organ which could win nothing and do much to cor-
rupt the "revolutionary consciousness" of the people.

The First Duma convened in the Taurida Palace on
April 27, 1906. The Kadets elected Muromtsev president
and wrote the rules of procedure. The government offered
no constructive legislative program to the duma but introduced a number of minor bills either as a token of contempt for the intruder in its legislative domain or to keep
it from meddling in more important matters. The duma,
on the other hand, censured the government after Goremykin's address and violently criticized all phases of its
activity. Numerous interpellations were hurled at the
various ministers, who only weakly defended their positions. Criticism, rather than constructive legislation, was

the order of the day. The granting of credits for famine relief in stricken areas was the only significant measure passed. Dissolution seemed imminent as the administration and duma were deadlocked. And the Kadets did what the government feared most; they raised the land question. Numerous bills incorporating the principle of obligatory expropriation were presented and a huge committee was elected to evolve a popular measure. The government condemned expropriation and offered an abundance of land at cheap prices. Moreover, the moderate and progressive wings of the duma debated bitterly over the wording of a reply to the administration's statement. The government, sensing a growing division, decided to act. On July 18, Goremykin was replaced by Stolypin who had impressed the tsar with his forceful behavior and his opinion that the duma must bow before the will of the administration as the representative of the throne. Finally, on the same evening the duma was dissolved by an imperial decree which fixed February 20, 1907, as the date for the convocation of the Second Duma.[23]

The indignant deputies of the opposition met on the following day in Vyborg, Finland, where the Russian police had no jurisdiction. Under the leadership of the Kadets they issued a manifesto calling on the population to refuse to yield taxes or recruits until a new duma should be assembled. But the masses failed to respond and the signers of the manifesto were prosecuted and deprived of electoral rights. The power of the revolution had definitely been broken. The people were exhausted by a year of violent revolutionary activity and the severe repression which attended it, especially in the west and south. Moreover, the opposition was deeply divided on the future course of the revolution. The moderates would accept the situation created by the October Manifesto. The Kadets, though striving for a more liberal duma, opposed the aim of the Socialists to struggle violently until a constituent assembly had been won which should establish a democratic republic. Each blamed the other

23. A. Suvorin, *Russkii Kalendar*, 1907, pp. 283–284.

for the failure of the movement. The Kadets held that the workers had overestimated their powers, and by the December uprising had demonstrated their weakness and brought on punitive expeditions.[24] But the Social-Democrats maintained that all that had been gained was the result of the violent activity of the masses; that after the defeat of the December uprising the Kadets had "perverted" the struggle for power into a parliamentary struggle which netted them nothing.[25] Some months were yet to pass before Lenin would admit that the revolution was on the ebb.

The left extremists were soon active. Counting on a wave of popular indignation and the effects of their organized propaganda, the Social-Democrats and Trudoviki issued proclamations on July 12, calling on the armed forces to arise and overthrow the government and convoke a constituent assembly. Futile and badly organized uprisings at the naval stations of Kronstadt, Sveaborg, and Reval (July 17 to 20) and a weak strike in the capital were the only results. The physical weakness of the revolutionaries was now apparent to all.

But in the face of fierce governmental repression by means of punitive expeditions and martial law, the Social-Revolutionaries began a campaign of assassination which lasted throughout the summer of 1906 and the election campaign. On the other hand, with the revolutionary spirit on the wane, and the government in complete control, the extreme nationalistic right organized the "Union of the Russian People" to fight parliamentary constitutionalism and Socialism. Dubbed the "Black Hundreds" they perpetrated race riots and assassinations which contributed to the general turmoil.[26] The country was shocked by the murder of a leading Kadet journalist and ex-deputy,

24. P. N. Miliukov, *Constitutional Government for Russia*, pp. 6, 8-9.
25. V. I. Lenin, *Sobranie sochinenii*, VIII, 490 (1922 ed.); cited hereafter as *Sob. soch.*
26. See following chapter. There had already been fierce riots in Poland during the sessions of the First Duma, and in July (26-28) the Polish town of Siedletz suffered an outbreak. In Odessa the Jews were subject to intermittent attacks.

M. I. Hertzenstein, on July 18.[27] But the toll of government officials taken by revolutionary terrorists made life a nightmare among the bureaucrats. From high commanding army and police officials to the gendarmes-of-the-line they fell in amazing numbers as the summer wore on.[28] Stolypin himself narrowly escaped extermination when a bomb was exploded in his summer home by unidentified assailants.[29]

The new chairman of the council of ministers was an imposing strong-minded man with an essentially bureaucratic background. A provincial, rather than a cosmopolitan figure like Witte, he resembled the October premier in his sensitivity to the necessity for reform and constitutionalism as the savior of monarchy. He liked to regard himself as a "middle-of-the-roader." He was determined to end disorders, to stamp out rebellion, but he also considered certain social and economic changes to be absolutely essential. That was his general policy.[30] And the emphasis which he placed on its various parts, and his approach

27. The Extraordinary Investigating Committee of the Provisional Government heard leaders of the "Union" confess at its hearings in 1917 that the murder was organized by Dubrovin, head of the Union, and carried out by its "fighting bands" under Iushkevich-Korsakovskii. See *Soiuz russkago naroda*, pp. 54–55, 98.

28. Among the prominent victims were M. N. Vonliariarskii, governor general of Warsaw, who was killed on August 14. General Min, who had put down the rebellion in Moscow, was murdered a day earlier at Neu Peterhof. On December 21, V. E. Von der Launitz, chief of police of St. Petersburg, fell as he emerged from the Academy of Experimental Medicine where he had been dedicating a new building. Then, on December 27, V. Pavlov, prosecutor general for the army, was killed in St. Petersburg. Up to the end of October, 16,922 persons had been killed and wounded in the political struggle. Of these 7,331 were murdered. Government officials of all ranks to the number of 3,611 had been killed or wounded while 13,381 citizens had been executed or killed by courts-martial, troops, brigands, etc. See A. Suvorin, *Russkii Kalendar*, 1907, pp. 285, 287, 290; *Ibid.*, 1908, pp. 305, 306; *Riech*, July 13, 1906; *Viestnik Evropy*, Nov., 1906, p. 446.

29. A. Suvorin, *Russkii Kalendar*, 1907, p. 285; *Riech*, July 13, 1906; V. I. Gurko, *Features and Figures of the Past*, pp. 497–498.

30. Stolypin's policy was developed in the government's program issued on August 24, and in several interviews with foreign correspondents. See *Riech*, Aug. 25, 1907, p. 4; V. N. Kokovtsov, *Out of My Past*, p. 166 (cited hereafter as *Memoires*); London *Times*, Jan. 14, 1907; P. A. Tverskoi, *Viestnik Evropy*, 1912, Part 2, pp. 188–195. See also V. I. Gurko, *Features and Figures of the Past*, pp. 494–495.

to the problem of reform resulted in wide popular opposition. Besides, like Witte, he was to feel the terrific pressure exerted by those circles near the throne who were opposed to all change. As long as he held the confidence of the tsar this group, led by P. K. Schwanebach and I. G. Shcheglovitov, gave up waging an open struggle against the new premier. But it was under pressure from them that Stolypin promulgated, under Article 87, the law of August 19, 1906, creating the dreaded field-courts-martial.[31]

In a program for the government which he issued on August 24, Stolypin justified field-courts-martial and continued repression.[32] They were necessary, he declared, in view of the revolutionary terror which would not cease with adoption of reforms but aimed at the complete overthrow of monarchy. Yet, since he would eliminate the seeds of the evil, he presented a series of reforms covering agriculture, civil liberties, education, local courts and class, race, and religious limitations which he would ultimately present to the duma. In the meantime he would enact urgent measures on land and liberty without delay —under Article 87. If he was grasping the initiative in legislative matters, Stolypin at least showed a desire to coöperate with the popular representative body.

Some of the premier's promises were fulfilled at once. On August 12, even before the publication of the program, the tsar had decreed the transfer of appanage lands to the Peasant Land Bank for sale among the land-short peasants,[33] and on August 27, state lands were added to the fund.[34] On October 5, 1906, some of the last vestiges of serfdom were abolished. The peasantry were equalized with other classes in domestic passport rights. They were made eligible for offices in local administration, some of which became elective. And they could no longer be pun-

31. *Pol. sob. zak.*, XXVI, no. 28,252; V. I. Gurko, *Features and Figures*, p. 499.
32. See footnote 30.
33. Brokhaus i Efron, *Novyi entsiklopedicheski slovar*, XVIII, 316. For a discussion of the Peasant Land Bank and other agrarian questions see Chapter VIII.
34. *Pol. sob. zak.*, XXVI, no. 28,315.

ished by land captains without trial.[35] The process was completed by the most famous of Stolypin reforms, the significant land law of November 9, 1906.[36] This measure allowed peasants to leave their communes with their lands as private property, and the scattered strips thus removed from communal jurisdiction were to be consolidated into one or two tracts of equivalent size and quality. Labor, too, was considered and on November 15, rules were published establishing "normal rest" for employees in commercial and craft establishments, stores, and offices.[37] Finally, a start was made in religious reform by granting freedom of worship to Old Believers and dissenters from the Orthodox Church.[38]

But if Stolypin enacted these reforms to attract popular support, and perhaps with an eye on the coming elections to the Second Duma, any good impression they might have created was overshadowed in the public mind by the proportions which official repression now assumed. Courts-martial took a striking number of victims, while states of "special" or "reinforced protection" practically annulled all civil liberties. The only effective mouthpiece for public opinion, the press, was assailed with remarkable ferocity. At the height of the electoral campaign and during the period of the Second Duma (half of January to the end of May, 1907) 226 dailies were stopped on "administrative" grounds, permanently or temporarily.[39]

Little wonder that, at best, the population received the government's program and viewed its policy with great

35. *Ibid.*, no. 28,392. For discussion of land captains see Chap. VIII.
36. *Ibid.*, no. 28,528.
37. *Ibid.*, nos. 28,548, 28,549.
38. *Ibid.*, nos. 28,424, 28,426; V. I. Gurko, *Features and Figures*, p. 502; *Vospominaniia, iz bumag S. E. Kryzhanovskago*, pp. 94–95 (cited hereafter as *Kryzhanovskii, vospominaniia*). Old Believers had broken from the established church in the latter half of the seventeenth century as the result of ritual changes introduced by Patriarch Nikon. See also Gurko, pp. 504, 506 and Kryzhanovskii, 94–95, for Stolypin's attempt to moderate Jewish legislation.
39. For field-courts-martial see Chap. XII. *Tovarishch*, Jan. 17, 1907, pp. 3, 4; Feb. 20, p. 3; March 3, p. 5; April 3, p. 3; May 6, p. 3; June 2, p. 3.

reserve. The opposition assailed the policy of force as cruel, futile, and dangerous. Its leaders held that the government had always tried to subdue its opponents with force and had only succeeded in creating anarchic conditions and wide discontent which led to further opposition. Meanwhile the most elementary guarantees of liberty and justice were removed.[40] On the correct policy to be followed, parliamentary or revolutionary, there were, as we have seen, wide differences of opinion. The wide application of Article 87 also aroused deep dissatisfaction. For it was felt that if the government was sincere in its desire to coöperate with parliament it had no right to predetermine the basic principles of such vital measures as land reform on which there was such a great variety of opinions. Under a truly parliamentary régime a bill in the duma would fully serve the government's purposes.[41] The most moderate elements were frankly skeptical. And when Stolypin tried, like Witte, to attract conservative public figures to his cabinet, he, too, met with failure. For even Octobrist leaders like Prince G. E. Lvov, D. N. Shipov, and A. I. Guchkov could not take the responsibility for a policy which included merciless repression.[42] Moreover, Stolypin failed to evaluate correctly the significance of the liberals. After the experience of the First Duma he regarded them as revolutionary, refused to legalize the Kadet Party, and repressed it at every opportunity. But since the Kadets were moderate liberals in the eyes of the public, Stolypin's policy only served to make the administration appear more reactionary and to discredit those elements it would patronize.[43] It seemed that Stolypin's definition of that "revolution" which he would crush included everything which differed with his views of what

40. Riech, Aug. 25, 1906.
41. See, for example, Viestnik Evropy, December, 1906, pp. 813–816.
42. D. N. Shipov, Vospominaniia i dumy o perezhitom, pp. 461–480; T. I. Polner, Zhiznennyi put Kniaza G. E. Lvova, pp. 123–124; V. I. Gurko, Features and Figures of the Past, pp. 491–493, appendix 4.
43. Cf. B. Maklakov, preface to La chute du régime tsariste, J. and L. Polonsky, translators, pp. 52–55.

a constitutional government should be. And that included the aims of all groups from the Kadets leftwards; that is, the majority of the population. As a result of Stolypin's policy many opposition circles felt that there was neither a constitution nor autocracy in Russia but an irresponsible government which resorted to both at its pleasure.

The fact was that Stolypin was trying to establish some form of limited monarchy but was severely handicapped by conceptions of administration arising from his bureaucratic background, by the difficulty with which the old bureaucracy adapted itself to the parliamentary régime, and by pressure from above. Russia had a parliamentary constitution under Stolypin, but it was in its first evolutionary stages and therefore indefinite. And it was not at all in accord with the desires of the vast majority of the population. The promises of October, 1905, foresaw, or gave rise to hopes for, a real parliamentary order as in the west. But the givers, the tsar and his counsellors, were too deeply rooted in the past to allow for so great a change. Thus there arose those contradictions and struggles which lasted to the day when Nicholas II was forced to abdicate.

I

RUSSIAN POLITICAL PARTIES

BY the fall of 1906 the political alignment under the new constitutional order was quite clear. Various elements of the population organized in parties and groups had definitely expressed themselves on reforms and the means of realizing them. The reactionary nobility would consider no changes. The conservatives, noble and middle class, were satisfied with those granted by the throne. The liberal intelligentsia looked for more fundamental concessions to the popular movement; the establishment of a monarchy truly limited by a popular representative body which was to enact vital reforms. The peasantry wanted land and freedom from bureaucratic oppression and they would support any organ which promised them relief. Finally, the left, the socialist peasantry and proletariat, preached reform through revolution. Insofar as they were interested in the duma they would use it to publicize their revolutionary aims.

What, then, were the parties which represented these basic currents in Russian political life? Each element, we observed, if it had not already done so, organized itself politically. Programs and tactics were evolved and broad propaganda campaigns launched to attract the bewildered populace. At the extreme right we find the "Union of the Russian People." This party was created by the reactionary elements among the Russian landowners and because of some of its features it may, at least in part, be marked as a forerunner of present-day Fascism. It developed as a movement to curb the activities of liberal and socialistic parties which had seriously threatened the existing political, social, and economic order during the Revolution of 1905. Consequently, it also drew much support from the lower-middle-class shopkeepers and some well-to-do peasantry (*kulaki*). These had suffered economically during the turmoil of revolution. Moreover, feeling like the landowners that their interests were being threatened by the revolutionary elements, they would unite with the gentry against the common danger.[1]

The principles which the Union professed were those of the reign of Nicholas I, namely, orthodoxy, autocracy, and nationalism.[2] The Union would preserve Russian Orthodoxy as the state religion in the Russian Empire. In proclaiming the principle of nationality, the supremacy of the Great Russian race in all fields of Russian life, as in latter-day Germany, the Union injected a biological element into their credo. In particular they would brook no challenge to the supremacy of Russian culture and consequently, they fiercely opposed all minority movements. But their wrath was especially directed against the Jews whom they accused of "destructive" and "anti-state" activity during the Revolution, and they demanded their political and economic restriction.[3] To the poorest elements in the village and the *lumpenproletariat* in the cities, the Jews were pointed out as the source of political and economic evil. Race riots frequently resulted from this propaganda. For despite peaceful protestations, the activities of the Union of the Russian People often took a violent turn in order that vengeance might be wreaked on political enemies, real or supposed.

Autocracy, the third principle of the Union, presupposed a ruler whose power was absolute and unlimited. In theory, the autocracy was entirely well intentioned and sought only the welfare of the nation. But, declared the Union, the bureaucracy had arisen to separate the tsar

1. Compare *Soiuz Russkago Naroda*, pp. 4–13.
2. See party proclamation issued in April, 1906, in V. Ivanovich, *Rossiiskiia partii*, pp. 117–118, and its program, *ibid.*, pp. 118–122.
3. V. Ivanovich, *Rossiiskiia partii*, pp. 117–118. The fourth congress of the Union (May 1–14, 1907) went on record as opposed to ownership by Jews of banks and loan offices, and to participation of Jews in state contracts. They would forbid them to acquire or rent land, directly or indirectly, and would restrict Jews in trade and ownership of industry. See *Soiuz Russkago Naroda*, pp. 5–6.

from the people and reduce the country to misery. Officialdom, therefore, was to be strictly controlled by a popular assembly through which the tsar was to be connected directly with the population. Some of the Unionists were, however, pure absolutists.

As is evident from the foregoing, the extreme right desired at most a consultative duma. For it held that a legislative body would necessarily infringe on the prerogatives of the tsar. Therefore, the Union bitterly opposed both the First Duma in which the right had no influence, and the Second where it was weakly represented but highly vociferous. The Second Duma, in particular, the Union found little to its liking. For that body included a strong, left, Socialist wing with scant regard for either autocracy, orthodoxy, nationality, or private property. Such a duma was anathema, and ought to be dissolved immediately before it played havoc with the historical privileges and property rights of the gentry. And for dissolution the Union strove with all of its energy, chiefly by creating disturbances in the duma to demonstrate that the latter was not fit for serious, legislative work, by raising issues which were intended to precipitate a clash between the duma and the government, and by impressing the tsar through its highly placed sympathizers of the danger which the duma presented to the throne.[4]

The great conservative party of the duma period was the Union of October 17, or the Octobrist Party, which attracted especially the representatives of the rising capitalism, and the conservative, as against the reactionary, landowners.[5] During the Revolution they had demanded

4. The program of the second branch of the extreme right wing, the Monarchists, differed little from that presented by the Union. They placed stronger emphasis on the preservation of the class structure, and stressed the belief that no legislation could bear fruit if enacted under the attack of the revolutionary movement. Therefore they demanded that the internal confusion be ended at once. In their legislative program they made a more specific demand for judicial reform. In the Second Duma they acted with the Union as a solid right wing. See V. Ivanovich, *Rossiiskiia Partii*, pp. 110–116.

5. See the proclamation of the Octobrist Party in V. V. Vodovozov, *Sbornik programm politicheskikh partii v rossii*, pp. 42–56; cited hereafter as *Sbornik programm*.

civil liberties and representative government, and when
these were granted in the Manifesto of October 17, we
have seen that they were quite satisfied. Thereafter, they
were interested only in completely realizing the promises
contained in the manifesto and in bringing the Revolution
to a speedy close. It had gone far enough for them, and
its continuation might well result in the complete overthrow of tsarism, capitalism, and large landownership.
Some great authoritative power, they held, was necessary
to end the revolutionary chaos and preserve the *status
quo* created by the October Manifesto. They believed that
this authority was to be found in a limited, constitutional
monarch. They maintained that the old autocracy had
weakened the principle of monarchy by separating the
ruler from the masses. Now that principle was to be
strengthened by a new unity with the population. Now
the dignity of the tsar was to be enhanced as the supreme
chief of a free people, as the symbol of imperial unity and
continuity, and as arbiter in the sharp political and social
struggle which beset the country.

The Octobrists did not minimize the urgency of reform
legislation as a means of satisfying the revolutionary
population. Therefore, they demanded the immediate convocation of the newly granted popular representative
body. But unlike other constitutionalists they accepted
the duma with all of the limitations imposed upon it by
the Fundamental Laws. Their legislative program was
concerned chiefly with the perfection of legislation governing popular representation and the enactment of important social and economic reforms. First among these
came legislation alleviating the economic plight of the
peasantry. The Octobrists would equalize the juridical
and civil status of the peasant, and abolish all administrative tutelage over him. They would help him to improve
his economy, create sources of credit, aid the peasant to
resettle, and increase his plot from a national land fund.
The Octobrists would also satisfy the workers with a pro-

gram of advanced labor legislation.[6] They called next
for the expansion especially of the primary, but also of
higher educational facilities. And they demanded class-
less, public, and independent courts. In local instances
they would create elective judges. In the administrative
field they would simplify the bureaucratic structure, subordinate the activities of officials to law, and create a
means of appealing their decisions and orders. If this
program were to be realized, the Octobrists maintained
that the budget might not be reduced Nevertheless they
would strive for a system of taxation in which the burden
would be more equitably distributed than heretofore.
Here, then, was a monarchistic party of moderate reform
which became, in fact, anti-revolutionary after the promulgation of the October Manifesto.

From this analysis of Russian political elements it is
obvious that the only true supporters of advanced parliamentary government in the western European sense were
the liberals organized in the powerful Constitutional
Democratic Party, the Kadets (known officially as the
Party of Popular Freedom). Although it attracted some
moderate and liberal landowners and industrialists, this
party was essentially that of the professional class and
included some of the leading legal, journalistic, and academic personages in the empire. And since they were
more fully acquainted with parliamentary forms and possibilities than other parties, and best understood the constitution and legislation regulating the duma, they proved
to be the most influential group in the Second Duma, as
they had been in the First. Their supremacy was questioned only when the heterogeneous socialistic groups on
the left found common ground for opposing them.[7]

Flushed by the successes of the liberation movement in
the Revolution—especially the realization of representa-

6. This included legislation protecting women and children, health and acci-
dent insurance, recognition of the right to strike and organize.
7. See immediately below discussion of leftist parties.

tive government—the Kadets employed energetic, oppositional tactics in the First Duma. But the ease and im-
punity with which the government dissolved that noisy
assembly led them to reconsider their parliamentary
methods.[8] Henceforth they fostered no illusions of gaining
wider freedom and truer parliamentary government by a
"direct attack" on the administration. The fate of the
First Duma showed only too clearly that parliament was
at the mercy of the government. Therefore, the Kadets
believed that they had henceforth to consider means of
preserving and strengthening the duma. As they expressed it, they would now inaugurate a "correct siege"
of the administration in order to gain their ends. Henceforth they would avoid open conflict with the government
and would embark on an effective legislative campaign.
They would now resolutely oppose attempts to utilize the
duma as a director of the popular revolutionary movement and a tribune for agitation. It was not to be considered as an auxiliary organ of the revolution. That
course, they felt, was based on an erroneous evaluation of
the comparative strength of the various social forces. It
might lead to the destruction of the entire parliamentary
structure or at best to a vital change in the electoral law,
making the duma as unrepresentative of the population
as was the upper house. True, when circumstances permitted, the duma might organize the developing social
and political forces of the opposition. But, in the opinion
of the Kadets, parliament might best serve the cause of
liberation by interesting itself in constructive, legislative
activity. For, though limited and not fully representative
at the moment, by enacting legislation beneficial to the
masses it would inevitably gain wide, popular support.
Thus, its position would be strengthened in the struggle
with the administration, and it might then attempt more
and far-reaching reforms. Then it might win more power.

    If, however, the foregoing aims were to be realized; if

8. See *Novaia duma, platforma partii narodnoi svobody;* V. Ivanovich, *Rossiiskiia partii,* pp. 15–18.

the duma was to legislate effectively, work efficiently together with the bureaucratic machine, and keep all of its prerogatives safe from bureaucratic aggression, the Kadets were convinced that a "duma ministry" was necessary—a ministry representing the majority elements in the duma and responsible to it. But since this was not provided for in the Fundamental Laws, it might be won, again, only with wide popular support, attracted by constructive legislation.

But in order to avoid open conflict with the government, the Kadets were careful to select those subjects for initial legislative activity which would not meet with opposition from on high and were at the same time practical. First in this category they placed laws safeguarding civil liberties and the independence of the courts. Next, they urged the use of the budgetary right in order to make the significance of the duma apparent to all. Then they would strive for bolder legislation including an electoral law embodying the principle of universal, equal, direct, and secret suffrage—the so-called "four point formula." For the national minorities they would seek complete political and cultural freedom. Since they regarded legislation which aimed to ameliorate the lot of the peasant and worker as extremely urgent and inevitable, they presented a complete program in both fields.[9]

The position assumed by the Kadets, that of a liberal center party, was indeed a thankless one. On the right they were assailed as revolutionaries, or charged with encouraging revolutionary demands, and on the left they were criticized for overcautiousness, or for outright "betrayal" of the revolutionary cause. But the Kadets were

9. Agrarian legislation included an increase in the size of the peasant plots, the land therefor to be drawn from a state land fund, and land expropriated from private owners who were to be remunerated justly. The Kadets also demanded a plan for resettlement of peasants in overcrowded areas, the protection of the peasant against exorbitant rents, and the protection of the agricultural laborer. Proposed labor legislation would include a guarantee of the right to strike and organize, worker's participation in factory inspection, legislation protecting woman and child labor, the creation of a labor relations board, and all forms of industrial and old-age insurance.

34 THE SECOND DUMA

true centrists in the Russian political scene. They tried to make violence unnecessary and impossible. They would reconcile the idealistic aspirations of the moment with the hard facts of reality and inaugurate a régime of political freedom. They felt that to achieve enduring results and to avoid a social and political cataclysm and an uncertain future they must, and could, in time acquaint the Russian people and even the government with western, parliamentary methods. They must win the respect of both for parliament and direct its growth along western, democratic lines.[10]

To the left of center,[11] besides the Social-Democratic Marxists at the extreme wing, stood the three so-called *Narodnik*, or Populist, parties: the Popular-Socialists, the Trudoviki, and the Social-Revolutionaries. Their tradition was derived from the peculiar Russian version of utopian Socialism fathered by P. L. Lavrov and N. K. Mikhailovskii in the seventies and eighties of the nine-

10. Despite its numerical weakness, the Party of Democratic Reform played a significant role in the debates of the Second Duma through its lone representative, Kuzmin-Karavaev. It was composed of intellectuals for whom the Kadet program leaned too far to the left. But on all major questions they agreed with the Kadets. They differed with the latter chiefly on the question of the structure of a political party. The Democratic Reformists held that the time was not yet ripe for the creation of strictly regulated parties. In their opinion, a party had first to demonstrate its ability to exist before it might demand unconditional obedience. This philosophy led, quite naturally, to organizational weakness and poor results at elections. Non-partisans who held the same views but felt the need for organization turned rather to the Party of Peaceful Restoration. This party which had no representatives in the Second Duma was formed during the sessions of the First Duma, drawing its adherents from the conservative Kadets and the liberal Octobrists who approved of "obligatory expropriation at a just remuneration" and opposed Stolypin's land reforms and violent repressive measures. See below Chap. VIII; V. I. Lenin, *Sochineniia* (1924 ed.), X, 475, note.
11. The picture would not be complete without mention of three minority groups: the Polish Kolo, Cossacks, and Moslems. The Kolo and Moslems were interested in their special racial problems, but on all important questions all three voted with the Kadets and may be considered as a part of the center. The only one of them to show any real independence was the Kolo which, as will be seen later, under the astute leadership of Dmovski chose its stand carefully on certain questions, and by its vote or abstention, was able to hold a real balance of power. This, among other things, hastened the dissolution of the Second Duma and the change in the electoral law.

teenth century.[12] Their chief interest and support lay in the peasant population. And in common they sought to defend the village commune as the foundation of the future socialistic society in Russia and as a means of avoiding capitalism in the village.

Of the *Narodnik* parties the most moderate was the Popular-Socialist, which was organized in St. Petersburg after the dissolution of the First Duma.[13] It consisted chiefly of socially minded intellectuals many of whom were willing to adopt even the principle of limited monarchy. They aimed ultimately at allowing each individual the most complete and harmonious development possible within the conditions of universal labor. Therefore, they would abolish all social and economic injustice. They would not, however, serve the interests of any one category of workers, but of all who worked; that is, of the peasantry and intellectual worker besides the industrial proletariat. For their hopes rested not on the dictatorship of any one class, but on the force and will of the whole people. They

12. They had argued that any general improvement in the conditions of those who labored which was to be derived from the social and economic organization and revolution must be accomplished by the people as a whole after it had been enlightened and instructed as to its true interests. This enlightenment, according to their views, was to be carried on by educated propagandists who were to live among the laboring people. This, they held, was their duty toward the masses who had enabled them to receive an education. Following their advice, hundreds of young people undertook social and revolutionary work among the peasants, the more radical elements joining the "Land and Freedom Society." But the movement was quickly crushed by mass arrests and exiles, and "Land and Freedom" resorted to terrorism. A split occurred at the Voronezh convention of the society in 1879 when the moderate elements formed the so-called "Black Repartition" group. They urged the peasants to seize the landowners' property and to divide it among themselves. The more radical group became known as the "People's Will." They would frighten the government into making concessions by systematic, terroristic attacks on officialdom. At the turn of the century this group was replaced by the Social-Revolutionary Party and more moderate *Narodnik* groups. See Brokhaus i Efron, *Entsiklopedicheskii slovar*, XXIII, 858–861; XXVI, 744–747; D. M. Wallace, *Russia* (1905 ed.), p. 523; D. S. Mirsky, *A History of Russian Literature*, pp. 280–281; T. G. Masaryk, *Spirit of Russia*, II, Chap. XV; G. Vernadsky, *Political and Diplomatic History of Russia*, pp. 337–338, 348–349, 352, 364.

13. A. V. Pieshekhonov, *Trudovaia* (*Narodno-sotsialisticheskaia*) *partiia;* Brokhaus i Efron, *Entsiklopedicheskii slovar*, XXVII, 945–946.

sought political and cultural autonomy for the minorities, and would reconstruct the state on federalistic principles. Society was to be organized on a "laboring" basis. All production was to be social, for the Popular-Socialists held this to be the only arrangement whereby all who worked would be free to develop. Therefore they would nationalize the soil, commerce, and industry. But unlike the more extreme leftists they would indemnify former owners for losses sustained. Finally, they demanded the equality of all citizens before the law, the complete preservation of civil liberties, and a unicameral representative body to be elected by universal suffrage. The appeal of the Popular-Socialists was not wide. But being neither entirely revolutionary nor liberal they served to aid in bridging the gap between the center and the left. And they played a significant role in the crystallization of public opinion.

The representatives of the peasant masses, the Trudoviki (laborites), were no party at all but a parliamentary group with a minimum of discipline and only a project of a platform. The Trudovik group was, in fact, a union of non-partisan elements which stood to the left of the Kadets, making decisive demands for agricultural reforms and adopting bold political tactics in the duma. Like the Popular-Socialist party it strove to fight for the interests and reflect the mood of all working classes. But its rank and file consisted, for the most part, of peasants who expressed essentially peasant demands under the leadership of Populist intellectuals. At its first congress in October, 1906, the Trudovik group took steps toward transforming itself into a political party. Its group character remained unchanged, however, and its projected platform was further developed.[14] Its political and economic demands were approximately the same as those voiced by

14. Brokhaus i Efron, *Entsiklopedicheskii slovar*, Supplement II, 787–789; N. P. Vasiliev, *Chto takoe trudoviki ?*, pp. 10–19. They are not to be confused with the Western European Laborites, for they were interested primarily in peasant, not factory, labor.

the Kadets with several additions. Complete amnesty was demanded for those accused of political, agrarian, and religious crimes against the state, and for those arrested for strike activity, violation of army rules, etc. The Trudoviki called for the abolition of all extraordinary "security" measures applied by the state in crushing the rebellion. They asked for all that the Kadets had demanded in the matter of labor legislation, and categorically opposed fines and child labor. Despite the outlawing of the Soviet they demanded its rehabilitation. The agrarian problem, their chief concern, was to be solved according to the project of 104 deputies presented to the First Duma; that is, on the basis of nationalization of the soil.[15]

The most radical of the *Narodnik* parties was the Social-Revolutionary.[16] Founded in 1898 as a direct descendant of the "People's Will," it adopted the terroristic tactics of the earlier organization, and an advanced socialistic stand not unaffected by Marxist principles. With the other *Narodniki* the Social-Revolutionaries called for the nationalization of the soil. But more than other peasant parties they carried on their propaganda and organizing activities among the city proletariat and even in the army. They were the most outspoken and definite revolutionaries among the Populists.

They especially deplored the condition of the peasantry as a result of the emancipation of 1861, and maintained that *kulaki*, landowners, and industrialists had united with the monarchy to oppose the peasant's just demands. Therefore they regarded the tsarist régime as a barrier to the social, economic, and cultural growth of the country, and to its destruction they dedicated themselves. They would "broaden and deepen" the social and property changes with which the overthrow of autocracy was bound.

Along with the more radical Social-Democrats, the Social-Revolutionaries had boycotted the First Duma as

15. See Chapter VIII on the land question.
16. See program in V. Ivanovich, *Rossiiskiia partii*, pp. 280–287.

ineffectual and likely to hinder the success of the revolutionary movement. But when the Marxists entered the field as a unit,[17] they, too, reconsidered their tactics and decided to participate in the second electoral campaign. They maintained then that the revolution was not yet feasible because of the weakness of the working class which would lead it. Therefore they would admit of some participation in legislative activity, but would restrict themselves to legislation which would aid in the development of the solidarity of the working class, raise its intellectual level, facilitate its organization, and prepare it for the liberation struggle. But the Social-Revolutionary legislative program did not differ materially from those presented by the Kadets and the other *Narodniki*.[18] Yet, like the Social-Democrats, they called for the convocation of a constituent assembly, democratically elected, for the purpose of "liquidating" the autocratic régime and reconstructing the social, economic, and political order.

To the left of the Social-Revolutionaries, at the extreme left, was the Russian Social-Democratic Labor Party, founded in 1883 by G. V. Plekhanov, L. G. Deitch, V. I. Zasulich, and others. Alone among the revolutionary parties it had proceeded along the path of Marxian Socialism, and with more or less success, toward the goal of becoming the sole spokesman for the proletariat. Dissension had continually marked the course of its development, and at the turn of the century its entire energy was consumed in driving off a Bernstein-revisionist attack carried on by an inner group who called their economic philosophy "economism." To fight that tendency and to direct the party's policy, a central organ, *Iskra* (The Spark), was founded in 1900 under the aegis of V. I. Lenin[19] and Plekhanov.

17. See below pp. 43, 51–52.
18. See S-R agrarian program below, Chap. VIII.
19. For biographies of Lenin see R. Fox, *Lenin;* D. S. Mirsky, *Lenin;* L. Trotsky, *Lenin;* G. Vernadsky, *Lenin, Red Dictator.* The significance and development of the struggle with the "economists" is discussed in G. Verndasky, *Lenin,* pp. 22–46.

But it was not until 1903, at its Second Congress,[20] called by the *Iskra* staff, that the unity of the party was dangerously threatened by a vital difference of opinion on the question of organization. The majority of the *Iskra* staff, under the energetic leadership of Lenin, demanded members who would actively participate in party organization, while the minority, following I. O. Martov (Tsederbaum), would require only regular, personal cooperation for membership, thus making for a less disciplined, less centralized organization. The congress supported Martov, but the two factions, henceforth called Bolsheviki (majority) and Mensheviki (minority), maintained an endless warfare with each other, interrupted by attempts at reunion. The Bolsheviki assumed an extreme, orthodox stand in their interpretation of the Marxian social and economic philosophy, and in applying revolutionary tactics which followed from that point of view. They would act independently and unite only with the peasantry against all other classes in the struggle for a socialistic society. The Mensheviki, like the Western European Social-Democrats, were less rigid in their interpretation of Marxian theories. They would compromise with less orthodox Socialists and even liberal, middle-class elements in order to realize the ultimate victory of Socialism.

Lenin and the Bolsheviki continued to dominate *Iskra* until the end of the year when Plekhanov lent his support to the Mensheviki, and Lenin resigned from its board. About a year later, in December, 1904, he left the party central committee when the Mensheviki achieved a numerical predominance in that organ as a result of increased party opinion in their favor. He now broke away from the main party and formed an independent Bolshevik group with a newspaper, *Vpered* (Forward), at Geneva. But

20. This First Congress was held in Minsk in 1899, but the delegates were arrested by the police before a program could be drawn up. See G. Vernadsky, *Lenin*, pp. 31–32. For a general narrative of the history of the Social-Democratic Party see E. Iaroslavskii, *Istoriia R. K. P.*; N. Popov, *Outline History of the Communist Party*; G. Vernadsky, *Lenin, Red Dictator*.

"Bloody Sunday," as we noted, had considerably increased radical sentiment among the people—which was all in Lenin's favor. He rejected an offer of reconciliation with the Mensheviki, presented by Bebel and the German Social-Democrats, for he would come to terms only if he might direct the party. At the same time Lenin agitated for a congress which he hoped would support him. In fact, party opinion had swung sharply behind him after the arrest of the central committee, predominantly Menshevik, at Martov's apartments in Moscow.

A congress was finally convened at London on April 12, 1905. But it was attended only by Bolsheviki who nevertheless insisted that it was the Third Party Congress.[21] At the same time the Mensheviki held a rival conference in Geneva.[22] Both groups called for an armed proletarian revolution to destroy autocracy. But the Mensheviki criticized the Bolshevik view that the moment for armed uprising was imminent and that the population should be organized for an immediate attack. The definite moment for the revolutionary outbreak could not be established, they declared, for the proletariat was still too weak and the movement too elemental and chaotic. The population, they held, had first to be thoroughly propagandized and prepared by means of agitation on current political issues, by controlling and guiding the trade-union movement, and by gaining wide support from non-proletarian elements for the fight for a democratic republic. If both factions were suspicious of liberal leadership in the revolution, the Bolsheviki would have no traffic whatever with it. Liberal intellectualism had, in their opinion, to be unmasked as anti-proletarian and counter-revolutionary. And the Leninists placed special emphasis on the support to be rendered to the peasant movement—to the point of condoning the confiscation and distribution of large

21. E. Iaroslavskii, *Istoriia V. K. P.*, II, 453; *Vsiesoiuznaia kommunisticheskaia partiia v rezoliutsiakh ee siezdov i konferentsii, 1898–1926*, pp. 32–41; hereafter cited as *V. K. P. rezoliutsii*.

22. Supplement to no. 100, *Iskra*, pp. 18–19; V. I. Nevskii, *Istoriia R. K. P.*, pp. 308–313; E. Iaroslavskii, *Istoriia V. K. P.*, II, 452.

estates. They would, moreover, organize the village poor against the village bourgeoisie. The Mensheviki, on the other hand, would seek support from all enemies of tsarism in the struggle with reaction.

There were further differences on the seizure of power and the utilization of representative institutions. Should the bourgeoisie emerge victorious over absolutism, the Mensheviki would dissociate themselves from the new government. For the middle class would oppose all elements threatening capitalism and the Social-Democrats could not become identified with their inconsistent and selfish policy. Therefore, the Mensheviki felt that they could best serve the progress of the proletarian revolution by refusing to seize or share power in a provisional government, and by acting as an extreme revolutionary opposition. But the Bolsheviki had advocated socialistic pressure on a bourgeois government, and they severely criticized the Menshevik decision. It was the duty of the Social-Democratic party, they asserted, to organize the revolution both from above and below, and they regarded the Menshevik resolution as a misconception of revolutionary duty if not sheer anarchism.[23] The Mensheviki expressed their willingness to utilize any popular representative body the government might grant in order to turn it into a constituent assembly. But the Bolsheviki regarded any popular organ convened by the tsarist government as a sop to disorganize the revolution, and they would consider nothing less than a constituent assembly. Finally, the essential differences in their views on organization were not yet reconciled. For some time, then, the mutual hostility of the Social-Democratic factions continued unabated; the Bolsheviki charging the Mensheviki with hesitancy and serious digression from the "true" revolutionary path.

As we have seen, in October, 1905, the Social-Democrats began to direct the course of the Revolution through the Soviet.[24] After its arrest Lenin, who had returned to

23. Compare Lenin, *Sobranie sochinenii*, VI (1921 ed.), 207–217, 233.

24. The Social-Democrats Khrustàlev and Trotskii took a leading part in its creation.

Russia, immediately organized a second council which called for a general strike on December 7. A few days later the Moscow uprising began, and with its failure the party was again curbed and forced underground. For the Social-Democratic factions the need for unity in the face of the common enemy was obvious. Accordingly, both branches held a conference in Tammerfors, Finland, which resulted in the creation of a provisional committee. This body was to prepare for a congress which would unify the party.

The Fourth Party Congress which met at Stockholm in April, 1906, was one of the most significant in the history of the Social-Democratic party. Here the breach between the factions was, at least outwardly, healed, and all of the Social-Democratic groups in the empire were united in one Pan-Russian party. Hence, the Stockholm gathering was officially known as the Unification Congress. Here, too, the rules of organization were evolved. Moreover, resolutions adopted at Stockholm were significant not only because they were binding for the party and fraction until the following congress met in May, 1907—late in the life of the Second Duma—but, as we shall see, they played an important rôle in determining the very fate of that duma. The Mensheviki obtained a majority in the party elections, placed seven of their number and three Bolsheviki on the central committee of the party,[25] and generally dominated the proceedings.

Of great significance was the resolution adopted on the attitude of the party toward the duma.[26] Like all other political and social matters touched upon, this question was considered entirely from the Marxist point of view of the inevitable class conflict, and the advancement of the revolutionary cause was the common aim of all deliberations. The government, the Social-Democrats believed, would certainly oppose the duma's reform program and

25. Protokoly obiedinitelnago siezda sotsial-demokraticheskoi rabochei partii, pp. 405–406.
26. V. K. P. rezoliutsii, pp. 62–63.

thus threaten the vital interests of the new bourgeois society. The latter would then be forced to call on the popular masses for support and cause them to turn the constitutional duma into a revolutionary weapon. The congress therefore decided that the party was to utilize the conflicts arising between the government and the duma for the purpose of "broadening and deepening" the revolutionary movement. To this end it was to aggravate the struggle so that the duma might become the rallying point of the popular revolution against autocracy. It was also to connect current political problems with the social and economic demands of the workers and peasants. And the partisans were to agitate among the people for the presentation of revolutionary demands in the hope that this outside pressure would render the duma more aggressive. But at the same time they were to point out that the bourgeois parties opposed to revolution were unfit to serve as spokesmen for the popular will. Finally, they were to emphasize the unsuitability of the duma as a permanent, representative institution and the necessity of calling a constituent assembly on the basis of the "four point formula."[27]

Moreover, the congress provided for the organization of a Social-Democratic group, or fraction, in the duma which would act under the permanent leadership and control of the party's central committee. It was to urge a more decisive opposition to the government, rally round itself all revolutionary elements, raise social and economic questions and support them in connection with political problems, sharpen the conflict between the duma and the government, and make contacts with the workers through party organizations. Therefore, wherever elections were yet to take place (elections to the First Duma had already ended in most localities) the party was to set up its candidates without entering into blocs with other parties. Thus the party officially favored entry into the duma in the face of bitter Bolshevik opposition. For the Lenin-

27. See above p. 33.

ists desired a complete boycott of the duma as a counter-revolutionary institution which would serve only the interests of the middle class and confuse the revolutionary masses.[28]

With the double aim of promoting the revolutionary cause and bettering the condition of the peasantry the congress passed an agrarian resolution which called for the destruction of the burdensome remnants of "feudalism" and the development of the class struggle in the village.[29] All class restrictions imposed on the peasant—personal, property, and financial—were to be abolished. And in order to increase the size of the peasant's plot all state, church and privately owned lands were to be turned over to organs of local self government for distribution among the peasantry. In Social-Democratic circles this was called "municipalization" of the land. Then, the congress favored the disintegration of the commune and its replacement by private, peasant property. This, the party believed, was the normal course of economic development. And Marxian theory held that the Socialist revolution would best develop in a capitalistic medium. Finally, at the insistence of the Bolsheviki, the congress agreed to organize the village proletariat separately and emphasize the "irreconcilability" of their interests with those of the peasant bourgeoisie. Moreover, they were to be warned against the attractions of the system of petty ownership which could never abolish peasant misery under the capitalistic system of production. Only a complete social revolution would destroy poverty and exploitation.

Since the agrarian reform was regarded by the Fourth Congress as the main question on the agenda the central problem of land distribution occasioned a long and heated controversy among the Social-Democratic factions. The Bolsheviki would "nationalize" rather than "municipalize" the land in the event of the victory of the "bourgeois

28. *Protokoly obiedinitelnago siezda*, pp. 237–239; *V. K. P. rezoliutsii*, pp. 54–55.

29. *V. K. P. rezoliutsii*, pp. 62–63.

revolution"—the establishment of the dictatorship of the peasantry and the proletariat. For only nationalization, they held, could effectively destroy the remnants of "feudalism," clear the way for the development of capitalism in agriculture, and thus facilitate the advent of the complete social revolution.[30] But the Menshevik majority in the congress saw in "municipalization" a firm basis for the future democratic structure. Local governing bodies, they held, were more democratic than the central state, and the numerous types of agriculture carried on in the empire necessitated local solutions of agrarian problems. Then, the Mensheviki feared that the reactionaries might arouse the peasantry against a government which would confiscate its lands. Moreover, they observed that despotism had, in the past, been created on the foundation of nationalized property. And finally, they felt that in the event of a successful restoration movement, the reactionary government would gain control of all peasant lands.[31]

From what has been said above it is quite obvious that in the minds of the Social-Democrats the peasant revolutionary movement was closely related to the question of agrarian reform. Without that movement the "feudal" régime might not be overthrown, and the bourgeois régime, vital to the development of Socialism, might not be established. Therefore, the Fourth Congress devoted special attention to this matter and the resolution on the "peasant movement" was unanimously adopted.[32] The Social-Democrats maintained that the peasants formed a revolutionary class whose economic and juridical demands might be met only by a general reconstruction of state life. Therefore the party was to organize them for revolutionary activity. But since the peasant movement was essentially bourgeois (although a peasant proletariat existed) and was being directed by bourgeois parties, the village population was

30. V. I. Lenin, *Sobranie sochinenii*, VII, 155–163 (1921 ed.); Lenin, *Sochineniia*, IX, 373–397 (1925 ed.); *Protokoly obiedinitelnago siezda*, pp. 39, 103–110; *V. K. P. rezoliutsii*, p. 56.
31. *Protokoly obiedinitelnago siezda*, pp. 39–42, 110–113.
32. *V. K. P. rezoliutsii*, p. 62.

to be separated into its component parts. The village proletariat were to be included in the proletarian party, the
Social-Democratic. But the bulk of the peasantry was to
be organized in the non-partisan Peasant Union, Soviets
of Peasant Deputies, etc., whose activities were to be co-
ordinated with those of the proletariat. The party was to
sharpen the struggle between the peasantry and the government and landowners, and it was to impress the first
named with the fact that its political demands might be
satisfied only by a constituent assembly. Yet the peasants
were to be urged to present extreme demands to the duma
to revolutionize it. The party also advocated elective, local
officials, the preaching of armed uprising among the
peasantry, and the creation of trade unions among the
agrarian workers which were to strike for shorter hours
and higher wages.

Likewise without dissent the congress adopted a resolution on the party's general attitude toward trade unions.[33]
It regarded trade unionism as a necessary and component
part of the class struggle, and of the class organization of
the proletariat. Trade unions, it declared, must strive
mainly for the broad organization of labor. But the Social-
Democrats believed that the economic struggle would result in the improvement of workers' conditions, and the
strengthening of their organization only if it were correctly coördinated with the political struggle of the proletariat. For besides defending the economic interests of
the workers, in a revolutionary epoch trade unions should
draw the workers into the direct political melée, and foster
their organization and unification. In view of these considerations, the congress resolved that the party was to
encourage the organization of the workers in trade unions,
and help to establish them. It was to strive for the abolition of all restrictions on their activities and to utilize their
legal status for agitation. Party members were urged to
join them, take an important part in their activities, and
attempt to bind them organically to the party.

33. *Ibid.*, pp. 64-65.

On the question of "partisan attacks," that is, raids by so-called party "fighting bands" (armed civilian partisans) on banks, arsenals, and troops, there was a serious difference of opinion among the delegates.[34] Accounts of these attacks were given a prominent place in the current press, and the public reaction was not entirely favorable. Of late, the Bolsheviki had taken a significant part in these raids. They regarded this activity as a means of preparing for armed insurrection; as fine, practical training for the "fighting bands." But the Menshevik majority saw in them only a disorganizing and demoralizing force, and the Fourth Congress condemned these attacks, and the wanton destruction of public property. Yet they excepted raids on arsenals and ammunition dumps.

Finally, the congress decided that the party was to agitate for an armed uprising among the workers, peasants, and soldiers.[35] The Social-Democrats hoped to make the population conscious of the "necessity" of realizing its demands by armed force. The party would not promise to arm the population but would organize fighting bands. Untimely clashes were to be avoided, and for the purpose of coördinated revolutionary activity "fighting agreements" were to be made with other revolutionary and oppositional organizations. The Bolsheviki regarded this resolution as too hesitant. They believed that the moment for armed insurrection had arrived, and that the party should concentrate on organizing the uprising and on realizing it.

The remaining business of the congress was entirely organizational and marked an important step in the growth of the party numerically and geographically. The Polish and Lettish Social-Democratic parties entered the Russian Social-Democratic Labor Party as autonomous organizations which were to participate in and act under the direction of the central committee of the party.[36] They

34. *Ibid.*, p. 64.
35. *Ibid.*, p. 63.
36. *Ibid.*, pp. 66–67. See Appendix I, B.

were to function on a territorial basis in Poland and in the Lettish provinces (Kurland and Livland). The Jewish Bund[37] relinquished the demand (made at the Second Congress) that it be the sole representative of the Jewish proletariat in the empire, and was merely recognized as an organization whose activity was not territorially confined.

Having thus united the party and embraced all Social-Democratic circles in the empire, the Stockholm Congress established the structure of the party organization and the rules by which it was to function. With few exceptions, the Rules of Organization adopted at the Fourth Congress remained unchanged until 1917.[38]

The rules defined a member in accordance with the Bolshevik formula, as anyone accepting the party's program, supporting it by material means, and taking active part in some party organization. The party was to be built on the principle of "democratic centralism"; that is, it was to be directed by a democratically elected, all-powerful central committee. But local, regional, and national organizations, similarly constructed, were to be autonomous in resolving their internal problems. New organizations were to be certified by regional (*oblast*) conferences, or by neighboring bodies. These certifications were to be reviewed by the central committee of the party. Organizations in the same district could form regional unions whose center was to be established at a regional conference. All organizations were to yield 10 per cent of their income for the support of the central committee.

The central committee and the editorial staff of the central organ of the party were to be elected at the party congress. The central committee was to represent the party in its relations with other parties. It was to create various party institutions and direct their activities. It was to organize and direct enterprises having a party-wide significance, and was to dispose of the resources and funds

37. *Ibid.*, pp. 67–68. See Appendix I, B.
38. *Ibid.*, pp. 65–66.

of the party and manage its central treasury. It was to
act as arbitrator in settling conflicts arising between
various party institutions and within separate institutions, and, in general, to coördinate all party activities.
The staff of the central organ was to act with the central
committee in solving party questions of a political nature.
If a member of the central committee resigned he was to
be replaced from a list drawn up by the congress and in
the order named. If a resignation from the staff of the
central organ occurred, the vacancy was to be filled by the
central committee together with the remaining members
of the staff of the central organ.

The supreme institution of the party was the party
congress which the central committee was to call annually.
An extraordinary congress might be convened after a
two-month notice at the request of at least half of the
party membership. Should the central committee refuse
to convene such a congress, the half of the party demanding it might create an organizational committee en-
joying the rights of the central committee at the congress.
All party organizations were to be represented at the
annual congress by one delegate for every 500 members
participating in the election. Organizations composed of
at least 300 voters might unite with neighboring bodies to
send a common delegate, if together they numbered 500
voters. The elections were to be democratic; that is, direct,
secret, and open to all party members. A congress was to
be valid only if it represented at least one half of the party.
The announcement of the convocation of an annual congress and its agenda were to be published at least a month
and a half before the date of the first session.

The Social-Democratic Party, then, was first and
foremost revolutionary and Marxian. It sought to overthrow the "feudal-monarchistic" order and replace it with
a bourgeois-democratic state under which the ultimate
Socialist revolution might be prepared. To that end the
entire program of the party was directed at the Stockholm
Congress. And to that end the parliamentary campaign

was to be subordinated. In the arena of national politics it is evident that the socialistic and revolutionary principles enunciated, and the tactics evolved at the Fourth Congress would inevitably result in a clash not only with the government and the right, but even with the liberal Kadets. For the Constitutional Democrats were parliamentary constitutionalists. They expressly opposed a duma which would lead the revolutionary movement and enact revolutionary legislation. They aimed to "besiege" autocracy, and predicted that constitutional government and the cause of liberation would suffer only a severe setback as a result of aggressive tactics directed against the administration. Constructive, reform legislation, not revolutionary demands would, in their opinion, preserve the duma and strengthen it. Accordingly, they also opposed continued revolutionary activity and advocated the attraction of the population to legislative work. Thus it came about that the Second Duma, marked as it was by the flowering of both Social-Democratic and Kadet tactics, witnessed a three-cornered clash (as the government and right opposed both groups) which dogged its every step and ultimately determined its fate.

II

THE ELECTION CAMPAIGN

AFTER the dissolution of the First Duma both factions of the Social-Democratic Party continued to
maintain the positions which they had assumed at
the Stockholm Congress in April, 1906. The Mensheviki
held the final goal to be the convocation of a constituent
assembly. But in the meantime they believed that no real
forward step might be taken in the liberation struggle
while the power remained in the hands of the reactionary
court circles and ministers appointed by them. Accordingly, the central committee called for the support of the
duma and a representative (duma) ministry. The Bolsheviki, on the other hand, opposed a duma ministry which
they held to be no real gain, and which they regarded with
suspicion as a "deal" between the government and the
bourgeoisie at the expense of the people. Moreover, they
maintained that such a ministry offered no guarantee that
the proletariat would be able to carry on its class struggle.
They believed that it would merely foster constitutional
illusions and thus pervert the revolutionary consciousness
of the people by arousing hopes of a peaceful passage of
power to the population and obscuring the basic aims of
the struggle for freedom. They demanded a national uprising which would establish a constituent assembly.[1] Only
by revolution, they declared, might the people win real
power.

But the attitude of the Bolsheviki toward the next duma
underwent a sudden and sharp change. In an article appearing in the first number of *Proletarii* [2] on August 21,

1. Lenin, *Sobranie sochinenii*, VII, part 2, 10–12 (1922 ed.); Lenin, *Sochineniia*, X, 26–32 (1924 ed.).
2. "On the Boycott" was the name of the article which appeared in *Proletarii*.
The latter was a Bolshevik sheet published in Finland until the end of 1907.

1906, Lenin defended the boycott of the First Duma as the only method then available for fighting the "constitutional illusions" built up by the Kadets during the first election campaign. From this point of view, he believed that the boycott had fulfilled its duty of warning the people against the tsarist constitution and in revealing Kadet "trickery" during elections. But the history of the First Duma had demonstrated that parliament might be used for agitational purposes, and that in it the revolutionary peasantry might be aligned against the Kadets by exposing the illusions which they preached. Therefore, Lenin called on the Social-Democrats to end their boycott of the duma and to open their eyes to reality. The duma was to be used, but its significance was not to be exaggerated, and it was to be subordinated to agitation for strike and uprising going on outside, in the country. Its uselessness as a means of achieving real gains was to be made patent to all, as was the necessity for calling a constituent assembly. Thus Lenin had now come to regard the duma as a valuable means of disseminating revolutionary, especially Bolshevik, propaganda, at a time when he had begun to admit that the revolution was on the wane.

If the Social-Democrats were to win a significant number of seats in the duma, their leaders realized that electoral agreements of some kind had to be reached with other anti-administration parties. But here again the choice of political bedfellows called forth a difference of opinion between the Mensheviki and the Bolsheviki which well-nigh threatened to divide the party in the midst of the election campaign when its solidarity was most desirable. The debates concerned the value of the Kadets, the most powerful of the opposition parties, as partners in the campaign. The Mensheviki would welcome them, while the Bolsheviki denounced them as traitors to the cause of revolution, and called for agreements with the *Narodnik* parties to combat them.

In that year it was moved first to Geneva and then to Paris where it appeared until the end of 1910. At that time it was replaced by the *Social-Democrat*. It was edited by Lenin, Kamenev, and Zinoviev.

In the fall of 1906, after a brief period of wavering between complete isolation and coöperation, the Mensheviki finally defined exactly their tactics in the coming campaign.[3] They reasoned that although the right, the "Black Hundreds," might be harmless in themselves they had the support of the highly organized government forces. But the people on the other hand, sadly lacked organization. And since the liberals, too, were bent on uniting the nation in a struggle against absolutism, the Social-Democrats had no choice but to coöperate with them. In war, manoeuvers were necessary. Thus, any non-proletarian party which was ready to fight for political freedom had to be supported. Moreover, by isolating themselves from the opposition, the Mensheviki feared that the Social-Democrats ran the risk of losing the confidence of the proletariat who would feel that the party was forsaking them in the struggle for freedom. Such a course might result in victory for the party's enemies and defeat for its allies. Should a Kadet lose an election, an Octobrist or a reactionary would win it. Therefore the Mensheviki recommended that the Social-Democrats act independently if they were sure to elect their candidate. But where they were uncertain, they were to enter into agreements with other opposition parties.[4] The central committee, dominated by the Mensheviki, allowed blocs with anti-administration groups in the lower electoral stages.[5]

Such an analysis of the interrelationship of political forces aroused in Lenin, and the Bolsheviki, boundless indignation.[6] He could conceive of nothing more non-Marxian, "unscientific." The Mensheviki, he asserted, had failed to analyze the class relationships of the various parties. Who were the Kadets? They were bourgeois in-

3. See E. Iaroslavskii, *Istoriia V. K. P.*, II, 671–672; *Tovarishch*, October 7, 1906.

4. *Tovarishch*, Oct. 31, 1906; *Riech*, Nov. 1, 1906, p. 3; L. Martov, *Izbiratelniia soglasheniia*, pp. 7, 13, 29.

5. *Sotzialdemokrat*, Oct. 27, 1906, quoted in Iaroslavskii, *Isoriia V. K. P.*, II, 672.

6. Lenin, *Sochineniia*, X, 91–94 (1924 ed.); Lenin, *Sobranie sochinenii*, VIII, 11–20 (1921 ed.); Lenin, *Sochineniia*, X, 204–209 (1924 ed.); *ibid.*, pp. 225–226.

tellectuals and liberal squires who would make "deals" with autocracy to end the revolution. They had no actual class foundations. They could not fight, therefore they were real "brokers" who would immortalize bourgeois exploitation and ordered, "civilized," parliamentary forms. They could not be called democrats for they would allow an upper house and restrictive press laws, and refused to accept local land-organizing committees. He maintained that the "Black Hundred" danger did not exist but was conjured up by the Kadets to attract peasant votes and thus ward off the danger from the left. But granted that the reactionary danger did exist; in Lenin's opinion the formation of blocs with the Kadets was not the correct means of combatting it. For the Kadets would surely compromise with the government. Furthermore, he believed that technical election blocs with the Kadets would soon lead to ideological blocs since the political forces of the country were disturbed and highly fluid. The real danger to the proletariat, he believed, arose from the Kadets who made a show of liberalism and were able to influence the peasants and small burghers with their ideas. They might convince them that freedom could be won and the monarch still be allowed to remain, and that redemption payments for soil to be expropriated would be most beneficial for the peasantry. The peasant was, after all, a small landowner, bourgeois by nature, and therefore particularly susceptible to Kadet influences from which the Social-Democrats had to wrest him.

But how were the Social-Democrats, representatives of the proletariat, to gain hegemony over the great masses of the peasantry? How were they to oust the Kadets from that position and replace them? Simply by uniting with the peasantry for the purpose of exposing and defeating the Kadets, declared Lenin, and he advocated electoral agreements for this end. In the lower stages, in the work of agitating before the masses, the Social-Democrats were to appear independently. In the workers' curiae there were to be no agreements at all, for here the Social-Democrats dominated the field. But in the higher stages, in the choice of electors to the city assemblies and of delegates and electors in the provincial elections, the Kadets were to be bested by agreements with the Social-Revolutionaries and the Trudoviki. These were the real bourgeois democrats— as opposed to the Kadets who were bourgeois monarchists —who ardently desired the creation of a democratic republic. But there was also the right wing of the *Narodnik* group, the Popular-Socialists; social-monarchists, half Kadet, Lenin termed them. These, too, were to be defeated at elections by special agreements with the Social-Revolutionaries. Blocs with the Kadets were under no circumstances to be allowed. For the sake of a few seats in the liberal duma the Social-Democrats were not to run the risk of interfering with the development of the "consciousness" and solidarity of the proletariat by supporting those traitors to the revolution, who would call for an end of revolutionary activity in the duma and who would enter the government's cabinet. Such tactics, he declared, would only confuse the proletarian and peasant masses.[7]

To resolve the debate on tactics and to prepare for the next party convention, the central committee called the first Pan-Russian Social-Democratic Labor Party Conference at Tammerfors in November, 1906. Here the Mensheviki, supported by the Bund, gained a majority for their tactical program.[8] According to the Tammerfors decisions the Social-Democratic party was to appear in the campaign. And following the dictates of the Stockholm Congress it was to broadcast the Social-Democratic program, dispel illusions concerning the peaceful outcome of the struggle between the people and the government, reveal the insufficiencies in the tactics and slogans of the bourgeois opposition parties, and contrast them with the revolutionary methods and goals of the proletariat. The reactionaries were by all means to be defeated, and the Social-Democrats were to organize all revolutionary

7. Lenin, *Sochineniia*, X, pp. 131–146, 245 (1924 ed.).
8. *V. K. P. rezoliutsii*, pp. 70–71.

forces, inside and out of the duma. Conditions were to be created for transforming that institution into a rallying point of the revolution. The complete powerlessness of the duma as a legislative institution under autocracy was to be revealed, and the necessity for a fully empowered constituent assembly. Likewise in accordance with the Stockholm decisions, alliances with single parties or groups of parties for the entire duration of the campaign were forbidden. During the first stages there were to be no agreements in the workers' curia with parties which did not accept the dogma of the class struggle of the proletariat. In other curiae agreements might be made with any opposition parties, but under the control of the party center, in order to prevent a rightist victory. No concessions of principle were to be allowed. Agreements were to be made for definite areas and on concrete lists of candidates and electors. Local organizations might make decisions within limits established by general regulations of the central committee. Because the Bolsheviki wished to preserve as much local autonomy as possible to allow for the application of their tactics they were able to wring from the conference a concession on local agreements. The central committee might forbid local organizations to compile lists which were not purely Social-Democratic but it could not bind them to compile lists including non-Marxians.[9]

But the Bolsheviki were completely dissatisfied. And since the resolutions of the conference were not binding, they introduced their special program, or opinion.[10] They officially announced the abandonment of the boycott tactics, emphasized the importance of attracting the peasantry by campaign propaganda and the danger for the revolution of the predominance and leadership of the Kadets in public life. They demanded absolute independence in the workers' curia and otherwise adhered closely to Lenin's rules for creating blocs with other political

9. Lenin, *Sobranie sochinenii*, VIII, 21–24 (1922 ed.); E. Iaroslavskii, *Istoriia V. K. P.* II, 672.
10. *V. K. P. rezoliutsii*, pp. 69–70.

groups. The agreements which they permitted were to be limited to the purpose of distributing places according to the proportionate strength of the parties to the pact. Finally, as a guide, the Bolsheviki grouped the parties according to their democratic consistency including in the first group the Social-Revolutionaries, in the second group the Popular-Socialists and the Trudoviki, while they recognized the Kadets as the least consistently democratic party in the opposition to the government.

The promulgation of two programs could not, of course, be expected to unite the factions of the party, and the struggle went on much as before with the exchange of charges, counter-charges, and imprecations, and even with the creation of a significant organizational split. All eyes were turned on St. Petersburg during the campaign, for, as the capital and chief metropolis of the empire, any precedent it might establish would have far-reaching effects. Consequently, both factions began to manoeuver for the control of votes and tactics of the St. Petersburg Social-Democrats. On January 8, 1907, a city conference, elected by the St. Petersburg organization, met with a Bolshevik majority.[11] An atmosphere of intense hostility prevailed. Each faction hurled charges of electoral irregularity at the other. But the Bolsheviki annulled only Menshevik mandates, and the Menshevik delegation refused to participate in the work of the meeting.[12] When the conference rejected a decree of the central committee separating the suburbs from the city for the purpose of making electoral agreements, the breaking point was reached. The central committee nullified in advance the

11. *Riech*, Jan. 9, 1907, p. 4; *Tovarishch*, January 9, 1907, p. 4. Unless otherwise noted dates used hereafter with references to *Riech* and *Tovarishch* will indicate issues during the year 1907. See also Lenin, *Sochineniia*, X, 501–503 (1924 ed.). Forty Bolshevik and thirty-one Menshevik delegates were elected.

12. The Bolsheviki maintained that many Menshevik delegates had not expressed themselves on the various points of the electoral program according to the rules established by the Bolshevik St. Petersburg committee, central organ of the local party. The Mensheviki charged that many Bolshevik delegates had been chosen by the executive organs of party cells rather than by the cells as a whole.

decisions of the conference, and the Mensheviki with-drew.[13]

Each side then proceeded to publish its own resolutions and to behave as an independent party, issuing appeals and explanations from a purely partisan point of view. The Mensheviki[14] proposed to elect an executive organ which would explain their stand and make contacts with all opposition elements in order to arrange for electoral agreements in the face of a "Black Hundred" danger. The Bolsheviki, on the other hand,[15] maintained their opposition to the Kadets, ridiculed the danger from the right, and otherwise upheld the resolutions adopted by the city conference. They would create an executive committee which was to make agreements with the *Narodniki*. They stated their terms for the distribution of places at the electoral assemblies, and continued to insist on the exclu-sion of the Popular-Socialists from any peasant bloc.[16] On January 18, the Mensheviki, acting independently with the Trudovik group, tried to form a bloc with the Kadets. But the attempt failed for the liberals would allow them but one of the six deputies to the duma allotted St. Peters-burg, while the Mensheviki expected at least three. The Social-Democrats, the Kadets declared, did not number one half or even one third of the capital's voters.[17]

13. *Riech*, Jan. 13, p. 4. The proposal was ostensibly only a technical improve-ment but it would have equalized the strength of both factions in the St. Peters-burg district for the suburbs were controlled by the Mensheviki and the Bol-sheviki maintained that the central committee was encroaching on the authority of the St. Petersburg organization.

14. *Riech*, Jan. 13, p. 4; Jan. 18, p. 4; Jan. 19, p. 4; Jan. 20, p. 4; *Tovarishch*, Jan. 19, p. 4.

15. *Tovarishch*, Jan. 10, p. 4; *Riech*, Jan. 11, p. 4.

16. *Riech*, Dec. 29, 1906, p. 4; Jan. 13, 1907, p. 4; *Tovarishch*, Jan. 13, 1907, p. 4.

17. It was this which prompted Lenin to write his brochure "The Election in St. Petersburg and the Hypocrisy of Thirty Mensheviki" in which he accused them of betraying the workers to the Kadets and of bargaining with them to "drag their deputies into the duma." (Lenin, *Sobranie sochinenii*, VIII, 148–152, 1922 ed.). For this the central committee put him on trial before a party court composed of three representatives of the Mensheviki, three of Lenin, and three appointed by the central committee from the Polish and Lettish Social-Demo-crats and the Bund. At the trial Lenin demanded that the Mensheviki and their

After these vain attempts a meeting of leftist groups on January 22 was attended by both Social-Democratic factions. The Bolsheviki were bluntly informed by the *Narodniki* that the Popular-Socialists must be included in any agreement they might conclude. Two days later the Leninists expressed their willingness to consort with all Populist elements.[18] But the party central committee now openly opposed blocs with only peasant groups.[19] Therefore, when a second meeting was called on January 25, the Mensheviki refused to attend on the ground that a bloc with the *Narodniki* alone was an insufficient guarantee for success in the face of a "Black Hundred" danger. Should a "left bloc" be formed they would act independently and would set up their organizations wherever they believed a rightist danger threatened.[20] The Bolsheviki proceeded to establish local electoral committees, and at the city conference which they alone attended they selected a candidate for the duma and invited popular support.[21] This state of affairs was a fair example of the disorganization existing in the party as a result of the attempt to hold two distinct groups with separate tactical principles under the same central institutions and general party program.

Elsewhere blocs were formed in the higher or lower stages, with or against the Kadets; or the party remained

leader Dan be tried also, but the central committee refused to prefer charges on the ground that the present court was called to analyze charges against Lenin. Only two sessions were held and only three witnesses examined when the trial was interrupted by the opening of the Fifth Party Congress in London. There Lenin's defensive speech, ridiculing the Menshevik electoral tactics, was distributed as a brochure, "Doklad v siezdu R. S. D. R. P. po povodu Peterburgskago raskola i sviazannogo s nim uchrezhdeniia partiinogo suda" (Report to the Congress of the Russian Social-Democratic Labor Party Concerning the Petersburg Schism and the Institution of a Party Court connected therewith). See *Protokoly V Siezda*, pp. 672–685, 758; *Riech*, Jan. 28, p. 2; Jan. 31, p. 2; *Tovarishch*, Jan. 31, p. 3. For the negotiations with the Kadets see *Riech*, Jan. 19, p. 4; *Tovarishch*, Jan. 19, p. 4; Jan. 25, p. 4.

18. *Riech*, Jan. 24, p. 4; Jan. 26, p. 2; *Tovarishch*, Jan. 24, p. 3.
19. *Tovarishch*, Jan. 25, p. 4; *Riech*, Jan. 25, p. 3.
20. *Riech*, Jan. 26, p. 2; Feb. 6, p. 4.
21. *Ibid.*, Feb. 14, p. 4; *Tovarishch*, Feb. 14, p. 4.

independent, according to the predominance of either faction in the local party organizations. In Moscow, after some delay, an agreement was reached between the Social-Democrats and the *Narodniki*. This, however, soon foundered on the question of the distribution of seats in the duma, since the Social-Democrats refused to yield ground after having demanded three of the four seats allotted Moscow, and felt strong enough to act without the left bloc.[22] Nevertheless, the Kadets drew upon themselves all of the bitter animosity of the Moscow Social-Democrats when they summarily rejected an agreement allowing the Marxists two seats in the duma. The Kadets also felt that they were strong enough without an agreement, and asserted that the principle of class representation was repugnant to them as was the Social-Democratic program in general.[23]

From the very beginning of the electoral campaign the administration actively interfered in an attempt to influence the results.[24] Stolypin, it is true, had issued orders to local officials, stressing the necessity for legality in all of their activities and for complete freedom of electioneering. They were to restrain only those who would use election meetings for agitational purposes. But these demands made little or no impression on the local grandees who found it difficult to acclimate themselves to the conditions of a constitutional régime.[25] Furthermore, all the resources of the bureaucracy, physical, legal, and spiritual, were brought into play in an attempt to create a duma with a majority to the right of center, a duma "acceptable" to the administration.

22. *Riech*, Dec. 16, 1906, p. 3; Jan. 12, p. 4; Jan. 21, p. 3; Jan. 25, p. 2; *Tovarishch*, Jan.1, 1907, p. 4.

23. *Tovarishch*, Feb. 4, p. 3; Feb. 6, p. 4.

24. Although preparations had been going on ever since the dissolution of the First Duma, the beginning of the election campaign may be dated from the publication of an imperial decree on December 8, 1906, establishing the date for elections to the duma as February 6, 1907. See *Riech*, Dec. 9, 1906.

25. A. Smirnov, *Kak proshli vybory*, pp. 81–82; *Tovarishch*, January 20, 1907, p. 2.

It was in the legal field that the manoeuvers of the administration were first apparent. In reviewing the electoral law we observed the possibility of multiple voting on the part of a single citizen as a result of the combined class, property, and territorial bases of that law. In itself the recasting of the electoral right to eliminate that weakness by the method of legal interpretation was a progressive step. But the government, through its highest interpretive body, the Ruling Senate, changed the law so that only those strata of the population known to be antagonistic to it were affected, the peasants and the workers. On October 7, the Ruling Senate declared that those peasants who held both allotment land in the commune and land purchased through the Peasant Land Bank could not, on the basis of such purchases, vote in the landowners' curia.[26] This deprived the peasants of an advantage still retained by the larger landowners who might yet exercise suffrage rights in several localities where their land qualified them to vote. Moreover, the squires might also vote in the city curia if they owned urban real estate. The same interpretation stated that "non-home owners" were to be excluded from the peasant curia; that is, peasants who did not permanently reside in the village or who were not permanently engaged in agriculture. This was obviously an attempt to exclude troublesome political leaders of peasant origin like Anikin and Aladin who from early youth had been attracted to the large centers.[27] The multiple voting right of workers was likewise limited by forbidding them to vote both at factories in the workers' curia and in the city curia as apartment renters.[28]

As a result of these moves many voters were indeed

26. *Riech*, Oct. 8, 1906; Smirnov, *Kak proshli vybory*, pp. 101–104.

27. *Riech*, Oct. 8, 1906; Smirnov, *Kak proshli vybory*, pp. 101–104. In the fifty-one provinces of European Russia, of the fifty-three peasants elected by the peasant curia, six were teachers, one was a physician, one an editor, one a student, and two were former students. See *Ukazatel k stenographicheskim otchetam, vtoroi sozyv*, pp. 1–25; cited hereafter as *Ukazatel*. Smirnov, *Kak proshli vybory*, p. 105.

28. *Riech*, Oct. 8, 1906; Smirnov, *Kak proshly vybory*, pp. 101–104.

eliminated from the groups involved. But so deep and widespread was the anti-governmental temper of the population—not a little enhanced by the indignation stirred up as a result of these interpretations—that they accomplished little toward bringing about a rightist victory in the elections.[29]

But not all of the activity of the administration directed at influencing elections was as subtle as that engaged in by the "highest spheres." From the provincial governor and city police chief down to the lower ranks of the bureaucracy, local officialdom, responsible to central governmental institutions, subjected the Russian population to varying degrees of pressure to obtain the desired results. Some of these acts were open and crude violations of the law, others involved less obvious trickery or rigid application of the electoral law in order to avoid or forestall elections, or to get rid of opposition elements. But generally speaking, these petty satraps demonstrated a lamentable lack of imagination and political acumen, and the ultimate results, as the elections were to make clear, hardly justified the huge effort involved.

In the first place, one of the peculiarities of the Russian political system was the legal status of the parties, as regulated by the law of March 4, 1906, on societies and unions.[30] By this measure the minister of the interior might

29. According to an investigation conducted by the Kadet party, in nineteen provinces (forty-two *uiezds*) embracing one third of European Russia, out of 187,000 small landowners only 131,000 remained (56,500 excluded). Individual provinces like Chernigov and Poltava suffered heavily, each losing 150,000 voters in the landowning class. In sixty-eight provincial towns, out of 478,000 voters, 437,700 remained after the Senate ruling. The largest cities with their own deputies were the worst to suffer. St. Petersburg lost 27,000 votes and Warsaw the same number. See Smirnov, *Kak proshli vybory*, pp. 101, 102, 104. In this work (How Elections to the Second Duma Went) Smirnov has drawn on sources used by the St. Petersburg liberal papers *Tovarishch* and *Riech*. These sources were not available to the author. Wherever possible Smirnov's figures have been verified and found accurate. Smirnov, according to a note received by the author from I. V. Gessen (Paris, Nov. 17, 1936), editor of *Riech*, was a provincial correspondent of that daily. There are no trustworthy official data on these elections. *Ukazatel*, pp. 17, 25.

30. *Pol. sob. zak.*, XXVI, no. 27,479.

close any organization which he regarded as dangerous or illegal. The law created boards of associations and unions responsible to the governors or city police chiefs. On the basis of information concerning organization, aims, rules, and finances submitted to them, the boards might grant or refuse to allow an applicant the right to found or open any society—political, social, or economic—or any branch thereof. In other words, the government was the sole arbiter in questions involving the legality of political parties. And it used that power to exclude the entire opposition, recognizing as legal only the Union of the Russian People, which, for a time, it aided most concretely;[31] the Union of October 17; the Party of Peaceful Restoration; and several semi-political organizations on the right.[32] Thus, the center and left parties did not legally exist, and a citizen who publicly claimed membership in any one of them ran the risk of being arrested for belonging to an illegal organization. Only the duma fraction of each party—the organized duma members of each party or group—was recognized as legal, composed as it was of duly elected, popular representatives.[33] Consequently, the government was able to exercise complete control over the campaigns of all opposition parties prohibiting meetings, the distribution of party proclamations, and lists of candidates.[34] Under this law it was also able to limit the political activity not only of bureaucrats, but also of those serving in state

31. The administration covertly supported the efforts of the Union of the Russian People wherever possible. That society already possessed a great advantage in the fact that it was legal, but its position was enhanced by direct government contributions to its press and by more or less open support from local officials who tolerated its pogromist activities. But Stolypin's constitutional inclinations resulted in estrangement from the Union. When part of its membership accepted the principle of parliamentary representation (after 1909) Stolypin again aided the rightists financially. He also probably regarded them as a counterweight to the developing liberalism in the duma. See *Padenie tsarskogo rezhima*, V, 402–416 (Kryzhanovskii); VII, 179–180 (Makarov); *Riech*, Dec. 12, 1906, pp. 4, 5; Dec. 16, 1906, p. 5; Jan. 24, 1907, p. 5; Jan. 31, p. 5.

32. *Riech*, Dec. 29, 1906, p. 4.

33. The duma fraction will be discussed in the following chapter.

34. For specific types of repression see *Riech* for Dec., 1906: 12, p. 5; 15, p. 5; 17, pp. 4, 5; for Jan., 1907: 25, p. 4; 30, p. 5; for Feb.: 6, p. 4; 9, p. 4.

institutions, including judges, by prohibiting them from joining opposition parties.[35]

The government also created direct barriers to the complete exercise of the suffrage by cancelling it at the slightest failure to observe the formalities of a complicated registration system. At the same time it closed information bureaus which might aid the bewildered voter, or located the polls at an unreasonable distance from the homes of a majority of the voters.[36] Then, in a circular of December 12, 1906, the Holy Synod required the clergy to defend the government in the election campaign.[37] The church as a whole readily complied with this demand, but in numerous instances the parish clergy set themselves up as champions of the popular cause.[38]

After elections had begun elevation to even the advanced stage of elector in the city or provincial electoral assemblies was no guarantee that one would vote for, or be elected as a member of the duma. For the committees on electoral affairs might still be counted on to annul elections on the ground that certain electors belonged to illegal parties. The accused might thereupon be arrested and exiled on that charge.[39] Finally, these committees used their power to invalidate uiezd and city curial elections after voting for electors to final provincial and city assemblies had begun, and the period remaining before election of duma members was too brief for the repetition of the entire electoral process.[40]

These, in general, were the chief methods employed by

35. *Riech,* Sept. 19, 1906, p. 3; Oct. 1, 1906, p. 4; Dec. 20, 1906, p. 2; Dec. 23, 1906, p. 4.

36. *Riech,* Dec. 5, 1906, p. 5; Dec. 12, 1906, p. 4; Dec. 20, 1906, pp. 3, 4; Jan. 9, 1907, p. 4; Jan. 31, p. 4; Feb. 6, p. 4.

37. Smirnov, *Kak proshli vybory,* pp. 133–134.

38. *Ibid.,* pp. 134–135, 138; *Tovarishch,* Jan. 19, p. 5; *Riech,* Dec. 10, 1906, p. 6; Feb. 9, 1907, p. 5; *Ukazatel,* pp. 1–25.

39. V. Mandelberg, *Iz perezhitago,* pp. 121–124; *Riech,* Dec. 29, 1906, p. 5; Jan. 21, 1907, pp. 4, 5; Jan. 24, p. 4; Jan. 20, p. 2.

40. *Riech,* Jan. 23, p. 5; Feb. 4, p. 5; Feb. 6, p. 5. Smirnov gives a number of examples in *Kak proshli vybory,* pp. 210–218.

the administration in its attempt to influence the outcome of elections. But so often and universally were they applied, that the population, aroused by the opposition press, came to regard them as an additional form of repression, and in most cases they served only to heighten that spirit of antagonism which was clearly reflected in the results of the elections. As the returns from the provincial and city electoral assemblies of the fifty-one European provinces came in, the victory of the opposition, center and left, became increasingly evident. In the twenty-six provinces they gained an absolute majority and showed themselves to be stronger than the right in eleven more. In only ten provincial electoral assemblies did the right appear with an absolute majority.[41]

Returns from the rural population showed that the peasant curia had elected 1,246 out of 2,258 electors.[42] They were strongly attracted by the radical solutions of the land question offered by the *Narodniki* and Marxists. But in the landowners' curia the government supporters fared better as a result of the senatorial interpretation of October 7, and the determined effort on the part of the large landowners to capture this curia where they knew that a victory was possible. Out of 1,726 electors (the maximum was 1,932) the right seated 814 at electoral assemblies.[43] In the remaining provincial curia, that of the

41. For specific provinces see *Riech*, Feb. 3, p. 4.
42. The peasants gave the Socialist left 23 per cent of their electors, the Kadets, 4.1 per cent, the right and moderate right 30.9 per cent, and the progressives and non-partisans 33 per cent. Many of the latter voted with the *Narodniki*. See P. Marev, *Krestianstvo i revoliutsii*, p. 132; A. Warskii, *Neue Zeit*, XXV, 873. According to a compilation made by the Kadet organ *Riech*, the center non-partisan opposition received 561 peasant votes, the Kadets, 103; the leftists, 482; the right, 563; Octobrists, 43; moderates, 158; and moderate non-partisans, 248. These figures are to be found in the supplement to *Riech*, Feb. 6. The table on election returns was compiled from local returns by correspondents and from local newspapers. Where the editors had no figures they used the semi-official St. Petersburg Telegraphic Agency reports but took no responsibility for their accuracy. Of 5,758 electors in 51 provinces, 5,286 are recorded—more than nine-tenths of the total. The results of elections in the workers' curia for 48 provinces are indicated in a separate list.
43. *Riech*, Feb. 6, supplement.

workers, the 144 electors chosen were leftists to a man.[44]

In the cities, both provincial and those with separate representation in the duma, lay the strength of the Kadets and workers. Consequently, the victory here of the parties in open opposition to the administration, especially of the two groups mentioned, was impressive. For out of a total of 1,302 electors in the provincial cities (the maximum was 1,346) the Kadets won 504 and the parties on the left 311.[45] And in fifteen cities of European Russia with separate representation the progressives won 42 electoral seats, the Kadets 684, and the parties to the left of them 260.[46] The sharp division of electors into left, right, and Kadet or center blocs only served to bring out the strength of the Kadets in the cities and the extent to which the opposition had exaggerated the "Black Hundred" danger. In twenty-seven metropolitan and provincial cities where three lists prevailed the Kadets won an absolute majority in seventeen and a comparative majority in two; in seventeen cities where the center and left voted together the right was universally defeated; in forty-four urban centers the right could count but six victories, two by only a comparative majority.[47]

The distinct opposition trend was even more apparent when the final ballots were taken in the city and provincial

44. *Ibid.* The provincial workers' curia elected 88 Social-Democrats, 51 *Narodniki*, two non-partisans, and three progressives.

45. *Ibid.* The progressives won 280 electors, the right 116, the Octobrists 55, the moderates 11, and the non-partisans 27.

46. *Ibid.*, for specific cities. The rightists elected 248 while the Octobrists won only 4 places. In St. Petersburg, out of 180 seats in the electoral assembly the Kadets won 169 and the left parties 11. *Tovarishch*, Jan. 31, p. 4; Smirnov, *Kak proshli vybory*, p. 205.

47. Smirnov, *Kak proshli vybory*, p. 205; *Tovarishch*, Jan. 30, p. 2; *Riech*, Jan. 28, p. 5; Jan. 31, p. 2; Feb. 2, p. 5; Feb. 4, p. 5. For specific cities see Smirnov, pp. 205–206. According to a compilation by Smirnov, in 38 cities with three competing lists the combined Kadet and left votes were double those received by the right: Kadets, 138,039; left, 74,807 (together 212,846); while the rightists together cast 94,887 ballots. In 42 cities where only two lists competed; that is, a combined left and center bloc against one on the right, the former polled 112,051 votes as against 38,954 for the right—more than twice as many as the latter. Smirnov, *Kak proshli vybory*, p. 208.

electoral assemblies for members of the duma. In all, 518
deputies were elected whose distribution was as follows :[48]

Social-Democrats ...	65	Kadets	98
Social-Revolutionaries	37	Cossack group	17
Popular-Socialists ...	16	Non-partisans	50
Trudoviki	104	Democratic Reformist	1
The Polish Kolo	46	Octobrists	44
The Moslem group ..	30	Rightists	10

All parties found most of their seats in the provincial
electoral assemblies (including the provincial cities) but
the Kadets were particularly strong in the cities with
special representation (fifteen deputies). To the average
burgher the call for reform without revolution and within
the frame of the traditional monarchy had wide appeal.
The Social-Democrats for their part drew heavily from
the suppressed minorities in the Caucasian towns, the mining population of Siberia and the Caucasus, and the great
Caspian and Black Sea ports with their aggressive seamen
and longshoremen.[49]

When compared with the First Duma there was noticeable in the Second a distinct increase on the extremes at
the expense of the center.[50] The Kadets, Democratic Reformists, and national groups who formed the bulk of the
center totaled 216 in the First Duma, but 192 in the Sec-

48. *Ukazatel*, pp. 27–33.
49. Smirnov, *Kak proshli vybory*, pp. 250–252; *Tovarishch*, February 17, 1907.
See following chap. for details on Social-Democrats.

	First Duma	Second Duma
50. Trudoviki and Popular-Socialists.......	85	120
Social-Revolutionaries................	2	37
Social-Democrats....................	17	65
Other Socialists.....................	7	
Kadets and Democratic Reformists....	184	99
Poles and other national groups........	32	93
Octobrists.........................	38	54
Non-partisans......................	112	50
Right and Monarchists..............	7	10

See *Riech*, Feb. 10, for figures on the First Duma. Those for the Second are from
Ukazatel, pp. 27–33.

ond. The leftist parties, including the Social-Democrats, Social-Revolutionaries, Popular-Socialists, Trudoviki, and other Socialists together numbered 131 in the First Duma, and climbed to 232 in the Second. The right, excluding the non-partisans who voted as often with the center as with the right, consisted of 45 members in the First and 64 in the Second Duma. Including the non-partisans they numbered 112 in the First, 114 in the Second. This gain by the extremes may be attributed to the abandonment of the boycott by the Socialists and to the efforts of the right extremists to play a more decisive rôle in the duma. But not a little of the increase on the left was due to the fact that the persecuted population often elected candidates simply because they had been, or were, victims of administrative oppression.[51]

Further differences between the two dumas were to be noted in the composition of each body. The age averages differed greatly in both assemblies. For the new duma was noticeably more youthful than the First. In the First Duma 42.4 per cent of its members were below forty years of age; in the Second 56.6 per cent were in that category. In the First Duma 15.1 per cent were over fifty years of age; in the Second only 9 per cent. The Second Duma also had a higher intellectual level than the First. While 42.1 per cent of the First Duma had received a higher education, in the Second 44.6 per cent had attended universities. In the First 13.8 per cent had received a secondary education; in the Second 18.6 per cent had completed a course of studies in a *gymnasium* or religious seminary. Finally, 2 per cent more had attended public schools in the Second than in the First (24.7 per cent in the First, 26.7 per cent in the Second).[52]

As for occupational differences between the two dumas we may observe that the landowner, industrialist and com-

51. In 25 provinces, of 203 deputies, 71 were punished for political offenses. The majority were imprisoned or exiled, others were only searched and placed under police observation, while still others were excluded from the universities or *zemstvo* work. See *Chleny vtoroi gosudarstvennoi dumy*, pp. xi–xii in preface.

52. *Ukazatel*, pp. 1–25; *Riech*, Feb. 16, p. 2.

mercial representation changed little. The percentage of industrial workers remained about the same, while the "white collar" workers increased their number somewhat (by six) in the Second, as did the professional classes and teachers. The greatest increase was registered by the allotment-holding peasantry whose number in the Second Duma was almost double that of the First.[53]

In sum, the second elections produced a duma even more hostile to the government and less amenable to cooperation than the first. The new duma now included the Social-Revolutionaries who propagated the doctrine of a violent agrarian movement. And the Marxist Social-Democrats now created a considerable fraction which grasped the lead in the left opposition, preached the irreconcilability of popular interests with those of the government, and chided the Kadets for their conciliatory tactics. On the other hand, a small but dangerous group of absolutists found their way into a duma which they openly regarded with extreme hostility and contempt. And the very division of the duma into right, center, and left camps, if effective, might easily result in a disunity which would paralyze its efforts, lower its prestige, and make its inherent weakness obvious to the enemies of parliamentary government.

53. The occupational distribution in the two dumas was as follows:

	First Duma		Second Duma	
	Number	Per cent	Number	Per cent
Landowners	62	12.4	65	14.4
Industrialists	6	1.2	2	0.4
Merchants	14	2.8	24	5.4
Peasant allotment-holders	64	12.8	111	24.8
Workers	24	4.8	25	5.6
Private service (clerical)	8	1.6	15	3.5
City, zemstvo or nobility institutional service	58	11.6	61	13.3
State service	18	3.6	15	3.5
Professors and instructors	11	2.2	14	3.1
Teachers	25	5.0	23	5.0
Physicians	25	5.0	19	4.2
Lawyers	27	5.0	38	8.5
Other professions	157	32.0	36	8.7

See *Ukazatel*, pp. 1–25.

III

THE SOCIAL-DEMOCRATIC FRACTION

THE election of sixty-five partisans and adherents was indeed a gratifying result for the Social-Democratic party in the first active political campaign in its history, and in competition with liberal and other Socialist parties. Moreover, the results showed a definite victory for the Mensheviki in the party, for there were elected eighteen Bolsheviki (including three sympathizers), thirty-six Mensheviki (including four sympathizers), and eleven adherents to the party fraction who took no definite stand but more often joined with the Mensheviki.[1] Of these, fifty-eight deputies were elected as party candidates and seven as non-partisan adherents.[2] By means of agreements with the Kadets fourteen were elected (five Mensheviki and ten Bolsheviki), and twenty-two by agreements with the *Narodnik* parties (sixteen Mensheviki and six Bolsheviki). The rest were seated as independent Social-Democrats or as non-partisans.[3]

The social and economic composition of the fraction was as complex as that of the duma. Twenty-five, or more than one-third of the Social-Democratic deputies were workers. And though most of them were classed as peasants, only five in the fraction were engaged in working their allotments in the villages. The intellectuals included ten journalists and literateurs, five teachers, six physicians, one lawyer, and one technician. Moreover, six members of the fraction were office workers, four were in the *zemstvo* service, and one—Nalivkin—had been vice-governor of

1. *Londonskii siezd, polnyi tekst protokolov*, pp. 451–452 (1909, ed.); cited hereafter as *Protokoly*. See Appendix I, A.
2. *Ibid.; Tovarishch*, April 20, p. 4.
3. *Protokoly*, p. 452; V. Voitinskii, *Gody pobied i porazhenii*, pp. 159–160; *Tovarishch*, April 20, p. 4.

Ferghana.[4] Next in number were thirteen burghers, while eight deputies were listed as nobles, five as sons of clergymen (and were therefore reckoned in a separate class with the clergy), and four as belonging to the official class (sons of high officials or having high official posts themselves).[5]

These representatives of the extreme revolutionary tendency came, generally speaking, from all over the empire. The largest number, sixteen, came from central and western European Russia. The next largest group, numbering fourteen, were from the Ukraine and the South. Nine hailed from Siberia and Central Asia, where the party was generally successful in the elections, and eight from the Caucasus where its victory was particularly brilliant. Fifteen were elected from the Volga and Ural provinces, while three were successful in the Baltic Region. On the other hand, in the great Polish industrial region where the Social-Democrats might expect some success, aggressive nationalism overcame or restricted class activity among the proletariat, and only National-Democrats (Kolo, in the duma) were elected. Here the Social-Democrats only suffered a loss of prestige as a result of the elections.[6] By nationality, thirty fraction members were Great Russians, eight Ukrainians, seven Georgians, six Lithuanians, two were Esths, one was a Lett, one an Armenian, and one a Jew.[7]

The fraction as a whole was surprisingly youthful. Thirty-five members ranged between the ages of twenty-five and thirty, twenty-two between the ages of thirty-one and forty, six were in their forties while only two were over fifty. Their leading orators—Tsereteli for the Mensheviki and Aleksinskii for the Bolsheviki—were only twenty-five and twenty-seven respectively.[8] And the edu-

4. *Tovarishch*, April 20, p. 4; *Ukazatel*, pp. 1–25.
5. *Tovarishch*, April 20, p. 4; *Ukazatel*, pp. 1–25.
6. *Ukazatel*, pp. 1–25; D. Koltsov, "Rabochie v 1905–1907 gg." in *Obshchestvennoe dvizhenie v Rossii v nachale XX-go veka*, P. Maslov, ed., II, part 1, 324.
7. *Ukazatel*, pp. 1–25; *Tovarishch*, April 20, p. 4.
8. *Ukazatel*, pp. 1–25; *Tovarishch*, April 20, p. 4.

cational level of the fraction was fairly low, for seven had received a lower education at home, twenty-two at public school, twelve had attended seminaries or high schools, and sixteen the universities.[9]

A characteristic of the Social-Democratic fraction which may be explained by its revolutionary philosophy and activity was the frequency with which its members suffered from repression at the hands of the government. Every member had been arrested, imprisoned, or exiled at one time or another in the course of his revolutionary career.[10] Then, as deputies, the Social-Democrats were ever under constant surveillance by the police. For the government was especially careful that the Marxist representatives should not commit any revolutionary act or utter any revolutionary word outside of the confines of the duma. And it broadly interpreted the nature of a revolutionary act[11] and the baffling rule that the duma must consent to yield its members before any arrests were made.[12] Thus, Makharadze's apartment was invaded on March 1, and occupied for several hours when the police "mistook" a meeting of deputies for an "illegal assembly."[13] For writing a pamphlet supposed to contain remarks insulting to the tsar, the minister of justice demanded on March 13 that the duma yield deputies Gerus and Kuznetsov for prosecution by the government.[14] But most of the deputies were sought for "illegal" public utterances, real or fictitious. On March 13 the government demanded that the duma yield the Lithuanian Kupstas for making a revolutionary address at Ponevezh, and a like charge was leveled against Kuznetsov.[15] Deputy

9. *Ukazatel*, pp. 1–25.
10. *Tovarishch*, April 20, p. 4.
11. *Riech*, March 3, p. 3, Duma Supplement; hereafter cited as Duma Sup.
12. *Stenographicheskie otchety*, I, 1427–1433; henceforth cited as *Stenog. ot.*
13. *Riech*, March 2, p. 3.
14. *Ibid.*, March 16, p. 3, Duma Sup.; *Tovarishch*, March 17, p. 6; *Stenog. ot.* I, 441–442. Henceforth all *Stenog. ot.*, citations refer to volumes for 1907, (Sozyv II).
15. *Stenog. ot.*, I, 1159, 1274–1275; *Riech*, March 30, p. 2; March 24, p. 3; *Tovarishch*, March 24, p. 5.

Zhigelev was twice detained by the police and held for several hours on the charge of attending "illegal gatherings,"[16] and Izmailov was arrested under like circumstances after addressing workers on the Warsaw Railroad. About a month later a warrant was issued for his arrest on the ground that he had advised a group of peasants to refuse taxes and seize the lands of the near-by landowners.[17] During the Easter recess all deputies were closely watched and, insofar as possible, isolated from the population.[18] It was shortly thereafter that Shpagin was hailed into court for delivering a "revolutionary" farewell address at Perm.[19] Direct contact with the government only served to increase the animosity of the Social-Democrats toward it.

Immediately before the opening of the duma, the Social-Democratic deputies who had already arrived at St. Petersburg organized a Social-Democratic fraction under the direction of the party central committee. This body selected a temporary executive committee of five members; the four Mensheviki Tsereteli, Dzhaparidze, Kirienko, and Mitrov, and the Bolshevik Aleksinskii.[20] It was not until March, however, that the fraction chose its permanent committee including Tsereteli, Ozol, Saltykov, Komar, Anikin, and the lone Bolshevik Aleksinskii. But the latter refused the honor and was replaced by Bielousov.[21]

Because there were no official party decisions on the matter, the fraction set about compiling its own rules,[22] which were to be binding until they should be replaced by the next party congress. It was decided that the fraction

16. *Riech*, March 16, p. 4; May 4, p. 5, Duma Sup.; *Tovarishch*, March 28, p. 5.
17. *Riech*, May 3, p. 4, Duma Sup.; *Tovarishch*, May 3, p. 3; *Riech*, April 20, p. 2; May 18, p. 2; June 1, p. 2.
18. *Riech*, April 21, p. 3; May 4, p. 4, Duma Sup.
19. *Riech*, May 3, p. 4, Duma Sup.; May 24, p. 2.
20. *Riech*, Feb. 20, p. 4; Feb. 21, p. 5; *Protokoly*, p. 185.
21. *Riech*, March 29, p. 2; *Tovarishch*, March 30, p. 3.
22. *Tovarishch*, Feb. 22, March 15, p. 4; *Protokoly*, p. 149.

was to act as an official party organization according to the decisions of the party congresses and under the constant leadership and control of its central institutions. The fraction would admit all Social-Democrats elected to the duma as party candidates and those deputies who would adopt the program and tactical decisions of the party and would be willing to act in the duma as its responsible representatives. But a deputy obnoxious to the voters might not be admitted. The fraction itself was to control the admission of members. In all of its activities the fraction was to act as a unit, the minority bowing to the will of the majority. Should the minority protest the tactics and decisions of the majority, such protest was to be examined by the central committee of the party and its decision was to be binding for the entire fraction. The executive committee of the fraction was given power to manage its affairs and in an emergency to make decisions which were later to be submitted to the general assembly of the fraction and the party central committee for confirmation.

The entire fraction was divided into four sub-committees, on the budget, the agrarian question, local self-government, and labor legislation.[23] These were to define the party's attitude and work out measures in their respective fields. On reaching a decision they were to inform the executive committee of the fraction and appoint one of their number to defend their opinion before the entire fraction. The executive committee invited experts to participate in these subcommittees so that the fraction might benefit by their special knowledge and advice. This was recognized and approved by all members of the party as necessary for the ultimate success of work in the duma. But the fraction committee aroused a violent controversy when it allowed these experts a deciding vote on equal terms with other members of the subcommittees in reach-

23. *Tovarishch*, Feb. 21, p. 5; *Riech*, March 15, p. 3.

ing decisions on all questions before them.[24] To the minority this seemed to be a clear case of "packing" the subcommittees.

The Bolsheviki objected first to the type of expert being called. They pointed to the "opportunist" S. N. Prokopovich[25] who had been an "economist," while the committee had passed by such significant leaders as Lenin. Furthermore, they demanded that experts be allowed only an advisory vote since they were merely to aid and advise deputies in the subcommittees and their personnel was too fluid to allow them a deciding voice.[26] The Mensheviki defended the action of the executive committee by pointing out that decisions reached by subcommittees were not binding for the fraction; their opinion was merely advisory. Therefore they felt that no great significance should be attached to powers granted to the experts. Finally, they saw no reason why Lenin should be consulted when the executive committee had avoided calling any Menshevik leaders. They noted that Viacheslav, representative of the St. Petersburg committee, had been invited, and felt that it was entirely his own fault if he had attended so few meetings. At any rate, the system adopted by the executive committee was continued.[27]

The central committee of the party was also sharply criticized by the Bolsheviki for its management of fraction affairs. They maintained that its representatives came to fraction meetings with no definite plan of activity, or with opinions so indefinite that it was difficult to ascertain whether they were those of individuals or of the central committee. The latter was also accused of employing its hand-picked executive committee only in acive work while the remaining members of the fraction attended meetings which consisted of boring addresses by representatives of

24. *Protokoly*, pp. 160–161.
25. An editor of *Tovarishch*. Lenin, *Sobranie sochinenii*, VIII, 568 (1922 ed.).
26. *Protokoly*, pp. 174, 185–186.
27. *Ibid.*, pp. 160–161, 182–184, 214.

the central committee. The Bolsheviki contended that attendance had begun to fall off badly with loss of interest.[28]

In reviewing the election campaign we noted that the basic difference of opinion between the Social-Democratic factions concerned the question of the suitability of the peasant parties alone or the entire opposition as allies in the struggle against the Old Régime. Such a fundamental difference was of necessity carried over into the duma where there were concentrated all shades of Russian political opinion. Consequently, when questions arose involving the attitude of the Social-Democrats in the duma toward the representatives of the "bourgeois" parties, the fraction presented two widely differing views.

Debates on this point began even before the duma convened and concerned at first the question of participation in an inter-fractional information bureau. All members of the fraction agreed that they could enter no such bureau until the fraction was finally constituted; they would merely inform it periodically of their plans and activities. But Social-Democratic factions differed on the question of which fractions they might inform and, consequently, with whom they would enter into a permanent information bureau.[29]

The Bolsheviki, adhering closely to their established doctrine, declared that they would enter a bureau with the *Narodnik* parties only, for they were true revolutionary democrats. They maintained that the Social-Democrats would have to struggle hand in hand with them against both the reactionaries and the Kadets. Therefore they uncompromisingly insisted on a bureau which would not include the latter. They believed, furthermore, that it would be far better to remain isolated if the *Narodniki* should insist on the inclusion of the Kadets.[30]

The Mensheviki, as resolutely adhering to their doc-

28. *Ibid.*, pp. 184, 185–186.
29. *Ibid.*, pp. 151–152; *Tovarishch*, Feb. 21, p. 5.
30. *Protokoly*, pp. 164–165.

trinal principles, held that the Social-Democratic fraction could participate in common activity with any group dissatisfied with the autocratic régime. They declared that the vital demands of the Kadets had not yet been satisfied and, consequently, they were to be considered an oppositional force which would support the revolution even though they held illusions concerning the possibility of a peaceful settlement of the liberation struggle. The Menshevik majority in the fraction adopted the latter viewpoint, and it was decided to enter an informational bureau of all opposition groups where the various fractions might learn of each other's plans. But special conferences were also held with left fractions only.[31]

The same fundamental difference of principles underlay the debate on participation in conferences of all opposition parties. These had been organized at the initiative of the Kadets, and the first was held on February 19, at the apartments of Prince P. D. Dolgorukov on the question of the duma presidium, which was to be elected shortly.[32] It was attended by all fractions, including the Social-Democrats, and also the Polish National-Democrats (Kolo) whose presence aroused the Bolsheviki. In general, they asserted, Social-Democrats should have nothing to do with the Kadets and should contrast their program with that of the liberals, thus winning the support of the revolutionary peasantry who would recognize the true defenders of their interests. Mingling with the Kadets, they declared, would only confuse the peasantry. But attendance at these conferences became absolutely intolerable to the Bolsheviki when they found themselves in direct contact with the National-Democrats. These, they asserted, had mercilessly crushed the Polish proletariat in their struggle to escape exploitation, and they charged the National-Democrats with being the instigators of pogroms in their homeland. Consequently, they

31. *Ibid.*, pp. 151–152, 245; *Riech*, March 1, 1907, pp. 1, 3; *Tovarishch*, February 28, 1907, p. 4.
32. *Riech*, Feb. 20, p. 3.

regarded participation in a conference with them as an insult to their Polish comrades. After the first conference the Bolsheviki fully explained themselves, and demanded that the fraction adopt a resolution stating that the Social-Democrats were not aware that National-Democrats would be present at Dogorukov's apartment, and had no intention of repeating the visit.[33]

But the Mensheviki saw the issue in another light. In general, said they, it was precisely because the Social-Democrats had mingled with the Kadets that the influence of the liberals over the peasant deputies had been weakened. They rejected the Bolshevik resolution, for although they admitted that from the Marxist point of view the National-Democrats were immoral, they regarded all bourgeois parties as equally so, including the Social-Revolutionaries and the Trudoviki. Consequently, the Social-Democrats would have to break off all relations with the latter, too, if they were to be guided by moral considerations alone without heeding those of expediency. They could associate even with the "devil and his grandmother," as Bebel and the German Social-Democrats had aptly put it, if the proletariat had anything to gain thereby. The National-Democrats were, indeed, reactionaries at home, but in the Russian duma they were a significant part of the opposition, and therefore had to be considered. Consequently, the Mensheviki saw no reason why their presence at the opposition fraction conferences should force the Social-Democrats to forego the advantages to be derived from participating in them.[34] Furthermore, the Mensheviki contended that their visit had brought no protest from the representative of the central committee of the Polish Social-Democrats.[35] In short, the Mensheviki, like their Social-Democratic comrades in the

33. *Protokoly*, pp. 152, 246.

34. *Ibid.*, 152, 182–184, 246, 253.

35. This brought the rejoinder from Kuiavskii, representative of the Polish S-D in Petersburg, that from conversations with members of the party central committee he understood that the visits were to be discontinued, and he therefore decided not to resurrect the issue. *Ibid.*, pp. 182, 253, 219.

west, regarded such questions from the point of view of expediency and could not imagine how their tactics might violate Marxist principles. On February 22, the fraction adopted a resolution, Menshevik in spirit, which declared that it would reserve freedom of activity for itself in the matter of meeting with other fractions to consider questions which it regarded as beneficial to its cause.[36] But eleven Bolshevik deputies were quick to present a minority report declaring that they would submit to the decision of the majority, but that they personally intended to keep away from general opposition conferences.[37]

Besides its regular legislative duties the Social-Democratic fraction was burdened with innumerable activities, both as a result of its effort to maintain the closest possible connection with the population, and because the general mass of voters had come to regard the duma as an all-powerful protector of the people against official oppression. But the majority of the population was illiterate[38] and the provincial press, though influential, was as yet undeveloped in comparison with that of Western Europe. Therefore, the most expedient method of reaching the voters was by direct contact through a highly developed party organization. Accordingly, the fraction was always busily engaged in informing its sympathizers and the public of the progress and significance of its activities. In return, it received innumerable instructions, letters, telegrams, and delegations—all complaining of official repression. Then, it was always necessary that the fraction be informed on party affairs, at the same time keeping the

36. *Tovarishch*, Feb. 23, p. 4; *Riech*, Feb. 23, p. 3.

37. *Riech*, Feb. 23, p. 3; *Tovarishch*, Feb. 23, p. 4; In this dispute the Lithuanian Social-Democratic deputies took an independent stand. On February 23, they expressed a desire to participate in the meetings of the Trudovik group and received permission on the following day from the latter. They maintained that they would not adopt the Trudovik platform, but approved of the group's tactics. Since they continued to adhere to the Social-Democratic platform and had only an advisory vote in the fraction, their status as Social-Democratic deputies was unimpaired, *Tovarishch*, Feb. 24, p. 2; Feb. 25, p. 2; *Ukazatel*, p. 11.

38. Thirty per cent to 40 per cent of the population over 9 years of age was literate. See *Kalendar Suvorina*, 1907, p. 216.

party posted on its business. To centralize these activities the fraction had established headquarters at 92 Nevskii Prospekt which soon became the humming rendezvous for the curious and the suppliant from all over the empire. From the moment of their election and arrival in St. Petersburg the Social-Democratic deputies were overwhelmed with requests to appear at workers' meetings. It would have been impossible to attend them all, but the situation was rendered more difficult by the fact that the government seldom allowed these gatherings to take place. Consequently, the deputies were often forced to resort to underground methods in order to satisfy their electorate.[39] The question of the manner of celebrating the opening of the duma called forth several such assemblies.[40] Some meetings were held on the premises of industrial establishments under the noses of the protesting management.[41] Again, a gathering of the organized unemployed in St. Petersburg might draw on the oratorical powers of a Social-Democratic deputy.[42] Occasionally, the administration saw fit to grant the workers the privilege of hearing their representatives report on the duma. But these assemblies always took place under the watchful eye of the district police captain who might curb the speaker's revolutionary zeal, or find grounds for closing the meeting.[43]

After electing their deputies, the workers often took great pains to instruct them concerning their precise de-

39. Aleksinskii on one occasion had to use a false worker's card in order to pass a factory gate. See V. Mandelberg, *Iz Perezhitago*, pp. 134–135; G. A. Aleksinskii, *Obrazovanie*, no. IV, part 2, "Iz Perezhitago," pp. 110–111; hereafter cited as "Iz Perezhitago."

40. For example, the meeting of the railroad section of the party in St. Petersburg at which two Social-Democratic deputies appeared, or that of the factory delegates elected in the past elections which welcomed eight Social-Democratic deputies. See *Riech*, Feb. 20, p. 3; *Tovarishch*, Feb. 20, p. 5.

41. Aleksinskii addressed such a meeting in the yard of the Semionovskii factory on February 26, and both he and Mitrov harangued the Nevskii shipyard workers on March 3. See Aleksinskii "Iz Perezhitago," pp. 110–111; *Riech*, March 6, p. 2.

42. *Riech*, March 9, p. 4.

43. Aleksinskii, "Iz Perezhitago," p. 112; *Riech*, March 6, 1907, p. 2.

sires. In many factories and shops the opening of the duma was marked by one-day strikes during which the workers met and composed instructions and letters to their representatives, demanding that they present and support legislation which would lighten the burden of labor and increase personal freedom.[44] At times attempts were even made to influence the parliamentary tactics of the fraction.[45]

But the Social-Democratic deputies like most others in the opposition, were more often recipients of numerous petitions. These were contained in letters or telegrams, or they were presented at the fraction headquarters by workers, their wives and relatives, and by peasant delegations from all over the empire. Their burden was chiefly a request for protection against one form of official oppression or another. Some of these the fraction regarded seriously; as specimens of particularly widespread abuses which required immediate intercession, or the presentation of interpellations to the proper ministers through the duma. But many of them, serious and petty, reflected an exaggerated idea of the rôle of the duma and the powers of a deputy by a people heretofore unacquainted with parliamentary forms. The more serious petitions often requested deputies to use their influence to bring about the liberation of relatives or friends from jails of preliminary detention. The prisoners were usually awaiting trial for petty political crimes and might pine away for months before action

44. Most often these instructions included demands for state insurance at the employers' expense; prosecution of employers for violation of safety regulations; an eight-hour day; prohibition of overtime work; arbitration boards; protection of woman and child labor; reform of factory inspection; abolition of fines levied on employees by factory managements; medical aid; protection of civil liberties; universal, equal, direct, and secret suffrage; abrogation of extraordinary states of "protection" and field-courts-martial; a representative ministry; abolition of the death penalty; the establishment of independent courts accessible to all, and a host of minor demands. See *Tovarishch*, Feb. 15, p. 3; March 4, p. 5; Feb. 16, p. 4; *Riech*, Feb. 2, p. 3; March 25, p. 2.

45. The Committee of the St. Petersburg party organization added to its regular demands a request that the treachery of the liberal parties be exposed, and the Lessner factory workers advised the fraction to join an information bureau of the left parties. *Riech*, March 2, p. 2.

would be taken on their cases. To these petitioners the
deputies had to explain patiently that intercession would
do more harm than good, and would ultimately be of no
avail. The less serious communications contained requests
to solve family problems, or to avenge mortal insults. A
boy from the Baltic region wanted a book on hypnotism,
since he knew that the Social-Democrats satisfied the needs
of the whole population.[46] Peasant delegations arrived
from the far steppe or the "black soil" (southern) provinces to air their grievances against neighboring landowners and local officials. Letters from villages described
their hard lot and asked that it be reported to the duma;
and all wanted land and freedom. Visits from groups of
St. Petersburg unemployed were frequent. These demanded work and complained of the inaction of both city
and national dumas.[47] Finally, there arrived the usual
crop of communications from the "lunatic fringe" with
complete solutions for all vital problems.[48]

When the importance of a particular case merited it,
as in a matter of life or death, or if the deputies thought
that pressure might yield beneficial results, they inter-
ceded directly with various ministers or provincial and
city officials. Thus, the widespread activity of the field-
courts-martial resulted in a number of petitions to the
minister of war, General A. F. Rediger. Here speed was
the essential factor and the deputies visited the general
personally. Their receptions were usually cordial considering the mutual hostility between the Social-Democrats
and the bureaucracy. But frequently they were sent from
one office to another and were finally informed that only
a petition to the tsar might save their comrade—if the
execution had not already taken place.[49] Again, the deputies often intervened in behalf of political prisoners or
exiles with demands for more humane treatment. They

46. Aleksinskii, "Iz Perezhitago," pp. 113–115.
47. *Ibid.*, pp. 116–121; *Riech*, March 17, p. 3; May 4, p. 3.
48. Aleksinskii, "Iz Perezhitago," pp. 123–137.
49. *Riech*, Feb. 24, p. 2, Duma Sup.; Feb. 25, p. 2; Feb. 27, p. 3; March 8,
p. 3; March 25, p. 2; *Tovarishch*, March 15, p. 5; March 31, p. 2;

were, after all, idealists and not criminals, and the Social-
Democrats lost no opportunity to prick the conscience of
the administration on the score of its harsh exile system.[50]
Finally, they were careful constantly to shed a fierce light
on all violations of civil liberties and human rights in general.[51] Great was the variety of cases which gave rise to
intercession on the part of the Social-Democratic deputies, but behind them all lay the common factor of administrative oppression in one degree or another.

The Social-Democrats regarded these petitions, above
all, as first-rate revolutionary material which might serve
as the basis for some piece of "advanced" legislation, or
as grounds for an interpellation in the duma. But they
were always given wide publicity. Moreover, the visiting
delegations from the ends of the empire offered a rare
opportunity for revolutionary agitation. The peasant who
complained that his chickens could not run about his
courtyard without trespassing on the property of the
neighboring "pomiestchik" was ready material for a lecture on direct action.

In order to maintain close connections with the population and carry on propaganda, the fraction adopted
the policy of appealing to the people for useful information, at the same time informing the nation of its work.
Many such requests were made by individual deputies
of their native constituencies in March.[52] These were
accompanied by a general fraction letter of March 18 on
famine relief, which maintained that only a social revo-

50. The fraction wired the governor of Tambov demanding that he improve
the living conditions of the Morshansk prison "politicals" or he would be faced
with a general strike. Again, Saltykov complained to Stolypin of the harsh
treatment of the Viatka exiles. See *Tovarishch*, March 2, p. 4; May 24, p. 4;
Riech, March 22, p. 3, Duma Sup.

51. In a typical case Aleksinskii visited the St. Petersburg chief of police concerning the arrest of a Lessner factory worker who had openly expressed dis-
approval of the suspension of a Menshevik paper. But the deputy was refused
an audience on the ground that duma members might complain directly to the
minister of the interior only, and not to his subordinate officials. *Tovarishch*,
March 31, p. 2; *Riech*, April 1, p. 4; *Protokoly V Siezda* p. 773 (1935 ed.).

52. *Riech*, March 24, p. 4, Duma Sup.

lution and the overthrow of the government would abolish widespread misery.[53] In mid-April the fraction issued an appeal to all trade unions, party organizations and private persons. This was, in essence, a detailed questionnaire on unemployment, issued for the purpose of gathering hard facts on the basis of which the fraction hoped fully to "illuminate" the question in the duma.[54] Finally, in the latter part of April a general proclamation to the people was published which explained its stand on the agrarian question.[55]

Soon after its formation the Social-Democratic fraction created a special organization which it dubbed the "railroad section" for the purpose of gathering information on bureaucratic oppression of railroad workers. It was, moreover, to criticize the budget of the ministry of communications, and to organize railroad men for economic and revolutionary activity. To this committee the fraction appointed four railway workers, all Mensheviki.[56] On March 16, they issued an appeal to all workers requesting examples of abuse, and that they write instructions for the guidance of the deputies.[57] A few days later the "section" issued a questionnaire to all organizations of railroad workers on conditions of employment, wages, housing, clothing, fines, etc. It intended to use the information obtained as material for interpellations to the ministry of communications.[58] On April 14, it addressed all workers in an open letter in which it noted the receipt of many complaints of individuals against their superiors, but confessed that the duma was powerless to aid them. It declared that the duma had no control over the acts

53. *Stenog. ot.*, II, 1,496–1,497.
54. *Tovarishch*, April 19, p. 3; May 6, p. 3.
55. *Riech*, May 1, p. 4, Duma Sup.
56. *Tovarishch*, March 2, p. 4; March 17, p. 6; *Riech*, March 11, p. 3. The four deputies were D. K. Bielanovskii, F. G. Prikhodko, V. N. Batashev, and N. S. Stepanov.
57. *Tovarishch*, March 17, p. 6.
58. *Ibid.*, March 22, pp. 4, 5; April 1, p. 5; *Riech*, March 21, p. 2.

of the ministry and could only gather glaring examples of official violence and present them to the government in the form of interpellations. It expressed the hope that the publicity given these matters would enable the public to understand the opposition which the duma had to encounter.[59] In a word, in this organization the Social-Democratic fraction had a model instrument for simultaneously befriending and organizing the railroad proletariat, and for revealing bureaucratic oppression at one of its sorest points.

As an autonomous party organization the fraction reported regularly on its activities in letters issued by the executive committee to all branches of the party.[60] The first of these appeared about March 14. It informed the party of the creation of the fraction and of its first political steps (on the amnesty question), and presented a motivation of the resolutions which it adopted on the matter of the election of the presidium and the secretariat of the duma, and on conferences with opposition groups. Finally, it described the formation of the four subcommittees.[61] This was followed by a second letter at the end of the month similarly justifying the fraction's tactics and decisions in the duma adopted after Stolypin had presented the government's declaration.[62] In mid-April two letters appeared; one explaining the fraction's stand on the agricultural question and the budget, the other giving a full report of the entire work of the fraction up to the Easter recess (April 18). On each resolution adopted a detailed analysis of Bolshevik and Menshevik arguments was presented.[63]

Thus, by meetings, intercessions, and direct appeals to

59. *Riech*, April 5, p. 2.
60. For a general review of the contents of these letters see the "Order" of Investigator Zaitsev, read to the duma on June 1, 1907; *Stenog. ot.*, II, 1,494–1,505.
61. *Riech*, March 15, p. 3; see following chapter.
62. *Riech*, March 30, p. 3, Duma Sup.; See Chap. V.
63. *Riech*, April 21, p. 3; April 20, p. 2; *Tovarishch*, April 21, p. 3.

the population, the fraction managed to remain in close connection with the proletariat which it represented, and to whom it hoped to preach its revolutionary message from the high tribune of the duma. And in pursuing this course in its non-parliamentary activity, the fraction was clearly following the instructions of the Stockholm Congress.

IV

THE ORGANIZATION OF THE DUMA

IN KEEPING with the autocratic origin of Russian constitutionalism the organization and general procedure of the duma were established by the law of February 20, 1906.[1] Although its terms were fairly generous, yet the interpretation placed on some of its articles by the government seriously handicapped the duma in its legislative efforts. According to this statute the general assembly of the duma elected from its midst a presidium consisting of a president and two vice-presidents who were to serve for a year, after which they might be reelected. The president generally presided over the duma sessions; announcing, opening and closing them, giving speakers the floor and interrupting or stopping them when they failed to observe the rules or respect the law. He had charge of the admission of the public to duma sessions, and of keeping order in the session hall. Rules, both on admission of outsiders and of preserving order, were compiled by the president together with the president of the council of ministers.[2] For the preservation of order the president appointed a sergeant at arms and several assistants who were directly responsible to him. Finally, he confirmed the stenographic reports taken at each session before their publication.

The Secretariat, consisting of a secretary and assistants (whose number was defined by the duma), was elected by the general assembly of the duma for a period of five years and held office until a new secretariat was elected. It had charge of the duma chancellery, the work of the latter

1. *Pol. sob. zak.*, XXVI, no. 27,424.
2. See also Article 1, law of Feb. 16, 1907, in *ibid.*, no. 28,890. This proved to be a real "joker" as Stolypin insisted on interfering in duma affairs.

being divided among its members. Clerks serving in this chancellery were to be appointed and discharged according to special rules evolved by the duma. General questions which arose concerning the work of the duma were settled by a committee formed of the presidium and the secretariat.

The general assembly of the duma was divided into committees, elected by the duma for the purpose of examining in detail and presenting conclusions or bills on matters presented to them by the duma. The duma was to establish their number and competence. Each committee elected a chairman and a secretary from among its members. At its meetings no "outside persons" or representatives of the press were allowed. The entire struggle for true parliamentary government often revolved around this article. The duma, striving to free itself from domination or interference by the administration, and the government, seeking to limit the independence of the popular legislative body and to hold it strictly to the word of the law, differed widely on the interpretation of "outside persons." The duma authorities held these words to mean the general public, and not experts called by the committees for their special knowledge. But the government, ever suspicious of the intentions of the public figures and of any connections between the duma and the population, would allow no person who was not duly elected to the duma to participate in its councils.

Members, on entering the duma, swore an oath whereby they promised to fulfill their duties, to retain the confidence of the tsar, and to strive only for the good of Russia. When the duma was in session its members might be deprived of freedom only with the permission of the general assembly. Members retired from the duma as a result of loss of citizenship, when they enlisted in active military service, entered a salaried civil service post, when they lost their suffrage qualifications, or if they were proven criminals or became insolvents. They were temporarily restricted from participation in assemblies when they were

under investigation or on trial, or until their insolvency
was liquidated. The power to expel its members, temporarily or permanently, was given to the general assembly
of the duma. This provision saved many an ardent re-
former or revolutionary from a long "preliminary detention." Yet, when it chose to do so in a crisis, the administration completely disregarded even this plain guarantee
of parliamentary immunity.

Bills were presented to the duma by its members or by
a minister on matters lying within the jurisdiction of his
ministry. Decisions on these bills were reached by a majority of the general assembly. When the duma was equally
divided on any issue, a second vote was taken, and if the
deadlock remained unbroken, the president decided the
matter with his vote. For the annulment of the election
of a deputy (a right allowed by the Fundamental Laws)
a majority of two-thirds of the members present was
required.

Members of the duma were given the right to interpellate ministers. A statement complaining of the commission of an illegal act by an official was presented to the
president of the duma with at least thirty signatures and
the latter placed it before the house. If the duma accepted
the interpellation it was sent to the minister to whom it
was addressed, and the latter was required to present a
reply within a month or explain why that was impossible.
If by a two-thirds majority the duma considered the reply
to be unsatisfactory, the statement was sent to the Imperial Council and ultimately reached the tsar. The duma,
especially its left wing, made full use of this handy instrument of propaganda, and it found especial favor in the
eyes of the Popular-Socialists. For, as the tension between
the duma and the executive increased, they would not
allow the administration to screen its views from the public.
They would demand a definite statement from the tsar himself on the vital issues.

Ministers were allowed to attend all duma sessions, but
they had no vote. Although they might be interpellated

they could refuse information on matters not subject to
publication, as state secrets. Such statements as they were
willing to make were delivered personally or through an
assistant. Moreover, the duma had to give them the floor
whenever they demanded it.[3] They might recall bills which
they had presented to the duma, but this right was withdrawn if the duma had already taken the matter under
consideration.

For a session of the duma to be valid a quorum of at
least one-third of its membership was required. If the
quorum was not obtained the business of the day was to
be postponed for no more than two weeks. If the duma
failed to obtain a quorum a second time for the same business, the matter, if introduced by the government, was
then presented directly to the Imperial Council by the
minister who introduced it.

The public was admitted by ticket to the sessions of the
general assembly. Members of the Imperial Council, senators, and diplomatic representatives were assigned special places. At closed sessions only ministers and the deputies might be present. Such a session could be called by
the duma itself, its president, or a minister who felt that
the subject of his project or message required a secret
sitting. Stenographic reports of all sessions were made
and published by the government and in the press. The
reports of secret sessions were not subject to publication
except with the permission of the duma, its president,
and the minister who called the session.

One of the peculiar and trying circumstances under
which the work of the duma had to be carried on was the
fact that the building in which it held its sessions was not
at its own disposal. According to the rules issued by the
government a few days before the opening of the duma,[4]
the latter, through its president and sergeant at arms, was

3. This aroused a controversy later when the duma contended that they had
to be heard only on matters under discussion. See Chapter XII on Political
Terror.

4. *Pol. sob. zak.*, XXVII, no. 28,890.

allowed to control only that part of the Taurida Palace
which it occupied: the session hall, committee rooms, offices of duma officials, etc. But the remainder of the palace
and entrance into it were in the hands of the administration of the Taurida Palace guard which was appointed by
the minister of the interior together with the minister of
the imperial household. This administration had at its disposal troops and police. This anomalous situation loomed
large in a number of irritating clashes, as in a dispute
over the right of the press to interview deputies in the
palace, or in the matter of admission of experts to the
duma committees.[5] In general, this tendency of the government to limit the powers of the duma and to interpret
its statute strictly often rendered the legislative powerless
to act efficiently and independently.

On February 14, 1907, the tsar issued an *ukaz* which
called for the opening of the duma on February 20.[6]
On that day the population turned out in a holiday mood
to welcome its second parliament. Workers marked the
event by one-hour or one-day strikes, or where that was
impossible, they held meetings and contributed their earnings for the day to the unemployed. Some factories voluntarily closed for the day.[7] The ministry of education ordered all schools closed, and the students of St. Petersburg
University decided to turn out in a body to greet the
representatives.[8] Crowds choked all streets leading to the
Taurida as many inhabitants of the capital gathered to
witness the colorful opening scene, for deputies from all
parts of the empire arrived in native costume. There were
lusty cheers especially for the members of the opposition
parties.[9]

The first day was chiefly given over to formal opening
with a prayer, reading of official documents and the tsar's

5. See below Chapter VI.
6. *Riech*, Feb. 20, p. 4.
7. *Ibid.*, Feb. 18, pp. 3, 4; Feb. 20, p. 4; *Tovarishch*, Feb. 20, p. 5.
8. *Riech*, Feb. 18, p. 4; Feb. 21, p. 3.
9. *Ibid.*, Feb. 21, p. 2, Duma Sup.

welcome, and the taking and signing of the deputies' oath.
And it was not until the moment for the swearing-in arrived that the Social-Democratic fraction filed in, each
member wearing a bit of red ribbon in his lapel.[10] That
gesture, and the failure of the opposition to arise and
respond to the cheers for the tsar from the right immediately aroused the displeasure of the "ruling spheres."
The work of provocation had already begun.[11] The only
real business of the day was the naming of a president.
The election of a Kadet as a member of the party which
contained the best parliamentarians was practically a
foregone conclusion. But the left fractions were insistent
that he be a Kadet acceptable to them. And among the
Social-Democrats the question of supporting a Constitutional Democrat called forth some debate and much mis-
giving.

Both the Bolsheviki and Mensheviki refused to enter-
tain any idea of presenting a candidate for the presidency
of the duma, for by law he would be in direct contact
with the throne, a state of affairs which they regarded
as unbecoming for representatives of a proletarian
party.[12] But the Bolsheviki also believed that this relationship offered a remarkable opportunity to a Kadet president for carrying on conversations with the reactionaries,
and for arranging compromises at the expense of the
people. Furthermore, they vividly remembered S. A. Muromtsev, Kadet president of the first duma, who interfered
with Social-Democratic orators, Ramishvili and Jordania,
when they referred to a "constituent assembly" and a
"democratic republic." Any other Kadet must act in the
same manner, they believed, for the liberals aimed at limiting the revolutionary and agitational significance of
the duma. Besides, the Bolsheviki held that the Kadets
should be made to realize that they no longer retained

10. *Ibid.*, Feb. 21, pp. 2, 2, Duma Sup.
11. *Stenog. ot.*, I, 1; *Letters of Tsar Nicholas and the Empress Marie*, J. Bing,
ed., p. 225.
12. *Riech*, Feb. 21, p. 3; *Protokoly*, pp. 152, 165–166.

their old hegemony, and that the Trudoviki should be urged to present their candidate for the presidency.[13]

The Mensheviki, too, favored a Trudovik president and, likewise, in order to impress the Kadets with the fact that they were no longer the recognized leaders of the duma. But when the Social-Democratic fraction presented the idea to the Trudovik group at a conference on February 18, the latter rejected the proposal partly because they, too, held contact with the throne to be abhorrent to their principles, and partly because they did not want their leaders distracted from fraction work. The most to which they would agree was the election of their candidate to the vice-presidency or to the secretaryship of the duma.[14] Consequently, the majority of the Social-Democratic fraction believed that they had no choice other than to vote for a Kadet candidate for the presidency. As vice-presidents the Trudoviki offered M. E. Berezin and A. I. Katavaev, while the Social Democrats agreed to nominate a candidate for the post of assistant secretary only.[15] The Bolsheviki asked to be allowed to abstain from voting so that they might not bear the responsibility for the election of a Kadet, but were persuaded, in the name of party discipline, to vote with the fraction majority.[16] Nevertheless, the Mensheviki openly declared that their action in voting for a Kadet candidate in no way bound them to support him as president. And should he demonstrate any of Muromtsev's "dictatorial" qualities they declared that they would denounce him at once.[17]

Although they might support a Kadet candidate, yet the Social-Democrats, and with them the Trudoviki, were adamant in their refusal to consider N. V. Teslenko, Kadet deputy from Moscow, because of the part he had played in refusing the Moscow Social-Democrats an additional

13. *Protokoly*, pp. 165–166.
14. *Ibid.*, pp. 152, 251; *Tovarishch*, Feb. 20, p. 5.
15. *Tovarishch*, Feb. 20, p. 5; *Protokoly*, pp. 152, 251.
16. *Protokoly*, pp. 165–166.
17. *Ibid.*, p. 152.

deputy in the recent elections.[18] But all groups and fractions present at the opposition conference on February 19, agreed on the candidacy of F. A. Golovin, another Moscow Kadet. Consequently, he was elected president of the duma on February 20 by 356 votes over the opposition of 102 rightists.[19]

The two vice-presidents were chosen at the second session of the duma on February 23, after the Trudoviki had reached an agreement with the Kadets at another opposition conference on February 22, which the Social-Democrats failed to attend. Here it was decided that the Trudoviki, M. E. Berezin and N. Poznanskii, were to be vice-presidents while the Kadet M. V. Chelnokov was to be elected secretary of the duma.[20] The Social-Democrats had refused to nominate a candidate for that post, too, and considered asking for one assistant secretaryship only, for the purpose of keeping informed on the internal affairs of the duma chancellery. At a fraction meeting on February 22, Saltykov was nominated for that office over the protests of the Bolsheviki who held that it was inconsistent to accept it after the others had been spurned. The modest request of the Social-Democrats could hardly have been refused by the other opposition parties.[21] The majority

18. *Ibid.; Riech,* Feb. 21, p. 2; *Tovarishch,* Feb. 21, p. 3; Feb. 23, p. 4.

19. *Stenog. ot.,* I, 7. F. A. Golovin was born in 1867 of noble lineage. He completed a law course at Moscow University in 1898. From 1904 to 1906 he was chairman of the Moscow provincial *zemstvo* board. He was one of the initiators of the Zemstvo Congress and an organizer and chairman of the Moscow committee of the Kadet party. All biographical material is derived from Granat, *Entsiklopedicheskii Slovar,* XVII, unless otherwise specified.

20. *Tovarishch,* Feb. 23, p. 2; *Riech,* Feb. 23, p. 3.

21. *Tovarishch,* Feb. 21, pp. 3, 4, 5. Poznanskii received 349 out of 446 votes cast; Berezin, 345; and Chelnokov, 379 out of 464. See *Stenog ot.,* I, 14, 18. At this time the Polish Kolo stirred a tempest in a teacup at an opposition meeting on February 20, by openly resenting the fact that the arrangements committee had seated them with the right parties. These they considered their hereditary enemies, and demanded seats at the extreme left. This met with instant opposition from the Social-Democrats, and after much debate it was decided that the order from left to right was to be the Social-Democrats, Social -Revolutionaries, Popular-Socialists, Trudoviki, Kolo, progressives and non-partisans, Octobrists and rightists. See *Tovarishch,* Feb. 21, p. 2; *Riech,* Feb. 21, p. 2, Duma Sup.

easily "steam-rollered" its list through the duma on February 23.

The election of assistant secretaries which had been postponed until the third session, February 24, was marked by a debate on the number of assistants to be created. The First Duma had limited them to five,[22] but now the Octobrist Kapustin and several Kadet leaders stressed the fact that the composition of the Second Duma was more heterogeneous than that of the First. Consequently, in order that each group might be represented, they asked that the number of assistants remain undefined. They would allow all who received an absolute majority to fill these posts.[23] This opinion was opposed by the Social-Democrat Ozol who held that five assistants were sufficient and that the remainder would become superfluous observers. He was supported by other spokesmen of the left. They did not relish the idea of right representation in the secretariat as the Popular-Socialist Demianov plainly asserted.[24] If such were their fears, they were quickly dispelled. For despite the adoption of the Kadet proposal,[25] in the balloting which followed only five candidates, all from the opposition, left and center, received an absolute majority.[26]

The duma turned next to questions of procedure. It had to confirm the first three chapters of the rules of procedure which had been compiled by Muromtsev in the First Duma. These dealt with the opening of the duma, the verification of the credentials of its members, the election of duma officials and duma committees.[27] For the further elaboration of rules, the duma chose a committee of nine-

22. *Materialy po sostavleniiu nakaza*, Article 22; hereafter cited as *Nakaz*.

23. The Kadet orators were Maklakov supported by I. V. Gessen, Kizzevetter, and Bulgakov. See *Stenog. ot.*, I, 22, 25–26, 27–28, 36–37, 38–39.

24. *Ibid.*, pp. 23, 28–29, 29–30, 30–32, 37.

25. *Ibid.*, p. 41.

26. Saltykov, the Social-Revolutionary V. N. Uspienskii, the Trudovik L. V. Kartashev, and the Moslem N. S. Maksudov were named. *Ibid.*, p. 43.

27. *Ibid.*, p. 44; *Nakaz*, pp. 1–24.

teen on March 19,[28] which reported to the duma on May 8
and 10. For the most part the committee's proposals were
adopted without protest, but any attempt on its part to
relegate debates to committees or to limit them—that is,
any attempt to limit the agitational possibilities of the
duma—met with strenuous opposition from the Social-
Democrats. Thus, when the committee proposed to limit
debates on the urgency of interpellations to one speaker
for and one against urgency, Ozol emphatically objected.
The motives for and against might be various, he asserted,
and some more convincing than others; therefore he believed that all who desired to speak on the subject should
be heard.[29] But he was overruled by the duma which
accepted the article in the form proposed by the committee.[30]

In like manner when the committee proposed to limit
to one orator for each side debates on the consideration
of urgent proposals, the Social-Democrats opposed the
measure. Through its reporter, Maklakov, the committee
had justified this limitation on grounds of expediency
and clarity in dealing with interpellations. Its majority
believed that the important moment in debates on an interpellation occurred when the government had given its
explanation, and all views were clear. That, they declared,
was the moment for unlimited debates on the subject matter. They maintained that all preliminary debates would
be untimely and would lose force, and should therefore be
limited to a few speakers on the order of dealing with
urgent statements.[31]

But the Social-Democrat Mandelberg saw in the committee's action only an attempt to diminish the significance
of interpellations which he regarded as the duma's most

28. *Stenog. ot.*, I, 980–981. The committee included 2 Social-Democrats (S-D),
Saltykov and Stashinskii, 2 Social-Revolutionaries (S-R), 2 Trudoviki, 1 Popular-Socialist (P-S), 4 Kadets, 2 Kolo, 1 Moslem, 1 Cossack, 2 non-partisans, 1
Octobrist (Oct.). See *Ukazatel*, p. 42.
29. *Nakaz*, p. 28.
30. *Stenog. ot.*, II, 332–333, 338.
31. *Nakaz*, p. 32; *Stenog. ot.*, II, 338–341.

serious weapon. These, said he, were introduced to "illuminate" portions of the government's policy, and for that purpose two orators were insufficient.[32] To V. M. Gessen's protestation that debates on the substance of an interpellation would not be limited but only postponed until after the government had presented its view,[33] Mandelberg replied that he regarded the moment when an interpellation was introduced and the government's activity brought to light, and the moment when the duma replied to the administration and presented its views on the interpellation, as equally important. Therefore he believed that both should be utilized by the duma to the fullest extent. He felt that the rule proposed by the committee would be detrimental in that respect.[34] But again the majority disregarded his objections and the article was adopted as presented by the committee.[35] Such was the temper and such the fate of all Social-Democratic objections to the proposals of the Rules Committee. Ozol sprang up four times to object to what he regarded as willful restrictions of parliamentary debates.[36] But each objection was overridden by a majority formed of the center and right which invariably accepted the committee's text.[37] Yet he managed to include one bitter truth in retiring when he reminded the duma that with all of its desire for smoothness and speed in the functioning of the legislative machine,

32. *Stenog. ot.*, II, 341–342.
33. *Ibid.*, pp. 343–344.
34. *Ibid.*, pp. 347–348.
35. *Ibid.*, p. 355.
36. He objected to the elimination of debates on urgent statements which were made out of order (Art. 93). He demanded that an article (115) allowing the president the right to suspend members for employing expressions "incompatible with the dignity of the duma" be phrased more definitely since he believed that the discretionary powers allowed the president were too broad. See *Stenog. ot.*, II, 270–271, 405–407. He tried to establish six as the minimum number of orators to which the duma might be limited on any given subject (Art. 203). See *Ibid.*, p. 418. Finally, he tried to establish fifty, rather than one hundred, as the number of deputies required to close a debate or terminate the registration of speakers on a single subject. For he maintained that the large number excluded small parties which he held would become more numerous in the future (Art. 125). See *ibid.*, pp. 421–422.
37. *Ibid.*, pp. 373, 409, 419, 428; *Riech*, May 11, p. 3, Duma Sup.

measures might be retarded not only in the popular body but elsewhere, that is, in the Imperial Council or in court circles.[38] The fact was that these rules, compiled and sponsored by the Kadets, did considerably limit debates for the express purpose of increasing to a maximum the legislative possibilities of the duma, a policy which was directly in line with the Kadet aim to "guard the duma." But to the Social-Democrats such a course meant a minimizing of the duma's significance as a platform for the widest dissemination of revolutionary propaganda. And in their eyes that was equivalent to a betrayal of the liberation movement.

The last step in the organizational work of the duma requiring immediate attention was its division into sections, each of which was to investigate and certify the elections of its members. The rules of the duma required that the deputies be assigned to the various sections by lot in the duma chancellery, the assignment having no political significance whatever.[39] Accordingly, on February 24, the secretary of the duma read out a list of eleven sections. Because of the continual arrival of new members from the distant corners of the empire, and the need for thorough investigation of elections of doubtful legality, this work continued up to the very last days of the duma's brief existence.[40]

Except for two occasions the Social-Democrats were not involved in the debates arising from the verification process. The first occurred during the section reports on March 6, when the Octobrist V. G. Vetchinin asserted that the election of G. A. Aleksinskii should be reviewed since he had been elected from the worker's curia to which

38. *Stenog. ot.*, II, 426.
39. *Nakaz*, pp. 14–15.
40. Reports were given on March 6, *Stenog. ot.*, I, 65–106; March 16, *ibid.*, pp. 646–676; March 30, *ibid.*, pp. 1,380–1,394; May 18, *ibid.*, II, 783–809; May 22, *ibid.*, pp. 958–980; May 29, *ibid.*, pp. 1,365–1,370. Distribution of new members by sections took place on March 22, *ibid.*, I, 894–895; April 9, *ibid.*, pp. 1,754–1,755; May 27, *ibid.*, II, 881, and May 29, *ibid.*, p. 1,365.

he did not, in reality, belong.[41] Aleksinskii explained in his usual sharp manner that he had been elected as a typographical worker, as a proofreader, to be exact. His election had been unanimous in the first stages and he had received a majority as elector and then as deputy for St. Petersburg. At the time of his election, he informed the duma, General Drachevskii, chief of police of St. Petersburg, had protested it to the Ruling Senate which had obligingly proceeded to "explain" that proofreaders might not be chosen as electors by typographical workers. Aleksinskii suggested that the Senate create a special curia for literateurs, and added that he fully understood that the desire to get rid of him concerned only reactionaries, outside of the Senate.[42] As a token of mingled sympathy and defiance, the duma confirmed his election.[43]

On the second occasion when the Social-Democrats took a leading part in the verification debates, on May 22, Ozol protested a section's findings on the Kurland elections. Despite the clear indication of the electoral law that the landless peasants of Kurland might vote at *volost* assemblies and there stand for election to *uiezd* assemblies, a senatorial interpretation of October 7, 1906, excluded these peasants from the latter gathering. The section found that the law had undoubtedly been violated but since only one *volost* had protested and since the landless peasants strongly influenced the elections at the *volost* assemblies, the representation for the entire province of Kurland should not be declared illegal.[44] Ozol emphatically disagreed. The Senate, he pointed out, had admitted its mistake though too late. Consequently, if the duma confirmed these elections it would stand as even more reactionary than the Senate when its clear duty was to fight all illegality. He argued, moreover, that the decree had

41. *Ibid.*, I, 84, 87; *Riech*, March 2, p. 3.
42. *Stenog. ot.*, I, 87–88.
43. *Ibid.*, p. 88.
44. *Ibid.*, II, 962–964.

definitely affected the course of the elections since many landless peasants did not use their active electoral right on being deprived of the right to stand for election to the *uiezd* assemblies. Finally, being about one-third of the peasant population, as the section had admitted, they could and did prevent the conclusion of electoral agreements between landowning peasants and the local nobility.[45] But the duma thought otherwise, for it accepted the elections and voted to inform the minister of the interior of the violation of the electoral law by local officials.[46]

With the exception of the formation of committees, which was attended to as various matters requiring their creation were presented for consideration, all further organizational work in the duma was of a minor though mechanically necessary nature and included the organization of the duma chancellery and minor changes concerning the time and program of the sessions. Both matters provoked debates in which Social-Democratic tactics and principles were reflected.

The Duma Statute fully empowered parliament to set up and administer its chancellery.[47] On March 22, therefore, the secretary of the duma introduced a bill on its organization which was reported by a joint conference of the presidium and the Budget Committee and adopted on May 1.[48] As was the case with most organizational questions, the Social-Democrats regarded the formation of the chancellery from a class-tactical point of view, rather than from that which its authors adopted—the point of view of expediency. Saltykov, Gubarev, and Mandelberg, aided by an occasional Trudovik, while offering no serious resistance to the committee's proposals, never failed to take advantage of an opportunity to reveal

45. *Ibid.*, pp. 964–971.
46. *Ibid.*, pp. 974–975.
47. *Pol. sob. zak.*, XXVI, no. 27,424.
48. *Stenog. ot.*, II, 2–53. The bill was first sent to the Committee on Arrangements for preliminary consideration. Its report was considered by the duma and given to the joint committee on April 10. See *Stenog. ot.*, I, 895, 1,849–1,880.

themselves as the representatives of an underprivileged class with "advanced" political and social principles. Thus, Saltykov attacked Article 4 of the chancellery rules which limited the positions women might hold to those involving purely secretarial work. He wished to exclude the article as being completely out of harmony with the views of the great majority of the deputies on the equality of the sexes in all branches of political life. He referred to the fact that a bill on universal suffrage had already been introduced and therefore maintained that such a restriction was illogical and a political error.[49] But Chelnokov (Kadet) observed that the exclusion of the article would deprive women entirely of the right to serve the duma. He suggested as a better solution that proposals be submitted by various fractions which would supplement this article, and the duma quickly rejected Saltykov's amendment.[50]

With the reading of the following article Saltykov was again on his feet. He would entirely exclude Article 5 which limited chancellery work to persons with an intermediate or higher education, or to those who had served in state, nobility, or *zemstvo* institutions for at least three years.[51] He supported the statement just made by the Trudovik Nebovidov that the article would not attain its aim of filling chancellery posts with educated persons because of the required preliminary examinations and because those who had been in the service of the government, *zemstva*, and nobility might qualify. Moreover, he held that the article did great injustice to the many who had acquired a higher education as auditors but because of empty formalities had no diplomas to prove it.[52] In Saltykov's opinion these arguments exhausted the question, but he added ironically that the nobility and *zemstvo* service requirements presupposed high land qualifications

49. *Ibid.*, II, 12.
50. *Ibid.*, pp. 13–14.
51. *Ibid.*, pp. 13–14.
52. *Ibid.*, pp. 15–16.

which would be useful in the chancellery only to demonstrate who it was that had had the fortune to expropriate
two or three hundred dessiatin.[53] Chelnokov countered
by explaining that in presenting this article the conference had only expediency in mind, and a general rule
which would modify the system of entry into the duma's
service. The article concerned the highest offices of the
chancellery and for efficiency it demanded that they be
filled by persons with high educational attainments. Because of their experience the ex-servants were also indispensable, Chelnokov believed.[54]

These arguments impressed the duma for it again rejected Saltykov's proposal.[55] But the left would take no
part in the voting. For the Social-Democrats, the Social-
Revolutionaries, and the Trudoviki announced that they
would abstain from balloting on the chancellery rules,
and on salaries of chancellery officials.[56] They would take
no responsibility for them.[57]

However, the Social-Democrats were successful in persuading the duma to make several minor changes. Saltykov was instrumental in obtaining the passage of an
amendment aimed at ultimately abrogating limitations
on female service in the chancellery. And Mandelberg
coaxed the duma to raise the salaries of duma journalist
and scribes.[58] Thus, refusing to take any responsibility
for the organization of the chancellery evolved in the conference, by abstaining from voting, the Social-Democrats,
as ever, impressed on the duma, and Russia, their position

53. *Ibid.*, pp. 16–17.
54. *Ibid.*, pp. 23–25.
55. *Ibid.*, pp. 18–19, 31.
56. *Ibid.*, pp. 32, 33, 41.
57. It was during this discussion that the rightist deputy from Bessarabia,
that unresting bundle of nerves, Purishkevich, exhibited a typical example of
his provocative and scandalous behavior by delivering himself of the opinion
that the left deputies, "Andalusian toreadors" (being a reference to the red
ribbons which they wore in honor of May 1) acknowledged only one qualification—prison—and thus caused pandemonium to break loose in the session hall.
See *Ibid.*, pp. 22–23.
58. *Ibid.*, pp. 42–43, 51–52.

as the champion of the underdog and spokesman of progress. Not even this apparently lifeless question was bereft of political and tactical significance for them.

One other matter arose in the course of the organizational debates which clearly emphasized the difference between those who would use the duma for legislative purposes and the groups who regarded it as an agitational platform. On March 30, thirty members introduced a statement which called for a limitation of the daily sessions of the duma to the afternoon hours because committee work was becoming highly complicated and burdensome, and would require the use of the morning hours.[59] This was essentially a technical change made necessary by the progressive accumulation of the business of the duma. Rodichev (Kadet) and Rein (Oct.) in defending the proposal maintained that the committees were fearfully overburdened with far too little time to devote to their tasks, and Stakhovich (non-partisan) pointed out that many members belonged to more than one committee and therefore required more time for committee work.[60]

But the Social-Democrats saw in the proposal another limitation on the use of the duma as a revolutionary tribune. To them it was a change in favor of the committees where the Kadets and other middle class parties might sidetrack dangerous questions, thereby avoiding a clash with the government; just such matters as the Social-Democrats would have aired before the entire country to rally it around the duma and gain its support for a more decisive anti-governmental policy. They objected that the duma, too, had much work on hand and had not succeeded in exhausting a single daily program. They placed great significance on debates in the duma as acquainting both the population and the deputies themselves with major problems and the party alignment on them. To accelerate preliminary work without limiting parliamentary debates they suggested that each fraction invite specialists to pre-

59. *Stenog. ot.*, I, 1,403.
60. *Ibid.*, pp. 1,404, 1,405, 1,407.

pare measures which would be openly debated in the duma. Moreover, they contended that speed in parliamentary activity did not ensure the immediate enactment of a measure which had first to pass the Imperial Council and then the "higher spheres." [61] But in the final vote a part of the Popular-Socialists and Trudoviki joined the liberals and the centrist proposal was adopted by a vote of 257 to 149.[62]

Here, then, was the essence of the varied debates on organizational questions. For they brought clearly into relief the Social-Democratic tendency, more noticeable with the passage of each session, to oppose the Kadets generally, and in particular the efforts of the center to limit the agitational significance of the duma and utilize it only as a smoothly functioning, legislative organ.

61. *Ibid.*, pp. 1,408, 1,409–1,411.
62. *Ibid.*, p. 1,418; *Riech*, March 31, p. 1, Duma Sup.

V

FIRST STEPS

WHILE all fractions were engaged in the first details of organizational work of the duma, the Social-Democrats were also considering their first political moves. In a fraction meeting on February 22, they decided to dedicate their first words to those whom they believed had made their election and inviolability possible—the political prisoners. Consequently, the fraction was determined to raise the question of amnesty for "politicals" independently of other groups and appointed a committee to decide on how the matter should be presented. It was resolved that the fraction would offer only a statement; a proposal to elaborate a bill on amnesty was rejected.[1]

This plan took the Kadet and *Narodnik* parties by surprise. Both protested vigorously against the Social-Democratic scheme to play a lone hand in the matter. They referred to it as a "party demonstration" and threatened to call the matter out of order on the ground that the duma was not prepared to consider it. But the Mensheviki did not want an offensive against the government to develop into a quarrel between opposition fractions. Therefore, on February 23, a statement was issued to the effect that although the Social-Democratic fraction had intended to speak on the liberation of political prisoners and exiles after the election of the president of the duma, their plan was not executed because of the objections of the *Narodniki*. But they hastened to affirm that they would most certainly address the duma on that matter in the near future. And it was finally decided to include the subject in a general party declaration in reply to the govern-

1. *Tovarishch*, Feb. 24, p. 4; *Riech*, Feb. 23, p. 3; *Protokoly*, p. 153.

ment's statement.[2] From then on the Social-Democrats played no great part in the debates on amnesty which took place late in the duma's existence.

With the support of all opposition fractions [3] the Trudoviki presented a bill on March 9, which would free from prosecution or punishment all persons arrested, fined, or sentenced to exile or imprisonment for criminal activity of a political, religious, or economic nature.[4] Persons sentenced by field-courts-martial were also included.[5] But the bill was not considered until May 24 when the Kadets, having reconsidered their stand, and fearing for the very existence of the duma, challenged the propriety of discussing it at all.[6] V. M. Gessen (Kadet) noted that the government had strenuously opposed a bill on amnesty in the First Duma and that under existing circumstances, the Second was powerless to liberate political prisoners. He believed that the adoption of this bill would only demonstrate the weakness of the duma.[7] He would follow to the letter the tactics of avoiding a clash with the government in order to preserve the duma as long as possible; in order to gain time and allow it to sink its roots deep into the consciousness of the people and win their unwavering support.

But, as ever, the Social-Democrats held these tactics to be treacherous, and that only by open clashes with the government on just such controversial questions as amnesty could the duma rally the people to its support. L. F. Gerus (S-D) challenged the notion that the duma

2. *Protokoly*, p. 153; *Riech*, Feb. 24, pp. 2, 2, Duma Sup; Feb. 25, p. 2; Feb. 28, p. 3; *Tovarishch*, March 1, pp. 2, 4.

3. This was gained at a conference on March 7.

4. That is, rural riots and strikes.

5. *Tovarishch*, March 8, p. 7; *Riech*, March 15, p. 3; *Gosudarstvennaia Duma, vtoroi sozyv, zakonodatelnyia zaiavleniia*, pp. 10–12; hereafter cited as *Zak za.*

6. At this time the duma awaited dissolution momentarily. A proposal was also offered to discuss the abolition of capital punishment on the same agenda. *Stenog. ot.*, I, 1,915; II, 1,156–1,164. The bill on the abolition of capital punishment was introduced on March 7, 1907. It would replace the death penalty by a punishment next in order of gravity. The bill was signed by 41 Kadets and centrists. *Stenog. ot.*, I, 748; *Zak za.*, p. 23.

7. *Stenog. ot.*, II, 1,148–1,152.

should be guided by the government's desires. He believed that any productive legislation that the duma might enact would be limited to insignificant matters and predicted that the important bills would be changed by the "police régime" to suit itself. The duma, in his opinion, was to be guided by the interests of the people who at the moment awaited a decision on amnesty.[8] Since he was supported by the entire left, as well as the extreme right which seized upon the occasion to demonstrate the "revolutionary" temper of the duma, the measure was scheduled for discussion in the near future.[9] But the Kadets persisted. They opened the debates on March 28,[10] by proposing that a special committee be created which was to decide only whether any part of the Trudovik bill infringed on the tsar's prerogatives. A bill of amnesty was to wait on the committee's decision.[11] But before the Kadets were able to defend their proposal Minister of Justice Shcheglovitov heatedly informed the duma that under Article 23 of the Fundamental Laws a bill on amnesty would definitely violate imperial prerogatives.[12] Maklakov (Kadet) quietly noted that there was a strong juridical support for the opposite view, and since the question was debatable it should be analyzed by the duma.[13] When the proposal was voted on most of the Trudoviki joined the center to form a majority which called for the appointment of a committee on amnesty. This body was named on May 29; too late for any significant activity.[14]

The duma had not yet undertaken any serious legisla-

8. *Ibid.*, pp. 1,162–1,163.

9. *Ibid.*, pp. 1,152–1,156; *Riech*, May 26, p. 2; May 25, p. 1, Duma Sup. The vote was 193 to 173. The duma refused to discuss the abolition of capital punishment by a vote of 194 to 165 as the right voted with the center.

10. The debates were to take place on May 26, but there was no time for them in that session.

11. *Stenog. ot.*, II, 1,246, 1,249.

12. *Ibid.*, p. 1,300.

13. *Ibid.*, pp. 1,300–1,305.

14. It is of interest to note that the Trudovik leaders voted with the minority formed by the extreme left and right. *Ibid.*, pp. 1,321, 1,437; *Riech*, May 29, p. 1, Duma Sup.

tive work when a near-tragedy occurred which might
have had far-reaching consequences had the fates been
less kind. At about 6 A.M., some five and one-half hours
before the opening of the fourth session of the duma, two-
thirds of the ceiling in the session hall collapsed and
demolished all but a few rows of deputies' seats. Rumors
flew fast and public indignation was aroused when it was
recalled that the palace administration had spent over a
million rubles on repairs during the past year and had
refused to allow the duma any hand in the matter.[15]

The deputies assembled as best they could and when
the session opened, K. K. Chernosvitov, speaking for the
Kadets, proposed its postponement and urged that the
presidium investigate the fall of the ceiling with the aid
of architects selected by the Arrangements Committee.
And Kadet Abramson suggested that the presidium be
empowered to search for a temporary meeting place.[16]

A proposal by Kapustin (Oct.) to end the session called
forth a bitter attack on the government by the Bolshevik
Aleksinskii. He did not wonder that the ceiling had fallen
in the hall where the people's representatives gathered.
He was certain that ceilings were stronger in police and
ministerial institutions. When the president warned him
to talk to the point, that is, on the continuation of the
session and search for a new meeting place, Aleksinskii
proposed that the duma seek out the very strongest structure in St. Petersburg, even if it housed a ministry, the
city duma, or any other organization, and there renew
its sessions. For the people were waiting for the duma to
speak and should they discover that the ceiling had fallen
over it, they would be able to draw their own conclusions.[17]
Amid cries of indignation on the right, Krupnskii (Oct.)
arose to call Aleksinskii's remarks "dirty insinuations."

15. *Riech*, Feb. 14, p. 4; March 3, p. 2; March 3, p. 3, Duma Sup. Expert
advice attributed the catastrophe to the expansion of supporting materials due
to the sudden change in temperature which resulted when, after a seven-month
absence, the duma and populace crowded into Catherine's old gift to Potemkin.
16. *Stenog. ot.*, I, 53–54, 58–59.
17. *Ibid.*, pp. 57–58.

But a scandal was quickly averted when the duma supported a move to end debates and by a great majority
adopted the Kadet proposals.[18] There was hardly a matter which the Social-Democrats could not turn to their
account. And the right rarely missed an opportunity,
such as this, to raise an outcry. As a temporary meeting
place the duma chose the Noble's Hall. Here they held
three sessions and returned to the Taurida Palace on
March 12.

The first important political event in the Second Duma
was the statement of the government's position by the
chairman of the council of ministers. In the First Duma
we observed that Goremykin antagonized the deputies
from the start by appearing before them without a serious
legislative program. But by his statement of August 24,
and by the succeeding enactments under Article 87, in
partial fulfillment of his promises, Stolypin was committed to a program of parliamentary reform. But now
the mere assumption of a "correct" position by the government would not insure a cordial reception of its policy
or avert a vote of non-confidence. After languishing for
seven months under a harsh régime of courts-martial and
states of "special protection"; after witnessing the cir-
cumscription of the duma's power, the electoral campaign,
and the violation of civil liberties and the spirit of the
October Manifesto, the opposition had sufficient grounds
for seriously doubting the sincerity of the government's
intentions. Thus, the possibility of a violent clash with
the administration on the basis of its declaration was ever
imminent.

It was just such a clash which the Kadets wished most
of all to avoid. They were frightened by persistent rumors
of immediate dissolution. Moreover, they felt that if the
duma met a liberal reform program with a vote of non-
confidence it might easily become discredited at home and
abroad. And finally, they realized that, if faced with a
vote of non-confidence, the government would be follow-

18. *Ibid.*, pp. 57, 59, 60, 61, 64.

ing established parliamentary precedents by calling for new elections with their accompaniment of disorder and repression, their uncertain outcome, and a possible change in the electoral law. On February 26, the Kadets met at the apartment of Prince P. D. Dolgorukov and decided to greet Stolypin's statement in silence, and to oppose any vote of confidence in the government which the right might offer with provocative intent. On the other hand, should the Social-Democrats propose a vote of non-confidence the Kadets were resolved to offer a formula of passage to the regular order on the agenda.[19]

But the Social-Democrats were as firm in their determination to act in the manner of the First Duma. It would have been contrary to their basic tactics to have allowed such a moment to pass without subjecting the activities and policy of the government to a severe criticism. They, too, met on February 26, and decided to act independently in regard to the government's declaration. However, should the duma not accept their formula for a passage to the regular order they would support one agreed upon by the opposition.[20]

Yet the *Narodnik* parties agreed on this occasion rather with the center than with the Marxists. They, too, held criticism to be necessary, but feared that an open attack on the ministry might result in immediate dissolution, thus preventing the passage of any reform legislation whatsoever. They would rather wait until the agrarian question had been settled before reckoning with the administration for its past sins. Accordingly, on February 23, the Social-Revolutionaries decided to meet the government's statement in silence, to adopt only a formula of passage to the regular order, and to "reveal" the right should they propose a vote of confidence.[21] On the following day, February 24, the Trudoviki likewise resolved to forego a

19. P. Miliukov, *Vtoraia duma*, pp. 62, 197; *Riech*, Feb. 27, p. 3.
20. *Riech*, Feb. 28, p. 3; *Tovarishch*, Feb. 27, p. 2.
21. *Riech*, March 1, p. 2.

reply to the ministerial declaration and criticism of its
inter-duma activity.[22]

To insure the success of their tactics and to persuade
the extreme left to give up what they regarded as a dangerous policy, the Kadets called several opposition conferences at Prince Dolgorukov's apartment on February
28 and March 1. The opposition parties and groups appeared en masse but the Social-Democrats were represented by only Dzhaparidze and Ozol or Tsereteli. The
Kadets, Kolo, Moslems, Social-Revolutionaries, and Trudoviki agreed not to attack the government's statement,
but having heard it to adopt a simple formula of passage
to the regular order. The Popular-Socialists were at first
hesitant but on the morning of the government's declaration they fell in with the majority.[23] But the Social-Democrats were unmoved. They informed the assembled deputies that their fraction was firm in its intention to reply
to the government's statement. They would, however,
abide by a formula of passage to the regular order agreed
upon by the opposition if their own formula, which was
essentially a statement of non-confidence, were not acceptable. They argued that silence would be taken as a sign
of approval by the population, and would be equivalent
to a refusal to express popular demands for the sake of
preserving the duma. These tactics, they believed, would
ultimately serve as a precedent for refusing to criticize
the government in any matter whatever. They were unaffected by Kadet pleas to avoid a dangerous situation
and by their suggestion that to avoid misunderstanding
the duma clearly reserve the right to criticize the government. At a final meeting in the duma on March 6, just
before Stolypin delivered his address, the Social-Democrats reaffirmed their stand and added that they would
present their own formula if the rightists should find that
of the opposition acceptable. They would in no way risk

22. *Ibid.*, March 2, p. 2.
23. *Tovarishch*, March 7, p. 3.

the appearance of joining the right in support of the government.[24]

Meanwhile, the Social-Democratic factions had been wrangling with each other over the exact nature of their fractional statement, on the necessity of which both were in complete agreement.[25] At the fraction meetings of February 26 and 28, the wording of a reply to the government was discussed.[26] The executive committee, supported by the Menshevik majority of the fraction, offered a project of a reply and a plan of activity which immediately precipitated a debate on tactical principles. It was their opinion that the statement should aim to deliver a telling blow at the government; therefore its declaration

24. *Riech*, March 1, p. 2; *Tovarishch*, March 1, p. 3; *Protokoly*, pp. 152–154. Some Kadets with the approval of the Social-Revolutionaries suggested that all fractions leave the hall in protest against the Social-Democratic speech, but the Trudoviki and Popular-Socialists objected. *Ibid.; Tovarishch*, March 2, p. 2; *Riech*, March 2, p. 3; March 6, p. 2; *Tovarishch*, March 6, p. 2; *Riech*, March 7, p. 1.

25. Before it became known that Stolypin would address the duma, the Social-Democrats supposed that the tsar would personally deliver an address from the throne as he had done at the opening of the First Duma, and they planned their activity accordingly. On February 19, a joint meeting of the representatives of the central committee of the party and the executive committee of the fraction proposed that a formula of passage to the regular order be adopted which would contain the party's program demands in ultimatum form. These included an eight-hour day, complete civil liberties and suffrage rights, freedom to organize and strike, aid to the unemployed, subordination of the executive authority to the duma, and the abrogation of the death sentence and field-courts-martial. The formula also included a demand for "all land to the peasants without redemption payments." But the representatives of the central committee suggested that if the Kadets and Trudoviki rejected the latter proposal the fraction should replace it with one which called for "obligatory expropriation of all lands for the benefit of the peasants." Aleksinskii, the only Bolshevik member of the temporary executive committee, declared that this move would violate the resolutions of the Stockholm Congress which clearly demanded expropriation without redemption. But the Mensheviki who dominated the meeting aimed to unite the duma opposition against the government at its first significant appearance, and thus strongly impress the population. They saw no need to develop the entire agrarian program of the party, especially the demand for expropriation without redemption to which the Kadets objected. A breach in the ranks of the fraction at the first important session of the duma seemed inevitable when the cancellation of the throne speech ended the controversy. See *Protokoly*, pp. 152–153, 168–170. See the S-D agrarian resolution in *V. K. P. Rezoliutsii*, pp. 60–61.

26. See below Tseretli's reply to the government.

and inter-duma activity were to be mercilessly criticized. In voting on a resolution of passage to the regular order the fraction was to unite all of the opposition forces of the duma, as a counterweight to the administration.[27]

The Bolsheviki saw a distinct danger to the revolution in these tactics. They feared that the population would not understand joint activity with the "treacherous," non-revolutionary, liberal bourgeoisie in the duma, thus, perhaps, undermining the leadership of the party in the revolutionary movement. They called for independent action on the part of the fraction. They demanded a statement characterizing the whole course of the revolution, and indicating the revolutionary aims and demands of the Social-Democrats; that is, a statement of their entire program. They would offer a resolution of passage to the regular order not only with democratic but also with socialistic content. The Menshevik project, they declared, contained none of these requirements. Finally, they argued that the dissolution of the duma was ever imminent. This might be the first and last appearance of the fraction and it should, therefore, fully expound its point of view and program in replying to Stolypin.[28]

The Mensheviki came to the defense of their project and tactics. They disagreed with the Bolsheviki on the necessity of including the party's program in the declaration. They would not read their program through in connection with every important statement they might make in the duma, but would explain it only on the basis of concrete problems as they arose. They declared that the reading of the party program in the First Duma was a correct tactical move. Then the party was appearing in the duma for the first time. Then, too, it was necessary to break down prejudices; to attract to participation in duma activity that two-thirds of the party which still boycotted it. But they maintained that the adoption of

27. *Protokoly*, pp. 154–155; Letter of S-D fraction to all party organizations, March 27, 1907, in *Leninskii sbornik*, XVI, 252–258.

28. *Protokoly*, pp. 154–155, 166–168.

such tactics at the opening of the Second Duma would
be a dull, perhaps humorous, repetition. It would be out
of place to talk about Socialism when the country was
awaiting the solution of vital problems; when, for example, it wanted to know whether or not the duma would
work with a government which did not enjoy the confidence of the people.[29] On February 28 the Menshevik
majority in the fraction adopted the committee's project
of a reply and voted to accept a simple formula of passage
if there were no hope for the adoption of a more decisive
statement.[30]

When Stolypin arose to speak in the Noble's Hall on
March 6, the duma realized that its first tense moment
had arrived. Pale and stern of demeanor, speaking with
precision, and loudly emphasizing important phrases, the
premier read his maiden address to the duma for half an
hour while the deputies listened in complete silence.[31] He
began with the assertion that when a country was in the
throes of reconstruction (and, consequently, of popular
ferment) and many changes were taking place, the general idea behind all government projects had to be explained and defended. The projects of the opposition had
also to be considered, and the government was to be the
arbiter of their compatability with the good of the empire.
The guiding purpose behind all government proposals,
he explained, was the creation of new material norms embodying the new relationships which resulted from the

29. *Ibid.;* fraction letter, *Leninskii sbornik*, XVI, 257–258.

30. *Riech*, Feb. 27, p. 3; March 1, p. 3; *Tovarishch*, Feb. 27, p. 2; March 2,
p. 4. As noted above, this decision was qualified on March 6, when they threatened to vote against a formula acceptable to the right.

31. *Stenog. ot.*, I, 106–120; *Riech*, March 7, p. 1. P. A. Stolypin was born in
1862 at Srednikovo near Moscow. He studied law at St. Petersburg University.
In 1885 he entered the ministry of public domains and was soon transferred to
the interior ministry. In 1889 he settled in Kovno, became an honorary justice
of the peace and marshal of the nobility. In 1902 he became governor of Grodno
Province and in the following year of Saratov. In May, 1906, he became minister of the interior under Goremykin after he had attracted attention by his
ability to control the population of Saratov during the Revolution of 1905. On
July 9, 1906, he was appointed chairman of the council of ministers. See A.
Suvorin, *Russkii Kalendar*, 1912, p. 587.

reforms lately undertaken. These norms, Stolypin declared, had to rest on clearly expressed laws in order to prevent clashes between the reformed society and state and the old institutions and laws. Therefore, the government was chiefly interested in presenting to the legislative bodies a whole series of bills reforming public life in Russia.

Before enumerating the government's bills, Stolypin stopped for a moment on important measures issued under Article 87 of the Fundamental Laws, especially the land law. He defended the promulgation of this measure on the ground of urgency. The tsar demanded it, and the peasantry, perishing from rural disorders, had requested reform. But the government, while crushing disorder among the peasants, was morally bound to indicate a legal means for satisfying their needs. Consequently, a land fund was created from state-owned lands, the Peasant Land Bank [32] was reorganized to allow for the sale and improvement of more fields, and finally, peasants were allowed to leave their communes and own land individually. All measures issued under Article 87 would be duly presented to the duma for its approval.

Stolypin then enumerated measures which the government intended to introduce; its legislative program for the duma. This included a series of political, administrative, educational, fiscal, and economic projects, especially agrarian and labor reforms, and those aiming at the improvement of trade and industry, and a number of public improvements.[33]

32. See below Chap. VIII, for the government's economic policy.

33. Besides those already enumerated he mentioned measures on the protection of civil liberties; on church property and religion in general; on reform of local administration; laws on roadbuilding, famine relief, and medical aid; police reforms; reforms of local and appellate courts; responsibility of officials and measures safeguarding correct judicial procedure. In the agrarian field he would also present a bill for improved land distribution; bills reforming land organization committees by making them elective and allowing them to propose and execute their plans. His labor bills included the control of administrative intermeddling in employer-labor relations; the right to organize and strike for economic purposes; labor insurance; medical aid; and woman and child legislation. But he would encourage the labor movement only insofar as it did not threaten

The enactment of so vast a reform program, the premier explained, depended directly on the condition of the
finances of the state. Therefore, he regarded the examination of the budget as a very important matter, and invited
the duma to undertake that task as soon as possible. He
explained the difficulty of finding new means for reforms
and the upkeep of the army while the normal income had
shrunk with the abolition of redemption payments on
November 3, 1905, and expenditures had increased as a
result of the necessity of meeting foreign obligations. The
obvious inference was that reductions were out of the question. But he promised that in the future the tax burden
would be more equitably distributed, and that, insofar as
posssible, the administration would refrain from placing
additional levies on the poorer elements of the population.
In concluding, he expressed the belief that the enactment
of reforms would pacify and revive the country, and to
that end he was ready to place at the disposal of the duma
all of the government's resources and experience.

Stolypin's statement was greeted with a vigorous applause on the right and a deep, studied silence in the rest
of the hall. Although this declaration of intentions was
less sharp than had been expected, and compared with the
usual governmental pronouncement might even have been
regarded as a distinct advance toward liberalism, especially since the administration now offered to consider the
proposals of the opposition, nevertheless it had several
obvious defects. In the first place, the government was
still allowed the final word in all legislative matters, and
there was no hint of a concession to the demand for a duma
ministry. Then, the government had emphatically declared
that it would brook no opposition to its agrarian program.
Finally, the duma's sensibilities were ruffled by Stolypin's

"public order" and "safety." The government would improve trade and industry
in the Far East by closing free ports and by constructing an Amur River railroad
from Lake Baikal to Khabarovsk (a completion of the Siberian Road within the
empire). It would improve Asiatic rivers and Far Eastern navigation. Stolypin
predicted reforms of all grades of educational institutions, and finally enumerated fiscal reforms which included changes in real estate and inheritance taxes
and a reform of the tariff system.

failure to congratulate it on its escape from possible catastrophe as a result of the collapse of the Taurida ceiling.[34] There was still too much of the bureaucratic, patriarchal spirit in the address to evoke a sympathetic response from any part of the opposition. But, as we have seen, the nature of Stolypin's speech had little to do with the duma's official reaction to it. That had been decided beforehand.

The chairman of the council of ministers was followed immediately by the Social-Democratic spokesman, I. G. Tsereteli. He delivered himself of a frankly revolutionary address which called forth shouts, imprecations, and thumping of hands and feet from the right, this tumult punctuating the more challenging portions of his speech, and trying the patience of the president.[35] In the opinion of the youthful Menshevik leader the "grave-like silence" which followed the government's first utterance was a demonstration of the depths of popular dissatisfaction. For it was clear to him that Stolypin spoke for "feudal" Russia, and that all of the administration's activities clearly demonstrated the connection between the government and large landowners. Had it not replied to the universal demand for obligatory expropriation with decrees organizing the sale of land through the Peasant Land Bank, and simultaneously stepped up the price of land? Had it not, in general, attempted to halt the historical development which inevitably doomed the landowning class? It threw out crumbs of reform, long overdue, yet by means of terrible repression tried to crush all manifestations of independent activity in behalf of the oppressed.[36] This

34. *Riech*, March 7, p. 1.

35. *Ibid.; Stenog. ot.*, I, 120–129. I. G. Tsereteli was born in the Caucasus in 1882, the son of a famous Georgian publicist. In 1902 he was exiled for participating in revolutionary student agitation. On his return in 1903 he edited the first Georgian S-D paper, *Kvali*.

36. He accused the government of interfering in the capital-labor struggle; of abetting and organizing lockouts; of persecuting the press and political organizations; of terrorizing two-thirds of the population while the country lay in a state of war at the tender mercies of uncontrolled satraps. He further accused the administration of organizing pogroms, and of failing to prosecute Hertzenstein's murderers.

government, he asserted, could not pacify the masses, but only exasperate them, and by obstructing historical developments, it made an explosion inevitable.

In the elections, he continued, despite all obstacles raised by the administration, the people had pronounced its sentence. It had expressed its will, but only by the organization and unification of the people could official tyranny be ended. For only the organized strength of the people could force the executive power to resign and guarantee the realization of a real constitution. The duma, assembled for legislative work, would analyze the government's bills which, in his opinion, took from the people the few gains it had made, and would point out the abyss between it and the administration. The duma would arouse the population for the struggle, and organize and unify it in order to win both land and freedom. Since the government would bow only before force, he called on the duma to weld that power which would help it to subordinate the executive authority to the legislative.

Tsereteli then read the Social-Democratic declaration which was essentially a sharp indictment of the administration containing all of the major charges which the opposition had ever brought against it.[37] It held that the people could have no faith in the promises of a government supporting such policies. For their part, the Social-Democrats expected nothing from it and saw salvation in the union of the duma with the people to end despotism, open prisons, establish freedom, solve the land and labor problems, and right the unjust tax burden. Therefore, the statement continued, the Social-Democrats would make use of the legal rights of the duma to awaken and organize the population, especially the proletariat, in order to win freedom and to subordinate the executive to the legislative branch of the government. Finally, in

37. Besides the accusations made by Tsereteli, the S-D statement charged the administration with mocking justice in applying medieval tortures and setting up field-courts-martial. It further accused the government of misusing state funds set aside for famine relief; of interfering in elections to ensure the victory of its protégés; of failing to aid the unemployed, and of placing the solution of labor problems in the hands of the employers.

payment of the debt of gratitude which the party felt that
it owed to political prisoners, the proclamation declared
that the duma would ever strive to free the exiled and the
confined by impressing upon the people the truth that
only by freeing itself could it hope to free its warriors in
the struggle for freedom. Thus, from the very start the
Social-Democrats showed how they would "reveal" the
cruelty of the government and point out its basic hostility
to the interests of the population.

First the silent reception of Stolypin's near-conciliatory
declaration, then the Social-Democratic reply; here, indeed, was a cold welcome for the government, from the
most representative body that the Russian people had
ever chosen. But the Kadets had never meant their opposition to go as far as the Marxists pushed it, and they
hastened to define their position and forestall further
harsh utterances. First, they proposed to limit the number of orators to the twenty-five who had already signified their desire to speak. But the extreme right voting
with the extreme left, easily mustered the fifty votes required by the rules to defeat the motion.[38] They had much
to say. Then, Prince Dolgorukov (Kadet), supported by
the *Narodniki*, the Kolo, and the Moslems, urged that
criticism be postponed until particular measures should
be discussed. And he proposed the simple Kadet formula:
"Having heard the statement of the chairman of the council of ministers on the introduction of bills, the duma
passes to the regular order." [39]

Debates on a formula narrowed to an exchange between
the extremes—right and left. For the milder right the
portly and anglicized Octobrist Count V. A. Bobrinskii,
and for the more extreme right the bald, neurotic, and
excitable Purishkevich pleaded for coöperation with the
government in enacting "ripe and inevitable" reforms.
Normality was their goal. They called for a swift solution
of the agrarian question. And they accused the left of revolutionizing the peasantry normally living at peace with
its landowners, and of terrorism which was universally

38. *Stenog. ot.*, I, 129–130. 39. *Ibid.*, pp. 130, 130–131.

considered criminal. Finally, Bishop Platon struck a familiar rightist note when he called on the duma to pacify the country and to condemn political murders by revolutionaries.[40] This, in general, was the temper of many other addresses from the right.

The Social-Democrats prolonged the assault begun by Tsereteli. In a long, rambling speech the Lett, Ozol, a weak-voiced, inexperienced orator, condemned the government for its sins against labor. For isolating the worker from the rest of the population, for suppressing trade unions and the labor press, for its fearful punitive expeditions which fell with especial fury on strikers, for its neglect of the unemployed and its failure to lower food prices, for allowing the workers no part in labor legislation, and for intervening actively on the side of the employer and encouraging organizations of great industrialist which precipitated serious lockouts; for these transgressions and many others Ozol assailed the Old Régime. He was certain that all believed with him that "Carthage must fall." [41] The fiery Aleksinskii jeered at rightist orators who had called themselves representatives of the people; those rich landowners and high church dignitaries who had to defend themselves against charges of pogromism. They would enslave Russia for they feared her people. The peasant, the worker, and soldier might expect nothing from the government which represented these elements, and would have to struggle against it for every gain. That was the single truth which the Social-Democrats had come to the duma to propagate.[42] Finally,

40. *Ibid.*, pp. 137–140, 140–142, 142–144.

41. *Ibid.*, pp. 134–137; *Riech*, March 7, p. 3. I. P. Ozol was born in Riga in 1878. He graduated from the Riga Polytechnical Institute, and became a merchant. During the Revolution of 1905 he became actively engaged in S-D activities.

42. *Stenog. ot.*, I, 154–156. G. A. Aleksinskii was born in the Caucasus in 1879. He attended Moscow University but his academic career was twice interrupted by arrest and exile for revolutionary activity. He later served in the Elets and Khotinsk *zemstva*. For propaganda among the workers he was repeatedly prosecuted. During the 1905 Revolution he became an active S-D journalist in St. Petersburg with Bolshevik sympathies.

Dzhaparidze had the honor of reading the Social-Democratic formula of passage to the regular order.[43] The extreme left could not resist presenting their special statement. They called unequivocally for an expression of non-confidence in a government which reflected the interests of only the nobility, landowners, and bureaucracy, and in which the country had already expressed a complete lack of confidence. But the duma, the Social-Democrats declared, with popular support would turn its will into law and would subordinate the executive authority to the legislative.

Through the daily press Stolypin must have been well posted on what to expect in the duma, and could prepare a reply accordingly. At any rate, before the end of the session he appeared on the tribune for a second time, with an olive branch, and defiance for the revolutionaries.[44] He had not intended to speak again, he began, but the course of the debate forced him to do so. He wished first to state that the government would always act strictly within the law. Then, he would like to find grounds for common work and a common language with the duma; but he was certain that it could never be that of hatred or malice. In order to make the administration's position perfectly clear he affirmed that the duma had no legal right to express non-confidence in the government which, of course, did not mean that this government, entrusted with power at a moment of great reform, would try to escape responsibilty. But he wished it remembered that when the entire country, from Kronstadt, a few *verst* from St. Petersburg, to the Caucasus, was embroiled in a revolutionary turmoil, the government either had to resign and yield before revolution, or defend the authority entrusted in it; that authority which was the preserver of Russian political and national unity. But the second choice brought accusations upon its head. In striking at revolution, it was impossible not to graze private interests, he

43. *Ibid.*, pp. 156–157.
44. *Ibid.*, pp. 157–160.

declared. Yet the administration aimed only to preserve the principles which underlay the reforms lately promulgated. Fighting with extraordinary means at an extraordinary time, he maintained that the government had won and made possible the Second Duma. He pleaded that there be neither accused nor accusers in the duma, and declared that like parliament, the government expected to reply before the judgment of history for its course.

He reiterated his contention that the part of the duma which desired to work, to enlighten the people, and solve the land problem would be able to declare its views even though they were opposed to those of the government. Even more, the government would welcome any revelation of maladministration. And he lightly excused past irregularities on grounds of human fallibility at a time when legal norms were not yet fully defined.

But, he declared, the government would regard differently attacks made for the purpose of arousing the population in order to facilitate the preparation for an open attack. And he closed with a peroration which rang as a challenge in the ears of revolutionaries to the last days of the Old Régime:

These attacks count on paralyzing the will and thoughts of the government. They all come down to two words directed at authority: 'hands up.' To these two words, sirs, the government with complete calm, with a consciousness of its uprightness can reply in two words: 'you will not frighten us' (*ne zapugaete*).

The session closed with the adoption of the Kadet formula.[45]

The government was as yet conciliatory. Stolypin's addresses were reassuring to those who had feared immediate dissolution. Yet the premier had displayed disturbing characteristics of the old bureaucratic type. He would co-operate with the duma, but basically on his own terms.

45. *Ibid.*, p. 172.

He would allow very little tampering with his all-important agrarian reform and he evolved a constitutional theory which was the very negation of the idea of a parliamentary ministry. A vote of non-confidence in his administration by the duma meant nothing to him for he represented and was responsible to the tsar alone. Then, his emphatic defense of repression and his vigorous assault on the revolutionaries made him appear more anti-revolutionary than pro-reform. The skepticism of the liberals increased and Stolypin attracted only the conservatives and reactionaries.

Hope soared on the right for it already knew the sentiments of the tsar. "One must let them do something manifestly stupid or mean, and then—slap and they are gone!" [46] That was the essence of his Majesty's attitude toward the Second Duma. And from the very start the reactionaries could point to a "revolutionary duma" where amnesty was demanded for political prisoners, "enemies of the state," and where the left had spent the first important session in assailing the administration. These vitriolic attacks from the revolutionary opposition did, indeed, render the duma's path more difficult. For they revealed an increasing disunity within the opposition. And they sorely tried Stolypin's patience while the alert reactionaries easily made them pretexts for "scandals" or for appeals to the ready ear of the throne. The extreme right henceforth assumed the offensive.

46. *Letters of Tsar Nicholas and the Empress Marie*, p. 229. See also V. Maklakov in introduction to *La chute du régime tsariste*, pp. 57–58.

VI

FAMINE RELIEF

W HEN the duma assembled on March 7, the day
following the delivery of the government's statement, the general atmosphere was more optimis-
tic. For the time being, at least, threatening clouds had
disappeared and the deputies turned to serious, constructive work. The first such task to occupy their attention
was the creation of the four permanent committees: the
Budget, Finance, Audit, and Editorial.[1] The Kadet and
center fractions attached great significance to the personnel of these vital committees. Therefore, at Prince
Dolgorukov's suggestion, elections to them were postponed
in order to enable the fractions to select their candidates
with care on the basis of proportional representation.[2]

Debates on the committees had apparently ended. But
President Golovin inadvertently touched upon a raw
wound in the body politic. While instructing the duma on
the manner of voting for the committees he explained that
Article 33 of the Duma Rules covered all regulations for
the election of permanent committees but that the duma
had yet to establish the order of electing temporary
bodies such as those on rules and famine relief.[3] The very
mention of "relief" was sufficient to whet the appetite of
the left for a thorough discussion and "revelation" of the
government's policy. But I. V. Gessen (Kadet) made
debates inevitable when he suggested that the duma had
also to define the functions of a committee on famine relief.[4]

1. *Ukazatel*, pp. 35–37.
2. The S-D V. I. Mitrov warned against ignoring non-partisans in selecting
candidates. *Stenog. ot.*, I, 183–184, 185, 198, 192–193.
3. *Nakaz*, pp. 17–18; *Stenog. ot.*, I, 196.
4. *Ibid.*, I, 196–197.

The Social-Democrats quickly entered the breach. They demanded the immediate election of a famine-relief com- mittee. And the Bolshevik leader Aleksinskii was surprised to find that there were any doubts concerning its duties. Representatives of peasants and workers clearly under- stood that it had first to examine the condition of the hungry peasants, and the activity of the government and public institutions in aiding them. Then, it had to con- sider means for further aid. He proposed, moreover, that a committee be created to investigate and relieve unem- ployment in the cities.[5] Comrade P. G. Izmailov supported him and charged the duma with assuming a cold-blooded attitude toward this vital human question. It had placed greater significance on the Budget Committee, and be- cause of the rules would elect it first.[6] The Trudovik Bulat agreed and proposed that the duma committee take over the feeding of the sufferers.[7]

The Kadets, foreseeing an interminable debate, called for an end of oratory while the population starved, and for the beginning of "productive" work. Rodichev ob- jected particularly to the proposal that the duma take charge of feeding the population. That, he declared, would be an infringement on the prerogatives of the execu- tive authority, and its adoption would only demonstrate the political and mental weakness of the duma. He pro- posed that a committee be created to investigate the han- dling of relief funds by the government as the only activity which the duma could legally undertake.[8]

But the flood of oratory was not so easily halted. Too many peasants, including some of the deputies, had suf- fered too often from famine, and the Social-Democrats were quick to realize the value of the committees as centers

5. *Ibid.*, p. 200.

6. *Ibid.*, pp. 199, 200–201. Izmailov was born in Novgorod in 1880. For six years he was a village teacher in the Caucasus and lost his position because of his revolutionary activities. He then took up farming on a village plot in the province of Novgorod.

7. *Ibid.*, p. 201.

8. *Ibid.*, pp. 210, 219–222, 227–230.

for propaganda. A solid Social-Democratic vote twice
prevented the limitation of orators to five minutes each.[9]
The bars were down, the deputies were inviolable, and all
of the pent-up anguish of the population was released in
a flow of speech-making which described the havoc
wrought by the famine, and the laxity of the government
in coping with it.[10]

Nor were the Social-Democrats behindhand in utilizing the occasion to the best advantage. They would inform
the entire country of the corruptness and cruelty of the
administration, and would press for the creation of local
investigating committees under the direction of the deputies. Aside from their practical value in directing local
relief work and thereby winning the gratitude of the population, the possibilities which these committees offered
as a means of collecting materials to be used against the
government and as media for disseminating revolutionary
propaganda made them highly attractive to the Social-
Democrats. They insistently demanded action of the duma
despite its apparent powerlessness and were little concerned with the question of competence. Their committees investigating on the spot would, they declared, reveal
not only widespread mismanagement and misappropria-
tion, but also the basic causes of the famine. They could
hardly be considered illegal, the Social-Democrats maintained, after Stolypin's request for a revelation of cor-
ruption. They held it an extravagant waste of time to appoint routine committees while thousands starved and
the government crushed all private attempts to aid the
sufferers; while Gurko [11] squandered sums set aside for

9. *Ibid.*, pp. 224, 227; *Riech*, March 8, p. 1.
10. See especially the description by the leftist Kadet, Dr. D. A. Pereleshin,
of the situation in his native Voronezh. Here crop failures and epidemics were
particularly severe, and the government had supplied bread which was 23 per
cent inedible grass. See Appendix II, A; *Stenog. ot.*, I, 232.
11. The reference is to V. I. Gurko, assistant minister of the interior. He contracted with one Lidval for the supply of provisions to the famine-stricken area.
The latter received an advance of 800,000 rubles from Gurko but was neither
able to meet the advance nor supply the necessary provisions. Gurko was tried
and dismissed for "exceeding his authority." See V. I. Gurko, *Features and Figures of the Past*, pp. 507–509.

the hungry and the Kazan peasants were forced to prostitute their daughters for bread. The government would do nothing for the people, therefore the duma must act. They realized, of course, that the duma could only enact half-measures at best. But because they wanted a healthy people capable of fighting for the new social order where there would be neither autocracy nor starvation, they regarded the committee as necessary. Specifically, the duma should create a relief committee which was to examine with care the government's activities in feeding the starving from 1905 to 1907, and investigate its expenditures not only by examining its accounts, but also by verifying its local disbursements. Secondly, the Social-Democrats proposed that the duma collect all available information on famine, unemployment, and profiteering on the vital needs, and obtain materials for considering the best method of aiding the starving populations, not only by studying available printed sources but also by investigating in the localities.[12]

The Kadets now moved energetically to parry what they regarded as a severe blow to the dignity of the duma. The young parliament, they felt, could not at this stage afford to violate the prerogatives of the executive branch of the government. And if it sent committees to the villages they would only raise hopes which the duma could not fulfill. It would thus impair its standing in the eyes of the population which expected so much from it. Therefore to avoid a hurried and radical decision on the question of creating a famine-relief committee, the Kadets resorted to formal technicalities. Rodichev declared that he wanted his proposal to follow the usual order for such matters. It had already been introduced in written form; now he held that it should be announced in the duma, then printed and placed on the agenda of some future session. He maintained that the question would thereby gain in clarity through discussion, and the rules of the duma would be respected. He remarked that the question had not yet been examined from the point of view of its political im-

12. *Stenog. ot.*, I, 208-210, 236-238, 235-236, 240-241, 245-248.

plications which might, perhaps, be highly significant.[13]

The Social-Democrats were quick to attack Rodichev's latest proposal. They believed that they had a majority behind their motion. They regarded the Kadet tactics as purely obstructive and charged them with flouting the will of the duma.[14] Struve's plea to the deputies,[15] and especially to the peasantry, to deal carefully with this matter involving a question of competence was viewed by Aleksinskii as an attempt to woo the *Narodnik* vote. He met it with a reminder that the peasants (Bulat) first proposed the organization of local committees. This, in his opinion, proved that the peasants had definite ideas on the matter and that Struve's plea was futile. Furthermore, he maintained that if the duma postponed decisions as long as possible when questions of competence were involved it would never accomplish anything, and the deputies would become something in the nature of assistants invited to sign official documents. Therefore, he moved that the committee be immediately elected.[16] But despite the calculations of the extreme left the liberal center was joind by the Kolo, Moslems, and right to form a majority which voted to postpone the election of a famine-relief committee until the following session.[17]

When debates on the nature of the committee's duties were begun on March 9,[18] Rodichev proposed that a committee be created to examine the entire expenditure for famine relief and planting, as well as its plans for future activity in these fields. Then he undertook a critical

13. *Nakaz*, pp. 25–26, Articles 53–55 inclusive; *Stenog ot.*, I, 249–250, 251.

14. See speeches of Zhigelev and N. S. Saltykov, *Stenog. ot.*, I, 251, 253–254.

15. *Ibid.*, pp. 255–256.

16. *Ibid.*, p. 257.

17. Eleven Kadets and 6 Moslems defected from the center and voted with all Social-Revolutionaries (except 2), all Social-Democrats, and all Popular-Socialists against Rodichev's proposal. *Ibid.*, p. 261; *Riech*, March 8, 1907, p. 4, Duma Sup.

18. On the preceding day there had been no session and the information bureau of the opposition fractions selected candidates for four permanent committees and the library committee. Therefore, when the duma met on March 9, elections were hardly more than a formality. *Stenog. ot.*, I, 267–268; *Tovarishch*, March 9, p. 2; *Riech*, March 10, p. 1.

analysis of the leftist plan to administer direct aid to the population. In the first place, he declared, it was illegal under existing laws. It could not be acted on until a new law was passed, and that would require at least six weeks.[19] Then, in following out the leftist proposal he noted that the duma would acquire all the responsibility for famine relief without being able to distribute either food or seeds, and this would only serve to undermine its authority. As for sending members to the localities, he believed that there were not enough deputies for the task of local investigation. Moreover, local officials who might feel that they were required to report data to a duma committee would yield nothing to individual deputies. Thus, they would be nothing more than travelling investigators who might only send reports to the duma. They would be powerless to meet the countless requests made of them in each locality, thus, again, demonstrating their weakness. Some, he said, would have the duma examine bills on famine relief. Yet none had been presented, and the duma had no time to investigate the causes of famine while material aid was necessary. Finally, he opined that rendering aid to the unemployed, as suggested in the Social-Democratic proposal, was also an executive function. It was, moreover, an entirely different question which would require a separate bill on the competence of a committee to aid the unemployed before it might be created. Rodichev explained that his committee would be entirely legal; that it would be elected by the sections of the duma on a non-partisan basis; that it would have full power to investigate, and should have twenty-two members.[20]

19. See Duma Statute, Article 56, *Pol. sob zak.*, XXVI, no. 27,424; *Nakaz*, Article 58. A bill had to be submitted to a cabinet at least one month before it could be discussed in the duma.

20. *Stenog. ot.*, I, 270–278. F. I. Rodichev was born in Tver Province in 1854 of noble ancestry. He entered *zemstvo* work and became marshal of the Tver nobility (1890 and 1906) and honorary justice of peace (1895), and was active in the liberal Tver *zemstvo*. He was a founder of the Kadet party and a member of its central committee. In 1906 he was elected to the First Duma. He failed to sign the Vyborg Manifesto since he was at the World Interparliamentary Congress in London when it was issued. He therefore escaped the fate of most of the Kadet leaders, temporary loss of political rights.

It was now the Social-Democrats who resorted to technicalities in an effort to overcome Kadet opposition. Aleksinskii and Dzhaparidze maintained that Rodichev had offered a new proposal which should therefore be printed, placed on the agenda, and considered after the proposals of the Social-Democrats and *Narodniki* which were already in order. The latter objected especially to Rodichev's contention that aid to the unemployed was a separate matter requiring a separate bill.[21] But Golovin upheld the Kadet claim that this proposal was only an exact formulation of the informal statement he had made in the last session, and the duma voted to discuss separately the question of aiding the unemployed.[22]

Foiled in their attempt to eliminate the Kadet proposal, the Social-Democrats could only resort to an attack on the centrist motion and policy and defend their own. Dzhaparidze continued to maintain that Rodichev's proposal differed from the topic on the agenda; for while the former dealt with a famine-relief committee, the proposal referred only to an investigative body. He readily admitted that the duma was powerless to relieve the starving but contended that parliament could warn the people that to save themselves they must take matters into their own hands. And the committees could reveal the immediate causes of the famine; not its basic causes, for that, he agreed, would require too much time. For a real examination of relief activities he maintained that a wide investigation in the localities affected would be necessary; not merely an examination of bureaucratic correspondence in St. Petersburg. Should local officials refuse data their behavior would only serve to open the eyes of the population to their obstructive activities. He objected at some length to the Kadet proposal that the committee be elected by the non-partisan sections of the duma. For he observed that

21. *Ibid.*, pp. 278–279, 279–280. Dzhaparidze was born in Tiflis in 1875. He was ousted from the university for revolutionary activity and completed his education abroad. He was on the staffs of many Georgian and Russian newspapers. He was arrested for radical activity in 1905.

22. *Stenog. ot.*, I, 278–279, 280.

the famine-relief question was highly controversial and, consequently, the views of each party should be represented. Moreover, the famine-relief committee was, in his opinion, fully as important as the Budget and Finance Committees which had been elected by the fractions. He warned the duma not to regard the question too lightly. For if it could not feed the population, the committee could educate it politically, and the materials which it collected might serve as an indictment against the government.[23] No clearer statement of the aims of the Social-Democrats in creating this committee was possible. Then Aleksinskii castigated the Kadets in true Bolshevik fashion. He mocked at their proposal as a fantastic method of solving the famine-relief problem. He bitterly observed that when economic questions were involved the Kadets were always on the side of the satisfied and opposed the hungry, the proletariat. He urged the duma, when questions of legality arose, to follow the laws of the people and not the legislation of the autocracy which the Kadets regarded with such great respect. In his opinion, the duma had to depend on the people or it would alienate them— and then it would be powerless indeed.[24]

Aroused by this attack, V. M. Gessen scolded Aleksinskii for utilizing the famine-relief debates to settle accounts with the Kadets. And he warned the duma that when their deputies appeared in the villages a popular "movement" would begin which might well result in bloodshed. For that the duma alone would then be responsible.[25]

While Rodichev was making a final summary of his proposal, Stolypin, Shcheglovitov, and other high officials filed into the session hall, and to the great surprise of the duma, the chairman of the council of ministers followed the Kadet leader to the tribune. In a friendly tone he informed the duma that he regarded Rodichev's proposal

23. *Ibid.*, pp. 290–296.
24. *Ibid.*, pp. 301–303.
25. The Duma, by now somewhat wearied, limited all speeches to five minutes. *Ibid.*, pp. 311, 312–313.

as an interpellation on the activity of the government in aiding the famine-stricken areas, and declared that it would reply in a few days in a report on the relief and seed campaigns. If further information was desired he pointed out that the duma committee might legally appeal to the proper ministers who would certainly give it all of the necessary information. He announced that the government intended to ask for further appropriations for famine relief and to change all defects in existing laws on the matter. Finally he expressed the belief that a committee such as Rodichev proposed was significant and would not be used solely to censure the government. Consequently, the administration fully supported the proposal.[26]

Stolypin's address caused an immediate sensation. This was the most definitely conciliatory move the government had yet made toward the duma. The Kadets were both elated and dismayed. By acting in agreement with the majority they maintained that Stolypin had behaved in the best traditions of true parliamentary government.[27] On the other hand, they fully realized the danger which the party ran in identifying itself too closely with the administration. In fact, the Bolsheviki believed that they now had certain proof of their contention that the Kadets were making "deals" with the government "at the expense of the people." Aleksinskii exultantly ran about convincing the Trudoviki to act with the left on all proposals and amendments.[28] And he achieved no small success. For, although they voted with the entire duma to create a famine-relief committee, they joined the left on the question of local committees.[29] But the Social-Democratic proposal to allow local investigations into the government's famine-relief activities was defeated by a majority composed of the center, the national groups, and

26. *Ibid.*, pp. 327–329, 330–331; *Riech,* March 10, p. 1.
27. P. Miliukov, *Vtoraia duma,* p. 199.
28. *Riech,* March 10, pp. 1, 4, Duma Sup.
29. This consisted of 168 *Narodniki* and Social-Democrats. *Riech,* March 10, pp. 1, 4, Duma Sup. The majority polled 287 votes.

the rightists. All other amendments from the left suffered the same fate, for this majority rejected those which would have the duma evolve a bill or temporary rules on famine relief, or would allow it to collect materials on the famine and high food prices. When Rodichev's proposal was put to a vote some of the leftists abstained and the measure was adopted. But the left derived some consolation from the fact that the duma decided to elect thirty-three members to the committee by fractions rather than sections.[30] If, by supporting Rodichev's proposal, Stolypin wished to impress both Russia and Europe with his liberalism his success was questionable. If, however, he sought thereby to drive a wedge between the liberals and the left he was, for the moment, eminently successful.

The Famine-Relief Committee first met and organized itself on March 18, chosing Dolzhenkov (Kadet) as chairman and Urazov (Trudovik) as secretary. It lost no time in requesting materials from the famine-relief department of the ministry of the interior, and was promised data on the following day. It also decided to appeal to the Zemstvo Union,[31] zemstvo boards, and the Free Economic Society[32] to supply all information, materials, and personal explanations possible. A representative of the ministry of the interior was invited to attend its sessions.[33] On March 20 the ministry sent down Assistant Minister A. A. Pavlov to inform the committee of the dimensions of the task involved and the progress made by the government in coping with it.[34]

But the committee soon found itself in troubled waters when it took action which precipitated a dispute on a fundamental parliamentary question and severely strained relations between the duma and the administration. Chair-

30. *Stenog. ot.*, I, 334–335, 444. The committee included 4 S-D's (Aleksinskii, Anisimov, Vinogradov, Izmailov), 2 S-R's, 5 Trudoviki, 3 P-S's, 7 Kadets, 3 Kolo, 1 Cossack, 3 Moslems, 4 Octobrists, 1 non-partisan. *Ukazatel*, pp. 41–42.
31. See Appendix III, A.
32. See Appendix III, B.
33. *Riech*, March 20, p. 4, Duma Sup.
34. *Ibid.*, March 22, p. 3, Duma Sup.

man Dolzhenkov, following the committee's decision, invited representatives of the *zemstva* and the Free Economic Society, and proposed that questionnaires be sent to various public organizations.[35]

When the government learned of the committee's decision it reacted immediately. Separated from the population by its peculiar interests and traditions, the bureaucracy of the Old Régime, responsible only to the tsar, was ever suspicious of the intentions of those elements of the population who undertook some public service or charitable work independent of the administration. This was especially true of its attitude toward the Second Duma with its great opposition majority whose left wing had proposed to undertake famine-relief work for the purpose of "revealing" the government. Under these circumstances the administration sought to exercise all possible control over the representative body. Consequently, on March 22, Stolypin sent a note to President Golovin calling his attention to the fact that the Famine-Relief— and Budget—Committees intended to invite experts and receive information from local institutions.[36] He contended that as a legislative organ the duma had no right to have direct relations with these institutions. If any explanations were needed the proper minister should be questioned according to Article 40 of the Duma Statute.[37] On the other hand, according to Article 61 of the Zemstvo Statute,[38] local and higher institutions could be addressed only through the provincial governor or the minister of agriculture. Therefore, he regarded the committee's act as a violation of both laws. He was confident that the duma would discontinue this activity and prevent its recurrence in the future. He informed Golovin that the administration had already taken steps to prevent the *zem-*

35. *Krasnyi Arkhiv*, XIX, 134; *Riech*, March 24, p. 2. The committee invited V. V. Khizniakov of the Free Economic Society, Vyrubov of the Penza *zemstvo*, and Tresviatskii of the Samara *zemstvo*.

36. See below Chap. IX.

37. *Pol. sob. zak.*, XXVI, no. 27,424.

38. *Ibid.*, X, no. 6,927.

stva from communicating with the duma and its chancellery.[39]

The duma's position was first stated by M. P. Fedorov (Kadet), chairman of the Budget Committee. When questioned by Stolypin on March 25, as to whether he was acquainted with the premier's note to Golovin, he replied in the affirmative, but retorted that as chairman of a duma committee he could not reckon with the government's demands since he regarded them as illegal. In his opinion, the activities of the duma were not within the jurisdiction of the ministry of the interior. Moreover, by law the duma might interpellate a ministry but there were no provisions for the interpellation of the duma by a minister.[40]

The Famine-Relief Committee, too, disregarded the note and invited Prince G. E. Lvov to report on the work of the United Zemstvo Organization. On March 26, the committee had received a telegram from Ufa describing the conditions there, and when Pavlov was questioned on the matter he refused to explain in the presence of "outsiders" (Lvov). A part of the committee then suggested that parallel sessions be held with and without experts, and on March 29, a minority insisted on sending out questionnaires to the zemstva. But the majority decided to await a settlement of the dispute before taking further action.[41]

Golovin replied to Stolypin on March 28, requesting the premier to inform him of the exact legal basis for his demand, and he adhered to the point of view that a minis-

39. *Riech*, March 24, pp. 2, 4, Duma Sup.; *Krasnyi Arkhiv*, XIX, 134–135; *Riech*, March 25, p. 2; March 27, p. 4, Duma Sup. These steps included the transmission of instructions to all provincial governors ordering them to be sure that all organizations which had acquired information concerning famine-relief activities in stricken provinces should send these materials directly to the ministry of the interior. Furthermore, the governors were ordered to remind the *zemstva* that until new laws were enacted they were to adhere strictly to existing legislation.

40. *Riech*, March 27, p. 4, Duma Sup.; *Krasnyi Arkhiv*, XIX, 134.

41. *Riech*, March 24, p. 1; *Gosudarstvennaia Duma, II sozyv, obzor dieiatelnost komissii i otdielov*, p. 158; hereafter cited as *Komissii*. *Riech*, March 28, p. 4, Duma Sup.; March 31, p. 4.

ter might not interpellate the duma.[42] Stolypin answered
on the following day. He now broadened his stand and asserted his right to intervene directly in the affairs of the
duma. He referred to Article 63 of the Duma Statute,
and section II of the Rules of February 20, 1906, on the
presence of outsiders at duma sessions.[43] According to
these laws he maintained that rules governing entry into
duma sessions were to be made jointly by the president
of the duma and the chairman of the council of ministers.
Consequently, he contended that they were to act together
when a difference of opinion on any rule existed, or when
rules were violated by either the cabinet or the duma. He
charged that Golovin had allowed persons to enter the
duma illegally without waiting for the tsar's statement on
his willingness to change existing rules, and without receiving the premier's consent. Therefore, he felt con-
strained to take measures to put an end to this "violation"
of the law and to prevent further "law-breaking" he had
ordered the Taurida guard, on the basis of the "Rules of
the Taurida Guard of February 16, 1907" to refuse entry
to any outsiders in general, except those mentioned in the
rules.[44]

Accordingly, on April 4, those invited by the committee were not allowed entry with the exception of Prince
Lvov whom Stolypin had appointed representative of the
Central Committee for Medico-Alimentary Aid to the
famine-stricken population. Lvov protested to Stolypin
against the abnormality of the situation, but the premier
replied that he, personally, could violate no law to solve
the question and would welcome any legislative proposals
for a change.[45] Further, he distributed copies of his letter
of March 22 among his cabinet members and informed
them that existing rules did not permit the participation

42. *Riech*, March 29, p. 3, Duma Sup.; *Krasnyi Arkhiv*, XIX, 134.
43. *Pol. sob. zak.*, XXVI, no. 27,426.
44. *Riech*, March 30, p. 2; *Krasnyi Arkhiv*, XIX, 134; *Pol. sob. zak.*, XXVII,
no. 28,890.
45. *Riech*, April 13, p. 3, Duma Sup.; *Krasnyi Arkhiv*, XIX, 134.

of experts in the work of the duma committees. None of their subordinates who might be invited to attend such meetings were to participate if outsiders should appear.[46]

Since the solution of the point in dispute hinged chiefly on the meaning of "outsiders," and until that should be settled by legislation Stolypin might appear to be formally correct; and since the latter was intent on using force to sustain his viewpoint, there was little that the duma majority might do (or care to do) short of appealing to the population for support. Therefore, on April 2, Golovin informed Stolypin that since the matter had been placed in the hands of the armed guards of the palace he considered the question of inviting experts to be temporarily closed. In reply, Stolypin declared that he, too, considered the dispute ended—by his letter of March 29.[47]

Stolypin may possibly have been formally correct. But this insistence on formalities; this display of official suspicion, interference with, and frustration of, a mechanically necessary part of the duma's legislative activity, smacked too much of the old bureaucracy. The large duma committees contained many inexperienced deputies who could hardly be expected to understand the highly technical measures presented by the government. They were sorely in need of any aid non-deputy specialists might offer. When the duma invited them to attend committee sessions it was not trying to extend its competence but to perfect its machinery and refute charges of "incompetence." Stolypin's stand, therefore, served only to deepen the chasm of distrust between the Russian people on the one hand, and the administration on the other.

On April 4, the government presented the Famine-Relief Committee with a bill which provided for the appropriation of 22,000,000 rubles for carrying on the relief campaign, and for covering contracts already fulfilled. A part of the committee held that the bill could not be ex-

46. *Riech*, April 4, p. 3.
47. *Ibid.*, April 3, p. 2, Duma Sup.

amined until the entire relief problem had been considered.
But others were willing to appropriate only five millions
for charitable aid and three millions more for purchases,
and to withhold the remainder until the entire question had
been considered. Many members believed that the demand
could not be examined while the proper materials and
experts were not available.[48]

At a meeting on April 10, a leftist minority desired to
reject the government's request without further examination. They argued that the government could not be entrusted with the expenditure of public funds without reports on the relief campaign and with no indication as to
how the appropriation would be spent. But the majority
held that the starving population would suffer from such
a policy since the contractors would cease supplying the
stricken areas. They would appropriate five million rubles
to the United Zemstvo Organization and Red Cross. All
other appropriations were to be postponed, and more information on the relief campaign was to be demanded of
the government.[49] A subcommittee reported a bill embodying the committee's decisions on April 12. After some
consideration the committee decided to assign six million
rubles as extraordinary credits for 1907 for the purpose
of satisfying the needs of the stricken population.[50]

At the duma session of April 17, the committee, through
Chairman Dolzhenkov, presented the bill to the duma and
asked that the appropriations be put at the disposal of the
United Zemstvo Organization, the Red Cross, and the
Central Committee for Medico-Alimentary Aid.[51] The
Social-Democrat Izmailov presented the views of the committee minority. He held that the Red Cross was purely a
bureaucratic institution and therefore he opposed the
placing of any appropriations in its hands. In the name
of his fraction he proposed that the entire sum be given

48. *Ibid.*, April 6, p. 3, Duma Sup. A ruble is $0.515.
49. *Komissii*, p. 160.
50. *Riech*, April 12, p. 2; April 13, p. 4, Duma Sup.
51. *Stenog. ot.*, I, 2,239–2,245, 2,264.

to the United Zemstvo Organization on the condition that
it would give the duma a complete account of its expenditures. He declared that his fraction was willing to vote
for the appropriation, even though the sum was insufficient, only because it regarded the need as urgent.[52] The
Kadets replied that this proposal would be equivalent to a
refusal of relief because the Zemstvo Organization did not
officially exist and the government might refuse to appropriate funds to it. They further noted that the organization was not equally developed in all localities and therefore could not assume the entire burden of administering
aid to the famine stricken.[53] And the duma majority
consisting of part of the Trudoviki, the center, the Kolo,
and the right carried the committee's proposals over the
opposition of the remaining *Narodniki* and the Social-
Democrats.[54]

In the interim the committee had been studying the
appropriation of the remainder of the twenty millions
asked by the government; the 17,500,000 rubles which
was to cover loans and contracts already fulfilled. The
subcommittee had examined these contracts after much
effort and a surprise visit to the ministry of the interior.
On May 1, it reported that despite evidence of incorrect
management and its own inability to review all expenditures these debts should be fully paid since they were
honorably contracted.[55] In adopting this report on the
following day, the Famine-Relief Committee decided that
the amount requested was to be appropriated. But the bill
was to be accompanied by an explanatory note informing
the duma that because of the incompleteness of the materials available the committee would take no responsibility
for the accuracy of the amounts demanded. It would, however, approve of the appropriations because it was necessary that they be paid, and would demand all available

52. *Ibid.*, pp. 2,245–2,246.
53. *Ibid.*, p. 2,248–2,250, 2,250–2,252, 2,252–2,253.
54. *Ibid.*, p. 2,264; *Riech*, April 18, p. 4, Duma Sup.
55. *Riech*, April 13, p. 4, Duma Sup.; May 3, p. 3, Duma Sup.

accounts at the end of the famine-relief campaign; at a date no later than January 1, 1908.[56] A bill embodying these decisions was reported to the duma on May 11.[57]

Again Izmailov appeared for the minority. He related how the government had hindered the committee from the start by requiring that it be satisfied with only official reports which painted a rosy picture of the progress of the campaign; how it prevented the committee from obtaining information in the localities; how the committee had decided to visit the offices of the ministry where it found no accounts on expenditures whatever. Only after the transactions had been completed would the ministry supply an account thereof. In a word, no exact information was available on the expenditure of 142,000,000 rubles on famine relief. That sum had already been expended for bread which was 25 per cent grass. Under the circumstances he maintained that the duma could not appropriate 17,500,000 rubles.[58]

Ozol asserted that if the duma assigned these sums to an irresponsible government whose expenditures it could not control, it would be sanctioning the government's destructive policy which raised prices of bread and salt atrociously. In the name of the Social-Democratic fraction he offered a resolution for passage to the regular order which declared that since the government had not presented the Famine-Relief Committee with a full account of its activities in relieving the stricken areas, and instead forbade local organizations to give the committee information on the state of relief affairs, and did not allow experts to attend committee meetings, the committee was unable to subject its activities to a real examination. Moreover, since the fragmentary information presented by the government did not include sufficient corroborative material, and since circumstances already known concern-

56. *Riech*, May 6, p. 3.
57. *Stenog. ot.*, II, 456–463.
58. See Dolzhenkov's report, *ibid.*, pp. 459, 464–466.

ing its administration of relief affairs indicated a general lack of economy and misuse of public funds, the duma did not believe that sums appropriated to the government would be used for the satisfaction of popular needs and refused its request for credits.[59]

The Kadets brought up their big guns to defend the voting of appropriations and to avoid what might be construed as a vote of non-confidence in the administration. Shingarev observed that the duma was not concerned here with the approval of accounts but with the granting of credits for the further progress of the famine-relief campaign. Refusal of credits, he maintained, would only mean more suffering for the starving population. And Rodichev warned the duma that confidence in the government might be destroyed if these credits were not granted.[60] In the final balloting, the Kolo and the Trudoviki abstained from voting on the committee's proposals. But the Kadets, uniting with the center and right, carried the measure over the opposition of the Social-Democrats and the remaining *Narodniki*.[61]

Kadet and Social-Democrat, liberal and revolutionary; it was quite clear by now that these were the two tendencies struggling for control in the duma—as in the Russian political scene in general. And as the Kadets became more resolute in defense of the duma's existence; as they stubbornly opposed open defiance of Stolypin's stand on experts, the rejection of the government's famine-relief demands, or the creation of local relief committees of questionable legality, they forced the more moderate Mensheviki to stand by the aggressive Bolsheviki in carrying out their party program. For if, as the Kadets feared, the local committees would emphasize the agitational significance of the duma and precipitate uprisings among the

59. *Ibid.*, pp. 503–507.
60. *Ibid.*, pp. 507–509, 509–510.
61. The vote was 174 to 142. *Ibid.*, pp. 515, 517, 526; *Riech*, May 12, p. 1, Duma Sup.

aroused peasantry, and if they were calculated to embroil the duma in a clash with the administration, they might threaten the very existence of parliament. But they were particularly happy media for the execution of the resolution which the Social-Democratic Party had adopted at Stockholm.

VII

UNEMPLOYMENT

IN 1907 the young Russian industry was recovering from an economic depression which had affected the entire continent since the turn of the century, as well as from the havoc wrought by the Revolution of 1905. Strikes and retaliatory lockouts, though decreasing in number and intensity, were still numerous and resulted in unemployment of significant proportions.[1] Moreover, chiefly as a result of the administration's tariff policy, poor communications, and low wages, the cost of living for the employed Russian worker had become extraordinarily high. And the gap between wages and prices of even vital necessaries widened as the decade progressed.[2] But the government had done very little to ease the situation, and regarded strikes with open hostility. In the large cities, however, especially in St. Petersburg, the unemployed organized councils which put great pressure on the local and central governments. Several public-works projects were begun and public kitchens were opened. But private contractors and bureaucratic indifference brought an end to effective state unemployment relief by the end of 1907.[3]

When the Second Duma convened the unemployed turned toward the Taurida Palace, especially, as we noted, toward the Social-Democratic fraction, with exaggerated hopes and expectations. They demanded outright aid of the duma which only the city governments might render, and they sharply criticised the fraction and

1. See Appendix II, B and II, D; D. Koltsov, "Rabochie v 1905–1907 gg.," *Obshchestvennoe dvizhenie v Rossii v nachale XX-go veka*, II, part 1, 325–328, P. Maslov, ed.; this article will hereafter be cited as "Rabochie."
2. D. Koltsov, "Rabochie," p. 334.
3. See Appendix II, C; Vl. Voitinskii, *Gody pobied i porazhenii*, pp. 188–191.

duma for their inactivity.[4] But we have seen that the Social-Democrats did not ignore the problem. In the duma they tied the question of unemployment to that of famine relief. For, in their opinion, both forms of human misery resulted from the same policy based on the self-interest of the ruling class. And, as a political problem, both lent themselves to the same parliamentary tactics. The debates on unemployment were, therefore, strikingly similar to those on famine relief.

On the evening before the duma was to take up the problem of unemployment, the Social-Democratic fraction decided that it would offer no concrete bills because of the complexity of the question. But the fraction was to demand the creation of committees like those which it had suggested in the debates on famine relief. They would send deputies to the localities to aid the population as they might. But they would also investigate the government's activities in aiding the unemployed, and the cause of the crisis, in order to "reveal" the administration.[5]

Newspaper reports forewarned the Kadets,[6] and they were resolved to sidetrack long and heated debates and, at any cost, to prevent the adoption of the Social-Democratic proposal. They believed that this project, like its predecessor, threatened to endow the duma with excessive authority and make a clash with the administration inevitable. Therefore, when the non-partisan deputy Petrochenko asked, at the beginning of the session of March 15, for immediate consideration of the land question, Prince Dolgorukov (Kadet) quickly supported him.[7]

4. D Koltsov, "Rabochie," p. 319; G. Aleksinskii, "Iz perezhitago," pp. 121–122; *Riech*, Feb. 18, p. 4.

5. Representatives of the St. Petersburg Council of Unemployed who were invited to attend the meeting proposed that the fraction introduce a project for public works to be administered by trade unions and the city dumas. *Protokoly*, p. 156, *Tovarishch*, March 15, 1907, p. 5; *Riech*, March 15, p. 3.

6. See preceding note.

7. *Stenog. ot.*, I, 538–540, Prince P. D. Dolgorukov was a an *uiezd* marshal of the nobility in Moscow province, 1893–1906. From 1896 to 1905 he held a position at court which he lost because of his activity in the liberation movement. During the Japanese war he was active in relief work. Later he became one of the founders of the Kadet Party and a member of its central committee.

Following the tactics employed by the Kadets in the famine-relief debates, he observed that the duma should first print all written proposals on the question of unemployment, distribute them among the deputies, and discuss them at a session in the near future. That was the usual order. He argued, moreover, that reflection was essential for the unemployment question was extremely complicated. It involved economic and social problems, and the duma's competence in dealing with the question had to be defined. Consequently, it would be necessary to elect a committee, to decide on how to elect it, and to consider its duties. In order to disentangle all of these matters and to avoid chaotic debates, he believed that the duma could follow only the order that he had suggested.

Tsereteli and Aleksinskii speedily let it be known that the Social-Democrats desired an immediate consideration of the question. The former noted that the election of the unemployment committee had already been twice postponed: once when the Social-Democratic proposal was removed from their bill on famine relief and again, when the Kadets had placed field-courts-martial on the agenda, out of the regular order.[8] He could find no formal objections to the immediate consideration of the unemployment question since a proposal had been printed and distributed, and because the problem had become acute and had to be solved without delay.[9] Aleksinskii added that he had received many instructions from the St. Petersburg workers, all demanding that the duma deal with the issue at once.[10] The Social-Democrats gained their point when the duma decided to postpone the discussion of the land question until March 19, and to consider unemployment immediately.[11]

Again the Kadets resorted to technicalities. Kizevetter was soon on his feet protesting that there existed no separate proposal on unemployment. He could remember

8. See below Chap. XII on Field-courts-martial.
9. *Stenog. ot.*, I, 280, 358, 540; *Riech*, March 16, p. 1.
10. *Stenog. ot.*, I, 544–545.
11. *Ibid.*, pp. 549–550.

only one statement in which the unemployment and famine-relief questions were united. Since the duma had already decided to separate these problems and then to print special proposals on unemployment, the Kadets would adhere to Dolgorukov's project.[12] But this time their efforts were futile. Discussion of unemployment was the order of the day, and the peasants wished to get on with the agrarian question. The duma heard Aleksinskii charge the Kadets with wilfully employing obstructive tactics, and demand that debates begin on this vital matter with only one printed proposal before the duma.[13] And it listened sympathetically to Tsereteli's contention that the separate Social-Democratic project on unemployment was, like Rodichev's second proposal on famine relief, merely a revision of the original.[14] In this mood the duma rejected Dolgorukov's proposal and passed to a general consideration of the unemployment question.[15]

Dzhaparidze presented the Social-Democratic point of view, and in a lengthy address he accused the administration of causing and prolonging unemployment.[16] At the outset he indicated the great proportions which unemployment had assumed,[17] and its horrible results in the form of malnutrition, disease, prostitution, suicide, and a higher death rate. For all of this suffering the government alone was to blame. Its general policy, he maintained, tended to impoverish the peasant and worker in order to satisfy the greedy appetites of the landowners whose interests it had at heart. Was it not for the benefit of these elements that it blocked the normal growth of industry? Was it not for these that it became involved in the Manchurian adventure which resulted in the disastrous Japanese war and the revolution, and thus thoroughly dis-

12. *Ibid.*, pp. 280, 552.
13. *Ibid.*, pp. 248, 552.
14. *Ibid.*, pp. 227–229, 552–553.
15. *Ibid.*, p. 553.
16. *Ibid.*, pp. 553–566.
17. He declared that there were 12,000 unemployed in the capital, 35,000 in Lodz, and 150,000 on the Volga. See Appendix II, B.

organized industrial and rural economic life? The government's post-revolutionary policy, he asserted, was directed at increasing unemployment for the purpose of breaking up labor organizations, and at preventing the spread of Socialism among the workers. To this end the administration had closed state factories, encouraged lockouts in private establishments, and persecuted those who would yield any concessions to labor. With the aid of the Union of the Russian People the government had entered into a campaign of forceful "union smashing." All over the empire it closed trade unions and simultaneously encouraged the formation of employers' organizations to meet the challenge of organized labor. And what of the great host who had lost their livelihood as a result of this policy? The government cared for them by burdening them with taxes, by exiling them from industrial centers so that they might migrate to the hungry villages, and by persecuting sympathizers who would mitigate their suffering. Only in the face of the danger of a hunger rebellion and under pressure from the councils of unemployed did the government and local administrations take inadequate measures which they soon abandoned.[18] These being the facts, he proposed that a committee be created to gather information on the causes and extent of unemployment, and to indicate measures necessary to alleviate the distress of the unemployed. He was certain that these data would reveal where the blame for the crisis lay.[19]

Proposals were now in order. The Social-Revolutionaries presented a project similar to that of the Social-Democrats. Theirs would also empower the duma to control relief funds and their distribution.[20] A third proposal

18. See Appendix II, C.
19. In concluding, Dzhaparidze precipitated an uproar by referring to the duma as an organization which would further the development of the revolution, seize executive authority, and subordinate it to the legislative. These remarks aroused Golovin to interrupt him and say that the duma would always remain a legislative body. *Stenog. ot.*, I, 565.
20. *Ibid.*, pp. 573–574.

had been introduced by the Kadets who would create a committee of nineteen to consider the amount the government should appropriate to aid the unemployed suffering from the industrial crisis, and to investigate the means and manner of aiding them.[21]

Kutler mounted the tribune to defend the Kadet plan. The question, he said, was far too complicated to be completely examined by the committee. That would require time, and it would be necessary to call in specialists. Furthermore, he averred, the duma as a legislative body could not assume such executive duties as the administration of work in the localities. Within the law the duma might only appropriate funds from the State Treasury and cite their destination and purpose. He believed, furthermore, that this complex problem should be narrowed in order to place the matter on a practical basis. Consequently, he proposed that the committee should render aid only to persons who were victims of the economic crisis since the task of aiding all unemployed would otherwise be too huge.[22] He warned the duma that the necessary funds could not be appropriated immediately from the treasury because they had not been included in the budget for the current year. This matter of aiding the unemployed he regarded as an elementary duty and he begged the duma to cease its speechmaking and to do something practical for the jobless.[23]

Aleksinskii and Tsereteli replied for the Social-Democrats.[24] The former was quick to make the most of the fact that the Kadets would not aid those who had suffered for political reasons and thus inferred that they assumed the view of the middle class which, according to the Marxists,

21. *Ibid.*, p. 551.

22. This attitude was held only by the more conservative Kadets. The liberal leaders, including Miliukov, would make no distinctions. See P. Miliukov, *Vtoraia duma*, p. 207.

23. *Stenog. ot.*, I, 584–587.

24. They spoke after a hour's recess had been taken and the duma had limited each speaker to five minutes. Both the S-D's and the extreme right opposed this move. A few Trudoviki had arisen in opposition to the proposal but on observing that most of the peasants were seated, quickly joined them. *Ibid.*, p. 589; *Riech*, March 16, p. 1.

they represented. For the Social-Democrats, he asserted, the problem involved more than an attempt to mitigate the consequences of the industrial crisis. They would repay the workers for the suffering to which the government had subjected them. For this reason he demanded that all of the unemployed be aided. Lest there should be any misunderstanding he explained that the projected committee was not only to consider the sums to be appropriated, but was also to examine the activities of the administration which brought about the present grave situation. If the duma should refuse to adopt that policy he believed that it would limit itself to Shidlovskii's offer to "collect rubles from the deputies in a hat." And against that labor indignantly protested.[25]

Tsereteli supported investigation in the localities because that would attract attention to the persecution of the unemployed. This, he believed, would at least prevent the recurrence of the more unbridled official excesses and serve to decrease the number of lockouts. Thus, the number of unemployed would be diminished and, consequently, the number of victims of the field-courts-martials which the Kadets were then interested in abolishing. The Social-Democrats were acquiring parliamentary habits in spite of themselves. For with the sad results of the careless motion on famine relief in mind, they presented a carefully worded statement which proposed a committee to carry out locally and in the capital those activities already suggested by Aleksinskii and Dzhaparidze.[26]

For the first time in the Second Duma, the minister of trade and industry, D. A. Filosofov, requested permission to speak. He stated that he could find no fault with the Kadet proposal but that the Social-Democratic project

25. Shidlovskii had agreed with Kutler that the duma should ascertain the extent of unemployment among the workers. But with some indelicacy he jeered at its efforts by proposing that the duma set an example for the entire country by contributing 25,000 rubles which should be given to the *zemstva* and city organizations for creating work. He offered the first contribution of fifty rubles. *Stenog. ot.*, I, 592–594, 600.

26. *Ibid.*, pp. 600–602.

was illegal, and he believed that its authors were aware of that fact. He objected to the "demand" for bread and work. The government would never, under any circumstances, consider it a duty to provide work. But he maintained that the administration had demonstrated its readiness to cope with unemployment and had included large grants for relief and public works in the 1907 budget. He assured the duma that the committee's investigations would prove that the extent of the need had been exaggerated. He referred to the numerous strikes in various parts of the empire and ended with the assertion that the government was willing to aid those who were unemployed as a result of the industrial crisis, but not those who had "voluntarily" brought unemployment on themselves by striking.[27] Again the government saw eye to eye with the Kadets.

The Social-Democrats lost no time in defending themselves. Dzhaparidze was immediately on his feet.[28] Filosofov's statement that the workers had brought misery on themselves by striking he called a false, threadbare argument of hired "pen-pushers" and bourgeois ideologists. Workers, he declared, had recourse to strikes and the suffering which they entailed only when necessity drove them to it in self-defense. It was not the strikes which caused economic misery and unemployment but the absence of a desire to allow for minimum economic and juridical protection, and the refusal to allow a normal outlet for newly developing forces which proceeded toward better governmental forms. Long hours, low wages, and enforced illiteracy seemed to Dzhaparidze to present sufficient cause for striking. He was not convinced that local investigation

27. *Ibid.*, pp. 611–614; Appendix II, D. The minister announced that the 1907 budget included a seven-million ruble appropriation for public works and that he would request 350,000 rubles and perhaps double that amount for relief of unemployment in Saratov.

28. *Stenog. ot.*, I, 615–619. He paid his compliments to Shidlovskii by noting that city administrations and the right would rather create free kitchens than public works for the unemployed. The workers, he asserted, wanted no gifts, but only the right to work productively.

by the duma was illegal. He regarded it as useful work since it involved the collection of scientific knowledge on unemployment from the government, city administrations, the press, and *zemstva*. Therefore, he was surprised to find that the Kadets were opposed to it. He could not forego the opportunity of noting the "solidarity" of the government with the Kadets on limiting aid to the victims of the industrial crisis. According to information derived from a questionnaire which he held indicated the general situation, he could say that 60 per cent of the unemployed had been discharged for participating in political strikes, and for their political convictions.[29] As for the "demand" for work, the hungry had a right to demand. "No matter how much the government declared from the height of its grandeur that they have not the right to demand, they will demand and it may come to pass that they will be satisfied."[30]

When Golovin closed debates, however, and read the various proposals, in the face of violent Social-Democratic opposition he steadfastly refused to allow the duma to vote on local committees because of the "manifest illegality" of the proposal.[31] But when the duma began to make final decisions on the unemployment question and favored a committee along Kadet lines, the Social-Democrats insisted on striking out the limitation of aid to "sufferers from the industrial crisis." And after two ballots, with the aid of the *Narodniki* and those Kadets who could not subscribe to Kutler's position, the Marxists won their point.[32] The politically unemployed had been bold enough to express their opposition to the existing order, and were, after all, without means of support. In the opinion of the

29. The questionnaire showed that 27 per cent of existing unemployment was due to lower production and 40 per cent to strikes, while 15 per cent were discharged for their political convictions, and 7 per cent for clashing with their management.

30. *Ibid.*, p. 619.

31. *Ibid.*, pp. 622–623.

32. *Ibid.*, pp. 623–624. On the second ballot by a vote of 223 to 202, with 11 abstaining, the duma decided to strike out the phrase.

duma majority these considerations outweighed those of "practicality" urged by the moderate Kadets. The duma then decided to elect a committee of nineteen which was to consider how much need be appropriated to the unemployed, to consider what forms this aid should take, to gather information on unemployment, and to investigate its causes.[33]

When the Unemployment Committee organized itself at its first meeting on April 3, Dr. Gorbunov (Social-Revolutionary) became its chairman and Aleksinskii its secretary. Thus, this committee, created to deal with a labor question, and therefore certain to be regarded with suspicion by the government, had clearly indicated its temper by electing two leftists as directors. Furthermore, for any plan its officers might have, they could always count on a solid bloc of eight leftists (two Social-Democrats, three Trudoviki, two Social-Revolutionaries, and one Popular-Socialist). Therefore it is not surprising that in its comparatively brief existence this committee was constantly at odds with the administration; especially since it, too, became immediately involved in the dispute on "experts" and refused to take the passive stand adopted by other committees and the presidium of the duma.[34]

At the same meeting, with the debates on "experts" well under way, the committee decided almost unanimously to appeal in local newspapers to *zemstva*, city dumas, councils of unemployed, and experts for information on the number of unemployed and the best method of meeting conditions in each locality. Struve (Kadet) disapproved on the grounds that the action was illegal and would only precipitate a new conflict with the government. He was, however, a minority of one. A subcommittee was created to receive all materials and report on the number of unemployed, the amount of credit and the kind of aid needed.

33. *Ibid.,* pp. 624–627. Elections to the Unemployment Committee took place on March 22. *Ibid.,* p. 937. The committee included 2 S-D's (Aleksinskii and Bielousov), 2 S-R's, 3 Trudoviki, 1 P-S, 4 Kadets, 2 non-partisans, 2 Kolo, 1 Moslem, 1 Cossack, 1 Monarchist. *Ukazatel,* pp. 42–43.

34. *Tovarishch,* April 5, p. 3; *Riech,* April 4, p. 3, Duma Sup.

Since some information was already available on unemployment in St. Petersburg, the committee decided to plan a local public-works project in the near future.[35] However, the duma presidium, already deeply involved in a dispute with Stolypin on information from local sources and specialists, refused to allow the committee either to print the appeal in its final form or to invite experts. Struve's suggestion that the subcommittee privately interview representatives of the various institutions was turned down as hurtful to the dignity of the duma.[36]

On April 7, the committee compromised with the presidium by limiting its appeal to a direct request for information from institutions independent of the administration, as trade unions, organizations of unemployed, newspapers, journals, and private persons. It further decided to acquire information on unemployment from Moscow, St. Petersburg, and Saratov city administrations through the ministry of the interior—in accordance with Stolypin's wishes. As for experts, the committee would disregard all prohibitions, including Stolypin's order, and invite them according to the original plan. Struve was a lone dissenter.[37]

The government then took an active hand in the matter and informed the duma chancellery through the administrator of the Taurida Palace guard, Baron Osten-Saken, that experts invited to attend the meeting of the Unemployment Committee on April 12, would not be admitted to the palace. The committee met in great indignation and, with Struve again in a minority of one, decided to raise the question of experts in the duma. If they were not to be admitted ultimately, the committee would raise the question of its own liquidation.[38] However, no such drastic

35. *Tovarishch*, April 5, p. 3; *Riech*, April 4, p. 3, Duma Sup.
36. *Riech*, April 6, p. 3, Duma Sup.
37. *Ibid.*, April 8, p. 3. On April 9, the committee invited S. V. Malyshev, St. Petersburg city administrator of public works, and the chairman of the city council of unemployed, V. C. Voitinskii. *Ibid.*, April 10, p. 3, Duma Sup.; *Tovarishch*, April 10, p. 2.
38. *Riech*, April 13, p. 4, Duma Sup.; *Tovarishch*, April 14, p. 2.

steps were taken, but it remained inactive for several weeks.

On May 5, the committee was informed that representatives of the St. Petersburg city administration would be allowed to appear at its meetings. Taking heart, it decided to hear these officials, and to use their reports and any private information it might have as the basis for a report to the duma.[39] Invitations were issued, but the administration evidently regretted its sudden liberality, for on May 8 Stolypin informed Golovin that he could not order St. Petersburg relief directors to the Unemployment Committee since, in his opinion, they did not belong to the category of administrators mentioned in Article 41 of the Duma Statute.[40] Stolypin apparently held that this article referred only to administrators of central and not local institutions. He declared, however, that he would be glad to communicate all information on unemployment and public works through the proper channels.[41]

The committee was thoroughly discouraged. But the administration had made an offer, and taking Stolypin at his word, a representative of the ministry of the interior was invited to appear at a meeting on May 12. No one appeared, however, and it was not until May 15, that the government took notice of the invitation. Then Stolypin informed Golovin that before ordering any of his subordinates to give information to the committee he wished to be informed of the legal grounds on which the unemployment question was being examined.[42] On the following day the indignant committee drew up a report on its activity and relations with the government. And it observed that although Stolypin had challenged the committee's legality in his last letter he was never concerned

39. *Riech,* May 6, p. 3; *Tovarishch,* May 6, p. 2.
40. This article declared that explanations were to be communicated to the duma by ministers, personally or through their assistants, or by chiefs of the various branches of the central administration.
41. *Riech,* May 9, p. 2; *Tovarishch,* May 9, p. 2.
42. *Riech,* May 13, p. 3; *Tovarishch,* May 13, p. 4; *Komissii,* pp. 569–572.

with that question in his previous correspondence.[43] Thereafter the committee's career was punctuated by neither false hopes nor challenges.[44]

The government was as obstinate and watchful as ever. It would allow no direct relationship whatever between the people and their representatives. And the Social-Democrats seeking the overthrow of that government maintained a position at the opposite extreme. Hence the reiteration of the proposal to create local investigating committees which inevitably resulted in a rehearsal of the chief themes of the famine-relief debates. Again the Kadets were forced to make the best of the unwelcome support of the administration, and again the firm stand which they assumed against proposals threatening the duma's existence forced the entire Social-Democratic fraction to assume an essentially Bolshevik position. They assailed both the government and the Kadets and wooed the support of the peasant parties. The opposition was apparently hopelessly divided. Yet, the Kadets seemed able to organize a sizeable, if fluid, majority on all vital issues. And should they succeed in restraining the left, in avoiding "incidents" which would antagonize the government, and in producing significant legislation, they might yet guide this noisy and vivacious duma through that perilous early period which proved fatal to its predecessor.

43. *Riech*, May 18, p. 2; *Tovarishch*, May 18, p. 3.

44. When overtaken by dissolution, the committee was examining a bill introduced by the Kadets on May 18, which provided for an appropriation of a million rubles to be loaned to city administrations for public works. It would commission the ministers of commerce and industry, finance, and interior to bring proposals into the duma on the conditions governing these loans, and to introduce bills on the organization of public works. *Stenog. ot.*, II, 829; *Zak. za.* pp. 216–217; *Tovarishch*, May 31, p. 5; *Riech*, May 31, p. 3.

VIII

THE AGRARIAN QUESTION[1]

BY FAR the most vital problem facing the Russian people between the Great Emancipation of 1861 and the Great Revolution of 1917 was the agrarian, or land, question involving the struggle of 100,000,-000 peasants for a satisfactory existence. The First Duma saw this problem in its true perspective and proportions, as did the administration which dissolved it on that issue, while the Second Duma followed exactly in the footsteps of the First. Since the agrarian question was complicated by many factors which were common knowledge and experience to the members of the duma it would be well to examine briefly the background of the conditions prevalent on the Russian countryside on the eve of the reforms of 1906.

The pivotal factor was, of course, the legislation of 1861. The Land Statute of the Peasants which regulated the emancipation of 1861 recognized the right of every peasant in Great, Little, and New Russia, and a part of White Russia, to an area of land representing the normal holding of a peasant for the given locality. If the holding at the time of emancipation was below the minimum for the locality, the peasant was entitled to an addition from his former master's estate to make up the difference. On the other hand, the former masters, the great landowners, or "pomiestchiki," took all land from their peasants which they held above the normal minimum. Maximum holdings were established in localities where the land meant

1. Standard works on the agricultural history of Russia in the nineteenth century, reviewed in the first part of this chapter, are J. Mavor, *An Economic History of Russia;* M. S. Miller, *The Economic Development of Russia 1905–1914;* G. Pavlovsky, *Agricultural Russia on the Eve of the Revolution;* G. T. Robinson, *Rural Russia;* A. N. Chelintsev, *Selsko-khoziaistvenaia geographiia rossii.*

little without the labor of the former serf, as in the northern, non-black-soil area where the peasants had worked the land entirely for a land rent or had acted as craftsmen for the master.[2] This land was not given to the peasantry gratis but was to be redeemed by a voluntary agreement with the landowner according to the original law, but such contracts were made compulsory in 1881. In these Land Statutes there are to be found the germs of many of the ills which later beset the Russian country- side and made life well-nigh unbearable for a great part of it. But the writing of this law and its results were, in turn, conditioned, in great measure, by economic develop- ments in the preceding century.

Until the second half of the eighteenth century most of the land in Russia was held by an absentee nobility, who allowed the use of their estates to the peasantry for a payment called *obrok*, which the landowner defined ac- cording to the serf's ability to pay. However, with the expansion of Russia southward by conquest in the last half of the century, large farming with serf labor began to develop in the virgin black soil of that region, and, instead of paying *obrok*, the serfs were required to do a certain number of days' labor, or *barshchina*, on the masters' fields. Although such labor was legally limited to three days a week, the law was weakly enforced. By 1861, *obrok* prevailed in the northern, non-black-soil re- gion, while in the southern, black-soil area, *barshchina* was most common.[3] Since the holdings allotted to the peas- ants by the Land Statutes were based on the average size of the local holding, the *barshchina* peasants were left

2. See Pavlovsky, *Agricultural Russia on the Eve of the Revolution*, map on p. 332; hereafter cited as *Agricultural Russia*. Generally speaking, Russia is divided into latitudinal strips which in order from north to south are: the arctic tundra, the northern forest, clay-soil, fertile black-soil, and brown steppe-soil regions. See *ibid.*, Chap. I.

3. In 1861, in 13 non-black-soil provinces 55 per cent of the peasantry worked under an *obrok* system while the same was true of only 26 per cent in 7 black-soil provinces. In the West, Southwest, and Little Russia, nearly all of the serfs worked under a *barshchina* economy. *Ibid.*, p. 71.

after emancipation with areas much smaller than they could easily cultivate. This land shortage was intensified by the fact that the powerful nobility put pressure on the legislators to reduce the size of the peasant allotments as the price of land steadily rose. By so-called "cut offs" (*otriezki*) the peasants were deprived of about one-fifth of their pre-emancipation holdings,[4] and their bitterness increased when the landlords included in these lands most of the wooded area, choice arable parcels, and in the north, where fertilization of the clay soil was particularly necessary, the *pomiestchiki* appropriated nearly all of the meadow lands. Then, to retain even more of their ancestral estates, the landowners allowed an arrangement whereby, instead of the standard transaction, the peasant might accept holdings which were one-fourth the size of the normal allotment, and thereby escape further redemption payments. These propositions were often accepted, since in 1861 land was still plentiful in the south, and leases could be easily obtained. About 6 per cent of the ex-serfs held these "gift" (*darstvennyi*), or "beggarly" allotments. When the south country became occupied and rents began to climb these peasants with their tiny holdings became the village poor. Besides these ex-serfs of large landowners, one-third of the 325,000 serfs of small landowners received no land at all, or too little land.[5]

Although the area of allotment land (land held by the village commune) rose from 116,720,996 desiatins in 1877 to 138,767,587 desiatins in 1905 [6] this expansion was not enough to offset the increase in the village population. This was reflected in smaller holdings for each household and with each redivision, the size per "soul" (male peasant) progressively diminished. In 1861 the average holding per male peasant was 4.8 desiatins; in 1880 it had decreased to 3.5 desiatins and in 1900 to 2.6. In 1887 the

4. *Ibid.*, pp. 72–73.
5. *Ibid.*
6. A. Suvorin, *Russkii Kalendar*, 1909, pp. 162, 164–165.

average peasant household held about 13.2 desiatins which had decreased to 10.2 in 1905.[7] In all, about 30 per cent of the peasants of European Russia held allotments which were not merely unprofitable, but, under existing circumstances, were too small to feed them. The remaining 70 per cent had either a sufficiency or surplus land.[8]

Then, redemption payments soon became a burden far too heavy for the average peasant to bear. With the peasantry working curtailed plots, and maintaining a low level of productivity, large arrears in these payments began to accumulate. By 1881 the government was forced to reduce payments by 27 per cent for the entire country. And, after having removed the collective liability of the commune for these payments (and taxes) on March 12, 1903, it abolished them entirely on November 3, 1905.[9]

Rural distress was further aggravated by the rapid growth of the population, unaccompanied by agricultural progress and increased opportunities of employment. The commune system presented all of the disadvantages of communal holdings with which medieval, western Europe had been familiar, including separated strips and compulsory cropping. Acting as the usual bar to progressive agriculture, it kept the yield per desiatin comparatively low. Moreover, industry and mining developed very slowly until the last decade of the nineteenth century, and therefore did little to relieve the rural congestion, while industry could find only a poverty-stricken market which, in turn, retarded its development.

With the rest of the western world, Russia was gripped by an agrarian depression in the seventies which lasted until the nineties of the nineteenth century, and drove many landowners from active farming. These began to find it more profitable to lease their lands or to sell them

---

7. *Ibid.*, p. 171; Chelintsev, *Selsko khoziaistvenaia geographiia rossii*, p. 109; hereafter cited as *Geographiia*. A desiatin is 2.7 acres.

8. Pavlovsky, *Agricultural Russia*, p. 180.

9. *Pol. sob. zak.*, XXIII, no. 22,627, no. 22,629; *ibid.*, XXV, no. 26,872.

through the Peasant Land Bank.[10] The land-hungry peasantry quickly snatched these plots on short-term leases, and as quickly exhausted the soil. This state of affairs also gave rise to usurious middlemen who further embittered the peasant. In the black-soil region 35 per cent of the private lands and in the remainder of European Russia 39 per cent of such lands were leased.[11] Yet, despite the depression, land prices rose as the more substantial peasants (*kulaki*) added to their holdings by buying land outside of the commune either as individuals or in partnerships.[12] Some signs of alleviation began to appear after 1891, when the extension of the railroad system stimulated the commercialization of farming. At the same time the acceleration of the industrial development resulted in the creation of several large factory centers such as Moscow, St. Petersburg, Donbas, Krovoi Rog, Baku, etc., which made their demands for agricultural products widely felt.

Meanwhile, in order to relieve the pressing demand for land, the government had taken several far-reaching steps. In 1882 Minister of Finance Bunge founded the Peasant Land Bank to assist the peasantry in buying land offered for sale and to control the buying movement. Credits were offered to communes, partners, and individuals. However, the bank could not deal in lands on its own account. Under the liberal direction of Bunge, keeping the peasant foremost in mind, the bank operated with a deficit, but under his successor Vyshnegradskii, it was treated as a purely financial operation, and in avoiding all losses, credit was restricted and its activities narrowed. In the decade 1882–1892 it was instrumental in purchasing 37 per cent of all private lands bought by the peasantry.

10. The difference in the amount of land held by the great landowners in 1877 and 1905 is notable. In the former year the gentry held 73.2 million desiatins, and in the latter, 46.2 million desiatins, a loss of 37 per cent. See Pavlovsky, *Agricultural Russia*, p. 111.

11. *Ibid.*, p. 106; Chelintsev, *Geographiia*, p. 120.

12. A. Suvorin, *Russkii Kalendar*, 1909, pp. 170–171; Pavlovsky, *Agricultural Russia*, pp. 108–109.

Under Witte, a radical change was brought about by the law of November 27, 1895,[13] which allowed the Peasant Land Bank to engage in land operations, to give mortgages on lands which were purchased without its assistance, and its credit was extended. This law consciously sought to create a well-to-do peasant element, a Russian yeomanry, by aiding the more substantial peasants to increase their holdings. Between 1885 and 1905, the bank helped the peasantry to purchase 5,864,245 desiatins; about three times as much annually as was bought in the preceding decade, and about 75 per cent of all the land purchased by the peasantry.[14]

The government also turned to resettlement as a means of relieving the land pressure. Its excursions in this field were ineffective, until the law of July 13, 1889,[15] legalized the natural colonization movement and established the basis of the Siberian emigration for the next sixteen years. It released emigrants from communal liabilities, allocated them plots of sufficient size, and granted loans for initial expenses. After 1889 credits were allotted annually for about 80,000 emigrants. The completion of the Siberian railroad in 1893 accelerated Siberian resettlement, which was organized by the Committee of the Siberian Railroad under the Tsesarevich Nicholas. Funds for carrying on resettlement activity were supplied through the "Fund of Auxiliary Enterprises of the Siberian Railroad," and when the committee was dissolved in 1903 it had prepared 11,500,000 desiatins for the occupation of about 1,200,-000 settlers.[16]

On the dissolution of the committee, the ministry of the interior took over the task of resettlement. A new policy was established in the law of June 6, 1904,[17] replacing that of 1889. Its purpose was to improve the economic condi-

13. *Pol. sob. zak.*, XV, no. 12,195.
14. Pavlovsky, *Agricultural Russia*, pp. 151–152.
15. *Pol. sob. zak.*, IX, no. 6,198.
16. Pavlovsky, *Agricultural Russia*, pp. 163–164.
17. *Pol. sob. zak.*, XXIV, no. 24,701. Because of the Japanese War and revolution, it did not come into effect until 1906.

tion of the peasantry in Russia by means of emigration and to strengthen the hold of the empire on its more remote sections. It reinforced the weak licensing system, in existence since the eighties, by allowing licensed migrants payment for the land they left behind, and required that scouts be sent out by licensed persons before resettlement, helping them to meet travelling expenses.[18]

By the *ukaz* of May 6, 1895,[19] in order better to coördinate the administration's agrarian policy, colonization was placed under the ministry of agriculture, leaving to the ministry of the interior the administration of the actual emigration from European Russia and the issuing of licenses which entitled the emigrant to reduced railroad fares. By this law Asiatic Russia was divided into many colonization districts, each under an official of the colonization department of the ministry of agriculture with a staff of administrative officers, surveyors, agricultural experts, etc., who were to prepare the territory for resettlement.[20] Finally, by the *ukaz* of March 4, 1906, central, provincial, and district land-settlement committees were established under the ministry of agriculture, which were to regulate all aspects of the government's agrarian policy, including colonization and improvement of agricultural methods and conditions.[21] The movement which this legislation attempted to regulate was becoming increasingly significant. In the decade 1896–1907, no less than 1,560,905 persons had resettled in Siberia. Of this number 125,800 had moved in 1906, and 415,287 in 1907.[22]

But the obvious mal-distribution of wealth in land, though not the only cause of peasant misery, remained as a great historical injustice to plague legislators and offer fertile soil for deep, social discontent. In 1905 the peas-

18. These had been encouraged since 1894, and in 1896 they were given reduced railroads rates. Heretofore the emigrants often abandoned their plots.

19. *Pol. sob. zak.*, XXV, no. 26,127.

20. Pavlovsky, *Agricultural Russia*, pp. 164–170.

21. *Ibid.*, pp. 222–223; *Pol. sob. zak.*, XXVI, no. 27,478.

22. A. Suvorin, *Russkii Kalendar*, 1909, p. 180.

antry of European Russia, forming 84.1 per cent of the population, held 35.1 per cent of the land while private landowners held 25.8 per cent. Of these private lands, the nobility, forming 1.5 per cent of the population, owned more than half, having as their private property 13.4 per cent of the total landed property in European Russia.[23]

With all of these facts the peasant was not acquainted, but he was ever conscious of the difference between his lot and that of his neighboring *pomiestchik*. With the struggle for existence growing more difficult yearly, it is hardly to be wondered at that when Russia openly rebelled, the peasant resorted to violence to obtain what he wanted most—land.

With the experience of the 1905 Revolution still vivid in his memory, and when agrarian riots were not uncommon in the Baltic, the central and black-soil regions, Stolypin, we have seen, sought after and found what he considered to be a satisfactory solution of the agrarian problem. He aimed at social reconstruction which would make of the land-hungry peasant, openly revolutionary, a law-abiding, independent farmer who would serve as a bulwark of the existing social, political, and economic order.

His plans involved the entire agrarian structure. Their chief purpose was to further a policy of enclosure, or at least to substitute a few compact holdings for many scattered open-field strips. Accordingly, he promulgated his famous land law of November 9, 1906,[24] under Article 87 of the Fundamental Law. To aid the peasant financially he revised the Peasant Land Bank by the law of November 15, 1906,[25] so that its credit operations might be extended to reach the poorer rural strata, and to help them purchase allotment or private lands or make improvements. To increase the amount of land available he encouraged and developed a system of assisted trans-Ural emigration on a

23. *Ibid.*, pp. 105, 163, 164–165.
24. *Pol. sob. zak.*, XXVI, no. 28,528.
25. *Ibid.*, no. 28,547.

large scale. Finally, to aid the peasant technically, he placed the administration of enclosure legislation in the hands of the land-settlement committees. This, in general, was the administration's agrarian policy, the heart of which was the first-named measure, the law of November 9, 1906.

Stolypin's land law provided that every head of a household holding allotment land in communal tenure could at any time claim his share of the common land as private property. In villages where no redistributions had taken place in the past twenty-four years, peasant households wishing to leave the commune might receive, along with their homesteads, all communal land in their possession at the time the request was made. In villages where a redistribution had taken place in the last twenty-four years, individual peasants were allowed a share of the communal land equal to the amount allotted them at the last redistribution. Any land which they held over that amount they had to purchase from the village at the average price fixed for redemption at the time of the emancipation. But peasants withdrawing from the commune might still claim their rights in undivided lands which the village exploited jointly; such as forests, meadows, pastures, etc. Lands to be awarded to the withdrawing household were to be designated by the commune within a month after the submission of a request for separation. In case of delay or of a dispute, the land captains [26] were to arrange the separation, and their awards might be appealed to the *uiezd* land settlement committee.

Lands withdrawn from the commune could be claimed, insofar as possible, in a single plot. If such a consolidation were found to be physically impossible, the withdrawing peasant was to be remunerated for the area which could not be consolidated, at a price fixed by agreement

26. The land captains, instituted in 1889, were appointed by the government from the nobility for the purpose of extending the state's control over the peasants. They were given administrative powers, and acted as local judges over the peasantry.

or by a court decision. All requests for withdrawal at the time of general redistribution had to be granted, and all land granted to the households withdrawing from the commune became their private property. Finally, by a two-thirds majority, an entire village might enclose the holdings of all of its members.

In this manner Stolypin thought he had found a means both of satisfying the peasantry and of preserving the existing order. At the same time he avoided the necessity of tampering with the interests of the large landowners which were jealously guarded by a powerful court circle. Thus, through necessity and, considering his bureaucratic and squire background, through conviction, Stolypin would allow no violation of *pomiestchik* property. And, in consequence, he could not even consider the plans of the opposition, all of which involved either expropriation or outright confiscation. If his opponents objected that he was violating the spirit of parliamentary government in predetermining the lines which agrarian reform must follow by issuing his project under Article 87, he replied that immediate action was imperative. He had, he declared, to bestir himself in the face of socialistic demands which aroused too great expectations among the peasantry. The good of the country seemed to him more important than "debatable" legal forms. And since the parliamentary system was not fully evolved he would resort to both old and new methods of administration according to the needs of the moment.[27]

The opposition was thoroughly aroused by the premier's bureaucratic stand. And when the Second Duma met, the Kadet, *Narodnik*, and Socialist parties were determined to replace Stolypin's law by what they considered more equitable and humane methods of giving the *muzhik* economic security. This they would do despite the experience of the First Duma for they believed that public opinion almost unanimously demanded a radical redistribution of landed property. Yet, Stolypin's position was

27. P. A. Tverskoi, *Viestnik Evropy*, 1912, no. 4, pp. 190–191.

strengthened by the great variety of opinions and bills; by the lack of unanimity on land reform.

The *Narodniki* were shocked by Stolypin's assault on the commune. They regarded it, we observed, as the basis for a future socialistic society, and felt that if it could be preserved until the advent of the new order the village would never have to know anything of capitalism. Nationalization of land and its equal distribution were their cardinal principles. Of their projects of land laws, the most highly significant because it represented so many peasant elements was the "Declaration of 104 Members of the Duma" introduced on May 3, 1907.[28] This measure provided for the abolition of all private property in land which was henceforth to belong to the entire population, and all were to have an equal right to its use. The assembly of the people's representatives was named as the supreme administrator of the disposition of the lands while organs of local self-government (commune, *uiezd*, city) were to dispose of it locally. They were entrusted with the task of dividing the land equally and with preventing its exhaustion. Land was to be used both publicly and privately. The former category was to be determined and set aside by local and central representative bodies according to their national and local significance. Among other purposes it was to be used to encourage agrarian progress.

The "Project of 104" defined private land use as land available for exploitation by private persons, households, associations, and coöperatives. Its distribution was to be based on a maximum "labor norm" for the locality, that is, an area which each of the above mentioned users could easily cultivate. The only exception allowed to this rule was a household having more unproductive consumers (as children, aged, sick) than workers. As a minimum norm the project established a "consuming norm" which was to

28. *Stenog. ot.*, II, 122; *Zak. za.*, pp. 203–208. The bill was signed by 37 Social-Revolutionaries, 6 Popular-Socialists, 59 Trudoviki, 2 non-partisans. It was first presented in the First Duma.

be based on the normal family budget of a given locality. No rent was to be paid for the use of the land, and only land held above the local "labor norm" was to be taxed. The distribution of this land was to be equalized within and between local self-governing units by the proper local administrative bodies, by means of land taxes on surplus holdings, resettlement, colonization, and boundary changes. The state was to extend credit aid and insure the land. Lands occupied by structures and homesteads were to be regulated by central and local organs of self-government and might be expropriated for public needs.

Like most land bills presented, the "Project of 104" provided for preliminary measures to be taken before the law should be carried out. These demanded the annulment of Stolypin's agrarian measures promulgated under Article 87, and the suspension of the activities of the State and Peasant Land Banks and of the sale of private property. Before local organs of self-government should be set up, there were to be created *volost, uiezd,* provincial, and *oblast* land committees which were to work out projects for bounding territorial units, for defining "laboring norms," and for the allotment of lands. They were to take over all state, appanage, church, and monastery lands, and each was to distribute them among the committees below it; the higher committees retaining the administration of lands of greater significance. Lands belonging to city administrations, *zemstva,* educational, and charitable institutions were to remain in the temporary possession of their holders. Before the execution of the law only an area of land equal to the "labor norm" was to be left in the possession of the landholders, the remainder was to enter a public land fund without redemption except for lands taken from charitable institutions.

The Trudoviki had presented a separate bill earlier, on March 6.[29] This measure provided for the creation of a committee to develop a land bill, and except for three major differences it was essentially the same as the "Proj-

29. *Stenog. ot.,* I, 177–179, 1,823–1,824; *Zak. za.,* pp. 8–9, 139.

ect of 104." Like the latter it abolished private property in land, gave the land over to the whole population, and allowed all who should cultivate it an equal right to its use. It likewise provided for a land fund which all state, crown, and church lands, and private lands above the laboring norm were to enter, and which was to be used for public and private needs. In the distribution of lands for private use, the Trudovik bill specified that the needs of old residents were to be met before those of resettlers. Surpluses in any locality were to be reserved as a fund to provide for the future growth of the local population and for resettlers who might wander from localities where there were land shortages.

Again, as in the "Project of 104," provincial, *uiezd*, and *volost* committees were to be democratically elected, and were to care for all preparatory work before the execution of the measure; deciding on the general principles and details of the reform. And they were to regulate rents and relationships between users, and between landholders and agricultural labor during the transition period.

There were several differences, however, between the Trudovik project and that of the 104 deputies. In the first place, private owners who had voluntarily yielded their lands to the national land fund might be reimbursed by the state. The decision as to whether or not such a remuneration should take place was to rest with the localities. Secondly, the Trudovik bill provided for a land tax according to the quality, quantity, and location of the land, and lastly, the entire national land fund was to be administered by local organs democratically elected.

The remaining *Narodnik* projects were quite similar. The Popular-Socialist bill was intended chiefly as a preliminary measure to give the peasants temporary relief until the duma should elaborate a final law.[30] It would suspend the action of all of the administration's agrarian laws, laws on agricultural labor, and the activities of the land settlement committees. And it would create land

30. *Stenog. ot.*, I, 1,842; *Zak. za.*, pp. 140–145.

committees which, in general, were given the same power
as those provided for in other *Narodnik* projects in regulating relations during the transition period, and before
the inauguration of the new order.

The Social-Revolutionaries introduced a project on
March 26, which provided only for the creation of land
committees. They declared that the fundamental principles
of the agrarian law which concerned the vital interests of
the population could not be correctly defined in a duma
elected on the basis of a very imperfect electoral law, and
without free, pre-election agitation. Any mistakes it might
make would lead only to new complications. Consequently,
the Social-Revolutionary fraction would elect these committees immediately and empower them to decide on basic
land reforms and the forms these should assume locally;
to collect information necessary for land reforms, and
assume those duties with which other *Narodnik* projects
burdened the committees.

Thus, the basic principles common to all *Narodnik*
projects were the nationalization of all land, and its con-
centration in a single land fund to be administered by
democratically elected organs, either local or central, or
both; the creation of local land committees to gather data,
offer projects for land reforms, and administer transitory
changes and relations between landholders, and between
landholders and agricultural laborers. The authors of
these projects were, for the most part, representatives of
the peasantry. As such, they demanded all of the land, and
that any reforms which the duma might enact be projected in the localities, on the soil itself.

The Kadets introduced their land bill on April 30.[31]
They had opposed Stolypin's measure for economic as
well as political reasons. With other opposition parties
they regarded the maldistribution of property as one of
the chief contributory causes of the peasant's misery, and
could not accept a measure which would allow the vast
estates of the gentry to go untouched. Moreover, they felt

31. *Stenog. ot.*, I, 2,293; *Zak. za.*, pp. 196–202.

that the government left the solution of the land problem largely to chance by creating a land fund of necessary proportions from voluntary sales to the peasant bank. That method, they held, would only lengthen the crisis.[32]

The Kadet bill, however, differed radically in many respects from other opposition projects. No nationalization of land was envisioned, only the establishment of a reasonable security for the peasantry, and private property in land was not doomed. The Kadets would increase the size of plots belonging to the population which cultivated the soil according to its "consuming" needs, and would use for this purpose state, appanage, cabinet, monastery, church, State Bank, and privately owned lands. They would demand the obligatory expropriation of private lands with the remuneration of the owners at the government's expense. Remuneration was to be based on a "just evaluation" of land. They believed, further, that it would be neither unjust to the peasant, nor an unbearable burden if he should contribute about one-half of the interest charges incurred by the government in financing the transfer. This was to be arranged by the establishment of a special payment for the land which each peasant was to bear according to his income and ability to pay. All land thus allotted was to be held in "perpetual use" (permanent ownership).[33]

The project proposed that in each *uiezd* a local, preparatory land institution determine the area to be allowed each landholder according to the average plot used by those cultivating the land, and according to their "consuming" needs. Voluntary resettlement was to be urged in case of an insufficiency in any locality. The minimum allotted any peasant was to be a full "consuming norm." Both individuals and communes were to receive land, and the latter were to distribute it among their members, satisfying first old settlers, and then resettlers. The com-

32. P. Miliukov, *Vtoraia duma*, p. 219.
33. See Kutler's address, *Stenog. ot.*, I, 739.

munes were to decide whether the land was to be held for life or inherited. Wherever possible the strip system was to be avoided or its inconveniences mitigated.[34]

On May 29, the Kadets introduced a second project which elaborated on the composition and duties of the preparatory committees on land affairs.[35] These were to be composed of representatives of the local agricultural population to the number of two from each *uiezd*, and were to be elected from among the representatives of the local population at *volost* assemblies. Besides these, each committee was to include a representative of the *uiezd* landowners, elected at *uiezd* assemblies; a provincial commissar of land affairs, and an assistant; the chairman of the provincial *zemstvo* board; two members elected by the provincial *zemstvo* assembly; and three members appointed by the minister of agriculture. The committee might also invite any specialists whose services it should need. This body was to carry on all investigative work, offer projects and administer local organization in each province under the guidance of the minister of agriculture.

Thus, in general, the Kadet plan for agrarian reform differed from those of the *Narodniki* (and the Social-Democrats) by its insistence on the payment of a just remuneration to the expropriated landlords, a small part of which was to be borne by the peasantry; by not providing for social ownership of the land; by allowing the landowning and governing elements, taken together, a predominant position in the land committees which were to be provincial in scope rather than local; and finally, by allowing the administration general supervision of land organization affairs. With the exception of obligatory expropriation, no revolutionary steps were foreseen by the Kadet

34. The Kadet project exempted from obligatory expropriation allotment and private lands up to the local "consuming norm," lands occupied by and necessary to factories and commercial enterprises, lands which local land committees wished to withdraw from agriculture, lands in cities, *zemstva* lands, and those of charitable and educational institutions.

35. *Stenog. ot.*, I, 1,434; *Zak. za.*, pp. 256–259.

project. But they believed that it contained the most that could be hoped for at the moment.[36]

The Social-Democrats regarded Stolypin's land law with mingled consternation and contempt. They realized at once that the creation of a strong yeomanry imperilled the cause of revolution. They had no objection to the destruction of the commune but they did not relish this particular method. And they maintained that Stolypin's solution was too crude to be effective. For it would, in their opinion, not solve the land problem and would only intensify the differentiation between the rich and the poor. Only the rich, they maintained, would be able to pay the high prices demanded by the Peasant Land Bank. And with the removal of the ban on the sale of village lands the rich, the *kulaki*, would accumulate large holdings. Thus the rich would become richer and the poor more impoverished. They demanded the confiscation of large estates. They would not commit themselves to any specific form of equitable distribution among the peasants until the quantity and quality of the land available were fully known. But they would control its distribution through public ownership.[37]

In the duma the Social-Democrats offered no elaborate project of a land reform for consideration. But in his first address on the agrarian question on March 19, Tsereteli read a short statement containing the principles which the Marxists regarded as basic for any agrarian reform.[38] They proposed the confiscation of all church, state, and crown lands without redemption and their surrender to the jurisdiction of local organs of self-government. Since a great part of this territory was unsettled, the Social-Democrats proposed that a land fund be created from it and other free land which was to be owned by the demo-

36. P. Miliukov, *Vtoraia duma*, p. 219.
37. N. Valentinov, *Krestianstvo i zemelnaia programma sotsial-demokraticheskoi partii v rossii*, pp. 22–51, 57, 69.
38. *Stenog. ot.*, I, 728–730. This was influenced by the Social-Revolutionary project.

cratic state. Likewise, without redemption, privately owned lands were to be expropriated (excepting small holdings and strips), and given over to the organs of local self-government. Deputies of the local population elected to these organs by universal, equal, direct, and secret ballot were to define the dimensions of plots, holdings in excess of which were to be confiscated. They were also to decide on the manner in which the lands were to be used. Finally, for the freer social and economic development of the peasantry, the Social-Democratic project provided also for the equalization of the rights of all citizens and the abolition of legal class demarcations. The peasants were to be allowed to settle where they pleased and participate in local self-governing bodies, in the unhindered management of their commune or private lands,[39] and of public lands, and in defining the conditions of their use.

The Social-Democratic congress at Stockholm had decided in favor of "municipalization" as against "nationalization," of confiscated lands,[40] and the Social-Democratic fraction was bound to adhere to its decision. But, since the fraction was free to adopt its own parliamentary tactics, the Bolshevik minority could not be prevented from sharply criticizing its stand, or from proposing a tactical policy involving coöperation with the *Narodniki* and opposition to the Kadets and right. For the demand for "nationalization" and the entire Bolshevik policy determined its criticism and tactics.

The Social-Democratic fraction turned to the agrarian question almost immediately after its organization. On February 25, it made a futile effort to prepare a left bloc on this issue by persuading the peasant deputies that the *Narodnik* programs were utopian and would result only in a civil war in the village. The Social-Democratic pro-

39. This was obviously a reference to the law of December 4, 1893 (*Pol. sob. zak.*, XIII, no. 1,051), which allowed peasants to sell their lands to other peasants only. Compare explanatory note on S-D agrarian bill in *Tovarishch*, May 1, p. 4.
40. See above p. 44.

gram, they maintained, would solve the problem in the
interests of all democratic elements, and aimed to develop
the productive forces of the country.[41]

The agrarian program was not again actively discussed
until the fraction meeting of March 18, two days before
it was to be considered by the duma, and the factional
debates on parliamentary tactics were renewed. The Bolsheviki had always maintained that the bourgeois-democratic (as distinct from the bourgeois-monarchistic) revolution preparing the way for the ultimate triumph of
the Socialist order could be successful only as a result of
the combined efforts of the proletariat and the democratic peasant masses. These elements, they contended.
were particularly interested in the success of the democratic revolution because of the repression which they endured under the "feudal-tsarist" régime. And we have
seen that they believed that the liberal bourgeoisie, the
Kadets, did not care to overthrow tsarism and large landownership, and to found a democratic republic; that is,
they did not desire a complete democratic revolution.
Therefore, the Bolsheviki had concluded that they must
first lure the bourgeois-democratic masses away from the
leadership of the bourgeois-monarchistic liberals which
they followed by force of tradition. They would subject
the masses to the influence of the proletarian Social-Democrats.[42]

Accordingly, when the fraction discussed its tactics on
this vital question directly involving the peasant millions,
the Bolsheviki proposed that in the duma debates the
Social-Democrats assail the Kadet and rightist programs
while avoiding any attack on the *Narodniki*. The Leninists held that the latter, in the main, occupied a position
identical with that of the Social-Democrats; they wanted
all of the land without redemption. The Bolsheviki had
no desire to bring out the differences between them. They

41. *Tovarishch*, Feb. 28, p. 4.
42. Lenin, *Sobranie sochinenii*, VIII, 233–235, 290–299, 595–596 (1922 ed.);
Lenin, *Selected Works*, III, 218–225, 238–239, 242–247.

would not complicate matters by developing their program, but would impress on the minds of the raw peasantry only its chief points: the expropriation of all non-peasant land without redemption, and the solution of the land problem by the people themselves in democratically elected local committees.

Moreover, the Bolsheviki believed that it was less important to oppose the utopian and essentially harmless *Narodnik* proposals than those of the Kadets, extremely harmful for the revolution. The Bolsheviki found the centrist plans for the retention of large landownership especially abhorrent for they regarded large estates as a hindrance to the development of free, capitalistic farming, the economic basis of bourgeois democracy which had to precede the socialistic order. Also unpalatable was the Kadet requirement of peasant payments which they believed would again place a heavy financial burden upon the village. The Bolsheviki advocated a comparison of these demands with those which the Social-Democrats held in common with the *Narodniki*. They placed great emphasis on maintaining their independence from the liberals. For if differences between them were artificially obscured, the activities of the Social-Democratic fraction would be nullified, or at best they would assume the rôle of an appendage to the liberal bourgeoisie; they would "play at the tail of the Kadets." [43]

But the Mensheviki, as usual, desired a unified attack on the common enemy, the "black hundred" right and the government, by the entire duma opposition. They proposed to point out in the duma the great abyss between these two elements, and to emphasize obligatory expropriation as the basic principle binding the entire opposition, and serving as a common basis for a general struggle with reaction. They believed that the plan of the Bolsheviki to divide the opposition in striking at the Kadets would play into the hands of the reactionaries who would

43. *Tovarishch*, April 21, 1907, p. 3; *Protokoly*, pp. 158, 171–172, 213; third letter to party organizations, *Riech*, April 20, p. 2.

use these differences to weaken the impression of the general attack directed against themselves. They maintained that the current political moment was not the time to settle accounts with future opponents in the face of the common foe. In their opinion, a difference on the land question within the opposition would acquire significance only when the time arrived to settle the agrarian question practically. They further pointed out that they had as vital differences with the *Narodniki* as with the Kadets.[44]

And, as was usually the case at fraction meetings, the Menshevik view prevailed. The fraction decided that its chief care in the duma would be to criticize the government's agrarian policy and to emphasize the solidarity of the entire duma opposition. They would advocate the obligatory expropriation of land without redemption and send their bill to the duma agrarian committee (when it should be created). Having agreed beforehand with all opposition fractions to direct their attacks at the government and right only, they further decided that if any fraction broke the agreement and developed its program, the Social-Democrats would do likewise. Finally, the fraction named as its three official orators on the agrarian question Tsereteli, Ozol, and Aleksinskii.[45]

The "agrarian debates" began on March 19, with an exposition of the rightist views by Prince Sviatopolk-Mirskii.[46] Like most of his colleagues on the right he was a large landowner [47] and, consequently, deeply interested in preserving as much of his ancestral wealth as possible. Accordingly, he proclaimed the basic cause of peasant

44. *Protokoly*, pp. 158, 171–172; *Tovarishch*, April 21, p. 3; *Riech*, April 20, p. 2.

45. *Protokoly*, p. 158; *Riech*, March 18, p. 3; *Ibid.*, April 20, p. 2; *Tovarishch*, March 18, p. 4.

46. *Stenog. ot.*, I, 696–707. As has already been observed, immediately before the opening of debates on unemployment the moderate peasant Petrochenko, supported by Prince Dolgorukov, had attempted to replace discussion on that question with a consideration of the agrarian problem. However, they succeeded only in setting the date for the beginning of the agrarian debates. See *Stenog. ot.*, I, 537, 539–541, 550.

47. *Ukazatel*, p. 4. Mirskii owned 2,768 desiatins.

poverty to be, not land hunger, the satisfaction of which would require obligatory expropriation, but the peasant's backwardness. He lectured the duma on the desirability of the English landownership system requiring the abolition of the commune and the introduction of private property in order to do away with unprogressive agricultural methods. And he managed to incense the left by assuring the duma that without *pomiestchiki* (squires) the Russian people would become a "flock without a shepherd." If the people received all of the land, he asserted, the total productivity of the Empire would be lowered.

After a cool, statistical analysis of the misery of the Russian peasant by the Trudovik *zemstvo* doctor, Karavaev,[48] Tsereteli arose to deliver the first Social-Democratic statement on the agrarian question.[49] He observed that although the government realized the significance of raising the peasant's living standards it nevertheless persisted in its refusal to consider any solution of the problem involving obligatory expropriation. Nor would it hear of any denials of the right of private property; property which the nobility held for rendering the state services unperformed since the days of Peter III; property which the state had "expropriated" from public lands. Thus, he contended, was laid the foundation of a "sacred" right in the name of which a hundred million peasants were denied a decent living. Although Catherine II and her son Paul had lavishly granted serfs and lands to their favorites, Tsereteli continued, yet when the peasants were emancipated they received only niggardly allotments burdened with huge redemption payments. And when the *muzhik's* lot became so unbearable that he demanded all of the squire's land, the government declared that property was inviolable. Tsereteli reassured the duma that if the peasant were given all of the land the interests of the empire would not suffer. Squiredom, using antiquated agricultural methods, for the most part, would certainly not ben-

48. *Stenog. ot.*, I, 707–723.
49. *Ibid.*, 723–730.

efit the country. He agreed that the peasant had to adopt better methods, but held that he had first to receive more land. Then he would have agricultural products to sell. Then industry, finding a growing domestic market, would develop and, in turn, offer a wider market to agriculture. He maintained, moreover, that by its pogromist-punitive-expedition policy the government had demonstrated its willingness to protect only squire property rights. Since these rights interfered with the nation's well-being he demanded their destruction and the overthrow of the government resting on squire-bureaucratic foundations. In the name of the Social-Democratic fraction he called for the election of a committee to consider the agrarian problem and, in conclusion, read his fraction's land reform project.[50] In presenting this purely socialistic and openly revolutionary address, Tsereteli had acquitted himself completely as a spokesman of the revolutionary proletariat.

The first word on the agrarian program from the center was uttered by N. N. Kutler.[51] To the surprise of the entire opposition and the embarrassment of the Kadets, despite the decision of the information bureau, he launched into a criticism of the Trudovik program with an occasional thrust at the Social-Democrats. He agreed with the Trudoviki in their demands for an increase in the area of land at the disposal of the peasantry and for the obligatory expropriation of private lands as both practical and attainable. But he objected to their detailed formulation of the problem, and their manner of solving it. He maintained that if the Trudoviki attempted to give land to anyone who would work it, other than peasants, there would not be sufficient lands to equal even the norms of 1861 which were below current "labor" and "consuming"

50. See above pp. 172–173.
51. *Stenog. ot.*, I, 730–742. N. N. Kutler spent much of his life in state service. He was director of the department of tax assessments, 1899–1904. Under Sviatopolk-Mirskii he became assistant minister of agriculture. A project to expropriate lands caused his retirement. Soon afterwards he became an editor of *Riech* and joined the Kadet Party.

norms. Moreover, to the Kadets "nationalization" and "equalization" appeared as impractical ideals. They were demands which needlessly complicated with hazy theories the clear problem of aiding the peasant population. Kutler admitted that it might be unjust to bar the city worker from the soil. But he believed that it would be more sensible to aid those who were already on the land than to allow the whole population access to it and help no one. In general, equalization seemed to him to invite bureaucratic interference, even though it be from a popularly chosen bureaucracy. He attacked the Social-Democratic proposal to abolish private property in land as unjust while property in the form of city real estate, capital, etc., was unmolested. Finally, he maintained that the peasant share of the redemption payments proposed in the Kadet land project would not be burdensome since rents were to be abolished.

Incensed by this attack on themselves and the Trudoviki, which they regarded as a breach of faith, the Social-Democrats privately complained to the Kadets who explained that they had somehow forgotten to warn Kutler in time. But the Marxists were unsatisfied and instructed Aleksinskii, to "curse-out" the Kadets. Nothing could be more congenial to the Bolshevik leader of the Social-Democratic fraction.[52]

To present the government's stand Prince Vasilchikov, minister of agriculture, mounted the tribune.[53] In an address which was, on the whole, careful and moderate, he welcomed the duma's apparent readiness to creat an agrarian committee for the consideration of the various land reform projects. But the time had arrived, he declared, to replace oratory with figures. He informed the duma that acquaintance with these would quickly dispel any false hopes concerning the results to be brought about by the various solutions. He assured the duma that the government was entirely concerned with the improvement

52. *Protokoly*, p. 158.
53. *Stenog. ot.*, I, 753–755.

of peasant landownership quantitatively and qualitatively. Moreover, since the administration realized the inevitability of clashes between the interests of private persons and groups, and between classes, it promised to change the "bounds" of private property when these did not coincide with the interests of the state. But he immediately reaffirmed the government's intention to regard the principle of private property as "sacred," allowing exceptions only to strengthen the rule. The government intended to distribute more widely the benefits of that principle in the belief that it endowed the agriculturist with a "wonderful force capable of turning shifting sands into gold, and naked rock to blooming garden." It was now quite clear to the duma that although there might be some hope for the Kadet plan the proposals of the Socialist left were henceforth outlawed.

Although the Kadets and leftists had made some effort during the recess which preceded Vasilchikov's address to stem the flood of oratory [54] over one hundred speakers were registered. And there followed an endless series of long, and repetitious addresses by peasant deputies who scolded Sviatopolk-Mirskii, bewailed the miserable lot of their neighborhoods, and described the repression which they suffered from the government's agents.[55] Each speaker, though paying scant attention to the efforts of his colleagues, would have the woes of his constituency written into the record. These rural deputies were quite vague as to the competence of the duma. They had been

54. During the recess, the information bureau met in an attempt to limit the increasing number of deputies who wished to be heard on the agrarian question. Up to that moment over one hundred had registered. After some discussion, the left (Social-Democrats and *Narodniki*) proposed to limit themselves to a total of nineteen orators while the center (Kadets and national groups) promised that only a few of their number would speak. See *Tovarishch*, March 20, p. 5; *Riech*, March 20, p. 4, Duma Sup.; *Stenog. ot.*, I, 748, 790.

55. *Stenog. ot.*, I, 755–761 (Baskin, P-S), 761–769 (Zimin, S-R), 769–772 (Afanasev, S-R), 772–777 (Kvorostukhin, S-R), 777–779 (Bogatov, Oct.), 779–780 (Nechitailo, Trud.), 780–782 (Rein, Oct.), 782–783 (Father Kolokolnikov, n–p).

told that it might accomplish much and they regarded it as all-powerful. It must hear them out.

It was apparent to a majority that the debates might proceed indefinitely, thus blocking all remaining legislative work. Therefore, when, at the end of the session, the president suddenly proposed that one day a week be set aside for agrarian debates, the motion was quickly carried.[56] But the peasants were dissatisfied. On March 22, thirty-two of them introduced a proposal demanding two days in each week for agrarian debates, and they found support in the Social-Democrats. On March 26, Aleksinskii asserted that his fraction could not accept a proposal made by Shingarev (Kadet) to end the registration of orators, shorten the time allotted them, and quickly select an agrarian committee. The Social-Democrats regarded preliminary consideration of the agrarian question in the duma as exceptionally important. Nor were the debates futile as V. M. Gessen would have the duma believe. Aleksinskii maintained that they were highly significant in that they would thoroughly illuminate this most vital problem.[57] For the Social-Democrats this question had far too much propaganda value to be lost in the dull, routine discussions of the committee rooms. Now, as at a peasant conference held on March 24, they were opposed to an immediate termination of debates on the agrarian committee.[58] And on that issue a majority agreed with them. For if the duma voted to end the registration of speakers and to elect a committee, it also decided to continue debates until all who had already registered should be heard. For this purpose two days in the week, Mondays and Fridays, were designated.[59] If it were not for the uproar caused by Purishkevich (right), the first "agrarian session" would have been dull indeed as debates dragged

56. *Ibid.*, p. 790.
57. *Ibid.*, pp. 1,050, 1,058, 1,061–1,062.
58. *Riech*, March 25, 1907, p. 4.
59. *Stenog. ot.*, I, 1,062, 1,063, 1,066, 1,068–1,069.

on interminably.[60] The left was able to muster ninety votes to block any motions limiting orators to ten minutes. Social-Democrat Vovchinskii protested against these proposals. If the duma believed that it had really exhausted the question, it should end debates entirely. If not, it should allow a speaker to unburden himself completely.[61]

Some progress was made at the beginning of the session toward establishing the composition of the committee. F. V. Tatarinov (Kadet) proposed that the Second Duma follow the example of the First and elect the committee not by proportional representation from each fraction but by a method which would allow representation to every locality; by elections according to relative majorities. He proposed a committee of ninety-nine, approximately one-fifth of the duma. Each deputy was to vote for one person. Those who received five votes or more were to be considered elected to the committee. If less than ninety-nine deputies failed to receive five votes each, those receiving four or three were to enter the committee.[62]

The extreme left regarded this proposal suspiciously— as an attempt to deprive it of its correct proportional representation, and they were quick to attack it. Social-Democrat Gerus maintained that the situation was different from that which existed in the First Duma. There the majority consisted only of Trudoviki or Kadets, while at the moment it was composed of many shades of political conviction. Moreover, two persons from the same locality might differ radically on the solution of the problem. Consequently, he believed that elections should proceed according to fractions, leaving each to elect its candidates by locality.[63] However, the Kadet view prevailed as the

60. He had too vigorously insisted that Golovin had shown favoritism in allowing Rodichev to speak out of order while he was not given that privilege (in an attempt to make a purely provocative motion to honor policemen who had fallen at the hands of the revolutionaries). For this statement he was expelled. See *Ibid.*, pp. 1,275–1,277.

61. *Ibid.*, p. 1,372.

62. *Ibid.*, pp. 1,280–1,282.   63. *Ibid.*, pp. 1,283–1,284.

Trudoviki, except for several of their leaders, joined with the center to adopt Tatarinov's resolution, and voted for a committee which was to consist of ninety-nine members, at most. This body was elected on April 2, when ninety-four deputies were chosen, including fourteen Social-Democrats.[64]

The agrarian debate rambled on incessantly. The Social-Democrats, contributing their share to the unending flow of words, maintained a steady fire on the proposals of the right and center. They charged that the rightists and the government had done nothing but oppress the peasantry and maintained that they could not abolish land hunger by a mélange of punitive expeditions, land captains, agrarian improvements, resettlement measures, and the break-up of the commune. Land, they cried, not culture, was the immediate, prime need. Kutler's redemption proposal they regarded as a new "noose" for the peasantry.[65] From the soil itself the Social-Democrat Sakhno bewailed the lot of the land-short *muzhiki* in the homely peasant accent of the Ukraine.[66] To land hunger he attributed their poverty and need, the stream of migration to the city, even murder. Their complaints were rejected on technicalities by the government which called them rebels when, as agricultural workers, they wanted more than thirty copeks a day, and beat them with *nagaikas* (whips) when they went on strike. Their ignorance, too, was a cause of their misery.

When they are in great need, when they are poor, when they are hungry, when there is nothing with which to heat their huts, nothing with which to cook soup to feed their

---

64. *Ibid.*, pp. 1,286–1,287; *Riech*, March 30, 1907, p. 4; *Stenog. ot.*, I, 1,379, 1,482, 1,594; *Ukazatel*, p. 39. In its final form the Agrarian Committee consisted of 14 Social-Democrats (Aleksinskii, Aframovich, Gerus, Golovanov, Zhigelev, Gudovich, Kirienko, Murten, Povilius, Serebriakov, Sierov, Fomichev, G. Fedorov, and Tsereteli) who had been selected at a fraction meeting on March 21; 6 S-R's; 19 Trudoviki; 5 P-S; 15 Kadets; 10 Kolo; 3 Cossacks; 5 Moslems; 8 nonpartisans; 10 Octobrists. See *Tovarishch*, April 1, p. 5; *Riech*, April 1, p. 3.

65. *Stenog. ot.*, I, 1,108–1,114, 1,342–1,347, 1,492–1,499.

66. *Ibid.*, pp. 1,482–1,486.

children, when they heard the priest who says: "Look first for the kingdom of heaven, for your home is in the heavens," they forsake the priest and begin to grumble. Why can the *pomiestchik* have so much land and to the lot of the peasant there falls only the kingdom of heaven?

Aleksinskii, offering the second official Social-Democratic contribution, summed up the Marxist attack at the session of April 5. Ever suspicious of Kadet motives he had just blocked a motion to fill the seats left vacant in the huge Agrarian Committee. And just as Kutler had criticized the left and the government, so Aleksinskii assailed the administration and the Kadets—as commissioned.[67] Behind all of the government's reforms he discerned a two-fold attempt to distract the attention of the peasantry from squire lands, and to divide the social structure of the village by creating a more substantial element which would offer a firm support for the government. Even resettlement which involved the lives of thousands of starving peasants was an attempt to remove them from the congested areas to the Siberian wastes. In each case he pointed out the change in the government's policy as it saw its faith in the commune as a stop-gap for peasant uprisings destroyed by the Revolution of 1905.

He attacked the Kadet bill as a revival of the emancipation of 1861 allowing the peasant only as much land

67. On April 5, opening debates concerned a Kadet proposal, introduced in the previous session, to increase the number of committee members to 99 since only 94, less than one-fifth of the duma, had been elected. The Social-Democrats regarded this as an attempt to increase the number of Kadets therein since they had received only 13 seats. Besides, Shingarev (Kadet) had proposed that the increase be carried out immediately since it would be long before newly elected deputies arrived from Siberia, and it was precisely in Siberia that the Social-Democrats had been successful. Aleksinskii attacked the proposal. He held that it was to allow for newly arrived members that several seats had been left vacant. He maintained that at the moment the various fractions were proportionally represented and that further elections would upset the balance. In the face of mounting opposition Teslenko withdrew the motion for the Kadets. See *Stenog. ot.*, I, 1,594–1,595, 1,606–1,607, 1,607, 1,614; *Ukazatel*, p. 39. Aleksinskii's speech was written by Lenin but revised by the speaker to avoid repetition. See *Leninskii Sbornik*. IV. 229–232, 233–268, *Stenog. ot.*, I, 1,623–1,640.

as the squire would give him, and requiring him to pay
for it. Here was no defense of high national interests, but
the protection of a landowning clique against the pressure
of the masses. In true Bolshevik fashion he analyzed agrarian legislation on a class basis. He quoted statistics to
prove that the personnel of the government consisted
chiefly of representatives of the landed classes, and observed that while a majority of the peasants in the duma
were on the left, the squires sat on the right, or in the
center. This alone seemed to him to offer sufficient grounds
for suspecting their solutions of the problem. He warned
the peasants against accepting redemption with its inevitable bureaucracy which would plague their children for
generations to come. He closed with a plea for purely
peasant land-settlement committees, as against the squire-
dominated bodies proposed by the administration, and the
Kadets.

With the passing of each "agrarian session" it seemed
that there would never be an end to repetitious speechmaking. The sessions assumed a most unparliamentary
aspect. The duma appeared to have lost all interest in the
proceedings. The speakers droned monotonously on, but
the assembly hall was, for the most part, empty, and those
present talked, read, wrote letters, or napped while the
corridors were filled with a milling crowd of deputies conversing or debating. Often the orators were scarcely audi-
ble above the din of the conversation. Yet any attempt to
limit the time at the disposal of the speakers, or to end
debates entirely, met with the firm opposition of the
combined right and left; the one for provocative reasons,
to prove the incapacity of the duma for productive work,
the other with propagandist aims in mind. No sooner had
those interested blocked such a proposal, then they would
file out into the corridors. So long as the country heard of
the oppression of the peasantry legislative work might
be interrupted indefinitely. So little interest was there in
the debate that by early May two consecutive sessions
(May 3 and 7), had to be prematurely closed for lack of

a quorum.[68] The nuisance had by then taken on such serious proportions that even the Social-Democrats began to weaken. On May 6, they resolved that agrarian debates should be closed and on May 9, decided to present only one more orator, unless Stolypin should speak, in which case they would introduce a second to reply to his remarks.[69]

It had been rumored before the Easter recess that the government, after hearkening to the innumerable demands made during the debates, would soon address the duma on the land question. The probability that it would yield on any point was slight, but the duma waited with aroused curiosity. At length, on May 10, Stolypin appeared and lectured the duma for three quarters of an hour on the immovable stand of the administration. When he had done, although his behavior and tone had been "correct," all hope of a rapprochement between the government and the duma had completely faded.[70]

Stolypin declared that it had come to his attention that the committee had reached an important decision.[71] From this and the debates in the duma it was evident to him that there was little hope of reconciling the various points of view. He turned first to the stand taken by the leftists. He asserted that their plan presupposed a revolution in all civil, social, and juridical relationships. Moreover, their equalization plans were unrealizable because of the uneven distribution of unoccupied lands in the various parts of the country. With the center and the Social-Democrats he regarded the commune as a bar to individual initiative. But with singular misunderstanding of the Social-Democratic project he charged that "municipalization" would equalize all at the lowest level since no one would develop improvements which they knew would go to others.[72] Pro-

68. *Riech*, April 13, p. 1, Duma Sup.; May 4, p. 1, Duma Sup.; May 8, p. 1, Duma Sup.; *Stenog. ot.*, I, 1,961; II, 122, 286; 130, 292.

69. *Riech*, May 8, 1907, p. 2; May 10, 1907, p. 4, Duma Sup.

70. *Stenog. ot.*, II, 433–445.

71. See below p. 194.

72. The Social-Democrats had never called for equalization.

gressive economy would be destroyed and Russia's strength, dependent on its wealth, would be impaired. He warned that any increase in the size of peasant plots through nationalization would be only temporary since it would be absorbed by the natural growth of the population, and the cities would be filled with a landless proletariat. Finally, he prophesied that any change in the system of government such as the left desired would leave Russia at the mercy of her neighbors. He held that the Kadet project was contradictory in that it opposed nationalization yet only partially recognized private property rights—those of the peasants, and not of the landowners. He maintained that the principle of obligatory expropriation would lead ultimately to nationalization since the peasant would demand all of the well-cultivated lands in his neighborhood rather than migrate.

The premier-minister then expounded the administration's program. It wanted a satisfied, substantial peasantry. But to that end the peasant had to be liberated from his present circumstances and his land had to be secured for him. The government had to aid the peasant with advice, credit, money. Land-short peasants were to be given as much land as they needed. He explained that he regarded the state as an organic whole, every part of which had to come to the aid of a sick member. That might be called state Socialism, he averred, but it would nevertheless yield substantial results. He informed the duma that the government would buy private lands out of which a land fund was to be created together with allotment and state lands. From this fund land-short peasants would first receive land, and then those who desired to improve their plots. Governmental institutions would ascertain what part of the financial operations involved in the purchase of land the peasant might bear, and the state would cover the remainder. That, in turn, would be covered by taxes, and thus, all classes would bear the burden of aiding the peasantry, not only 130,000 landowners. He regarded his plan as more just and elastic than the Kadet project. Obligatory expropriation would be resorted to only in exceptional cases; to help the peasant improve his economy by granting him woods, water, meadows, etc. Stolypin closed with a warning to the left that the government would not tolerate revolutionary activity among the peasantry, and in a burst of patriotism cried out: "The opponents of organized government would like to take the path of radicalism, the path of digression from Russia's historical past, from its cultural tradition. They need a great upheaval, we need a great Russia!" For reasons of policy, obvious and hidden,[73] Stolypin had dampened all hope for agreement between the people and the government on this gravest of all problems. Stolypin, the government, supporting the view of the conservative gentry that property was inviolable threw down the gage to the land-hungry commune peasantry which was only beginning its acquaintance with the principles of private property.

The left reacted at once to the premier's challenge. His address resulted immediately in a scramble of 120 deputies to the orators' registry.[74] A new wave of speechmaking threatened. In the second place, it solidified the left opposition better than any tactics the Social-Democrats had yet devised. The *Narodnik* and Social-Democratic members of the Agrarian Committee immediately assembled and decided to hold periodical meetings to plan for common activity by the left in both the committee and the duma.[75] On May 13, this group resolved to limit debates. They would hear fifteen orators on the land question, and then introduce a proposal to end debates, allowing concluding words to reporters on bills introduced by the various fractions. The deputies further decided to offer

73. Stolypin was then considering not whether he should dissolve the duma, but how it should be done. See Chapter XIV.

74. *Riech*, May 11, p. 3, Duma Sup.; May 15, p. 3. According to Article 128 of the duma rules, if a minister spoke after debates had been closed, they might be renewed at the request of a single deputy. This rule had been adopted just before Stolypin spoke. See *Stenog. ot.*, II, 432; *Nakaz*, p. 44.

75. *Tovarishch*, May 12, p. 5; May 15, p. 4.

a resolution of passage to the regular order on which the
left might agree and which should guide the activities of
the Agrarian Committee. It was to recognize the necessity
of obligatory expropriation of squire land and the abrogation of the agrarian laws issued under Article 87 of the
Fundamental Laws.[76] Three days later the leftists agreed
to support a Trudovik formula embodying these principles.[77]

Prolonged debates were definitely averted when, on
May 14, the opposition (except for the Social-Democrats)
met at Prince Dolgorukov's apartments and decided to
make no tactical changes as a result of Stolypin's address.
No additional debates would be allowed. Moreover, each
fraction promised to present only two speakers thus limiting the total to twenty-four.[78] In harmony with this
plan a proposal to designate a special agrarian session was overwhelmingly defeated, and during the following regular session on land reform, May 16, there was
almost no reference to the premier's remarks.[79]

In fact, the session of May 16 was especially notable
for the duma's decision to close debates on the land question. This action, considered inevitable for some time, was
hastened by the president's announcement that ninety-
four additional signatures had been added to the list of
speakers. The duma immediately put an end to further
enrollment, and limited each member to ten minutes.[80] But
debates "died hard," and to close them three ballots were
required. The first proposal was rejected by the Social-
Democrats who wished first to hear Ozol reiterate the

76. Berezin (Trudovik) noted that the resolution on obligatory expropriation
would demonstrate whether the Kadets had changed their stand after Stolypin's
speech. As for the annulment of laws under Article 87, the Social-Democrats
pointed out that some workers sympathized with them, but they would take no
initiative in defending these measures since they were illegally adopted. *Riech*,
May 15, p. 3; *Tovarishch*, May 15, p. 4.

77. *Tovarishch*, May 22, p. 2.

78. *Riech*, May 15, p. 3.

79. *Stenog. ot.*, II, 527, 531.

80. *Ibid.*, pp. 618, 619; *Riech*, May 17, p. 2, Duma Sup. Only Krupenskii
(right) objected.

Social-Democratic attack on the government and center.[81] When he had finished a second proposal was offered, and although the Social-Democrats voted for the first time to end debates, the Moslems were intent on hearing Karataev tell of the iniquities suffered by the Kirghiz tribes whose lands were being absorbed by the resettlement administration and the colonists. With the right they were able to defeat the motion.[82] Following this address a third ballot taken and, with only the right opposing, the debates were closed amid loud applause. As the president explained, only one member of each fraction might speak hereafter.[83]

The final address of the last "agrarian" session, and considered by some the finest in form and phrasing uttered on the land question, was that of the chairman of the Social-Democratic fraction, Tsereteli, whose intense sincerity had won for himself the respect of all opposition elements. At the moment he merited especial attention since he had recently returned, after a month's absence, from the Fifth Party Congress then being held in London, in the face of the threat of dissolution and probable arrest.[84] His address, though impressive, offered nothing that had not been said before. It was, in fact, an excellent resumé of the Social-Democratic position. Obligatory expropriation was the *sine qua non* for the enlargement of the peasant plots. It was absurd to raise the peasant's cultural level as long as he lived on a plot which could not feed him. He chided the Kadets for their willingness to preserve squire landownership which was unprogressive, kept the peasant in poverty, and thus deprived industry of a domestic market. The Kadet redemption proposal would

81. The first proposal was rejected by 88 votes (38 more than the 50 required by the rules). See *Stenog. ot.*, II, 657.

82. They mustered 59 votes against the motion. See *Ibid.*, pp. 673–675, 665–669, 672; *Riech*, May 17, p. 2, Duma Sup.

83. *Stenog. ot.*, II, 676; *Riech*, May 17, p. 2, Duma Sup. To be more exact, one representative might speak for each group which had presented a project.

84. *Stenog. ot.*, II, 1,220–1,236; *Riech*, May 27, pp. 3, 2, Duma Sup. See Chapter X, for London Congress.

soon become a burden to the *muzhik* and would increase the national debt payable by the masses. He took special care to oppose the *Narodnik* (and Bolshevik) demand for nationalization. He feared that it would result in a counter-revolutionary movement and a fratricidal war in the village. He contended that the projected *Narodnik* "labor norms" would equalize the peasants only in poverty, and regarded equalization, in general, as a utopian ideal which, if applied, would depress the condition of the peasantry and retard the entire economic development of the country.[85] The Social-Democrats opposed nationalization, Tsereteli explained, because the management of a land fund by the central government would require a large bureaucracy. These agents would be separated from the local population, they would be unacquainted with local needs, and therefore unconcerned with the welfare of the population. Furthermore, nationalization would be unjust to national minorities who would not tolerate it. Finally, it would bestow upon the government a vital economic power which, in the event of restoration, would become a dangerous weapon in the hands of the enemies of the people.

The Social-Democrats, he explained, desired the obligatory expropriation of land which would be given to local organs of self-government democratically elected. From these organs the population would rent land and the revenues thus derived would be applied to local needs such as unemployment relief, maintenance of communications, schools, hospitals, model farms, etc. The Social-Democrats

85. He maintained that the poorer peasants who would not be allowed to sell their lands, according to this project, would soon find their fields useless. Even if all received equipment he foresaw the development of inequalities under a competitive system. Those nearer the markets would become wealthier, and the poor would again be bound to their unprofitable plots by the prohibition of land sales. Tsereteli made this attack on nationalization in fulfillment of a promise made at the London Congress. Here he had upbraided Aleksinskii for not having elaborated on "municipalization" as the basis of the Social-Democratic agrarian reform in order to counteract the *Narodnik* campaign for nationalization. He regarded this omission as a violation of the resolution of the Stockholm Congress.

would give the land-short peasants necessary land and inventory, and by uniting the peasantry on the question of land distribution, and by joining them with the "advanced" proletariat, the projected "municipalities" would form a bulwark of democracy capable of preventing restoration. Tsereteli concluded with a formula of passage to the regular order which repeated the basic principles of the Social-Democratic agrarian project.

The introduction of formulae [86] by both the Social-Democrats and the Trudoviki containing instructions for the Agrarian Committee was challenged by the Kadets. Kizevetter held that there was no need for them since they were essentially the program demands of the fraction presenting them. The adoption of any one of them would limit the application of all remaining programs, and a general formula satisfactory to all fractions would have to be so broad as to satisfy no one. Therefore he urged that the committee be allowed to reach its own decision. These statements of principle were significant in themselves, he argued, and needed no confirmation by the duma.[87] Over the heated opposition of the Trudoviki, the duma majority consisting of the right and center concluded that a directive formula of passage to the regular order was unnecessary.[88] Debates on the land question were now ended.

Meanwhile, the Agrarian Committee had been quietly proceeding toward the adoption of a measure to be submitted to the duma. The Kadets took charge at once. At its first meeting on April 14, the Popular-Socialists had offered Volk-Karachevskii for chairman. The Kadets proposed N. N. Kutler, but Aleksinskii noted that he was

86. *Stenog. ot.*, II, 643. The Trudoviki had presented theirs on May 16.

87. *Ibid.*, pp. 1,236–1,239. A. A. Kizevetter, historian, publicist, and politician was born in 1866. At Moscow University he studied under Kliuchevskii and soon after graduation occupied a chair in Russian history. He wrote significant studies of the commune, and of the cities of the eighteenth century. He was also co-editor of several political and literary journals, and was one of the founders of the Kadet Party.

88. *Ibid.*, pp. 1,239, 1,242–1,245, 1,246. The majority vote was 238 and the left minority, 191.

already chairman of the Finance Committee and that under Article 38 of the rules, he could not hold two chairmanships. Kutler thereupon offered to resign from the Finance Committee post and was elected chairman by a Kadet-right combination. Several Trudoviki who joined the majority were expelled from their group.[89]

In the next few sessions subcommittees were created to consider the government's land law and local land committees.[90] Over the objections of the left deputies who desired elections to the latter subcommittee by a majority vote, the committee supported the center in creating it with each fraction represented in proportion to its strength in the committee. Thus the Kadets were assured of several seats. The center was again supported when the committee decided to limit its functions to an investigation of the possibility of increasing the size of peasant holdings.[91] On May 8, after lengthy debates in the subcommittee on Stolypin's law, that body appointed Volk-Karachevskii and Khominskii (Kolo) to investigate and report on the results of the law and the juridical grounds for its abrogation and replacement by another measure regulating separation from the commune.[92]

A crisis developed on May 9, when the Kadets and leftists voted to end debates on obligatory expropriation of private property before the Poles and rightists were given an opportunity to express themselves. Fourteen members of the committee indignantly stalked out, leaving Stetskii of the Kolo behind. However, a compromise was reached on May 12, when the committee adopted a Kadet suggestion (the left opposing) that debates on obligatory expropriation be renewed in connection with the discussion on the dimensions of the area to be expropriated.[93]

89. The vote was 46 to 36. Other officers were the P-S Baskin, the Kadet Iunitskii, and the Octobrist Teterevenkov, secretaries. Beliaev (Trud.) was chosen vice-chairman on the following day. *Riech*, April 14, p. 4 Duma Sup.; April 15, p. 3; *Komissii*, pp. 69–87.
90. *Riech*, May 3, p. 3, Duma Sup.; May 4, p. 3, Duma Sup.; May 6, p. 3.
91. *Ibid.*, May 6, p. 3.
92. *Ibid.*, May 9, p. 2.
93. *Ibid.*, May 13. p. 3.

Then there followed a series of seven sessions at which
the land fund was discussed and the seemingly endless
debates and points of view presented in the duma were
duplicated. The principle of obligatory expropriation was
adopted. And on May 30, the debates having ended, the
committee decided on the necessity of a land fund, and
rejected both *Narodnik* nationalization and Social-Democratic "municipalization." [94]

On May 28 the subcommittee on government measures
called for the annulment of the law of August 27, 1906,
regulating the sale of state lands to the peasants. At the
same time it would establish guarantees for those who had
already concluded preliminary arrangements. In like manner the subcommittee decided to ask for the abrogation
of the law of November 15, 1906, which allowed the peasants to obtain mortgages on their holdings from the Peasant Land Bank. The subcommittee held that these measures would not provide sufficient lands and might burden
the peasant financially. Therefore, they were to be regarded as serious hindrances to the solution of the agrarian question.[95] Other important matters involved in the
land question had not yet been introduced or discussed
when the axe of dissolution fell.

Although treated in the duma as a separate problem,
the resettlement question, as noted above, was regarded
by the government as a vital part of its agrarian policy.
It was therefore inevitable that the duma should refer to
the matter in discussing the general agrarian problem,
and deputies Kosmodomianskii and Karataev had talked
almost exclusively on it. But the chief debates on resettlement began on April 6, when thirty-six deputies presented
an interpellation to the minister of agriculture and an
explanatory note.[96]

94. *Ibid.*, May 31, p. 3; *Komissii* pp. 73–74. The meetings took place on
May 12, 14, 17, 18, 19, 23, and 25. *Riech*, May 13, p. 3; May 17, p. 2; May 18,
p. 2; May 19, p. 2, Duma Sup.; May 20, p. 2; May 24, p. 2; May 26, p. 2.

95. *Ibid.*, May 30, p. 2, Duma Sup.

96. *Stenog. ot.*, I, 1,743–1,747, 2,270–2,271.

THE AGRARIAN QUESTION 195

The statement charged that the minister of agriculture had issued a circular letter to all Siberian governors in December, 1906, ordering them to put an end to all activities directed at the provision of land for "old dwellers" (inhabitants long established). For the purpose of increasing the land fund for colonization he had ordered land-settlement committees to take surplus lands in the hands of the population, land occupied by natives, and state lands where land-settlement work had not yet been carried out. In proceeding the minister had advised the committees to halt before no "formal difficulties," which he and the council of ministers would take steps to remove. The interpellation maintained that these orders were contrary to the law of May 23, 1896, which assigned state lands to the "old dwellers" as a reserve whence they were to draw in case of need, and of the law of June 4, 1898, which protected the surplus lands of the village.[97] Consequently, the interpellators would know why the activity of the land settlement committees had been diverted from aiding "old dwellers" to the resettlement of new ones, why the rights of the old settlers were being violated, and on what legal grounds.

On April 17, after a brief discussion, the urgency of the interpellation was recognized by the duma and it was forwarded to the minister of agriculture, Prince Vasilchikov.[98] In justifying his activity before the duma on May 24,[99] Vasilchikov held that the complaint contained in the interpellation was founded on a misunderstanding of the law of 1898. For Article 3 of this measure clearly allowed for the creation of resettlement sections both of non-allotment and of other unsettled lands. He explained

97. *Pol. sob. zak.*, XVI, no. 12,998; XVIII, no. 15,539.
98. *Stenog. ot.*, I, 2,278. On the day before Vasilchikov was scheduled to reply to the duma, the Social-Democrats decided to broaden the question by introducing a proposal to create a special committee for investigating the condition of the colonists and for examining the activities of the resettlement administration. *Tovarishch*, May 24, 1907.
99. *Stenog. ot.*, II, 1,099–1,108; *Riech*, May 27, p. 4 contains information given out by the resettlement administration.

that according to the same law, and that of 1896, no land subject to inclusion in the allotments of the local population could be considered in the resettlement plans, and he had ordered his subordinates to adhere strictly to the law. Therefore, in his opinion, there was nothing to fear from the engagement of the land settlement committees in resettlement work. He was careful to note that his order to "halt before no formalities" was issued not to encourage officials to digress from the law, but only for the purpose of avoiding unnecessary and detrimental formalities. The increase in the colonization land fund, he observed, was due to the unexpectedly large number of colonists who went to Siberia in 1906 and 1907, and he warned the duma that more funds would be required.[100] Finally, he challenged statements made in the duma to the effect that with false propaganda the government had lured the peasantry away from the squires' lands to the Siberian wastes. The government, he said, had posted placards with large, thick characters, legible to all, which informed the peasants that they might settle in Siberia on free lands, and with fewer formalities than heretofore, but that the undertaking was a risky and difficult one, involving much hardship which many could not endure. This movement, he asserted, was a natural one, three centuries old, begun not by the government but by Iermak.[101]

Replying to the minister in a long address the Siberian Skalozubov (Popular-Socialist) stated that the Siberian deputies regarded the government's order as contradictory to the law on the land settlement of "old dwellers." In the opening of resettlement work in occupied areas they saw a new attempt to restrict the economy of the established population in order, somehow, to settle colonists in Si-

100. See above p. 162.
101. Iermak, a Cossack, was sent by the Stroganovs, Novgorod fur merchants, at the head of a private army to crush the Trans-Ural tribesmen, who were marauding the Russian villages of that region. In 1584 he not only completed the task assigned, but conquered the entire region for the Muscovite state. In that year he was drowned. See J. Mavor, *An Economic History of Russia*, pp. 211-212; G. Vernadsky, *History of Russia*, p. 52.

beria. These, he asserted, would receive lands unfit for agriculture. Further, the use of the surplus lands of the old settlers was, in his opinion, proof of the fact that land suitable for immediate colonization was exhausted. He pointed out that the state lands and woods, and the steppe in the settlement area required much improvement before they could become productive. All this indicated to him that the ministry was settling the land without plan, and without due consideration for the interests of the native population. He believed that normal colonization in Siberia would be possible only with the organization of public life in that region; that is, with the introduction of local self-government.[102]

The Social-Democratic position was presented by another Siberian, Dr. Victor Mandelberg, out of Irkutsk.[103] He believed that he could do little more than emphasize a few circumstances after Skalozubov's exhaustive discussion of the Siberian situation. He first noted the importance which the government attributed to this question as a solution of the agrarian problem. In its hurry to resettle the population he maintained that the administration had disregarded the interests of both the old and new dwellers. In his opinion the minister's order to obey the law was insufficient, for the bureaucracy, separated from the population, and considering only its own interests, would not reckon with formalities of the law. And if specifically relieved of the necessity of observing them it would act most arbitrarily. He explained that all complications arose from the fact that good land was not as plentiful in Siberia as the government believed and many hoped. Consequently, the colonists put great pressure on the older population, thus generating a hostility between the two elements. Moreover, the area available was further diminished by the fact that the land in use was primitively and extensively cultivated. Any attempt to improve agriculture locally was met with bureaucratic opposition.

102. *Stenog. ot.*, II, 1,113–1,132.
103. *Ibid.*, pp. 1,133–1,137.

Resettlement, like unemployment, were, in Mandelberg's opinion, basically due to the prevailing economic
structure; they were ills which only Socialism might ultimately cure. But he maintained that the administration
had failed to regulate the flow of emigration because it
had always held its petty aims foremost in mind. At an
earlier period it had hindered resettlement activities since
it required a great landless proletariat for the development of capitalism. But after the late revolution it clearly
saw a necessity for colonization. He maintained, despite
Vasilchikov's statement to the contrary, that the government had painted Siberia in glowing colors in order to
encourage emigration. Proof of the administration's failure to regulate the movement was to be seen in the ever
increasing number of peasants who returned from Siberia,
and the high death rate which prevailed among them. Only
a duma committee could organize land settlement, he
believed. Then, reverting to the Marxist tactics of the
famine relief and unemployment debates, and in accordance with the Social-Democratic agrarian project, Mandelberg proposed the creation of a committee which would
take over all resettlement work.

In closing debates the duma adopted a formula of
passage to the regular order presented by the Siberian
deputies. It branded Vasilchikov's reply to the charges
made in the interpellation as unsatisfactory, and declared
that measures taken by the ministry for the organization
of resettlement did not safeguard the interests of the
colonists and violated those of the native population.[104]

Thus, the entire opposition was in direct disagreement
with the basic principles of the government's land reform,
the most vital of the Stolypin administration. And this
state of affairs, naturally, boded none too well for the
duma's future. For the First Duma had foundered on this
rock. And Stolypin was adamant on the enactment of his
ingenious land program which he hoped would simultaneously solve the agrarian problem, protect his political

104. *Ibid.*, pp. 1,137–1,138.

position, and establish a sense of conservatism and respect for law among all classes, from which the government could not but benefit immensely. Moreover, he could not fail to notice that the opposition, though vigorous in its objections to his plan, and at one on the necessity of the expropriation of large estates, was, nevertheless, otherwise deeply divided on the solution of the agrarian question. Liberal, peasant, and Marxist, each strenuously advocated a separate bill. And the Social-Democrats, not even in agreement among themselves, were reviling not only the government, but also the Kadets—for political dishonesty and betrayal of the peasantry. But if all were at odds in the duma, in the Agrarian Committee the Kadets controlled the situation and were slowly evolving a measure, including obligatory expropriation, and on which a majority could agree. But if, as is not improbable, this hastened the ultimate fate of the duma, it was chiefly because the administration had come to regard the committee's action as the expression of a parliament as dangerously rebellious as the first with which no compromise was possible. The points of view on this, as on all vital questions, proved to be too divergent, and the government guessed its strength. Yet, popular opinion forced the solution of this most important question on a duma which would have been able to realize the execution of its aims only after years spent at proving the value of parliament as an organ of reform.

IX

THE BUDGET

THE PROBLEM regarded by the duma as second in importance only to the land question was the examination of the administration's annual list of revenues and expenditures. For in order to be legal in accordance with the Fundamental Laws, these had to receive the duma's approval. Although the budget was partially "iron clad" and if unconfirmed the last budget became automatically effective for another year, the duma, in using its budgetary right, might ease the burden of indirect taxation which weighed heavily on the peasantry. Moreover, by withholding confirmation, as the extremists proposed, it might demonstrate to the world that the majority of the Russian people had no confidence in its government.[1]

In this, as in all vital questions, the tactical differences between the Bolshevik minority and the Menshevik majority in the Social-Democratic fraction manifested itself. The former, as always, chose the line of individual class action, distinguishing the party from all other opposition elements as the leader of the revolutionary, proletarian movement which was to lead all other true revolutionaries to victory, and opposing the leadership of the Kadets. The Mensheviki, on the other hand, would strive for the same victory of socialism by first joining with all other opposition elements, including the Kadets, to destroy the feudal régime; the dreaded "Black Hundred" danger.

Accordingly, when tactics on the budget question were discussed at the fraction meetings of March 19 and 21, both factions agreed to reject the budget of a govern-

1. See M. Mikhailovskii, *Dieiatelnost sotsialdemokraticheskoi fraktsii*, pp. 27-28.

ment whose revenues they believed financed its oppressive policies. They would explain their stand in a formula of passage to the regular order.[2] But the Bolsheviki recommended that the rejection be based entirely on socialistic grounds. That was how Social-Democrats behaved in Western Europe in rejecting the budget of a class state, and precisely there lay the distinction between the Russian Social-Democrats and other parties; a difference which should be emphasized in either a resolution or a special declaration.[3] The Mensheviki, however, objected. They declared that the moment had arrived not for pronouncing socialistic phrases and slogans, but for action in the cause of socialism. It was not a time for futile speeches about tactics, but for the application of principles. If Bolshevik tactics were applied, they would merely make for the defeat of the fraction by isolating it from the rest of the opposition. The existing régime was "feudal," the Mensheviki held, and had, consequently, earned the enmity of the bourgeoisie. And since that régime had to be destroyed, the fraction should strive to retain a united opposition with all bourgeois parties; even if at the same time it pointed to the unacceptability of a bourgeois budget for the proletariat. Accordingly, they regarded a resolution containing socialistic demands as unfeasible since it could not possibly be acceptable to the bourgeois opposition. If, on the other hand, the bourgeois parties should refuse to reject the budget, their inconsistency and failure to fulfill their democratic duty would be revealed before the democratic masses. Moreover, the Mensheviki felt that should they reject the budget on class grounds, the government might triumphantly claim that the Social-Democrats had rejected a bourgeois budget, whereas the entire revolutionary significance of the fraction's activity in this matter consisted in discrediting the government as *feudal;* as satisfying not even the bour-

2. *Tovarishch,* March 20, p. 2; March 22, p. 4.

3. *Riech,* March 27, p. 3, Duma Sup.; April 21, p. 3; *Tovarishch,* April 21, p. 3; *Protokoly,* pp. 157–158.

geoisie. Besides, they held that such a course would be a tacit recognition of the "constitutionality" of the régime.[4] The usual Menshevik majority was at hand to adopt a proposal to their liking. Budget debates were to be ended with a formula of passage to the regular order in which the duma, basing its action on democratic principles, was to reject the government's budget as a whole, and was to refuse to give it the committee.[5]

But if the Social-Democrats felt that refusal to confirm the budget would develop the "revolutionary consciousness" of the people, the Kadets regarded its rejection as a futile motion which would only cast discredit on the duma and do incalculable hurt to the parliamentary development of the country. The duma, in their opinion, had altogether too few significant rights to strengthen its position, and could hardly afford the luxury of refusing to utilize it budgetary powers. For the liberals regarded the right to confirm the budget as a basic prerogative of the new duma—a vital foundation stone for the new parliamentary structure. If they were willing to accept that right in a limited form, as a pale shadow of the financial powers of western parliaments, it was only because this was the most that could be had at the moment and would serve as the basis for future gains by a stronger duma with greater prestige. And strength and prestige could be acquired only through beneficial and progressive legislative activity. The responsibility for refusal to examine the budget was, according to the Kadets, far greater than the responsibility for confirming it. Thus, in this, as in all vital issues, the opposition to the government was hopelessly divided.[6]

4. *Tovarishch*, April 21, p. 3; *Riech*, April 21, p. 3; *Protokoly*, pp. 157–158, 213, 252–253; *Ternii bez roz*, pp. 45–46.
5. On March 9, the duma had quietly elected the Budget, Finance, and Audit Committees; the three connected with its right to examine the budget. According to an agreement made on March 7, at an opposition conference, each of these committees was to consist of thirty-three deputies. *Tovarishch*, March 22, p. 4; *Riech*, March 22, p. 3, Duma Sup.; *Stenog. ot.*, I, 267–268, 442–443; *Ukazatel*, pp. 35–36; *Riech*, March 9, 1907, p. 2.
6. See P. Miliukov. *Vtoraia duma*, pp. 109, 146.

Before delivering his address on the budget on March 20, the minister of finance, Kokovtsov (influenced to a certain extent by the moderate foreign minister, Izvolskii), called for a special session of the council of ministers in which the speech was carefully reviewed to make it as dispassionate and uncontroversial as possible, and to avoid any intimation of arrogance.[7] When the session opened, most of the cabinet was present with many aids who filled the government's benches and remained there throughout the discussion.[8] Kokovtsov began in a tired, monotonous voice with a statement that he would not anticipate criticism of the budget before the committee had reported.[9] But in his opinion, the budget with all of its ramifications was too complicated for the understanding of the average deputy, inexperienced in financial matters. This he held to be a temporary state of affairs which would be remedied by an impartial, unprejudiced analysis of the budget together with healthy debate. He demanded that this very difficult work be carried on outside of any regular order because of its importance to the welfare of the state. Nor did he fail to remind the duma that the administration had all of the necessary means at its disposal to meet the budgetary needs for 1907. And foreseeing an attack on that provision of the constitution, he justified it as a technical necessity. A great modern state, he declared, could not risk financial embarrassment because of an unapproved budget.

After these preliminary remarks, he undertook an an-

7. Before the opening of the session, a copy was presented to the tsar for examination. He approved of the tone, but doubted that a clash would be avoided. Kokovtsov, *Memoirs*, p. 173.

8. *Ibid.*, pp. 173–174; *Riech*, March 21, p. 1; *Stenog. ot.*, I, 793–809. Kokovtsov was born in Novgorod province and spent most of his life in government service. He served in the prison department of the ministry of justice from 1872 to 1891 when he became a state-secretary of the economic department of the Imperial Council. In 1896 he became assistant minister of finance under Witte. In 1904 he was appointed minister of finance, and in October, 1905, he became a member of the Imperial Council. From April, 1906, to January, 1914, he served a second term as finance minister. See *Padenie tsarskogo rezhima*, VII, 355–356.

9. *Riech*, March 21, p. 1.

alysis of the projected budget for 1907.[10] The administration, he declared, thought only to be moderate in compiling the budget. Despite war, revolution, and famine,
the total expenditure for 1907, ordinary and extraordinary, would be 2,471,000,000 rubles, or 39,000,000 rubles
less than that of the preceding year (which had been
burdened with some of the expenditures of the 1905
budget). The ordinary expenditures, he conceded, were
140,000,000 rubles higher than those of the past year
as a result of increased expenditures in liquidating the
war debt, operating the railroads, and administering the
state liquor monopoly. Expenditures in other departments, he declared, had increased only 34,000,000 rubles
over those of 1906. To impress the duma with the government's moderation he compared the 1907 budget with
that of 1903, the last normal year. This showed an increase of only 89,000,000 rubles in four years, and of
this amount, 39,000,000 rubles had been assigned to the
war ministry. Anticipating the charge that the budget
contained a number of unnecessary expenditures, Kokovtsov recommended that the duma point them out and
he promised that the government would make the required
changes. But he warned that increased expenditures resulting from the war would make further reductions difficult, for at the moment, all expenditures were considerably restrained. He predicted, however, that when conditions were favorable reductions would be realized. With
the plans and demands of the left in mind, Kokovtsov
conceded that reform would be necessary but dismissed
a refusal of funds as absurd. He maintained that as in
other countries during periods of transition cries of
extravagance and new theories of financial reconstruction
were heard along with promises of broad satisfaction of

10. *Stenog. ot.*, I, 80. Summary of project in *Riech*, Feb. 21, p. 2. The government had sent it to the duma on March 7. All expenditures for 1907 were 2,471,-
684,872 rubles (1906—2,510,972,775). Ordinary expenditures for 1907 were
2,174,963,544 rubles (1906—2,027,858,774 rubles). Extraordinary expenses were
298,554,701 rubles (1906—478,242,219 rubles).

new demands and the removal of the tax burden from the poor to the rich. But such promises, he asserted, were seldom fulfilled.

The minister of finance then turned to the extraordinary expenditures which he declared were 180,000,000 rubles below those of 1906 (478,242,219 rubles). But he observed that further loans would be necessary since there were insufficient funds to cover several items involving war liquidation, famine relief, and railroad construction. He warned the duma that the amount of the deficit was directly dependent on the means which it would allow the government, and on the ability to collect revenues. And in closing he requested that the duma, with the credit and prosperity of the state foremost in mind, regard the budget as above party strife.[11]

Kokovtsov's hope of avoiding a sharp attack from the opposition by presenting a simple, dry statement of fact concerning the current budget was immediately blasted when N. N. Kutler (Kadet) arose to deliver a long tirade on the government's financial policy in general and the 1907 budget in particular.[12] His arguments were regarded as especially significant by both the administration and the duma, since his long service in the ministries of finance and agriculture, only recently terminated, gave him special knowledge of the workings of the governmental machine and the bureaucratic mind.[13] The budget, he declared, was but a reflection of the government's financial policy. He noted first defects in the mechanics of compiling the budget. Lists of expenditures established in 1851 had only recently been revised, he declared, and the duma could not alter classifications established by the administration. He charged that certain items such as the expensive Foundation of the Empress Marie had been omitted, and he enumerated many irregularities practiced in the

11. This was made in the form of a quotation from the Belgian minister of finance.
12. *Stenog. ot.*, I, 809–832.
13. See above Chapter VIII, footnote 51.

compilation of the budget.[14] The laws governing all expenditures, he asserted, overlapped and contradicted each other in great confusion.

The revenue system, he went on, was indeed burdensome. Indirect levies on articles of general use, "which drag the last kopek from the poor man's pocket," consisted of 89 per cent of the tax list. And of these the greatest was the liquor excise to which the wealthy contributed but 1½ per cent. The high tariff system was equally unbearable since it reduced the consumption of articles of general use thereby affecting the prosperity of the country and lowering the standard of living. Higher income taxes would yield comparatively little, he believed, but the lowering of direct levies would result in greater consumption and state revenues. Indirect taxes were, of course, necessary. But he held that the masses who paid them should derive the most benefit from the administration's expenditures. As for direct taxes, he observed that the poor paid two-thirds of the land tax, most of the city real-estate and craft taxes, and bore the burden levied on the wealthy manufacturers and home owners through increased prices and rents.

In all state operations, declared Kutler, there prevailed a lack of economy, recklessness, and administrative inefficiency. Liquor contractors were overpaid, railroads were incompetently handled. Strategic lines were built which brought no immediate return. In his opinion there were too many oversalaried posts with too little work and too many undersalaried officials who were overburdened. There was also a surfeit of obsolete positions, including the censorship office and the land captains, anachronisms in the new order. The entire civil service, he averred, had

14. This was established in 1860. The Foundation held a monopoly over the manufacture and sale of playing cards. It was supported by an amusement tax and, in turn, maintained various educational institutions. The irregularities mentioned by Kutler included the participation of unauthorized persons, the establishment of expenditures only orally confirmed, the granting of salaries outside of the official list, and the inclusion of "great expenditures not subject to publication."

to be reformed, and the same was true of the military whose inefficiency had been revealed by the Japanese War. He agreed that the government's credit was not exhausted but maintained that it was being applied to unproductive ends as war and bad financing. Amid loud applause he declared that the state's credit rose when a correct relationship was maintained between the administration and the people's representatives in order that the latter might be responsible for the government's economy.

For all of the government's vast expenditures he held that the people received comparatively little in return, except, perhaps, liquor at higher prices. For educational purposes only 5,500,000 rubles had been appropriated and, of this, some 90,000 was unaccounted for. Finally, he charged the ministry with shifting 1906 items to the 1907 budget to hide the losses of the former year. Yet, despite these defects in the financial system, Kutler, in closing, declared that it was the duty of the duma to point out necessary reforms in those parts of the budget which it could not examine, and to analyze carefully those sections which it might legally review. Here, indeed, the duma might begin to fortify its position.

The administration hardly expected such an attack. Moreover, Kokovtsov felt personally offended by this sally from a former colleague whom he had once succored in a moment of need.[15] The charge of diverting educational funds (the location of the 90,000 referred to by Kutler was immediately revealed to him by his chief accountant) also served to arouse the habitually placid minister of finance, and moved him to request a second hearing.[16]

This time in a more enlivened tone Kokovtsov defended his policy. He took great satisfaction in pointing out that the funds which Kutler had missed in the education budget

15. Kokovtsov had used his influence in placing Kutler in the State Loan and Discount Bank after his forced resignation from the ministry of agriculture in 1906 as a result of his "expropriation" project. See Kokovtsov, *Memoirs*, pp. 174–176.

16. *Ibid.; Stenog. ot.*, I, 834–850.

had been appropriated for teachers' pensions. He justified fund transferences from the budget of the preceding year on the ground that they were entirely within the same department and covered items for which the 1907 budget made no provision. He stated that the budget of the Foundation of the Empress Marie had never been included in the general budget and if the duma wanted to put it there it had a right to do so. The legality of the separate expenditures could not justly be criticized, he asserted, until the budget had been carefully examined by the committee. But he admitted the existence of archaic laws providing for archaic institutions which the duma might abrogate. If the rich paid so little in taxes, he averred that it was because they were so few in poverty-stricken Russia. Kokovtsov particularly resented the charge that the government had raised the price of liquor, thus mulcting the poor. And he remarked, unguardedly, that although he had heard of that "last kopek" to which Kutler had referred, he noted that with the help of God the peasant had managed heretofore to spend it on drink. As for strategic railroads, the country could not get along without them. Bad handling was the exception and occurred in every European country. This was especially to be expected in Russia after waging a war far from the base of supplies, and after a famine-relief campaign. He ironically expressed his gratitude to Kutler for recognizing that the debt burden was not excessive, and maintained that it was incurred by Russia while assuming the rôle of the protector of Europe. High interest rates, Kokovtsov charged, were a result of the revolution, and he held that every country had experienced a fall in its credit. He closed with the emphatic assurance that the Russian financial system was quite sound.[17]

17. Kokovtsov's counter-attack was reinforced by Stolypin who appeared as minister of the interior. He derisively expressed his disappointment in Kutler for not enlightening the duma more on the budget since from his past experience he was eminently qualified to do so, and he denied a minor charge Kutler had made to the effect that the press censor had received an increase in salary. *Stenog. ot.*, I, 850–851.

But the Kadet attack had not ended. Peter Struve arose to expound the duma's meager budgetary right.[18] It had no power to change the administration's proposals, he declared, or the laws on which they were founded. For the law of March 8, 1906,[19] delimiting the budgetary right of the duma, was originally meant for the consultative Bulygin duma and had been grafted bodily on to the legislative Witte parliament. Under the changed conditions the duma should be allowed to abrogate all lists and should be able to take the initiative in budgetary matters.[20] At present the duma was prevented from abolishing many harmful laws. It could not even decrease estimates and depended entirely on the government's whim in that respect. But despite the defects of the law, Struve would not have the budget made the grounds for an "aimless demonstration" by the duma. It should undertake a campaign of reform in order to carry on a "correct siege" of the old order and clear away its remnants in the interests of the popular purse and national economy.

The first Social-Democratic statement on the budget was heard on March 22, when Aleksinskii engaged the attention of the duma (for an hour and a half) with a biting attack on budget and the entire policy of the administration.[21] He demanded the repudiation of both. In this statement, as in his speech on the agrarian question, Aleksinskii analyzed the class basis of the government's policy as reflected in the budget. That was good Marxist tactics. True, he admitted, Russia had incurred a heavy debt while

18. *Ibid.*, pp. 851–864. Peter B. Struve was born in 1870 and received a legal education at St. Petersburg. He was one of the early Russian Marxists, but soon fell out with the more radical elements as a result of his reformist views. By 1905 he was in full agreement with the liberals and was one of the leaders of the Kadet Party. He now opposed revolutionary Marxism in his journal *Poliarnaia Zviezda* (Northern Star).

19. *Pol. sob. zak.*, XXVI, no. 27,505.

20. He explained that the practice of foregoing the initiative in England was due to the fact that their government was one of a parliamentary majority and if Parliament gave up the initiative in budgetary affairs it was simply a matter of technical simplification.

21. *Stenog. ot.*, I, 937–960.

playing the rôle of the protector in Europe, but it was
a reactionary, gendarme rôle. The two-and-one-half-bil-
lion-ruble war debt was the result of an expensive adventure which, considering the suffering it entailed, was certainly not in the interests of the population. An analysis
of the government's domestic policy likewise revealed that
it was carried on solely in the interests of a clique of squires
and capitalists who squandered the people's money to satisfy their greedy appetites. The huge standing army, for
example, was necessary only to the government in its
struggle with the masses. When the state had constructed
a vast railroad net in the nineties it had paid twice the
normal price for all equipment, and the revenues therefor
had come from a tax on vodka. The State Bank, he observed, supported twelve different enterprises, and its
funds were used to found, secure, and reconstruct all
sorts of capitalistic undertakings. Aleksinskii then presented data [22] to prove that the government was one of
squires, for squires, and which handsomely remunerated
squires—at the people's expense. He enumerated some
of the services which the government had rendered the
nobility in the past, including the redemption and financial aid. He observed that considerably more was spent
on police than on education in which Russia lagged badly
behind the West. Aleksinskii then assured the duma that
Kokovtsov wanted the budget quickly confirmed so that
he might administer finances in the bureaucratic spirit as
of yore, and obtain loans in Western Europe. But he remarked that the English, at any rate, were not entirely
in sympathy with the government's course.[23]

22. He quoted from *The Trepov Party in Figures* by N. A. Rubakin.
23. Aleksinskii quoted the London *Economist* as saying that the Russian
government had promised not to make further loans without the duma's consent, and to submit the government's finances to the duma for its approval. On
these conditions it received the loan of April, 1906. The *Economist*, he observed,
regarded the dissolution of the First Duma as a breach of faith. See *Economist*,
July 28, 1906, p. 1,247. Aleksinskii's remark precipitated an uproar. Bobrinskii,
Purishkevich, and Krushevan exclaimed that since the tsar alone might dissolve
the duma, Aleksinskii had insulted his Imperial Majesty, and they would remain no longer. Thereupon, followed by a few other rightists, they stalked out

As the Bolshevik whip Aleksinskii could not forego an attack on the Kadets. Since so much of the budget was "iron clad," he declared, and the government could obtain funds legally even if it were unconfirmed, the Social-Democrats believed that the duma was powerless and would plainly inform the population of this sad state of affairs. Consequently, he differed with Kutler and Struve on the tactics to be followed. A refusal to sign the budget, he maintained, was not a "demonstration" but a duty. And even Struve had admitted that the duma could do little more than compare estimates with the laws on which they were based. The duma's task, Aleksinskii declared, was to criticize the entire budget and the financial policy of the government; to expose its true character to the West. The Kadets, he held, were as willing as ever to make an arrangement with the old order on conditions which were unfavorable to the population.

In closing Aleksinskii read the official Social-Democratic statement which would have the duma declare that it would not take any responsibility for the government's financial policy and therefore would refuse to confirm the budget. For it was part of an economic system which for decades had destroyed the productive forces of the country and ruined the masses. It consisted of revenues derived from direct taxes, duties, and vodka excise; that is, from the meager earnings of the population. And these revenues supported the bureaucratic-autocratic order in a struggle with the people. Then, the law of March 8, 1906, and the Fundamental Laws had deprived the duma of any control over the government's expenditures. And, finally, the Social-Democrats believed that it was the government's purpose to curtail the duma's authority over its economy, and to establish credit in the West in order to obtain fur-

of the assembly hall. However, Golovin upheld Aleksinskii on the ground that he had not expressed his own opinion but had quoted from a foreign periodical. And Aleksinskii added that the book from which he had gathered his information had been printed in St. Petersburg and passed the watchful eye of the censor. See *Stenog. ot.*, I, 954–955. At the end of the session the right protested in a declaration against both Aleksinskii's statement and Golovin's stand.

ther means for a struggle with the people. The Marxists would allow the state not one kopek.

The session of March 23 was poorly attended by the Social-Democrats and for a while resembled the agrarian debates as a great number of deputies, especially the peasants, began to leave the hall.[24] Little new was offered on the question. The rightists Bobrinskii and Purishkevich said nothing that Kokovtsov had not already touched upon.[25] Kutler was grieved that the minister had taken his remarks as a personal insult, and Struve maintained that refusal to confirm the budget would be little more than an "ineffective gesture." [26] But the threatening torrent of oratory was cut off when the duma decided to stop the registration of speakers.[27]

The second, and last, Social-Democratic orator on the budget question, A. G. Zurabov, appeared on March 27.[28] Aleksinskii, he informed the duma, had explained what the government did with its revenues; he would say more about how it obtained them. In the West, he declared, states usually investigated into the needs and then discovered the sources at hand to meet them. But in Russia it was just the opposite; the government got what it could and then distributed its funds among the various departments. It extracted as much as it could, and more, from the people which it regarded as its property, its slave. Like Aleksinskii he analyzed each field of state economy and concluded that in every case it was the government's aim to extract as much as possible from the population and divide the revenues between the Treasury and the squires or the capitalists. It received its chief income from indirect taxes when the rest of Europe was abandoning

24. *Riech*, March 24, p. 1, Duma Sup.

25. *Stenog. ot.*, I, 1,002–1,014, 1,025–1,027.

26. *Ibid.*, pp. 1,027–1,035, 1,035–1,039.

27. *Ibid.*, p. 1,047.

28. *Ibid.*, pp. 1,160–1,175. A. G. Zurabov, an Armenian, was born in Tiflis in 1873. He was expelled from a teachers' seminary for revolutionary activity and was imprisoned several times. He edited a number of Armenian newspapers including the Marxist *Osnak*.

them and the saturation point had been reached a decade before. He assailed the creation of the liquor monopoly as an "expropriation" of 100,000 booth owners as well as of *zemstva* and communes, which had used liquor revenues for cultural purposes. And he maintained that the liquor policy led only to widespread poverty and the illegal distillation of unhealthful brews. The state's incautious railroad construction, he held, resulted in the creation of a huge debt and annual deficits. Without funds to repair and improve the roads the economic development of the country was retarded and the hazard of travel by rail increased. The sugar syndicate [29] was in his opinion nothing more than the union of the government with a few capitalists for robbing the people. Russian sugar, which the peasant could not afford, was used by English farmers to feed their swine. And the administration's oil-land policy was evolved for the benefit of the great international oil companies while the peasant's cultural development was hindered because kerosene was too expensive for him. In a word, the government was like a *kulak*, a greedy, village money-lender, sucking the very marrow out of the population. But the productive forces of the country had opposed this exploitation and had rebelled; that is, the disorganized national economy led to revolution, and not the opposite, as the government claimed.

Zurabov concluded by directing several "warm words" at Struve for his address on March 23.[30] Struve, he declared, had called the Social-Democratic proposal an "affected gesture" without analyzing it or considering the motives behind its presentation. Deep in their souls, he had said, the Social-Democrats knew that the Kadets would not vote for it. That was not true, asserted Zurabov, and because they wanted wide support Aleksinskii

29. The sugar syndicate was formed in 1887 at the government's suggestion in order to control prices. See M. S. Miller, *Economic Development of Russia*, p. 238.

30. *Stenog. ot.*, I, 1,035–1,037.

had called on every true democrat to vote for his fraction's resolution. Since the Kadets found this proposal inconvenient they tried to prove it undemocratic and unacceptable to democrats. Struve wanted to "besiege" the government, but Zurabov believed that he had adopted very poor tactics for he would allow the "besieged" bread and means. True besiegers should allow nothing to pass. "He gives food to the enemy and says 'open the gates to me alone for that. I won't go in that door but will eat *kasha* with you at the gates!' " If he did not want to subscribe to the Social-Democratic proposal and wanted to express confidence in the government, Zurabov challenged him to have the boldness to inform the whole people that he was carrying on a political game at their expense.

In this last session of the "budget debates," the deputies displayed singular forbearance as, one after another, they yielded their right to speak, thus considerably curtailing further discussion.[31] But before debates were finally closed, and before the duma voted on its plans for the budget, Kokovtsov added a final word.[32] In his usual moderate tone he explained that his remarks about the "last kopek" which brought a violent barrage from the left were not uttered in a spirit of contempt. He had been wholly misunderstood since he had simply meant to infer that the tax system did not leave the peasant altogether penniless. But he reaffirmed the government's sole monopoly of the initiative in budgetary matters, and maintained that he had to be careful and conservative in presenting the lists since many demands were being flung at him from opposite directions. He objected to "winged words" on the "iron clad" portions of the budget, and held that it was only a fifth part; about a billion and a half rubles was at the complete disposal of the duma. He again stressed the exceptional difficulty of the task, and in closing requested the duma to give the budget to a

31. *Riech*, March 28, p. 1, Duma Sup.
32. *Stenog. ot.*, I, 1,249–1,268.

committee where it should be very carefully analyzed. In
the final vote which followed a great majority, including
the *Narodniki* and center, accepted the minister's advice.[33]

Control of the Budget Committee which the duma had
elected on March 9, was in the hands of the duma center.
On March 16, Kadet M. P. Fedorov was chosen chairman, and Kadet F. Tatarinov, secretary. Subcommittees
were elected to examine particular parts of the budget and
it was decided to invite specialists to committee meetings.[34]
The latter decision, as usual, resulted in a conflict within
the committee and with the government. The committee
was informed of Stolypin's objections and, after protracted debates on March 24, decided that only the general assembly of the duma had the right to regulate the
internal affairs of its committees, and that until receiving further notice from the general assembly, chairmen
of the subcommittees by agreement with the presidium
of the committee had the right to invite experts. It noted
that although Article 42 of the Duma Statute required
the absence of "outsiders," the following articles clearly
indicated that the term referred to the public. Furthermore, it maintained that when the Senate examined the
duma rules it had found no contradiction between Article
42 of the Duma Statute and Article 44 of the Rules of
the Duma which allowed committees to invite experts
through the chancellery.[35] However, having presented
its point of view, the committee took no further steps
which might cause Stolypin to complain.

But the Budget Committee was faced with still another type of vexatious and obstructive activity on the
part of the government. On March 26, it requested Ko-

33. *Ibid.*, p. 1,268; *Riech*, March 28, p. 1, Duma Sup.
34. *Riech*, March 17, p. 3; March 18, p. 3; March 22, p. 3, Duma Sup.;
March 23, p. 4, Duma Sup. The Budget Committee consisted of 4 Social-
Democrats (Gerus, Dzhugeli, Mitrov, Ozol), 2 S-R's, 5 Trudoviki, 2 P-S's, 6
Kadets, 1 Democratic Reformist, 4 Kolo, 1 Moslem, 2 Cossacks, 5 Octobrists,
and 1 non-partisan.
35. *Komissii*, pp. 11–12; *Nakaz*, p. 22.

kovtsov to allow it to examine the journal and papers of the interdepartmental conferences at which the budget was compiled. He referred the matter to the council of ministers which promptly rejected the petition on the ground that the records were a part of the internal activity of governmental institutions during the preparatory stages of the compilation of the budget, whereas the duma might review the budget only in its final form, as presented by the cabinet.[36] The exasperated committee submitted a complaint to the duma on April 6, which reviewed the history of the incident and pointed out the significance of the journals and the obstructive nature of the government's action. It maintained that the government's behavior could only arouse suspicion since the journals were never regarded as secret documents and the 1905 edition was accessible to all in the duma's library. The committee maintained that the cabinet's stand was indeed unexpected after the promise of coöperation held forth during the debates. No further action was, however, taken in this matter.[37]

The budgetary was by far the busiest of all duma committees and the only one to hold meetings during the Easter recess.[38] It held sixteen general committee sessions, while the subcommittees met fifty times to examine thirty-four estimates and fifty-seven credit items. These were very minutely analyzed, and often, as in the case of the administration of the liquor monopoly and the war ministry the subcommittees curtailed expenditures significantly. Yet they increased the estimates of other depart-

36. *Komissii*, p. 15; *Riech*, March 27, p. 4, Duma Sup.; April 6, p. 3, Duma Sup.; April 7, p. 4, Duma Sup.

37. *Stenog. ot.*, I, 1,747–1,750. Another question of order which troubled the committee was the choice of a correct attitude toward expenditures based on laws issued under Article 87 of the Fundamental Laws. This problem was resolved, at least temporarily, when the subcommittee reviewing the budget of the ministry of finance refused to cover losses sustained by the Peasant Land Bank as a result of its decision to lower interest payments, since that decision was introduced under Article 87. See *Riech*, March 3, p. 4, Duma Sup.; May 4, p. 2, Duma Sup.

38. *Ibid.*, April 19, p. 3; April 26, p. 2.

ments as those of the administration of forests and the budget for the ministry of trade and industry.[39] When the committee as a whole was called upon to approve various items, the Social-Democrats and Trudoviki refused to vote on the ground that they were in principle opposed to the confirmation of the budget.[40]

Although the duma was dissolved before the committee was able to report on the budget as a whole, its work was not entirely negative and unproductive. For it introduced special reports on items which it considered important and more or less convinced the duma of their urgency. We have already witnessed the difficulty with which it won the adoption of its recommendations on famine relief and shall see that the debates which raged around its report on the government's demand for recruits very nearly led to the duma's immediate undoing. On a number of minor items, however, it was more successful, despite the continued opposition of the left in both the committee and the duma. When, for example, the committee supported the government's request for 239,000 rubles to maintain sea routes between Vladivostok and ports on the Sea of Okhotsk, the Trudoviki and the Social-Democrats objected that the administration had not presented enough data to enable the duma to reach a final decision.[41] The same objection met the request for the maintenance of urgent communications on the Lena and Amur Rivers and on Lake Baikal.[42] The Social-Democrats also contended that the establishment of monopolies on the Siberian waterways would pauperize thousands who earned their bread by hauling freight and mail.[42]

39. *Komissii*, pp. 8, 15; *Riech*, April 11, p. 2; May 1, pp. 3–4, Duma Sup.; April 26, p. 2; May 12, p. 3, Duma Sup.; May 18, p. 2, Duma Sup.; May 20, p. 2, Duma Sup.; May 25, p. 2, Duma Sup.

40. *Ibid.*, May 16, p. 3, Duma Sup.

41. *Stenog. ot.*, I, 690. The bill was introduced by the minister of trade and industry on March 1, and was given to the Budget Committee on April 9. *Riech*, April 11, p. 2; *Stenog. ot.*, II, 837–839, 839–849.

42. *Stenog. ot.*, I, 1,474–1,475; *Riech*, April 28, p. 2; *Stenog. ot.*, II, 874–875. Introduced on April 2, this bill was also given to the committee on April 9. *Ibid.*, pp. 856–859, 878–879.

Finally, the committee reported a series of measures calling for credits to be expended on trade and craft schools supported by the ministry of trade and industry. Of the ten items listed, involving some 125,530 rubles, the committee urged the rejection of only one grant to an artistic publication, *Khudozhestvennyia Sokrovishcha Rossii* (Artistic Treasures of Russia) because, as the reporter Fedorov later explained, it was allowed the immodest subsidy of twenty rubles per copy.[43] Against these items, too, the Social-Democrats offered the most outspoken opposition. They would gladly support any educational institution which gave the proletariat an opportunity to raise the value of its labor and better its condition. But the amount granted was too small and the number of beneficiaries far too limited; for these schools were inaccessible to the workers. Moreover, the instruction was poor and the inspection weak. Grants were made on the basis of political influence rather than merit or need, and the duma knew nothing of the applicants, their qualifications, and the conditions of the grants. Finally, the Social-Democrats would not confirm any of its parts before debates on the entire budget had taken place. For by confirming specific items of expenditure they felt that they would bind themselves to approve corresponding revenues in the budget of the irresponsible, "autocratic" government.[44] But in all of these matters the committee was eminently successful as the duma decided to attribute greater weight to its arguments for urgency than to the objections of the extreme left.[45]

Besides expenditures, the administration's budget contained, of course, a program of taxation—of revenues—consisting of fourteen measures which were given to the Finance Committee for preliminary examination. But the

43. *Stenog. ot.*, I, 182–183; II, 1,280–1,281; *Riech*, May 27, p. 3. For a detailed account of the ten measures see *Ukazatel*, pp. 284–285.

44. *Stenog. ot.*, II, 1,254–1,258.

45. *Ibid.*, pp. 846–847, 870–871, 879–880, 1,249–1,290.

duma found time to examine only three.[46] A minor matter of a tax on non-irrigated lands in Turkestan was quickly disposed of. The government had been engaged for seven years in the difficult task of assessing this wilderness and was asking for the extension of the right granted the minister of finance to establish temporary levies. The committee approved the measure on May 2 and urged the duma to adopt it with the stipulation that the government present more data on the matter in the budget for 1908.[47] Here, again, the Social-Democrats objected that the duma could not confirm an item with insufficient data at hand; when it knew nothing of the fairness of the levy. And again they opposed the practice of passing on separate articles of the budget before it had been reported by the committee in its entirety. This method, they complained, contradicted the committee's decision to introduce the budget as a whole before presenting any part of it. It was their plan to reject the entire budget and they vigorously opposed a piecemeal confirmation.[48] However, as was usually the case with questions of local significance, the duma followed the advice of the committee majority and adopted the measure after two readings on May 26.[49]

More significant were the other tax measures examined. One involved a revision of the average tax per desiatin on cultivated lands and forests; a change affecting the entire peasantry. The bill was introduced by Kokov-

46. This committee had been organized on March 21, when Kutler was chosen chairman and Saltykov secretary. However, on April 17 Kutler was replaced by Zhukovskii when the former accepted his election as chairman of the Agrarian Committee. The committee consisted of 4 S-D's (Makharadze, Mitrov, Saltykov, Sierov), 2 S-R's, 3 Trudoviki, 3 P-S's, 9 Kadets, 3 Kolo, 2 Moslems, 1 Cossack, 6 Octobrists. *Riech*, March 23, p. 3, Duma Sup.; April 18, p. 3; *Ukazatel*, p. 289.
47. The bill was introduced by the minister of finance on April 2. *Riech*, April 13, 1907, p. 4, Duma Sup.; *Komissii*, p. 48; *Pol. sob. zak.*, XXVII, no. 28,843; *Stenog. ot.*, II, 1,027–1,030.
48. *Stenog. ot.*, II, 1,033–1,037.
49. *Ibid.*, pp. 1,042–1,043, 1,252.

tsov on March 7, and turned over to the Finance Committee on March 29.[50] On May 2, after some deliberation, the committee proposed that the duma reject the measure, and named ex-chairman N. N. Kutler to report thereon. On the evening session of May 22, Kutler defended the committee's stand.[51] He explained that although it was true, as the government contended, that land values had risen since the current tax system was established in the eighties, yet the present bill would more than double the total amount of the tax.[52] He explained that the measure was presented to the First Duma and was to take effect on January 1, 1907. Consequently, after its dissolution, temporary measures were adopted under Article 87. Nine provinces suffering from crop failures[53] were freed in 1907 from the higher tax, and the remaining provinces were to carry half the loss in revenue involved. Therefore, the government would receive twenty instead of thirty millions in 1907. However, the committee considered that the existing burden was already too heavy and that further levies were unthinkable. Moreover, it believed that no increases should be made without corresponding decreases. Kutler reported that the committee could not agree with the government's contention that the tax burden on the land was light as a result of the abolition of the redemption payments. True, the government's land tax was not high, but the land was also burdened with a *zemstvo* tax four times greater than the state tax and a *mir* (commune) tax almost as large. Furthermore, the committee believed that projected reforms of self-government and the agrarian reforms would have to be paid for by land taxes. In closing, he declared that land reform was necessary to help the peasant out of his poverty-stricken state and therefore, this tax would be a backward step; the duma could not

50. *Stenog. ot.*, I, 181, 1,278–1,279.
51. *Riech.* May 3, p. 3, Duma Sup.; *Stenog. ot.*, II, 1,044–1,047.
52. More detailed figures in *Stenog. ot.*, II, p. 1,044.
53. *Ibid.*, Voronezh, Orel, Penza, Pskov, Riazan, Samara, Saratov, Tambov, and Tula.

reply to the request for land with higher taxes. With these arguments in view, the committee proposed the rejection of the bill.

Assistant Minister Pokrovskii defended the measure.[54] He reiterated the government's claim that there could be no discussion of an actual increase in taxes, for land values had risen much since the current rates were first levied in 1884. He maintained, further, that the bill would better equalize the distribution of the levy.[55] In the person of Pokrovskii the government refused to admit of any intention on its part to forego future increases in view of the greater demands of state economy. He contended that the loss of 90,000,000 rubles with the abolition of redemption payments was hardly mentioned by the committee, and new taxes totaled only 73,000,000 rubles. He admitted that land taxes were heavy but held that this fact should not lead to a prohibition of further increases, but to a speedier consideration of the government's land project which divided the land into small units with equitable tax burdens. The administration, he warned, would not transfer any of its levying power to the *zemstva* until the taxes for each province were established according to ability of the landowners to pay them, and the change would be made only when the government believed that the proper time had arrived.

Pokrovskii saw no basis for the committee's fear that land reforms meant increased taxes since the ministerial project contemplated no change in the method of assessment. The proposed levies, he declared, amounted to only 3,800,000 rubles which was a small part of the loss sustained when redemption payments were abolished. Finally, it was his opinion that, in general, the levying of taxes and the demand for land had nothing in common. At any

54. *Ibid.*, pp. 1,047–1,056.
55. Under the 1884 law the central, black-soil provinces bore 36.6 per cent of the tax; fifteen remaining black-soil provinces, 36.6 per cent; and non-black-soil provinces, 27.5 per cent. According to the new law ten central black-soil provinces would pay 25.7 per cent and the other two categories 43.4 per cent and 31 per cent respectively. *Ibid.*, p. 1,048.

rate, the government was doing all in its power, short of obligatory expropriation, to give the peasant all the land he needed. In conclusion, he pointed out that it would be unjust to raise the taxes of large landowners on the eve of a projected obligatory expropriation. The assistant minister's arguments were, however, in vain, for this increase in the land tax was distasteful to all elements including the landowners on the right. Sinadino (Oct.) believed with the opposition that the population could bear no more taxes, and that increases would have to be accompanied by corresponding cuts.[56]

For the Social-Democrats, Mitrov and Mandelberg maintained that according to Pokrovskii the government intended to cover redemption losses by increasing taxes. The peasants, they held, would undoubtedly bear the heaviest burden, if for no other reason than because taxes were apportioned locally by *zemstva* in which the nobility held the majority of votes. To prove that taxes were burdensome the Social-Democrats produced figures covering the comparatively prosperous region of Livland, and revealing the great number of peasant holdings sold there for arrears in taxes.[57] Moreover, they felt that this debate justified their contention that no part of the budget could be discussed while basic questions involving the duma's attitude toward that budget remained unanswered. Because of these prime considerations the Social-Democrats refused to support a single item.[58] The duma rejected the government's bill unanimously.[59]

The final tax measure considered, that on city real estate, had also been issued under Article 87 on November 22, 1906.[60] It was presented to the duma on April 2 and given to the Finance Committee which decided to propose

56. *Ibid.*, p. 1,062–1,064.
57. From 1894 to 1896 in Livland 3,936 desiatins were sold for arrears. See *ibid.*, p. 1,067.
58. *Ibid.*, pp. 1,057–1,060, 1,065–1,067.
59. *Ibid.*, p. 1,070.
60. *Ibid.*, p. 1,474; *Pol. sob. zak.*, XXVI, no. 28,570.

the adoption of the bill with some reductions. It appointed Zhukovskii to report to the duma.[61] On the evening session of May 29 he explained that the bill asked that 1906 levies on city real estate be repeated in 1907, the total amount being 12,957,000 rubles. He explained, further, that he fully understood that the taxes were unjust since in 1905 they were indiscriminately raised everywhere by 33 per cent and not according to the relative growth in property values. Yet the committee had learned that the administration was considering a reform measure and would consequently ask the duma not to reject the current tax on grounds of unjust evaluation. Such a course would make privileged characters of the untaxed. He argued that if the duma were to attempt to rewrite the bill the tax would not be collected until 1908 when all real-estate holders would be taxed for two consecutive years. With these considerations in mind he declared that the committee had decided to change the estimates only in obviously overtaxed provinces.[62] Accordingly, the Finance Committee had lowered the government's figures by 126,999 rubles and avoided placing the burden on other elements of the population. The committee believed that this would indicate to the government the correct assessments for 1908. In that form he proposed that the duma adopt the bill.[63]

Saltykov followed to present the minority viewpoint.[64] He enunciated the strictly Social-Democratic views that the bill should not be considered at evening sessions since it was neither of local significance nor urgent; that the government would collect the levy under Article 87; and that, in general, the bill should not be considered before the duma's attitude toward the entire budget had been defined. He noted that Kutler had objected to the latter ar-

61. *Riech*, April 13, p. 4, Duma Sup.; April 19, p. 3; May 3, p. 3, Duma Sup.
62. He referred to Samara, the Don Cossack Region, and Nizhegorod where many small property holders were affected.
63. *Stenog. ot.*, II, 1,448–1,457. The text of the bill as presented by the committee is to be found on pp. 1,476–1,479.
64. *Ibid.*, pp. 1,458–1,462.

gument on the ground that the duma might only examine
and verify the correctness of expenditures.[65] That, Saltykov declared, reduced the complicated budget question to
one of simple arithmetic. Moreover, since the government
was bringing in a reform bill on city taxes he believed that
the duma should be guided by those general considerations
which moved it to reject an increase in the average land
tax. He declared that he could understand the administration's anxiety to have this bill passed but he could not understand why the committee which admitted its injustice
supported it. Since 1904, he said, the government had
twice revised the assessment of city property and increased
it by a billion and a third; once when it applied the 33 per
cent increase and again by 3,400,000 rubles when a revision was made in 1905–1906 according to *zemstvo* evalua-
tions which it hastened to accept. Consequently, he recommended that the duma ignore the bill, if it would not reject
it. Most provinces, he pointed out, were obviously overtaxed. And he felt that the committee's belief that the
lowering of taxes in the cities would somehow relieve the
poorer elements was groundless. For the duma would not
be able to force the city governments to grant refunds to
the poor property owners, and everywhere the city administrations were in the hands of the richer bourgeoisie.
Moreover, as a final consideration, he reminded the duma
that the taxes would go into a general treasury to be used
by the government as it pleased. Under existing circumstances, he declared, the Social-Democrats could not possibly confirm this bill, and the duma, too, he concluded,
should reject it.

Ozol added the Social-Democratic contention that the
poor would hardly benefit as the committee hoped, since
the city dumas, consisting of the wealthier elements, would
not overtax themselves. Moreover, he contended that property owners passed the tax burden on to those who rented
property from them. He believed that the bill should be

65. *Ibid.*, pp. 1,039–1,040.

rejected on the principle that to change a bad law as quickly as possible it had to be cast out in its entirety. He warned the duma that if it persisted in voting the budget by items the government would soon revise all lists by presenting special articles for the duma to vote on, or would present no budget at all, only individual laws. If the duma should confirm this bill, he maintained that it would simply be handing a 12,000,000-ruble gift to the irresponsible ministry, whereas if it were rejected the people would be the beneficiaries.[66] But with the peasants abstaining,[67] and with few Social-Democrats or *Narodniki* present, only sixty-three votes could be mustered against the bill by the left as it passed on the first reading.[68]

The duma Audit Committee, the last of those created in connection with the examination of the budget was organized on March 16, and elected Saveliev (Kadet) chairman and Peterson (Popular-Socialist) secretary.[69] On March 21 it decided to limit its activities to an examination of the correctness of the accounts and bookkeeping of the state auditor. Accordingly, subcommittees were formed for examining the accounts of the civil, military, naval, and railroad administrations, and of the special funds of the various departments, as well as those involved in credit and state banking operations.[70] The Audit Committee began its stormy career by deciding on the same day to invite specialists to its meetings, and when Stolypin's attitude became known it continued to maintain that accord-

66. *Ibid.*, pp. 1,466–1,468.

67. Just before the duma voted the Trudovik leader Bulat declared, in the name of his group, that the projected tax was based on data collected in 1893. And although real estate values had greatly changed since then, yet the government had collected no further information but levied a general increase of 33 per cent. Since it could not be considered equitable he maintained that the tax should not be confirmed at all. But since that would liberate a wealthy element from its due share of the tax burden which might then fall on the poorer classes, the Trudoviki would abstain from voting. A burst of laughter greeted this wily evasion of the necessity of voting on the measure which simultaneously ranged the Trudoviki solidly with the left. *Ibid.*, p. 1,471.

68. *Ibid.*, pp. 1,475–1,479; *Riech*, May 30, p. 1, Duma Sup.

69. *Riech*, March 17, p. 3.

70. *Ibid.*, March 22, p. 3, Duma Sup.; March 29, p. 4, Duma Sup.

ing to Article 42 of the Duma Statute it was acting within its rights.[71] Unlike most other committees it never relinquished that view, and as late as May 3 decided to invite Professor Ozerov of the University of Moscow. Should he be refused entry into the duma they agreed to meet him in private.[72]

But the major difference between the committee and the government concerned the former's request for all reports of the state auditor for 1905 as well as the annual reports of all governmental accounting institutions for that year. After considering the matter for several days, on March 27 Schwanebach, the state auditor, categorically refused all materials despite Article 31 of the Duma Statute which specifically mentioned the reports as being subject to the duma's examination. He declared that the reports were secret, and were, consequently, on the basis of Article 40 of the Duma Statute, not subject to publication.[73]

In reply the committee observed that submission of these reports to the duma committee was not equivalent to their publication since meetings of the committee, and later, those of the duma, might be held behind closed doors. Finally, the committee held that it could demand all reports, for prior to the publication of the October Manifesto they had been presented to the old Imperial Council whose functions had been assumed by the duma and the reformed Imperial Council. The committee contended that these reports were necessary in order that the duma might obtain a complete picture of the administration's economy during the past few years, and examine the legality of its expenditures, and statistical materials on the various appropriations. Besides, it observed that it had already received reports from the State Bank, the ministry of justice, and the horse-breeding department.[74]

71. *Ibid.*, March 22, p. 3, Duma Sup.; *Komissii*, p. 61.
72. *Komissii*, p. 61.
73. *Pol. sob. zak.*, XXVI, no. 27,424.
74. *Riech*, April 3, p. 3, Duma Sup.; *Komissii*, p. 63.

Another specific request for reports was submitted on April 14. The committee offered to review them in the government's offices if that were more convenient. But on May 3, it learned from the duma chancellery that the request had again been rejected.[75] Taking another tack the committee decided to investigate the legality of the refusal and to begin work on available materials.[76]

The matter had reached an impasse and thus it remained until dissolution. The impression created on the population by this incident, as by the numerous controversies on experts, was extremely unfavorable to the government. For although the auditor—known to all as an extreme reactionary—might have been able to prove the formal correctness of his stand, his interpretation was regarded by opposition groups as particularly narrow, and his tactics as purely obstructive and bound to arouse popular suspicion. This was especially true since investigations of the accounts of the ministries of the interior and justice, and of the Holy Synod, revealed arbitrary transferences of funds from one account to another and generally chaotic bookkeeping.[77]

Then, as usual, these disputes offered excellent material to the Social-Democrats for emphasizing the irreconcilability of the interests of the ruling classes and those of the people. And the Bolsheviki could find grounds for opposing the Kadets. In point of fact, liberal and revolutionary policy clashed sharply on this as on every major issue. And again, with the Mensheviki opposed in principal to such a stand, the entire fraction found itself firmly aligned against the Kadets. Yet the whole opposition, including the Kadets, was unanimous in condemning the government's policy as ruinous to the population. Thus, with the duma but a month old, its majority was attacking the fiscal policy of the government, and its extreme left was calling for a refusal to confirm the budget; a clear mani-

75. *Riech*, April 5, p. 3; *Komissii*, pp. 59–60; *Riech*, May 4, p. 3, Duma Sup.
76. *Riech*, May 9, p. 2.
77. *Ibid.*, April 11, p. 3; May 11, p. 2.

festation of non-confidence. And although later, under the influence of the Kadets, the duma confirmed several urgent estimates, after two months the Budget Committee had not reported on the budget as a whole. Consequently, as the administration chafed at the delay and smarted under the attacks, its animosity toward the duma increased. The reactionaries pointed to its inability to work with the government. And as evidence accumulated which seemed to support that contention, the manner in which the duma dealt with the budget loomed large in the minds of those who would be responsible for its dissolution.

X

THE DUMA AND PUBLIC OPINION

WITH debates on the Agricultural and Budget Committees ended, the Second Duma had considered the major portion of that work which it was fated to accomplish. And the chief characteristics of its activity were quite clear. What, then, we may ask, was its position? What had it thus far accomplished? How did it now stand in relation to the government and to the people? The positive legislative achievements of the Second Duma were, even at the end of its sessions, notably few. Several minor budgetary items had been approved, and a grant for famine relief. But considering the circumstances under which it labored it is indeed remarkable that the duma made any progress at all; that despite numerous tumultuous, and chaotic sessions its debates— thanks to the efforts of the Kadets—not infrequently resembled those of more mature legislative bodies. The parliamentary idea was at least beginning to take hold.

For the difficulties which the young parliament faced, and the circumstances which determined its fate were evident from the start. The conditioning factor of nearly all of the duma's activity was the constant threat of dissolution. Fear of the fatal decree and the parliamentary changes which might accompany it determined the policy of the Kadet Party. And because they invited dissolution, the activities of the extremists endangered the duma's existence.

The Social-Democrats adhering faithfully to the Stockholm resolutions utilized the duma as an arena for disseminating their revolutionary plans and doctrines, as the spearhead of revolution. And the effects of that policy on the parliamentary development of the duma were not particularly happy. By blocking orderly, legislative activity the Social-Democrats interfered seriously with the enactment of any program of reform. Time and again, they were responsible for long-winded, aimless debates by preventing any limitations on the time or number of speakers. And since they favored open debates on the duma floor to quiet discussion in the Kadet-controlled committee rooms they precipitated long and involved arguments on the comparatively simple matters of creating special committees and of sending bills or interpellations to permanent bodies. The duma's enemies easily found sufficient material to prove that it was incapable of realizing creative results; that it was "unworkable." And as proof that the duma was revolutionary they had but to point to the vitriolic attacks on the government in which Social-Democratic orators were wont to indulge and which marked their official statements. Social-Democratic pleas for votes of non-confidence in the administration, and for the creation of legally questionable committees not only served the purposes of the right but alarmed liberals who valued the existence and dignity of the duma. Finally, by their uncompromising attitude the Marxists did much to divide the opposition. When the Kadets sought to restrain them or interfered with their tactics, they charged the liberals with betrayal of the popular cause and lined up solidly against them in approved Bolshevik fashion—despite strong conciliatory currents among the Mensheviki. From the very start, in line with the best teachings of Lenin, they waged a relentless campaign against the Kadets for the control of the opposition majority. The breach widened with every new issue and revealed to its foes the inherent weakness of the duma. With the passing of each session the government waxed bolder and more intransigeant in its attitude toward parliament.

The right, we know, was numerically weak in the duma. Yet it was evidently extremely dangerous because of its provocative tactics and its influence at Tsarskoe Selo where it continually pointed to the unproductiveness of the duma and its revolutionary nature, and called for immediate dissolution. Moreover, as time wore on its hopes for early dissolution were fostered by none other than the premier himself.

Peter Arkadievich Stolypin maintained, at first, a patronizing attitude toward the Second Duma despite its strong oppositional nature. For he had, apparently, staked his political fortune on the possibility of compromise with the popular representative body; and in the face of strenuous opposition from the reactionaries at a sympathetic court. But Stolypin was too much the bureaucrat to find a "common tongue" with the popular assembly. While the most moderate elements of the opposition demanded a ministry responsible to the duma, he maintained that he could be answerable only to the tsar. And he would compromise only on his own terms. For the most vital of his reforms, the agrarian, he found no support whatever among the vast majority of the deputies. Yet he would allow no tampering with its basic principles. And the supporters of the duma awaited debates on the report of the Agrarian Committee with great trepidation. But Stolypin revealed his bureaucratic predilections most clearly in his deep suspicion of any connections between the duma and the people. It was because of this mistrust of the intentions of the popular spokesmen, long traditional with the bureaucracy, that he hounded deputies who were so indiscreet as to address their constituents at meetings or picnics. And, more significant, it was because of this feeling that he forbade the presence of experts at committee meetings and seriously hampered their activity. Thus, under the damocletian sword of dissolution and between the Scylla and Charybdis to the right and left the young and weak parliamentary body had to thread its careful way. The slightest miscalculation in its course might result in complete destruction.

What, then, of the public during this period of the Second Duma? What was its general mood, and how did it regard its chosen representatives? The first half of 1907

was marked by a steady decline in the revolutionary spirit
of the people. Revolutionary manifestations, expropria-
tions, assassinations and, as we have seen, strikes, though
still significant during the first three months of the year,
became noticeably irregular in April and May of 1907.
In all branches of industry the employers assumed the
offensive, with the aid of the government, direct or indirect, and workers turned to defensive tactics or retreat.[1]
There were several large labor demonstrations on the second anniversary of "Bloody Sunday" (January 9). And
May Day was celebrated eagerly but quietly with one day
"walk-outs," peaceful mass meetings, and a minimum of
friction with the police.[2] But these were exceptional instances. Reactionary forces dominated the scene, martial law prevailed, unemployment was widespread and its
victims suffered intensely as the cost of living rose, while
trade unions were too poor and public works too few to
render significant aid.[3] Little wonder that deaths from
hunger and suicide were a daily occurrence and that an-
archistic trends appeared here and there in the large centers.[4]

But the majority of the workers reacted less violently.
Beaten in open combat they turned to trade unionism for
organization in the political and economic struggle. And
in Poland the unions were purely economic, non-partisan,
and anti-terroristic. In the first months of 1907, the 652
unions in European Russia boasted of over 200,000
members, about 3.5 per cent of all industrial labor. At

1. See "Russkaia lietopis" (Russian Chronicle) in A. Surovin, *Russkii Kalendar*, 1908, pp. 292–296; D. Koltsov, "Rabochie," pp. 328–329. See daily
column on the revolutionary movement in *Riech* for this period. For statistics on strikes see Appendix II, D; G. T. Robinson, *Rural Russia*, p. 203; A.
Shestakov, *Krestianstvo v revoliutsii 1905 goda*, p. 33; D. Koltsov, "Rabochie,"
pp. 325–328.
2. D. Koltsov, "Rabochie," pp. 336–338. *Riech*, April 19, May 3.
3. V. S. Voitinskii, *Gody pobied i porazhenii*, II, 193–196. For differences between prices and wages see D. Koltsov, "Rabochie," p. 334.
4. Voitinskii tells of the "worker's plot" group which seized necessaries of life
and wreaked revenge on worker's "enemies." Voitinskii, *Gody pobied i porazhenii*, II, pp. 193–196.

the same time the coöperative movement began to attract wide attention.[5] Extremists might continue to call for armed uprising, but the Russian worker faced the realities of the moment.

The peasant movement, likewise, abated. The decline in village rioting and attacks on the estates of neighboring *pomiestchiki* began in June, 1906, and by the middle of 1907 the number of disturbances was negligible. This was due, to some extent, to the increased volume of land on the market, the fall of rents, and the rise of wages for agricultural labor.[6] But field-courts-martial and punitive expeditions figured not a little in the "pacification" of the countryside.

Under the circumstances, therefore, it was quite natural that there should be no evident, immediate reaction to the duma's activities. During the first half of 1907 the political life of the country moved not so much around the duma as in it. The popular masses were sympathetic but silent observers of the drama. There was no mass action in the face of definite demands. Political parties found no active response to their appeals to support the duma. And there was no strong revolutionary force to react positively to the fiery speeches of the extremist opposition in the duma. Individual acts like the labor demonstrations had, as we have seen, lost that inspiring force which a year earlier would have mobilized the population. The people, as a matter of fact, came to regard parliament with fatalistic resignation. The ease with which the government had dissolved the First Duma implanted a widely held belief that another oppositional duma would be dissolved either immediately or at the first favorable opportunity. Moreover, the failure of the Second Duma to pass significant

5. S. Piontkovskii, *Istoriia rabochego dvizheniia v rossii*, pp. 170–179; D. Koltsov, "Rabochie," pp. 325, 335–338.
6. P. Marev, in *Krestianstvo i revoliutsiia*, V. Gorn, ed., charts pp. 57–62, 126; G. T. Robinson, *Rural Russia*, pp. 196, 203; A. Shestakov, *Krestianstvo v revoliutsii 1905 goda*, pp. 33, 95; E. Morokhovets, "Krestianskoe dvizhenie 1905–1907 gg. i sotzial demokratiia," in *Proletarskaia revoliutsiia*, No. 2 (37), pp. 94–95, 160.

reform legislation was not calculated to attract active popular support. And the public was not as well informed on the intensive activity of the committees as it was on the dramatic plenary sessions.[7]

The proceedings of the duma, in fact, were accorded as wide publicity as the opposition press could afford. Debates were summarized and whole sections of the daily and periodical press were given over to dicussion of events at the Taurida. But here, again, newspapers were hampered by governmental interference. For it was to combat the dissemination of opposition speeches and views expressed in the duma that officialdom—local and central —stubbornly sought to limit information on debates and to isolate the duma and its deputies. News about parliament was often meager in the provinces as papers containing reports were either confiscated, severely censored, or forced to print only official statements.[8] And we already know that connections between the population and deputies for discussion of political affairs were either interfered with or flatly forbidden.[9] Yet, generally speaking, the government achieved no great success in attempting to block channels of information. And the many "instructions," petitions, and projects which flowed into the various fractional headquarters reflected the seriousness with which the duma was regarded by the people, and the wide interest in national affairs which was stimulated by the Revolution of 1905 and developed rapidly thereafter among all classes.

While the extremist fractions were at work in the duma and strongly influenced the course of events, those groups of the population whom they represented did not reflect the quiescent mood of the great majority. But the Social-

7. D. Koltsov, "Rabochie," pp. 336–338; F. Dan, "Vtoraia duma," in *Obshchestvennoe dvizhenie v rossii v nachale XX-go veka*, IV, part 2, 138; cited hereafter as "Vtoraia duma"; M. Kovalevskii, article in *Revue Politique et Literaire*, Serie 5, VII, 804.

8. V. Obninskii, *Novyi Stroi*, pp. 197, 200; *Riech*, May 16, p. 2.

9. See, for example, Obninskii, *Novyi Stroi*, p. 198; *Riech*, May 17, p. 3; May 30, p. 2.

Democrats were, to a great extent, demoralized by the decline in the revolutionary temper of the population and especially by active government repression. In many large centers their party headquarters were raided and destroyed, their presses seized, and large quantities of literature confiscated.[10] Yet the Marxists were not idle. Some attempts were made to organize the peasantry and to influence them against buying land from the Peasant Bank, against resettlement, and against placing too great faith in the duma. In no respect were they particularly successful and the peasant organizations they set up were at best weak and ephemeral.[11] But in the period of the Second Duma the Social-Democrats subordinated underground work to that of establishing connections between the duma and the population.[12] Seconding the work of the fraction, the party turned to the duma with the request that it issue a proclamation presenting its program of immediate demands and asking for popular support. Frequent demands were made for aid to the unemployed and famine stricken, and copies of Tsereteli's reply to the government's address were distributed in the thousands.[13]

Most significant for the affairs of the duma, however, was the development of party policy during this period, especially as expressed by the Fifth Congress. A strong moderating current which developed in the St. Petersburg organization was instrumental in healing the breach between the Mensheviki and Bolsheviki created in the course of the election campaign.[14] And it was in the same spirit that the Fifth Party Congress held at London in May, 1907, refused to follow Lenin and a group of Bolshevik extremists in condemning the fraction for "unsocialistic"

10. A. I. Spiridovich, *Istoriia Bolshevizma*, pp. 168–170.

11. E. Morokhovetz, "Krestianskoe dvizhenie 1905–1907 gg. i sotsial demokratiia," *Proletarskaia revoliutsiia*, no. 4 (39), p. 83; no. 6 (41), p. 87; no. 8 (43), p. 35.

12. *Ibid.*, no. 7 (41) pp. 77, 85, 89; no. 7 (42), p. 30.

13. *Ibid.*, no. 6 (41), p. 77; D. Koltsov, "Rabochie," p. 328.

14. V. S. Voitinskii, *Gody pobied i porazhenii*, II, 175–176, 197–199; *Krasnyi Arkhiv*, LXII, 204.

errors and a tendency to become interested in the parliamentary activity of the duma. Instead, the fraction was lauded for the care with which it had watched over the interests of the proletariat. It was, however, openly censured by the congress for attending conferences of opposition fractions especially since they were frequented by the Polish Kolo. But the Bolsheviki had won a majority at London (with the support of the Polish and Lettish Social-Democrats) as a result of the resolute stand which they assumed during elections to the congress, and because of Lenin's merciless criticism and energetic propaganda. And they were in no mood to compromise on the basic principles which they held concerning the position of the duma in the revolutionary movement. Accordingly, the congress adopted a series of resolutions which aimed at continuing those Bolshevik tactics which the fraction had, for all practical purposes, already adopted. The fraction was instructed that it was to serve the interests of the proletariat as heretofore, and also those of the petty bourgeoisie, especially the peasantry. It was to explain to all who would listen the impossibility of achieving political freedom by parliamentary means under the existing political circumstances. And it was to reveal the inevitability of an armed clash for the purpose of wresting power from the hands of the autocratic government and giving it to the people who were to create a constituent assembly. Social-Democratic deputies were to emphasize the organizational, agitational, and propagandist rôles of the duma rather than its legislative possibilities, and all of their activity within the duma was to be subordinated to the mass struggle taking place outside of its walls. They were to undertake a more resolute struggle against the Kadets, to have as few contacts with them as possible, and to destroy their hegemony over the petty bourgeois representatives. The fraction was, moreover, to place less emphasis on the demands for a "duma ministry" and for the subordination of the executive to the legislative branches of government. For the party held that these slogans expressed the tendency of the bourgeoisie to compromise with the reactionaries at the expense of the people, and could, in fact, be realized only by a direct revolutionary attack.[15] Thus, Social-Democratic deputies were instructed by this final party congress before the Great Revolution to follow a strong Leninist line. And the effects of these tactics were shortly to be revealed.

At the other extreme two groups were actively striving for the same general ends: the dissolution of the duma and its abolition, or at least a change in the electoral law which would result in a predominance for the landowning class in the duma. The electoral laws of August and December, 1905, marked the victory of those court advisers among the nobility who desired a liberal statute with a minimum of legal, class differentiation. The conservative nobles who felt their interests threatened by this law and especially by the parliamentary reforms which followed the October Manifesto met in May, 1906, and founded a "Congress of the United Nobility." [16] In November, 1906, and in February, 1907, just after the opening of the Second Duma, the congress held sessions which demanded the suppression of revolutionary activity, the protection of property, the break-up of the village commune, the immediate dissolution of the duma, and the revision of the electoral law to place parliament under the control of the propertied classes.[17] Stolypin had, as yet, no inclination to dissolve the duma. But the demand of the November meeting that representatives of all social orders be elected at provincial assemblies in which the nobility should predominate strongly marked later parliamentary legislation.[18] Moreover, the permanent council of the congress was influential in securing the dissolution of the First

15. *V. K. P. rezoliutsii*, pp. 43–45; See debates on Duma in *Protokoly;* See my article, "The Fifth Social-Democratic Congress and the Duma," *Journal of Modern History*, Dec., 1939, pp. 484–508.

16. P. Miliukov, *Vtoraia duma*, pp. 160–169.

17. G. T. Robinson, *Rural Russia*, p. 197; P. Miliukov, *Vtoraia duma*, p. 134.

18. Compare Miliukov, "The Case of the Second Duma," *Contemporary Review*, October 1907, p. 466.

Duma and the creation of field-courts-martial, and it interfered successfully with Stolypin's attempt to place moderate public figures in his cabinet.[19] Like other reactionaries, the United Nobles feared a duma deporting itself "so correctly and decorously that there would be no fault to find," and they entered it for provocative purposes.[20]

But most of the provocative elements in the duma represented the Union of the Russian People. This party, as we know, sought for a complete return to autocracy with the exception, perhaps, of a popular advisory body and firmer executive and judicial control over the bureaucracy. Numerically this extreme nationalistic group was insignificant. But its strength lay in the fact that its influence among the "ruling spheres" was all out of proportion to its popular influence. Among the bureaucrats, with whom the Union had close, often official, connections, it found many ardent sympathizers. And it was a more or less open secret, verified years later, that the administration supported the Union's press financially throughout the period of "reaction"—1906–1911.[21] Minister of Justice I. G. Shcheglovitov had, throughout this period, close relations with Union leaders, Dr. Dubrovin and V. G. Orlov. Moreover, the secret police, the *Okhrana*, was continually supplied with information concerning revolutionary activities by Union members.[22] Finally, the position of these "True

19. Miliukov, *Vtoraia duma*, p. 169; L. Kleinbort; *Obrazovanie*, no. 8, 1907, p. 138.

20. Miliukov, *Vtoraia duma*, p. 171; Miliukov, "The Case of the Second Duma," *Contemporary Review*, October, 1907, p. 460.

21. From 1906 to 1911 the government expended 3,000,000 rubles in support of the rightist press. This support was discontinued for some time during the period of the Second Duma because of the notoriety which the Union attracted by its terroristic tactics. See *Padenie tsarskogo rezhima*, V, 175–206, 404–413; V. P. Viktorov (ed.), *Souiz russkogo naroda*, introduction pp. 11–12; S. E. Kryzhanovskii, *Vospominaniia*, pp. 100–104. The government attacked the opposition and supported its own policies in pamphlets which it secretly published, *ibid.*, 102–103.

22. *Padenie tsarskogo rezhima*, VI, 120–123; VII, 267.

Russian People" was greatly enhanced by the fact that Nicholas II had more than once welcomed their support and approved of their nationalistic principles.[23]

Secure in the knowledge that they could rely on official support and protection the branches of the Union were often emboldened to call on local authorities to aid their so-called "fighting rings." For like latter-day nationalists they frequently resorted to violent methods to attain their ends.[24] They played on the religious superstitions and economic fears of the small proprietors, merchants, and hopelessly unemployed and often incited them to anti-labor and race riots. We have already had occasion to refer to the Union's rôle in the assassination of the liberal journalists Hertsenstein and Iollos.[25] Other liberal and revolutionary leaders and deputies were threatened and the Union's press directed a steady stream of abuse not only against the opposition but also against individual ministers whose policies did not meet with its approval.[26]

The chief object of the Union's attack was, of course, the duma. And far from limiting its activity to vitupera-tive editorials it tried to mobilize its following in an effort to demonstrate to the tsar the unpopularity of the repre-sentative body. On February 28, the chief council of the

23. On December 23, 1905, the tsar and his heir received medals from the Union of the Russian People, for which his Majesty thanked Dr. Dubrovin "very kindly." And on that date and on February 16, 1906, he assured the "Russian People" that no changes would be made in the autocracy and informed them that he counted upon them for help in "vanquishing the enemies of Rus-sia." It is also interesting to note that a few days after the dissolution of the Second Duma, in reply to Dubrovin's telegram thanking him, Nicholas II wel-comed the Union's support in helping him to realize the "peaceful renovation" of Russia. Stolypin angrily but tardily objected. Petrishchev, *Russkoe bogatstvo*, July, 1907, p. 87; Miliukov, *Constitutional Government for Russia*, pp. 19–20. Sympathy for the Union was also expressed in a letter from Nicholas to his mother on March 1, 1907. See E. J. Bing, *Letters of Tsar Nicholas and the Em-press Marie*, pp. 223–224.

24. Miliukov, *Constitutional Government for Russia*, p. 19.

25. See Chap. I.

26. G. A. Aleksinskii, "Iz perezhitago," pp. 128–132; Miliukov, *Constitutional Government for Russia*, p. 19.

Union of the Russian People issued a circular telegram to all branches ordering that when a "black cross" should appear in *Russkaia Znamia*, the party's organ, they were to deluge the Emperor with telegrams urging the immediate dissolution of the duma and a revision of the electoral law. They were to declare that under the present law its majority would always consist of "social outcasts" and "criminals." The appearance of the symbol on March 16, brought a response which evidently impressed Nicholas II, but he felt that the moment for dissolving the duma had not yet arrived.[27]

Having failed in their efforts to end the duma immediately, the Union's cohorts within the Taurida, we have seen, were ever on the alert to utilize every occasion to brand the duma as unpatriotic, revolutionary, and incapable of performing its appointed task: the enactment of reform legislation. With the approach of the Easter recess the Union, fearing the direct contact of the leftist deputies with the population, noised it about that the revolutionaries were preparing for a wide agitational campaign and they insisted on immediate dissolution.[28] Finally, at its Fourth Congress in April and May the Union of the Russian People called again for the end of the "rebellious duma" and the abrogation of its statute to allow for an advisory body. They would deny the franchise to "politically unreliable persons" and for an indefinite period would place the entire country under martial law.[29] And the "higher spheres" heard these demands with unconcealed sympathy.

Thus, if the left presented a real threat to the duma's existence, moderate elements might at least find means to curb or counteract it. But the danger from the right

27. *Riech*, March 24, p. 2; *Tovarishch*, March 24, p. 2; Kizevetter, *Na rubezhe dvukh stoletakh*, p. 454; P. Miliukov, *Vtoraia duma*, pp. 107, 173–174, 175. Bing, *Letters of Tsar Nicholas*, pp. 223–224.

28. *Padenie tsarskogo rezhima*, VI, 300.

29. G. T. Robinson, *Rural Russia*, p. 197; A. S. Izgoev, *Russkoe obshchestvo i revoliutsiia*, pp. 29–30.

was quite beyond their control. And working together it would seem that these extremist forces would doom the young, inexperienced, and divided duma. Therefore, on the ability of its parliamentarians to outwit powerful political groups on the right and to restrain and outbid the revolutionaries hung the fate of the progress of the liberal, parliamentary idea in tsarist Russia.

XI

INTERPELLATIONS

W E TURN again to the increasingly dramatic developments within the duma. Among the more important powers granted the duma, without qualifications in the Fundamental Laws, was the right to interpellate ministers; to question them concerning charges of illegal activity involving themselves or their subordinates.[1] If, after formal presentation of interpellations containing charges, the duma regarded them as urgent it turned at once to a consideration of the form in which they were to be presented to the government. If considered non-urgent they were reviewed by a special Committee on Interpellations which recommended their adoption or rejection according to their foundation in fact. The committee's recommendations and edition of interpellations were generally accepted by the duma.[2]

The large, liberal majority in the First Duma was quick to realize the value of interpellations as a means of arousing wide resentment against an unpopular and arbitrary government, and presented them with increasing frequency. The Second Duma followed this precedent closely. The revolutionary left made use of the right of interpellation on every possible occasion despite the strenuous efforts of the Kadets and center to limit their number and temper their language in order to "legislate" and avoid clashes with the administration. Although the liberals forced the duma to differentiate sharply between

1. *Pol. sob. zak.*, XXVI, no. 27,805, Article 33.
2. See Duma Rules Articles 77 and 78 adopted May 8. See *Stenog. ot.*, II, 354–355. The Committee on Interpellations was elected on March 19, 1907, It consisted of 3 S-D's (Anikin, Nalivkin, E. Petrov), 2 S-R's, 6 Trudoviki, 2 P-S's, 8 Kadets. 3 Kolo, 1 Cossack, 2 Moslems, 2 non-partisans, 3 Octobrists, 1 Monarchist. See *Stenog. ot.*, I, 752–753, 987; *Ukazatel*, p. 42.

urgent interpellations and non-urgent, and considerably moderated and clarified their texts, discussion and heated debates involving interpellations occupied the duma for many long, and often fruitless, sessions. Thirty-seven times the duma addressed itself to nine ministries, individually and severally.[3] Stolypin, as minister of the interior and chairman of the council of ministers was, by far, the major recipient of these statements. As occupant of both offices and together with other ministers he was interpellated no less than thirty-one times.[4] The ministry of justice, in turn, was presented with grave charges on thirteen different occasions.[5]

In fact, with the mass of this material in mind, the center offered a proposal on March 16, "acknowledging the necessity for beginning active legislative work . . ." to set aside one day of the week for interpellations.[6] But no action was taken on the matter, and after twenty-five urgent statements had already been introduced, the deputies of the center presented a second proposal on April 30, and the duma reserved Thursdays for interpellations.[7]

But this change was accompanied by vigorous objections on the part of the Social-Democrats who held that interpellations were a necessary means for controlling a lawless executive. They contended that through them the duma would reveal itself the friend of the people and its true representative, thereby ranging the population behind it and adding more importance to its legislative work.[8] To the Social-Democrats, regarding the duma primarily as a platform for revolutionary propaganda, the significance of interpellations as a means of "revealing"

3. *Ukazatel,* pp. 308–313. The ministries of justice, agriculture, war, navy, the Over Procurator of the Holy Synod, and the ministers of finance, and education were addressed.
4. *Ibid.*
5. *Ibid.*
6. *Stenog. ot.,* I, 630.
7. *Ukazatel,* pp. 308–311; *Stenog. ot.,* I, 2,342–2,343; II, 570, 577; *Riech,* May 16, p. 1, Duma Sup.
8. *Stenog. ot.,* II, 570–573.

official repression was quite obvious. Accordingly, they attributed much importance to the fullest possible use of this right, both for the practical benefit it yielded as a means of relieving the population from excessive bureaucratic oppression, and for its agitational value.[9] Consequently, they sought to avert limitations on debates involving interpellations, as in the debates just mentioned, and when the duma rules were under consideration.[10] Thus, on April 12, the fraction proposed an amendment to the rules to the effect that interpellations be considered immediately on the day of their introduction without first printing and distributing them.[11] However, when Mandelberg discussed the proposal on May 15, Golovin refused to submit it to a vote. For, he declared, the procedure involved had already been established by Articles 77 and 78 adopted on May 8.[12] In all, the Social-Democrats presented, or participated in the presentation of fourteen interpellations to the duma, and they were ever on the alert for new material which filtered into their headquarters in the mass of petitions and instructions from all parts of the empire.[13]

The great majority of the interpellative statements presented by the opposition sprang from the administration's efforts to combat all forms of what it regarded as revolutionary activity. Accordingly, there appeared in the duma a number of interpellations involving field-courts-martial, complaints against violations of civil liberties, charges of government interference in labor disputes on the side of the employers, and, finally, attacks on the political prison system.

9. *Protokoly*, pp. 158–159; *Tovarishch*, March 18, p. 4.
10. See above p. 96.
11. *Stenog. ot.*, I, 1,929, 1,930, 1,975.
12. *Ibid.*, II, 347–348, 355.
13. The authorship of the various interpellations is not always clear. Participation of the Social-Democrats in fourteen statements was established definitely when signatures of the authors were published, or by information given during the debates.

It was an interpellation of the last-mentioned category which, with one exception,[14] held the interest of the duma and the population more than any other. And the consideration by the duma of interpellation "number five" concerning the "riot" in the central prison at Riga and the system of torture applied there illustrates with striking clarity the procedure followed in such discussions, the clash of policy among the opposition groups, and the attitude of the administration toward accusatory statements. This interpellation, moreover, involved, in part, the volatile question of terror.

The interpellation was evoked by a riot which broke out in the prison on the morning of March 31, 1907, when a scuffle occurred between political prisoners and a guard, Sokolov by name. The latter was overcome, as were soldiers guarding the corridors. But other soldiers, attracted from the outside by the din, fired into a group of fleeing prisoners. The press reported that on the arrival of the warden, Colonel Ernst, with an armed guard, other prisoners were shot in their cells, and that all were removed from one cell whither some of the prisoners involved in the attack had fled, and executed as they emerged. The prison administration regarded the affair as an attempt at flight. As a result of the incident seven were killed and seventeen wounded, while, at the moment, sixty prisoners awaited trial.[15]

On April 2, fearing that the prisoners would be given over to field-courts-martial, the Social-Democratic fraction presented an urgent interpellation. This statement declared that the clash had occurred as a result of the unbearable prison régime and the system of torture to which the prisoners were subjected by the police in their efforts to extract information on underground political

14. The interpellation on the police raid on the S-D headquarters is referred to here. See Chapter XIV.

15. *Tovarishch*, May 27, p. 1; Report of the Committee on Interpellations, April 10, 1907, in *Stenog. ot.*, I, 1895–1896. See below p. 249.

activities. Further, it expressed the fear that the prisoners being held for the incident would be executed by field-courts-martial without trial. The authors wished to know what measures the administration intended to take to abolish torture and provocation in prisons, and what measures it had already taken to investigate the facts and prevent the execution of the innocent.[16]

Debates on the urgency of the interpellation began on April 3, when Rodichev expressed the Kadet point of view. He called for care in composing the interpellation. He explained that the slightest error, as, for example, directing it to the wrong ministry, would simply merit a reply that it was incorrectly formulated. He did not believe that the interpellation involved a matter of life or death and declared that since the government would take advantage of the thirty days allowed it before it should reply, a few days made little difference. He asked that the statement be given to the Committee on Interpellations for careful editing.[17]

The Social-Democrats held the opposite view. Ozol of Riga replied that a matter of life or death was, in fact, involved since the sixty prisoners held would be tried by a field-court-martial and the committee might report after the executions had already taken place. He believed that the formulation of the interpellation was correct, and that it had been rightly addressed to the council of ministers since the entire government was involved in the case.[18] Dzhaparidze added that at the moment the duma dare not be guided by formal considerations; editorial errors were easy to correct.[19]

At this juncture Kuzmin-Karavaev (Democratic Reform) caused a sensation by announcing that he had wired the governor-general of the Baltic Region, Meller-Zakomelskii, asking that he spare the lives of the prisoners. He

16. *Stenog. ot.*, I, 1,475–1,476, 1,549, 1,562; *Riech*, April 4, p. 1, Duma Sup.
17. *Stenog. ot.*, I, 1542–1544.
18. *Ibid.*, pp. 1,544–1,546.
19. *Ibid.*, pp. 1,549–1,550.

informed the duma that he had just received a telegraphic reply in which the governor declared that there was as yet no cause for binding anyone over to field-courts-martial. Consequently, Kuzmin-Karavaev saw no need for urgency in the matter.[20] The Social-Democrats hastened to counteract the impression created by this announcement. Aleksinskii read a wire from the "progressive voters of Riga" which held that fifty-six prisoners had already been bound over to military courts.[21] And Ozol pleaded with the duma to disregard the governor-general's telegram since he might turn the prisoners over to the temporary courts-martial which were as deadly as the other military courts. Moreover, the matter of tortures had yet to be looked into.[22]

But Aleksinskii's statement caused some consternation among the Mensheviki. They called a fraction conference during the session and agreed that it might be difficult to prove that the "voters' " telegram was correct. To stand by it, therefore, after having practically given the lie to the government might place the fraction's dignity in great jeopardy. Therefore, they decided that the only proper solution was the withdrawal of the urgency of the interpellation.[23] Although he was subjected to a torrent of reproach from the Bolsheviki, Tsereteli arose to inform the amazed duma that the Social-Democrats had come to the conclusion that Meller-Zakomelskii's reply had to be taken into account and that they would therefore withdraw the urgency of their proposal.[24]

20. *Ibid.*, pp. 1,550–1,551.

21. *Ibid.*, pp. 1,551–1,552.

22. *Ibid.*, pp. 1,553–1,554. The Social-Democratic arguments were followed by a provocative outburst from the right in the form of a statement by Shulgin, who asked whether those who talked of saving others could openly say that they had no bombs in their pockets. Immediately there were loud demands for his expulsion, and at the advice of Vice-President Poznanskii who was then in the chair, a proposal to that effect was presented. Despite profuse apologies and an explanation that he meant no one present, the duma voted to expel Shulgin for a single session. *Ibid.*, pp. 1,554, 1,562, 1,563.

23. *Protokoly*, pp. 158–159.

24. *Ibid.; Stenog. ot.*, I, 1,561–1,562.

As non-urgent, the interpellation was now subject to examination and verification by the committee. This body reviewed it on April 4, and decided to generalize the statement since it had come to the conclusion that beating of political prisoners was an habitual part of the imperial prison system. It also drew up a report of its investigation and edited the interpellation.[25]

On April 10, Pergament (Kadet) mounted the tribune to deliver the committee's findings, and told a tale so horrible as to be hardly credible had it not emanated from so high a source.[26] He informed the duma that the committee's investigation had clearly established that the interpellation was based on factual evidence; that a system of brutal treatment of political prisoners prevailed throughout the Baltic Region, not only in prisons but also in jails, precinct stations, and detective headquarters. He reported that when punitive expeditions were sent to the Baltic in 1905–1906,[27] the police, especially the detective departments, simultaneously adopted a system of fearful tortures to extract evidence from political prisoners so as to enable the government to execute those suspected of revolutionary activity. At the end of 1905, he declared, a "committee" had been created by the Riga detective department which included such high officials as the chief of the detective bureau and an assistant captain. According to its own statement, the governor, the prosecutor, and the gendarme administration had empowered the "committee" to examine political prisoners and execute them without trial.

He then launched into a description of what he termed the "Riga museum of horrors" through which, he declared, many political prisoners had passed. The picture

25. *Stenog. ot.*, I, 1,757; *Riech*, April 5, p. 3; April 10, p. 3, Duma Sup.

26. *Stenog. ot.*, I, 1,879–1,898. O. I. Pergament was born in Odessa in 1869. He was graduated from the mathematical faculty of Novorosiisk University in 1891 and then entered the legal faculty. He gained great renown as a criminal lawyer and participated in numerous political trials.

27. These were despatched by Durnovo following uprisings in December, 1905. See B. Pares, *History of Russia*, pp. 436–437.

he painted recalled the inquisition, and the torture chambers of the despots of the Renaissance. No bone or member of the body was spared and the torments were often prolonged for eight days on end. When marks of torture became too obvious, the victims were shot on the pretext that they had attempted flight. Pergament declared that since the appointment of Meller-Zakomelskii as governor-general these tortures had been applied with increasing frequency but the government had carefully concealed them from public view.

He maintained that normal prison conditions were equally dreadful. For months political prisoners were deprived of books, correspondence, and exercise in an attempt to isolate them. In that time they lived on bread and water in dank, dark cells, and waited for months in overfilled jails for investigation and trial, sometimes without even knowing the charges on which they had been arrested. The mockery and brutality practiced upon the prisoners by the guards and prison administration were more than enough to provoke them to extreme actions. The Riga Central Prison, Pergament noted, had already been the scene of several bloody outbreaks.

As for the events of March 31, the committee had discovered that the riot ensued when the guard Sokolov struck a prisoner whom he was conducting with others to the washroom. The latter defended himself. Soldiers in the corridor called by the guards were overcome and their guns taken from them. Other soldiers, on hearing the noise from the outside rushed in and fired on the fleeing prisoners, killing seven of them and wounding seventeen, of whom two had already died.

In closing, he declared that the Committee on Interpellations hardly needed to prove the illegality of the measures described. These, he observed, were definitely criminal under Article 345 of the Statute on Punishments,[28] which subjected to imprisonment any official who inflicted

28. *Svod zakonov rossiiskii imperii*, statutes on Punishments, XV, 87.

cruelties while performing his duty. He made no claim
for the infallibility of the committee's material, but
pleaded with the ministers of the interior and justice—
to whom the interpellation had been directed—not to avail
themselves of the month allowed them but to calm the
people's representatives by replying immediately.

It was now the administration's turn to speak. And its
representatives assumed an uncompromising, defensive
attitude which typified all government replies to the
charges hurled against it. Assistant Minister of the Interior Makarov was most moderate. He declared that an
investigation conducted by the government in the Baltic
prisons revealed that although some violence had been
resorted to, press reports concerning it were highly exaggerated. He could not justify this policy but held that it
was highly understandable in view of the fact that the
police had lost many comrades in their struggle with the
revolutionaries. He informed the duma that Meller-Zakomelskii was already investigating the matter and would
bring it into a court which would also verify the sources of
the committee's report.[29] Assistant Minister of Justice
Liutze was more unyielding. He called Pergament's report
unlikely. The soldiers in Riga had killed in self-defense
and evidence on hand made it clear that an escape had
been anticipated.[30] In a word, the committee had been
entirely misinformed. The government could regard interpellations only as malicious and provocative statements
and did its utmost to disprove them.

The debates at the following session were scarcely calculated to enhance the dignity of the duma as the Social-
Revolutionaries and Social-Democrats on the one hand,
and the Monarchists on the other, matched imprecations
and insinuations. They wandered in and about the subject
under consideration, and their orations were accompanied
by roars, hisses, and whistles; especially from the right.[31]

29. *Stenog. ot.*, I, 1,900–1,901.
30. *Ibid.*, pp. 1,902–1,904; *Riech*, April 11, p. 1, Duma Sup.
31. *Riech*, May 14, p. 1, Duma Sup.

The Social-Democrats reverted to their old demand for a committee to investigate the matter on the spot. And despite the adoption of the Kadet resolution to examine the affair in the Interpellations Committee, they persisted in pointing out the advantages of their proposal.[32] They charged the government with resorting to a medieval judicial procedure which the civilized world had long since abandoned; a procedure which made criminals of its agents. They charged the deputies on the right with identifying themselves with the police, and expressed the hope that by adopting the interpellation the duma would make it clear to western bankers that they were supporting a torture machine with their loans to Russia. When Minister of Justice Shcheglovitov demanded the sources of the committee's information,[33] they replied that they had used letters from the victims, court records, and testimony given by state institutions. But they were careful to add that a local investigating committee would reveal these sources, and might also discover the legal grounds on which field-court-martial executions were carried out.[34]

The temper of the committee's report and that of the duma majority during the discussion left little doubt concerning the outcome of the debates despite the bitter tirades from the extremes. The duma adopted the committee's edition of the interpellation, and by a decisive majority decided to ask the chairman of the council of ministers if he intended to remove from their posts those accused of torturing prisoners in Riga before the investigation into the affair should begin in order to avoid a repetition of the resort to brutalities.[35]

There the question rested until May 17, when the government offered a reply. Minister of Justice Shcheglovitov declared that he would answer the charges that tortures had been applied during investigations of revolu-

32. *Stenog. ot.*, I, 1,977, 1,977–1,978, 1,980.
33. *Ibid.*, p. 2,047.
34. *Ibid.*, pp. 2,025, 2,044–2,047, 2,050–2,052, 2,052–2,056, 2,066–2,068.
35. *Ibid.*, pp. 2,079, 2,080.

tionary activities with the knowledge and consent of the
Riga district prosecutor, and that he, together with the
gendarme administration, had empowered a special committee to examine political prisoners. According to an investigation undertaken by the Senate, he asserted, all of
these charges were disproved. The alleged committee had
never been created, and the prosecutor had never attended
an investigation of the detective department. Nor had he
ever ordered an investigation of "politicals." He had simply prosecuted revolutionaries with especial energy and
for this he deserved high praise. The minister publicly
protested against the committee's report. Moreover, he
informed the duma, the Senate's investigation completely
exonerated the prison administration and guards from
any illegal activity with which they were charged. No
one had been executed illegally, and none without cause.[36]
In short, the minister would accept information from governmental sources only and regarded others as hardly
meriting consideration. His every assertion was corrobo-
rated, according to Assistant Minister Makarov, by a
special investigation of the ministry of the interior. Some
violence had been admitted by the chairman of the Riga
field-court-martial, and it was being investigated. It was
unfortunate, he declared, but explicable in view of the
behavior of the revolutionaries.[37]

"Dear sirs, we do not believe you," declared Social-
Democrat A. A. Kuznetsov,[38] and thereby sounded the
keynote of the resentful oratory which followed the government's statements. The opposition flatly challenged
every assertion of the administration. But having heard
the replies from the various ministries the duma could do
little more than register its opinion of the government's
attitude in a formula of passage to the regular order. But

36. *Stenog. ot.*, II, 685–692.
37. *Ibid.*, pp. 602–700. In their struggle with the revolutionaries, Makarov
declared, the police had lost 153 comrades in the Baltic Region and 214 of their
number were wounded. Moreover, they had to cope incessantly with riots,
explosions, and assassinations.
38. *Ibid.*, pp. 732–735.

on the form which this statement was to take there were many opinions. No less than eight formulae were presented.[39] The Social-Democrats, representing the extreme point of view, would openly condemn the government. It had admitted the use of violence in investigations. Members of the prosecutor's staff had witnessed the application of tortures. Testimony of witnesses gathered by the government could not have been impartial. And, finally, events revealed in the Baltic Region were only a part of a system prevalent in all Russia. Therefore, the Social-Democrats felt that the explanations offered by the administration were not worthy of the duma's confidence, and that only a duma committee investigating on the spot could discover the truth.[40] The Kadets, striving, as usual, to avoid a clash with the government, and to appear as impartial and conciliatory as possible, condemned illegal police activities revealed by Makarov's statement. But they also scored murders and crimes frequently committed in the Baltic Region.[41] The formula of the Popular-Socialists attracted attention because of the singularity of its purpose. They would simply state that the explanation was unsatisfactory.[42] As Demianov explained, they had in mind Article 60 of the Duma Statute which ruled that if two-thirds of the duma declared an explanation given by the government to be unsatisfactory, its decision was to be examined first by the Imperial Council, and then by the tsar. In this manner the duma might learn of his Majesty's attitude toward the representative body.[43] This formula was immediately rejected, and the Popular-Socialists, in turn, voted down all other opposition formulae as they were presented and defeated one after the other.

A brief recess was called, and when the duma reassem-

39. *Ibid.*, pp. 765–768.
40. *Ibid.*, pp. 766–767.
41. *Ibid.*, pp. 767–768.
42. *Ibid.*, pp. 765, 727–728.
43. *Ibid.*, pp. 765–768.

bled the Trudoviki presented a new, simplified statement
on which all opposition groups might agree. It declared
that since the explanations of the ministers of the interior
and justice had clearly established the existence of illegal
police activities in the Baltic Region, the duma passed to
the regular order. To this the Social-Democrats would add
the words of the Popular-Socialist formula: "acknowledging the explanations of the ministers unsatisfactory." [44]
Here was a direct, militant challenge to the government,
and the Kadets sought strenuously to prevent its adoption.
Maklakov observed that the duma had already rejected
both the Trudovik formula and the Social-Democratic
amendment. The Committee on Rules, he declared, was
about to decide on the order to be adopted should all formulae for passage to the regular order be rejected. But
he was certain that no one in the committee believed that
it was permissible to present a new formula after all had
been set aside. The committee would soon recommend that
in such a case the duma was simply to turn to the next
question on the agenda. It was not necessary that a formula of passage be adopted since it was only a medium
favored by the duma for expressing its opinions.[45] But
when the duma voted to consider the new formula, the
Kadets announced that they would abstain since they believed that the deputies were following an irregular order,
and the remainder of the opposition majority adopted
both Trudovik and Social-Democratic proposals.[46]

Social-Democratic tactics were on this occasion crowned
with success. The horrors of the prison system were widely
publicized and the government was rebuked. But at the
same time the disunity of the opposition majority had
again been clearly revealed to all who would exploit it.
Only the revolutionary left could find a basis for agree-

44. *Ibid.*, p. 769.
45. *Ibid.*, pp. 769–771.
46. *Ibid.*, pp. 775, 776–777, 777–778. On May 21, those on trial for participation in the Riga riots were sentenced by a temporary court-martial. Eight were
executed, four received life imprisonment at hard labor, and four were to serve
for twenty years at hard labor. See *Tovarishch*, May 27, p. 1; May 29, p. 3.

ment; a dangerous sign in the eyes of an executive unified
in purpose; an executive which felt that its power over
the population was increasing rapidly, and which believed
that it might now deal with the popular representative
body as it would.

Other interpellations which attracted less popular interest followed approximately the same course. Their texts
were considerably moderated by the center. The debates
which preceded their inevitable adoption were marked by
fierce attacks on the government's "pacification" policy.
And the administration, when it deigned to reply, invariably defended its agents. The incidents involved in these
statements were often quite insignificant. But taken as a
whole the interpellations are important for the frequency
with which they were presented; that is, for their agitational rôle. Even more important is the broad picture
which they present of the grievances which the Russian
people nursed against the tsarist government.

Several examples will suffice. The ministry of justice
was addressed for a second time concerning prison conditions. On April 5, the Social-Revolutionaries complained
of the inhuman beating of several "politicals" including
Pleve's famed assailant, Sazonov, at the Siberian prison
of Algachinsk. They had been singled out as irreconcil-
ables and resisted attempts at treatment as common criminals.[47] A month later, on May 7, Shcheglovitov cleared
his subordinates of all guilt. His account of the incident
agreed essentially with that presented by the duma committee. But he denied that unnecessary violence had occurred, and he placed all of the blame on the prisoners for
their failure to submit to prison discipline.[48] The duma,
following the lead of the Kadets, simply observed that
the government had admitted the existence of brutal treatment of political prisoners.[49]

As the party of the proletariat it was to be expected

47. *Stenog. ot.*, I, 1,602, 1,667, and 1,603, 1,667–1,669.
48. *Ibid.*, II, 253–259.
49. *Ibid.*, p. 286.

that the Social-Democratic fraction would introduce a number of interpellations concerning the government's interference in the struggle between capital and labor. One, presented as urgent on April 2, informed the duma that gendarme General Taube had been sent to Baku where a merchant-marine strike was in progress, and was empowered to take "energetic measures" to restore order. The authors of the statement, fearing that Taube would use his authority to break the strike, demanded that the government inform the duma of the exact powers granted the general, and give specific reasons for interfering in a peaceful situation.[50] When the Kadets observed that no illegal activity had been charged, the duma rejected the urgency of the statement.[51] The committee and duma then limited the interpellation to a request that the administration elucidate on the "special powers" granted Taube. But the government chose to ignore the matter entirely, despite the requirements of the Fundamental Laws.[52] Again, the ministry of the interior was interpellated on April 12, soon after the brutal clubbing administered by the gendarmerie to the workers of the Chesher woolen mills in St. Petersburg. These had gathered in the factory yard to discuss a wage reduction with the management. The latter called for the police who acted with apparently very little provocation. Punishment of those responsible was demanded by the interpellation, as well as measures to prevent a repetition of that sort of incident.[53] Its urgency was voted in the face of Kadet objections, for the incident had deeply stirred the deputies and the people of St. Petersburg.[54] But popular excitement soon diminished, and the government did not find it necessary to reply.

50. *Riech*, March 29, p. 2; *Tovarishch*, March 30, p. 3; April 1, p. 5; *Stenog ot.*, I, 1,477.
51. *Stenog. ot.*, I, 1,570–1,571, 1,578.
52. *Riech*, April 5, p. 3; *Stenog. ot.*, I, 1,711.
53. *Tovarishch*, April 12, p. 5; April 4, p. 2; *Stenog. ot.*, I, 1,983–1,985.
54. *Stenog. ot.*, I, 1,987–1,988. As was often the case the Kolo's vote was decisive in this matter. *Ibid.*, pp. 1,994–1,997; *Riech*, April 13, p. 1, Duma Sup.

The greatest number of interpellations dealt not especially with economic oppression but with violations of civil liberties in general. The slightest symptom of popular unrest, the least resistance to authority, civil or military, quickly brought a punitive expedition to the locality, or the immediate arrest and prosecution of individuals. And in those localities where various states of martial law had been declared following the upheaval of 1905, violation of civil rights and establishment of arbitrary judicial procedure were not infrequent occurrences. It is not strange, therefore, that the popular representative body was, as we have already seen, the recipient of countless complaints concerning major or petty oppression on the part of local satraps. Some incidents threatening the security or economic welfare of large populations, or involving exceptionally brazen violations of liberty and justice were brought to the attention of the government and public in the form of interpellations. Thus, when the little Caucasian village of Lanchukhti was visited by a cavalry detachment and threatened with a fine of 45,000 rubles, the duma adopted a Social-Democratic statement on April 6, questioning the minister of the interior concerning the reasons for the burdensome levy.[55] On May 24, the State-Secretary Baron E. I. Nolde replied that a cavalry detachment in search of hidden recruits had, indeed, illegally posted itself on the village for one night. That would be thoroughly investigated. He explained, however, that the village had been fined some 47,000 rubles for illegal woodcutting and if it defaulted the matter would be reviewed by regular judicial institutions. At any rate, he assured the duma, no bloody fate or economic disaster awaited Lanchukhti.[56] Although the Social-Democrats continued to maintain that the village was really threatened with physical violence and ruin, and wished to condemn the government's policy, Nolde had made some impression and Kadet moderation prevailed, for the duma adopted

55. *Stenog. ot.*, I, 1,478, 1,583, 1,584; *Riech*, April 5, p. 3.
56. *Stenog. ot.*, II, 1,077–1,079.

a simple statement of passage to the regular order.[57] A similar interpellation charged Governor-General Meller-Zakomelskii with illegally fining two Estish *volosts* 3,000 rubles each for the failure of their populations to apprehend the murderer of the Baltic Baron Stenghausen, member of the Imperial Council. Since the statement was presented on May 15, and the government might avail itself of a period of thirty days before replying, the duma had not yet received a response when dissolution overtook it.[58]

Spectacular violations of individual rights likewise provided the duma with significant and useful material for interpellations. With other leftist deputies to the number of 131 the Social-Democrats joined in presenting an interpellation about an apparently calculated violation of the freedom of opinion guaranteed in Article 14 of the Duma Statute. For the Holy Synod had issued a decree on May 12 prohibiting five leftist deputy-priests from adhering to the parties of their choice, and the duma angrily protested the act three days later.[59] But the statement was submitted too late for a reply. Finally, the duma protested against the perversion of even military justice in the case of the brothers Kablov and Tarakanov. The four Muscovites had been sentenced to an unlimited term at hard labor on May 28, 1906, for wounding a policeman. But on the same day Governor-General Gershelmann, exceeding his legal authority, had annulled the decision and set up a new court which ordered the execution of the accused for the death of the same officer. The sentence was carried out immediately. On April 3, the duma demanded an investigation of the general's behavior.[60] On April 30, the ministers of war and justice appeared

57. *Ibid.*, pp. 1,079–1,084, 1,097, 1,098.

58. *Ibid.*, I, 1,755–1,756; II, 594; *Ukazatel*, pp. 310–311.

59. *Stenog. ot.*, II, 594–596. The clergymen involved were Arkhipov (Trudovik), Brilliantov (S-R), Grinevich (Trud.), Kolokolnikov (left non-part.), and Tikhvinskii (Trud.). *Ibid.*, p. 596; *Ukazatel*, pp. 312–313.

60. *Stenog. ot.*, I, 1,470–1,472, 1,592; *Pol. sob. zak.*, XXVI, no. 28,252, especially Article 5.

as apologists for the government. Both maintained, amid
jeers from the opposition, that no law had been violated
but that the first court had been improperly convened and
had incorrectly accused the prisoners of wounding an officer, while the second had been properly called, according
to military regulations, and had accused the brothers of
their real crime—the murder of the policeman.[61] In reply
the entire opposition roundly scored the court-martial
system in general and adopted a formula of passage to
the regular order which observed that the governor-general had exceeded his authority and had thereby violated
the law.[62] The duma branded as illegal an act which the
government condoned and defended.

Thus, for the most part, the Social-Democratic tactics
in dealing with interpellations were successful. The First
Duma had demonstrated their value as propaganda, and
in the Second, the Marxists eagerly seized upon them as
means of emphasizing the despotic and tyrannical character of the government. And they strenuously opposed
the Kadet tactics of directing them to the Committee on
Interpellations where their tone might be softened. They
deplored the formal grounds on which the Kadets acted,
and charged them with forgetting the interests of the
population. Their own interpellations were often carelessly
written for they reckoned little with the government's
reaction to them. A refusal to reply on formal grounds,
it seemed to them, would serve to prove that the administration was evasive in the face of concrete charges, and
they rather expected that it would defend its agents. It
was enough for them that the duma focused the attention

61. *Stenog. ot.*, I, 2,294–2,296, 2,306–2,307.
62. See addresses by Kadets Maklakov and Gessen, *Ibid.*, pp. 2,297–2,305
and 2,318–2,321; by S-D's Mitrov and Serebriakov, *Ibid.*, pp. 2,321–2,322 and
2,336–2,337. For formula see *Ibid.*, pp. 2,338, 2,342. Article 5 of the field-court-
martial law forbade appeals from the sentences of these courts. And within two
months after the publication of the law Stolypin explained (Oct. 12, 1906) that
it was forbidden to abrogate a field-court-martial sentence and, consequently,
to have it reviewed by a second military court. See *Pol. sob. zak.*, XXVI, no.
28,252; A. I. Kaminka, *Vtoraia gosudarstvennaia duma*, p. 246.

of the country on one arbitrary act or another, and expressed its dissatisfaction with the administration's policy.

On its part, the government regarded interpellations as a provocative weapon of the revolutionary left employed to arouse the population against it. It saw in them no real desire to control wayward officials. Therefore, the ministers usually questioned the veracity of the charges made against their subordinates, and were at great pains to defend them. The use which the duma made of interpellations only increased the distrust for that body in governing circles as an irresponsible and revolutionary organ. Such sallies as that precipitated by the interpellation on the Riga tortures in which the entire opposition participated, and revealed its disunity, only hastened the day of dissolution.

XII

POLITICAL TERROR

O N March 9, 1907, forty-four Kadet deputies introduced a bill, accompanied by an explanatory note, which called for the abrogation of the law of August 19, 1906.[1] Introduced under Article 87 of the Fundamental Laws, this statute provided for the creation of field-courts-martial, the most terrible of the repressive instruments devised by Stolypin in his struggle with the revolutionary movement. According to this law, in all localities declared to be under martial law, civilians whose guilt in the perpetration of a crime was evident were to be bound over to a court-martial composed of a chairman and four officers. These courts were to be established at the request of the chief civil or military official of a city or province. The accused were to be tried within twenty-four hours of their apprehension, and sentence was to be passed no later than forty-eight hours after the court had convened. The proceedings were to be entirely secret, and the sentence was to be executed within twenty-four hours after its pronouncement.[2]

Aside from the natural fear which they inspired, these courts were met with general contempt and loathing because they were so flagrantly opposed to the liberal spirit which had by now become an intrinsic part of Russian public opinion. Moreover, in giving justice into the hands of local military officials, Stolypin had obviously contradicted his oft-repeated statement that he strove ever to end the rule of bureaucrats.[3] And, as the explanatory note accompanying the Kadet bill pointed out, these military

1. *Stenog. ot.*, I, 269; *Zak. za.*, pp. 16–20 (text); *Riech*, March 10, p. 4, Duma Sup.
2. *Pol. sob. zak.*, XXVI, no. 28,252.
3. See above pp. 21–23.

men were inexperienced in juridical matters and would make gross judicial errors which not even practiced jurists could always avoid. The Kadets, and with them enlightened public opinion, were convinced that these courts aimed only to crush the revolution by terrorizing the population, and that they were an anachronism when viewed in the light of modern judicial procedure.

According to information derived from six major St. Petersburg newspapers, from the day of their institution until they were abolished on April 20, 1907, the field-courts-martial sentenced to death and executed 1,102 persons in all Russia. They sentenced 127 to hard labor, 7 to exile, and acquitted 71. To this there may be added the record of the naval-courts-martial which executed 42, sentenced 202 to hard labor, and jailed 443; all under the general charge of uprising.[4]

The charges on which these military courts acted were numerous. For acts of political terrorism 459 were executed; 382 for attacks on state and private property including peasant-mob violence; 84 for agrarian murders, and 41 for other crimes. The Baltic provinces with 324 executions and Poland with 212, the Caucasus with 195, and the province of Ekaterinoslav had suffered most from the establishment of extraordinary courts.[5] In these regions the uprisings had been particularly fierce for they were widely affected by the industrial and agricultural depression. Moreover, the situation was complicated by strong nationalist movements among the native populations in Poland and the Caucasus, and in the Baltic Region with its feudal German barons, who exploited a Lettish and Esthonian peasantry. In general, these courts were most active until the end of January, 1907.

In introducing their bill to abrogate the law on field-

4. *Novoe Vremia, Birzheviye Viedemosti, Strana, Riech*, and *Tovarishch*. These statistics were compiled by A. B. Ventin of the *Tovarishch* staff from monthly reports compiled, in turn, from the daily issues of these papers. For monthly lists see *Tovarishch* for Jan. 17, pp. 5–6; Feb. 20, p. 3; March 3, p. 5; April 3, p. 3; April 20, p. 3. See also *Byloe*, Feb., 1907, pp. 70–81.

5. *Tovarishch*, April 29, p. 3.

courts-martial the Kadets had a double purpose in mind. First, it would obviously put an end to further needless killing. Then, since the law would automatically lose its force on April 20, as the government had not yet requested its prolongation,[6] the Kadets would test the administration. They would discover whether or not it would show a desire to coöperate with the duma by proclaiming that it was prepared to abandon this measure before it should legally expire. From the Kadet point of view the government would then have taken a great stride toward the re-establishment of a more normal political and social life.[7]

To the Social-Democrats the Kadet action appeared as an attempt to prove their liberalism and to disprove rumors to the effect that they were, or hoped to be, a "governmental" party, and that they were forsaking the opposition. The Marxists believed that these efforts were especially necessary after the government had sided with the liberal views on the famine-relief question. Nevertheless, they realized the significance of the move, and even agreed to the removal of the debates on unemployment from the agenda to make way for an immediate discussion of the Kadet bill.[8]

Consideration of the measure was begun on March 22, and with only the right opposing, the duma decided to examine the bill immediately.[9] A long and bitter debate followed which occupied the duma for the greater part of two sessions. The list of those who signified a desire to speak grew rapidly, but any attempt to close registration was resolutely fought, as in the agrarian debates, by the combined action of the right and the extreme left.[10] The

6. Bills introduced under Article 87 were to lose their force automatically if the government did not ask for their prolongation within two months after the duma convened: that is, by April 20, in the case of the Second Duma.

7. P. Miliukov, *Vtoraia duma*, p. 86; M. Mikhailovskii, *Dieiatelnost sotsial-demokraticheskoi fraktsii*, pp. 16, 19–20.

8. *Protokoly*, p. 156; *Ternii bez roz*, p. 57.

9. *Stenog. ot.*, I, 254, 358.

10. *Ibid.*, p. 377; *Riech*, March 13, p. 1.

Marxists demanded unrestrained expression of popular hatred for this most flagrant example of tsarist tyranny. The right, on the other hand, would just as ardently defend the military courts and prove that the duma was revolutionary.

The Kadets repeated the arguments presented in the explanatory note. V. M. Gessen appealed to the duma to value every moment for the sake of the lives involved, even though field-courts-martial would cease to exist in a month.[11] Maklakov warned the administration that although it might destroy revolution by means of extraordinary courts, it simultaneously undermined the elementary principles of government, and that they would ultimately act as a boomerang to ruin the state.[12] Kuzmin-Karavaev (Democratic-Reform) would amend the Kadet proposal with two articles. One provided that all field-court-martial sentences not yet executed were not to be carried out, and according to the second, all such sentences and cases pending were to be turned over to the regular, civil courts.[13]

The right, which had come to regard these courts, somewhat hysterically, as the bulwark of their interests after the nightmare of revolution, vigorously attacked the Kadet proposal. In their opinion, the courts were a necessary evil. Shulgin was surprisingly frank. When regular courts had failed extraordinary courts were always a measure of last resort; especially in a period of revolutionary upheaval. He believed that their greatest advantage lay in the fact that the punishment immediately followed the crime. "One throws a bomb today, tomorrow he hangs so that he will not throw one on the following day."[14] Krushevan generously admitted that all cultured people who were raised in the literary tradition of Europe and Russia favored the abolition of field-courts-martial. But

11. *Stenog. ot.*, I, 359–362.
12. *Ibid.*, pp. 385–392.
13. *Ibid.*, p. 269.
14. *Ibid.*, p. 373.

he demanded that before their removal the duma should first openly condemn the crimes they were meant to crush. Moreover, he was willing to vote for their abolition if only to allow the peasants to reckon with greedy middlemen, mainly Jews, whom he asserted overcharged for land and controlled the press in order to screen their acts from the public.[15] Purishkevich delivered an historical discourse on the death penalty in England and concluded that capital punishment was merited there by crimes for which the duma would not apply it in Russia. The left, he declared, might call those representatives of law and order on the right "murderers" and point to Hertsenstein. But he contended that there were also murderers on the left since the program of the Social-Revolutionary Party called for active political terror.[16] And on the following day the right took up Krushevan's proposal and more insistently than before demanded that the duma condemn political murders before it abolish courts-martial.[17] To this Shingarev (Kadet) replied that the duma had sworn to improve conditions of life by legislation; but it was not a public meeting, and was not bound to present resolutions consisting of "sorry words."[18]

L. F. Gerus presented the Social-Democratic point of view.[19] He contended that by their own arguments from foreign sources rightist orators had refuted their own statements. It was true that terrible laws existed in Western Europe, but they were introduced not by the long-suffering population but by the upper classes. These laws, he maintained, were directed against the natural tendencies of the oppressed masses in their quest for a bit of bread. In a word, the right was defending laws which pro-

15. *Ibid.*, pp. 377–379.
16. *Ibid.*, pp. 379–383.
17. *Ibid.*, pp. 446–447, 469–477.
18. *Ibid.*, pp. 477–480. For the development of the Kadet idea see below pp. 271–272.
19. *Stenog. ot.*, I, 417–420. L. F. Gerus was born in Kuban in 1876. He received a secondary education and became a public school teacher. He joined the S-D Party in 1905 and during the Revolution was active in Ekaterindodar. He was elected as a Menshevik from Kuban.

tected only the interests of the great landowners. In Russia it was not the peasantry who called for field-courts-martial, but the nobility. Furthermore, he contended, the courts did not pacify revolution, but provoked it. Terroristic acts were inevitable when the government hindered the development of the revolutionary struggle along cultural lines. Not by force, but by reforms alone could the people be pacified. Gerus declared that the Social-Democrats fully supported both the Kadet bill and Kuzmin-Karavaev's amendment. But they would go even further. They would propose that the binding over of civilians to a court-martial be forbidden even under extraordinary laws. But with all of this legislation, the Social-Democrats believed that the cruelties to which Russia was being subjected would be abolished only when the political power passed from the hands of the ruling classes to those of the people.

Aleksinskii replied to all arguments presented by the right.[20] He agreed with Shulgin that field-courts-martial were a weapon against revolution and terror. But he refused to place terroristic acts and field-courts-martial sentences in the same category. The latter, he argued, were carried out not by the courts themselves, but by officers troops, prosecutors, and priests, while terrorist committees executed their own orders. He attacked Bishop Evlogii for classing all murder alike from the Christian point of view. To Aleksinskii that was equivalent to placing the people's executioners and their champions on the same level. He informed the duma that his party was opposed to terror and reminded it that when the First Duma was convened, even the Social-Revolutionaries had abandoned violence in the hope that they might attain their ends by parliamentary means. They had resumed their struggle only after the First Duma had been driven out. They had replied with terror from below to terroristic acts from above. He referred to the readiness of the right to take all that was obnoxious and dastardly from the

20. *Stenog. ot.*, I, 460–469.

West. If they were told that these countries cherished inviolability of person and democracy they immediately replied that these were incompatible with the "Russian spirit." He observed that even common criminals held field-courts-martial in contempt; these same courts which the right, influenced by the high ideals of "European and Russian literature," regarded as only slight divergences from the regular judicial procedure. The "cultured" Krushevan he charged with designing to exterminate the duma, Jews, and the whole revolutionary population in general. And after pointing to several glaring examples of the miscarriage of justice by field-courts-martial in the Baltic region and the Caucasus, he concluded that since the government would exploit the people for the benefit of the ruling classes, the duma could not afford to leave this murderous weapon in its hands. In closing he warned the administration that dissolution of the duma would merely reveal to the people that it could rule only by force to retain its power. The Social-Democratic attitude was clear. They would not soil their hands with terroristic deeds. At the same time they absolutely refused to condemn acts of "heroism" performed by champions of the people's interests. These, they held, were driven to desperation by a reactionary administration which would go to any extremes and use any vicious weapon at hand to defend itself. Two wrongs did not make a right. But one, in their opinion, could be clearly justified.

Stolypin had appeared on the ministerial benches during the debates of March 13, and when they had ended, he arose to present the government's views on field-courts-martial.[21] He stated at once that, in his opinion, under Article 87 the duma could not abrogate the law of August 19, for it had to be cancelled automatically. Even if the order for the abrogation of permanent measures were followed, the process could not be completed until April 12, a month after the introduction of a statement similar to one presented on the preceding day. He fully understood,

21. *Ibid.*, pp. 512–517; *Riech*, March 14, p. 1.

he said, that the duma was anxious to learn the government's attitude. He would not reply to attacks on the administration charging it with having violated the law since these were groundless. Rather, he would consider attacks on the nature of the law; that it was shameful and threatened the very foundations of the empire. But the government had to regard the matter differently. When a state was in danger, he cried, it had to adopt the most exceptional measures to defend itself from attack, for that was the universal law of self-preservation. "When a house is burning you smash the doors, you smash the windows," and when a man was dangerously ill it was often necessary to cure him with a dose of poison. He admitted that the defense measures led to repression, even to dictatorship. But he contended that a dictator had often saved a state from danger, and that there were moments in the life of a state when its needs stood higher than the law. Yet, he explained, he had never regarded these exceptional measures as anything more than temporary. As for the future, he contended that the measure could not be given up immediately because the bloody ferment still persisted. If given a free hand, he maintained that the Social-Democrats would undermine the allegiance of the army, and establish a democratic republic, while the Social-Revolutionaries would urge terror and uprising. Under these circumstances the government could not afford to take a demonstrative step. In closing, he called on the duma to end the terroristic madness, and he likened the "bloody" hands of the government to those of a conscientious surgeon who would resort to extraordinary means to cure a very sick patient.

The Kadets had beckoned, but the government had refused to meet them half way, and their disappointment was voiced by V. M. Gessen.[22] He declared that it was

22. *Stenog. ot.*, I, 517–524. V. M. Gessen was born in Odessa in 1868. He was educated at Novorosiisk University where he taught law from 1894–1896. In the latter year he began to lecture in the St. Petersburg University, at the Alexander Lyceum, the Polytechnical Institute, and in the Higher Courses for Women. He was also an editor of several legal journals including *Prava* (Law), and was one of the founders and leaders of the Kadet Party.

precisely for the pacification which Stolypin desired that the Kadets had introduced their bill. Further, a strong authority did not fear concessions. If Stolypin had taken half a step forward in acknowledging that field-courts-martial should not be applied, he should now take a full stride with the duma and abolish them.

Yet, despite Stolypin's irrevocable statement, the duma voted to create a committee which was to report out a measure on the abolition of field-courts-martial.[23] On April 9, this body decided to present the Kadet bill along with Kuzmin-Karavaev's amendment. And on April 17, the duma was urged to consider the committee's proposal out of the regular order. Kuzmin-Karavaev held that immediate action was necessary to forestall the presentation of a bill by the government before April 20, which would prolong the existence of the courts.[24] He would also prevent the government from attempting to delay the adoption of his amendment by regarding it as a separate measure. This the administration might well claim if the matter were to be taken up after the Easter recess. For by then (after April 20), there would be no extraordinary courts. There would then be no necessity for the Kadet measure and only the amendment would remain.[25] The duma agreed and voted to consider the project immediately.[26]

Kuzmin-Karavaev reported the matter briefly, holding that it had been thoroughly reviewed during the preliminary debates. The measure he proposed in the name of the committee asked for the abrogation of the law of August 19, 1906, and for the removal to regular judicial

23. *Ibid.*, pp. 525–526; *Riech*, March 14, p. 1. This committee was elected on March 15, but was not organized until March 31, when it chose V. M. Gessen as chairman and Shirskii (S-R) as secretary. *Riech*, April 1, p. 3.

24. See footnote 6.

25. *Riech*, April 10, p. 3; April 13, p. 4, Duma Sup.; *Stenog. ot.*, I, 2,280–2,282.

26. *Stenog. ot.*, I, 2,282. V. D. Kuzmin-Karavaev was born in Tver in 1859 of noble lineage. He received a legal and military education and from 1890 taught law in the St. Petersburg Military Academy. He was active in the liberal Tver *zemstvo*. During the Japanese War he was appointed head of the Court-Martial Committee in the Far East. He was the author of many works on criminal law and was an editor of the Brokhaus and Efron Encyclopedia.

instances of all cases being considered by the courts-martial as well as all sentences not yet carried out. The bill
was adopted unanimously.[27] But on May 7, Golovin announced that it had been rejected by the Imperial Council.[28] For the first time in the history of the Second Duma
the selective upper house was able to demonstrate its
veto power and the helplessness of the young duma in this
parliamentary system conceived by the tsarist bureaucracy. And those who regarded the duma as the best possible, and the sanest, medium for reform fully realized that
years of unhampered, progressive parliamentary activity
lay ahead before the Imperial Council should be made to
bow before public opinion as expressed in the will of the
popular representative body.

On a number of occasions heretofore we have observed
that the right entered the duma chiefly to destroy it by
proving that it was essentially a gathering and sounding
board for revolutionaries. Nowhere was this more striking than in the debates which raged around the issue of
terrorism. On March 13, in the midst of the debates on
field-courts-martial, the rightists introduced a statement
embodying their principle thesis. It declared that the
desire to abolish these courts might arise from a high and
humanitarian conviction or simply from a hope to mitigate the punishment due revolutionaries. Consequently,
in order to avoid the accusation that it was encouraging
revolution, the duma was bound, while considering field-
courts-martial, simultaneously to express its attitude toward murders perpetrated by revolutionaries. The actual
statement of condemnation was to declare that in view of
the increase in the number of political murders and ex-
propriations which resulted in the deaths of innocent victims, the duma considered it necessary to condemn all
revolutionary murders and violence.[29]

In presenting this proposal it was evident to all that

27. *Stenog. ot.*, I, 2,283–2,284, 2,284–2,285.
28. *Ibid.*, II, 199.
29. *Stenog. ot.*, I, 527.

the right had only a purely provocative purpose.[30] For despite a widespread, if suppressed, popular sympathy for terrorism, only a handful of Social-Revolutionary fanatics officially approved of assassination as a political weapon. And all parties had at one time or another publicly announced their positions or had denounced resort to terror. Liberal and revolutionary groups held that the suggestion that the duma encouraged terrorism was insulting to it. The duma's supporters maintained that the parliamentary campaign obviated terrorism.[31] But the opposition also understood that any debate on the rightist proposal in the duma would bear only evil fruits. The Kadets realized at once that should they vote to condemn terror they would identify themselves with the right and thus weaken their political position. Time and again they had maintained that to condemn political murders together with the right which was responsible for a number of assassinations would be to adopt a short-sighted policy which would only result in more murder. They regretted and opposed individual terror. But they were quick to observe that the existence of official terror in the form either of field-courts-martial or of support of the terroristic Union of the Russian People was intolerable for it threatened the very idea of organized government. Moreover, they charged that the continual wavering of the government between concessions and taking back what it had given helped to create an indefinite, chaotic situation resulting in that anarchy which the administration would have the duma condemn.[32] Then, it was felt that it would be extremely difficult to find a formula on which all could agree. Finally, a clash between the extremes was seen as inevitable, for the left, aware of the wide sympathy for terrorists, was certain to attack the measure and its authors.[33] In a word, there was a dangerous possibility

30. See Miliukov, *Vtoraia duma*, pp. 227–228; B. Pares, *Memoires*, pp. 142–143.
31. See Miliukov, *Vtoraia duma*, pp. 201–202.
32. *Ibid.*, pp. 104, 224, 230.
33. *Ibid.*, p. 228; *Stenog. ot.*, I, 527.

that if the project were discussed a majority would reject it. If not, the duma would at least reveal that it contained extreme elements guilty of the charge of encouraging and protecting terrorists. This, in turn, would reinforce the arguments of those powerful court elements who believed that the duma was not worth sparing. Consequently, the opposition, with the Kadets in the lead, squirmed and wriggled for almost the entire duration of the Second Duma, and led the proposal through a tortuous legislative career in an effort to avoid a debate on it.

On the very day of its presentation, Golovin incurred the enmity of the government on a matter of constitutional prerogative. After stating that the proposal would be printed, distributed, and placed on the program of a future session, he closed debates and allowed Kizevetter (Kadet) the floor on a personal question. The latter unexpectedly asked the chairman of the council of ministers to explain whether the adoption of such a statement of a general, ethical nature lay within the competence of the duma.[34]

Golovin immediately sensed the danger of establishing the precedent involved in Kizevetter's request. This would make the irresponsible premier a "competent" authority on the rights of the duma and would thus strengthen any claim he might make of jurisdiction over the acts of the duma. Therefore, when Stolypin asked to speak Golovin quickly tabled the request.[35] He declared, amid loud applause, that he regarded Kizevetter's question as superfluous since the only competent authorities on matters subject to the duma's consideration were the duma itself and its president. Therefore, he could not allow the chairman of the council of ministers to speak.

Stolypin was taken aback by this resolute course. He sent an angry note to Golovin on March 4, stating that according to Article 40 of the Duma Statute ministers

<hr />

34. *Stenog. ot.*, I, 528–529.

35. As noted above, Stolypin presented just such a claim later in the debate on committee experts. *Krasny Arkhiv*, XIX, 136–137; *Stenog. ot.*, I, 529.

had to be given the right to speak wherever they so desired. To this Golovin replied that Article 40 referred to explanations directly concerning questions on the agenda for the day which were under discussion. Since the question raised by Kizevetter had been removed by the president from the consideration of the duma, and was thus not being examined by it, explanations thereon could not be given. Any other interpretation, he added, would not permit the president to maintain order in the duma's affairs.[36]

When a week had passed without any action on the proposal offered by the right, Purishkevich impatiently reminded the duma thereof on March 19, and asked that it be considered as soon as possible.[37] Golovin replied that the matter would have to wait its turn and would be taken up after the more important business of the duma had been considered—such as legislation and interpellations.[38] Yet exactly a week later, the president read a statement of the right agreeing that the discussion of the proposal, scheduled for the following day, be postponed in order to allow the duma more time to prepare materials and speeches on it.[39]

The duma was greatly relieved, but in the following week, on April 2, the right again called for consideration.[40] Accordingly, when Golovin reported on April 5, that the proposal was on the order paper for the following day, the duma awaited the inevitable with great anxiety.[41] However, the same agenda contained several of the interpellations presented by the left including the Algachinsk, Lanchukhti, and Taube questions—enough cause for prolonged debates. Therefore, it was not until an hour before the end of the session that debates on interpellations were ended. Then, Kuzmin-Karavaev arose,

36. *Krasny Arkhiv*, XIX, 138–139. Golovin had closed debates. See p. 272.
37. *Stenog. ot.*, I, 791.
38. *Ibid.*, p. 792.
39. *Ibid.*, pp. 1,152–1,153.
40. *Ibid.*, p. 1,533.
41. *Ibid.*, p. 1,661; *Riech*, April 17, p. 1, Duma Sup.

the hero of the day, to propose that since the statement
of the right was of such importance it had best be postponed and discussed more fully at some future session. He
advised the duma to turn to the verification of the credentials of deputies. Bobrinskii supported the proposal, and
the duma adopted it unanimously.[42]

But when, at the following session, on April 9, the right
asked that the statement be placed first on the agenda for
the following day they found unexpected opposition. Berezin believed that the matter was not urgent and should
make way for other, more important questions. This proposal involved only a moral condemnation of political
murder, not a law forestalling such murders in the future.[43] The right raged. Krupenskii asserted that refusal
to consider the matter would mean that the duma did not
desire to act on an urgent "interpellation" of the Russian state. Purishkevich, amid indignant cries, declared
that the duma was bound to consider the proposal since
political murders continued to take place. Bobrinskii was
calmer. He maintained that it was logical that the statement was to come first in the following session, but that the
duma could, if it so desired, remove it.[44]

The Social-Democrats, too, were spoiling for a clash
on the issue of political murders. The debate would allow
them to state their position clearly and to castigate the
right and government for their brands of terror. Accordingly, Dzhaparidze declared, amid cheers from both extreme wings, that Berezin's argument was unconvincing,
and that the proposal should be placed on the agenda for
the following day. The Social-Democrats, he said, would
support a move to that effect. But the duma rejected the
motion in short order.[45]

42. *Stenog. ot.*, I, 1,714–1,715, 1,715; *Riech*, March 7, p. 1, Duma Sup.

43. *Stenog. ot.*, I, 1,826, 1,826–1,828.

44. *Ibid.*, pp. 1,828–1,829, 1,829. In proof of his statement Purishkevich informed the duma of a telegram he had just received telling of the assassination
of the chairman of the Union at Zlatoust. *Ibid.*, p. 1,830.

45. *Ibid.*, pp. 1,831, 1,837. The vote was 345 to 128. The minority consisted
of the extreme right, the Octobrists, the Social-Democrats, and some Social-

Nevertheless, the right persisted doggedly, and after being rebuffed on two further occasions,[46] the protracted struggle was finally brought to a close on May 15, when the rightist proposal was placed on the program and considered in order. But by that time the question had lost much of its original spice. The duma had already aired the matter of condemning terror in discussing field-courts-martial and the Riga tortures, and its leading proponents were, for the most part, absent. Therefore, after a brief debate, the duma refused to consider a statement denouncing political murders.[47] Further discussion of the proposal would have made little difference to the right. The main purpose of their stratagem had been achieved, for the duma had refused to consider a problem which concerned the very existence of every important bureaucrat, and thereby inevitably increased the growing displeasure among the "ruling spheres" with the popular representative body.[48]

A final measure aimed at combating revolutionary ter-

Revolutionaries. The unanimity of the Social-Democrats and the right on this matter in which they were utterly opposed was so striking that they could not avoid smiling at each other when a rising vote was taken. See *Riech*, April 10, p. 1, Duma Sup.

46. On April 10, they proposed that their project be considered after the Easter recess. Golovin postponed discussion on this proposal until April 12, when the duma rejected it. Yet on May 1, the right proposed that the Duma immediately set a date for the discussion of their project to condemn political murders. But the matter rested until May 11, when Krupenskii's proposal to consider it was also rejected. *Stenog. ot.*, I, 1,842–1,843; *Riech*, April 10, p. 1, Duma Sup.; *Stenog. ot.*, I, 1,929; II, 52–54, 454–456.

47. *Stenog. ot.*, II, 608. Kelepovskii, Sazanovich, and Purishkevich were expelled on May 4 for creating a disturbance, and Bobrinskii was not in the hall. *Ibid.*, p. 188; *Riech*, May 16, p. 1, Duma Sup.

48. Realizing that they might be publicly accused of condoning terror several opposition orators offered an anti-climax to the debates by explaining their fractions' positions. The Social-Democrats were unexpectedly solicitous for the powers of the duma. They had rejected the proposal not in order to work any change in public life or to gain support for the duma but because they believed that every important public matter lay within its competence. The Kadets simply stated that they were interested only in legislative matters. And the Social-Revolutionaries had only discussed terror because of its historical significance in Russia. Finally, the Popular-Socialists had debated the question in order to bring out the causes of terror and demonstrate the guilt of the government. *Stenog. ot.*, II, 608–609, 609, 609–610.

ror was presented to the duma by the minister of justice on April 17. It proposed the prolongation of the temporary rules, issued under Article 87, which punished by fine or imprisonment any praise of criminal activities in writing or speech.[49] It was directed chiefly at the opposition press where one might have found outright advocacy of "partisan attacks" as a form of struggle, in the illegal sheets of the extreme left, or the guarded and vindicative utterances and daily columns dedicated to revolutionary acts in Kadet *Riech*.[50]

But the measure was not turned over to the Committee on the Inviolability of Person until May 3, and on May 18, O. I. Pergament informed the duma of the committee's attitude toward this bill.[51] He explained that laws issued under Article 87 could be amended only by the duma. If a law had any undesirable elements, the whole measure had to be rejected and replaced by a new law. The government's measure, he declared, added nothing new to the legislation contained in Article 133 of the Criminal Code and the Code on Punishments. The latest ideas were summarized in the former which punished serious crimes with only the usual detention.[52] He maintained that the compilers of this code believed that promiscuous prosecution of those who praised crime would be unjust. But the government's law would punish any such pronouncements no matter how insignificant. Further, it would increase the prison sentence from six to seven months and add a fine to the list of punishments applicable. Consequently, he held these changes to be unacceptable and urged their rejection. A law which would punish the slightest crime with the highest possible pun-

49. *Stenog. ot.*, I, 2,235; *Komissii*, p. 525, contains text; fines up to 500 rubles, imprisonment for 7 months.

50. For example see Lenin, *Sobranie Sochinenii*, VII, Part 2, 77–86 (1922 ed.) or *Riech* in commenting on Trepov's murder, Sept. 3, 1906, p. 1.

51. *Stenog. ot.*, II, 809–814. This committee was chosen on March 22. It had 33 members including 4 S-D's (Vinogradov, Gudovich, Dzhaparidze, Zurabov) 3 S-R's, 4 Trudoviki, 1 P-S, 9 Kadets, 1 Democratic Reformist, 4 Kolo, 2 Moslems, 1 non-part., 4 Octobrists. *Stenog. ot.*, I, 896; *Ukazatel*, pp. 37–38.

52. Both codes are to be found in *Svod zakonov rossiiskoi imperii*, XV.

ishment had no place in the reformed order, he declared.

Assistant Minister of Justice Liutze defended the bill.[53] Praise of crime, he asserted, was immoral. Further, he believed that it should be punished as it was abroad because it often led to further criminal activity and was especially dangerous in a revolutionary period. Because of the great degree of criminality involved he held that the judge was given wide latitude in applying punishments. He saw no theoretical basis for making a difference between praise of serious and minor crimes. Moreover, in his opinion, it was inexact to say that punishments exacted in the new law were more severe than those in the criminal law since the latter supplemented not the Criminal Code but the Code on Punishments.[54] Compared with the latter, the new law lowered both prison sentences and fines. In general, however, he believed that the committee's argument had no significance since the courts usually applied lighter punishments.

The Social-Democratic viewpoint was presented by V. A. Stashinskii.[55] In his opinion, praising of "criminals" must have become widespread and organized if the government found it necessary to legislate on the matter. He therefore saw a deep disagreement between the legal principles accepted by the people and those of the legislators; whom the latter considered a criminal the former regarded as a hero. He held this discord to be symptomatic of a deep-seated, social disease, for a lawgiver could do no other than abide by the judgment of society. No one would think of praising arson and robbery, he declared. But this bill dealt with political crimes alone, and if the legislators were out of tune with public opinion, they might regard important popular demands as criminal, and praise of "crime" would inevitably result. Then, however, their prohibitions would be of no avail. So it was with the question of civil liberties and so with that of the propagation of

53. *Stenog. ot.*, II, 815–819.
54. *Pol. sob. zak.*, XXIV, no. 24,732; Article 1,035.
55. *Stenog. ot.*, II, 896–898.

minority cultures.[56] The one solution, he declared, was to direct legislation according to public opinion. For if the government promulgated laws contradictory to popular interests, it might close the mouths of the dissenters, but it could never silence their faith. In the balloting which followed the duma, as usual, accepted the committee's advice and rejected the temporary censorship rules of December 24, 1906.[57]

Thus, in this as in all matters involving political terror, the government and the duma occupied completely contradictory positions. With the Social-Democrats utilizing the debates to stress the tyrannical character of the government and to explain, if not justify, terror; with the opposition refusing to be drawn into a direct condemnation of terror and looking askance at official means of combating it; and with the government ready to go to any lengths to annihilate it, the outlook for the future was not bright. This state of affairs could only serve to increase the mutual distrust existing between the legislative and the executive. And with all of the organized force in the hands of the latter, the danger of dissolution loomed greater than ever.

56. See Appendix II, E.
57. *Stenog. ot.*, II, 898.

XIII

THE ARMY

IN his statement of March 13, on field-courts-martial, Stolypin had observed that he could not allow complete freedom of action to the Social-Democrats for their official sources proved without a doubt their intention to undermine the loyalty of the army.[1] And the Stockholm resolutions did, in fact, demand that the army be brought over to the side of the people.[2] Such pronouncements were not unusual among revolutionary groups, for the army, especially the gendarmerie, had always been the chief instrument of the tsarist government for crushing revolutionary activity. But since it consisted, in large measure, of peasants who had been called to the colors, the leftists never lost hope that it might some day be turned against the "supreme power." And early in its career the Social-Democratic Party took steps to create a revolutionary sentiment among the soldiery and in the navy.[3]

In the revolutionary period of 1905–1906 the local Social-Democratic organizations began, on their own initiative, to establish party cells among the soldiers. By the early months of 1906, there existed a complete network of such "military organizations" carrying on organizational and propaganda work in the largest cities of the empire.[4] They labored intensively, publishing sheets,

1. *Stenog. ot.*, I, 515.
2. *V. K. P. rezoliutsii*, p. 63.
3. The bulk of the material in the first part of this chapter is drawn from E. Iaroslavskii, *Istoriia V. K. P.* Iaroslavskii was an active leader in this particular branch of revolutionary work. Therefore, his chapters on army work are very complete and contain much original material.
4. Lomzh, Samara, Sevastopol, Aleksandrovsk, Tiflis, Ekaterinoslav, Kazan, Riga, Libau, Grodno, Lodz, Moscow, Petersburg, Vilna, Warsaw.

brochures, and newspapers, mainly illegal. By the end of 1905, there were six Social-Democratic army papers, and by 1906, their number had increased to thirty-three. Some, the Bolsheviki claimed, were published continuously for two years and had a circulation of from five to twenty thousand.[5] Of these, the St. Petersburg *Kazarma* (Barracks) which began publication in February, 1906, was the most influential. At first it had a distinctly Menshevistic bias. But as the local organization became increasingly Bolshevistic, with the resignation of Menshevik elements, the paper assumed a like coloration; first under the editorship of N. F. Nasimovich (Chuzhak) and after his arrest under that of E. Iaroslavskii.[6]

Although these organizations acted at first without any central direction, persistent efforts made at organizing the more or less chaotic movement soon began to bear fruit. In the autumn of 1904 after the Kiev Social-Democratic Military Committee had established like organizations in Warsaw and its vicinity, an attempt to keep them united by correspondence failed. But in 1906 the St. Petersburg organization took the lead in the movement by establishing close connections with provincial groups, and in March, the Moscow organization invited those in St. Petersburg, Vilna, and Warsaw to a conference. Here they were to discuss local work, organization, literature, propaganda among officers and relations with central and local organizations and with military associations of other parties. The delegates met and Iaroslavskii had begun a report on the Moscow group when the police, acquainted with the organization's affairs through informers, raided

5. The military organ of the central committee of the party, *Soldatskii Put* (Soldier's Way) had, according to the Bolsheviki, a circulation of 20,000. Others were *Soldatskaia Besieda* (Soldier's Chat) 7,000; St. Petersburg, *Kazarma* (Barracks), 20,000; Libau, *Shtik* (Bayonet), 6,000; Moscow, *Soldatskaia Mysl* (Soldier's Thought), 5,000; Riga, *Golos Kazarma* (Voice of the Barracks), 6,000; Moscow, *Zhizn* (Life), 5,000; Warsaw, *Slodatskii Listok* (Soldier's Sheets), 10,000. See Iaroslavskii, *Istoriia V. K. P.*, II, 613.

6. *Ibid.*, p. 614.

the meeting arresting all present. But a few days later, Iaroslavskii and five others escaped.[7]

The outbreaks at Sveaborg and Kronstadt, in the first days of Stolypin's administration, though not ordered by these organizations were largely guided by them. In the Sveaborg mutiny on July 17, both the local and Finnish Social-Democratic military groups coöperated to revolutionize the garrison. So effective was their work that Gerasimov, director of the police, believed that 50 per cent of the soldiers and 80 per cent of the sailors in this region had been affected.[8] At the end of June, the Finnish organization created a committee to evolve plans for an uprising. However, the matter got out of hand, and the Social-Democratic Military Organization, recognizing an accomplished fact, took the lead in a hopeless situation. The mutiny at the Kronstadt base which occurred on July 19, was also largely influenced by the Marxist organization.[9]

In the wake of these outbreaks the alarmed government sought to crush the illegal societies. On the night of July 21, the Security Department (*Okhrana*) destroyed the center of the St. Petersburg fighting group, and on July 26, arrested eight members of the committee of the Kronstadt Military Organization. But in August and September work was renewed. A new city committee of nine was chosen in St. Petersburg in September. An "assembly of agitators and propagandists" was organized as was a "literary committee" for publishing agita-

7. The delegates to the convention were as follows: from Moscow, Iaroslavskii, Zemliachka, Kobrin, Sommer-Liubich, Drier; from St. Petersburg, Veltman-Pavlovich, Shapiro, Bruk, Dalnitzkii (Antonov-Ovseenko), Zhdanovich (Adamov); from Vilna, Captain Klopov; and from the Lettish organizations Tomlin (Muzikant). See *ibid.*, p. 615. The Social-Revolutionaries too had a strong "military organization."

8. Report of May 29, on Sveaborg and Helsingfors Military Districts, 1906. *Ibid.*, p. 695. For this purpose, the Sveaborg committee had distributed in the first months of 1906, 12,000 brochures, 24,000 copies of *Kazarma*, while the Finnish organizations to October, 1906, had distributed more than 200,000 proclamations and nine numbers of *Kazarma* with a total of 13,500 copies. *Ibid.*, p. 697.

9. *Ibid.*

tional literature and a "technical division" for distributing that literature. Finally, a secretarial section was created. The work was carried on in districts and subdistricts and each branch group consisted of organizers, secretaries, and propagandists.[10]

As noted earlier, the Mensheviki were opposed in principle to any preparation for an immediate uprising as a form of adventurism, and, of course, condemned the Bolshevik-dominated military organizations as leaders of such a movement. However, when the St. Petersburg Bolsheviki, under I. M. Laliants (*Mysh*—the Mouse), began to head a movement for the unification of all military organizations, the Mensheviki tried to control it. They called for a conference of military associations at Terioki which proved a fiasco since only eight Menshevik leaders appeared, and the great organizations of St. Petersburg, Finland, and Kronstadt ignored it. But the St. Petersburg Committee of the Social-Democratic Party invited the delegates at Terioki to a conference which would be held at the capital within three weeks.[11]

The First Pan-Russian Conference of Military and Fighting Organizations gathered on November 22, and continued through thirteen sessions to November 29, 1906. It consisted of representatives of local organizations in all parts of European Russia.[12] Even the party central committee which forbade local groups to attend an unauthorized gathering, sent a representative to say that it was paying no attention to questions of technical preparedness for an uprising. The most important organizational result of this conference was the creation of a provisional bureau of military and fighting organizations which was to plan a national society to be subordinated to the party congress. The bureau was to work out a project

10. *Ibid.*, p. 700.
11. *Ibid.*, p. 701.
12. Voronezh, Kazan, Kronstadt, Kaluga, Libau, Moscow, Nizhni-Novgorod, St. Petersburg, Riga, Sevastopol, Finland, the Ural Region, and the South of European Russia. *Ibid.*, 702.

of organization and was to have a central organ. After declaring its faith in the rising tide of revolution the conference recognized as its main problems first, the creation of strong cells in the army through which it was to organize revolutionary support for the demands of the people. The organization was also to coördinate the activity of the military groups with that of the proletariat. It was to subordinate all of its work to the political problems of the moment and to the political leadership of the central organs of the party. In the face of Menshevik propaganda, the conference decided to broadcast a "correct understanding of armed uprising." [13]

The program was, however, interrupted at the start. As a result of the activity of informer I. V. Brodskii mass arrests were made of the St. Petersburg Committee and of district organizers in December, 1906. Again, as the government grew more watchful, local groups became inactive. By 1907 only nineteen papers were published in a few large cities.[14] Along with other revolutionary activities the campaign in the army slackened considerably in the period of the Second Duma.

In its struggle with the military phase of the revolutionary movement, the government tried twice to enlist the aid of the duma. On April 17, when army affairs were occupying much of its attention, the minister of the interior introduced for confirmation a measure issued under Article 87 on November 6, 1906. This law extended the competence of Articles 169 and 194 of the 1897 rules on military service. These articles forbade persons under judicial investigation or trial to fulfill their military obligations, and the law of November 6 would also include persons under police investigation or merely observation.[15] The measure was obviously enacted for the sole purpose of keeping "politicals" out of the army.

13. *Ibid.*, pp. 703–704.
14. *Ibid.*, p. 705.
15. See *Pol. sob. zak.*, XXVI, no. 28,526; *Stenog. ot.*, I, 2,177; *Svod zakonov rossiiskoi imperii, ustav o voinskoi povinosti*, IV, 61, 69; contents of bill are in *Komissii*, prilozhenie, pp. 534–535.

On May 3, the bill was given to the Committee on the Inviolability of Person, and on May 21, Adzhemov (Kadet) reported that it was highly dissatisfied with the measure.[16] Russian law, he declared, allowed only those persons to lose their civil rights who were under judicial investigation or trial. By extending the competence of Articles 169 and 194 to persons under police investigation or observation the law confused judicial and administrative (police) jurisdictions and thus destroyed that clear demarcation between these two branches of government which was a fundamental characteristic of Russian law. The committee also believed that the places left vacant by the recruits involved would have to be filled by many who should remain at home according to lot and family position, thus violating their rights. Moreover, a citizen might be called at twenty-six or thirty-one as a result of prolonged investigation, though the law specified that they be called at twenty-one. In this manner, too, individual rights would be violated. Finally, the committee believed that the physical quality of the army would be impaired if men of thirty-one years of age were called in great numbers. With all of these considerations in mind the committee proposed that the duma reject the bill.

Lykoshin of the ministry of the interior was quick to reply.[17] He disagreed with Adzhemov's juridical theses, for to his mind police investigation and preliminary judicial examination were very much alike. In the former the rights of the police holding the inquiry were the same as those of the judicial inspector in the latter. The whole procedure of police investigation had a judicial character and was carried out under the supervision of the judicial inspectorate. Moreover, in most cases, he argued, information gained at police investigations served as materials for judicial examinations; that is, they had, in his opinion, the significance of a judicial examination and replaced it. He contended, moreover, that rules governing persons

16. *Stenog. ot.*, II, 124, 922–925; *Riech*, May 13, p. 3.
17. *Stenog. ot.*, II, 925–932.

under police observation were incompatible with the requirements of military service, for such persons could not carry arms and had always to be within the jurisdiction of the police. As for postponing service, the government often did that for educational or business reasons, he declared. He admitted that the interests of others, innocent persons, might be harmed, but not their rights, for the government was able to fill all quotas by lot. Finally, he hardly believed that men at thirty were detrimental to the service.

Since the committee had said nothing about it, Lykoshin offered to explain why those who had committed political offenses should be kept out of the army. He frankly informed the duma that the bill aimed to keep its ranks free of anti-governmental, revolutionary elements.[18] The interests of the army, he asserted, and the maintenance therein of a spirit of unity and discipline were closely connected with the interests of the government. At the moment he had reason to believe that a revolutionary organization operating within the army had intensified its activities by issuing a whole literature of propaganda. Thus, the government had to interfere in self-defense and to preserve the very existence of the state. It could not do otherwise.[19]

The Social-Democrats joined in the chorus of indignant opposition statements which followed.[20] They charged the government with interpreting and changing laws to suit its own selfish interests. At the moment, the change in military service laws would affect not only the revolutionaries but all who opposed "official" views; that is, all those parties which the government refused to legalize. Yet, if the administration alone were to decide who should be allowed to serve, the army would soon be com-

18. This brought cries of "politics" from the left, and Lykoshin agreed with some vehemence.

19. Lykoshin aroused the duma at the end of his address by shouting in an unnecessarily loud voice that aside from the fine-spun theories of the committee it was evidently desirable to keep revolutionaries out of the army.

20. *Stenog. ot.,* II, 936–939, 939–941.

posed only of those who had no political faith or conscience, or worse, members of the Union of the Russian
People, so popular among the officers. The government,
the Social-Democrats asserted, endeavored to keep out
of the army just those elements which best understood the
interests of the people. But its efforts were in vain, they
believed, for it was impossible to eliminate all who lived
in an atmosphere of revolutionary ferment. They held
that the army should be closely bound to the people and
that its popular personnel was the best guarantee of that
union. Any attempt by the government to adapt the army
to its group interests should be stoutly resisted. Therefore, the Social-Democrats supported the committee and
formed part of the duma majority which rejected the
government's proposal.[21]

The administration's second bid for aid against the
revolutionaries in the army came with the introduction
of a bill which established more severe penalties for underground military activity. It called for the prolongation
of the period of validity of the temporary law of August
18, 1906, introduced under Article 87. This statute increased the punishment for distributing anti-governmental propaganda among troops from the three years
established for such crimes in the Criminal Code to six,
and bound over the guilty to military and naval courts-
martial.[22]

On May 3, the Committee on the Inviolability of Person
received this bill along with the preceding measure and
Kuzmin-Karavaev (Democratic Reform), the specialist
on army affairs, reported the committee's decision to the
duma on May 22. He noted at once that the bill did not
change the content of existing laws on criminal agitation
in the army but merely increased the punishment for agitation. This propaganda, he informed the duma, included
any call for traitorous or rebellious activity designed to

21. *Ibid.*, p. 948.
22. This bill was introduced on April 17, *ibid.*, p. 2,235; *Pol. sob. zak.*, XXVI,
no. 28,247; *Komissii*, pp. 536–537; *Svod zakonov*, XV, 130–131.

overthrow the state and social order. He observed that espionage and insulting the throne were evidently lesser crimes if judged by the penalties they merited.[23] For merely reading a propagandist sheet harsh punishment could be visited on a soldier. Arguing from these considerations he proposed that the duma reject the bill.

He then analyzed the second part of the measure which, he explained, bound over persons carrying on propaganda in the barracks to courts-martial. If caught red-handed, the criminal was to have no preliminary investigation. He noted that according to the supreme decree of 1862 only citizens in localities under martial law might be subjected to courts-martial. That rule was to be found in existing statutes on criminal judicial procedure and the law on field-courts-martial. Yet the bill presented by the government would establish military trial, applied only in exceptional circumstances, as a permanent, legal norm. He noted that the government had declared that the bill was designed to deal with the more dangerous manifestations of revolutionary agitation and to accelerate court procedure. But he regarded these justifications as too general and declared that they reflected a lack of faith in the civil courts. These, too, could be made to accelerate their pace if the government so desired. This bill, he asserted, would bring the legal system back to the pre-reform (1861) court-martial system when the government used courts to persecute undesirable citizens. The army, he maintained, should be kept out of politics, and should be respected. Therefore, he would not place it in the unnatural position of a state within a state. He would not create a situation wherein a citizen harming the interests of the army could have no recourse to civil courts.[24]

The chief military prosecutor, G. D. Rylke, came to the defense of the bill.[25] To him the arguments of the committee were unconvincing. Until the means proposed

23. *Svod zakonov*, XV, Articles 101, 102, 108 for exile; 103 for espionage.
24. *Stenog. ot.*, II, 995–1,004.
25. *Ibid.*, pp. 1,005–1,008.

had been tried by long experience they could not be regarded as inexpedient. He held that a more severe punishment was necessary for revolutionary propaganda in
the army, since it was indeed a more serious crime than
those provided for in the articles of the Criminal Code.
The bill gave the army more power to combat this evil,
he admitted, but from this it did not follow that the military would have recourse to the punishments permitted
to the exclusion of all others. He pointed out that the
alternative to this measure would be an undesirable limitation of army life in an effort to ward off revolutionary
propaganda. The government might even find it necessary
to shut off the army physically from the entire population. But according to the government's bill, he contended,
only the guilty would suffer.

Stung to the quick by the charge that the bill reflected
a lack of faith in civil courts, Vice Minister Liutze appeared on the tribune to answer it. He realized that the
law had its defects, but increased agitation in the army
leading to such unheard of events as the Sveaborg and
Kronstadt mutinies had forced the government to pro-
mulgate the law of August 18, 1906. Because of its defects
it was issued only as a temporary measure which included
military trial, undoubtedly unjust as a permanent, legal
norm. The government would gladly have dropped it if
agitation in the army were decreasing, but since that was
not the case, even the ministry of justice opposed its abrogation.[26]

The only Social-Democrat to reply was I. N. Nagikh.[27]
He compared the bill with its twin measure which he declared was designed to keep revolutionaries out of the
army while this bill dealt with those who somehow had
penetrated its ranks. He believed that the increased agitation to which Liutze had referred came not from revolutionaries, but from ordinary troops who were ill-fed, ill-
clothed, and badly paid, and were treated with scorn by

26. *Ibid.*, pp. 1,008–1,009.
27. *Ibid.*, pp. 1,016–1,018.

their officers. If these evils were abolished he believed that there would be no occasion for mutinies. In the name of his fraction he urged the rejection of the bill.

Like other laws issued under Article 87, the duma saw in this measure only an aggravated form of oppression adopted during the days of reaction following the ebb of the Revolution of 1905. Therefore, it was rejected.[28] But among the court and administrative circles the defeat of these two measures could not but help to strengthen the growing conviction that only by dissolving the duma and by creating a more pliable legislative body could they hope to govern Russia as they saw fit. To the Social-Democrats these bills on propaganda were an unmitigated evil. They were a further encroachment on the civil liberties of the citizenry. But even more important, they interfered with the attempt of their party to inform the army that, as a part of the people, it must look to its interests and aid the "advanced elements" in their struggle against autocracy. Consequently, juridical fine-spun theories aside, they had a particularly practical aim in opposing these measures.

The administration bill on army affairs which attracted most attention both because of its significance and the dramatic turn of the debates, was that on the quotas of recruits to be called to the colors in 1907. It was introduced on April 10, by Minister of War Rediger who asked that it be examined in secret session.[29] I. V. Gessen immediately arose to propose that it be sent to the Budget Committee at once in order that the duma might demonstrate its right to establish quotas, since Article 86 of the Fundamental Laws allowed the tsar to call the necessary number if it was not defined by May 1.[30] But Aleksinskii believed that the agrarian question which would be displaced on the program was far more important. Besides, if the minister wanted a closed session he should present

28. *Ibid.*, p. 1,019.
29. *Stenog. ot.*, I, 1,844.
30. *Ibid.*, pp. 1,844–1,845.

his reasons for this extraordinary request. For, in Aleksinskii's opinion, publicity of the duma's debates was one of the most important conditions of its work.[31] However, the duma majority adhering to the Kadet view, decided to give the bill to the subcommittee on army affairs in the Budget Committee.[32]

On April 16, Kuzmin-Karavaev reported to the duma in a closed session.[33] He analyzed the problem from all angles. The defects revealed by the Japanese War, he asserted, had to be corrected by the duma, and of the general problem of military reform, this on recruits was a vital part. The ministry had requested 463,050 recruits for 1907. This was larger than the quotas demanded in former years,[34] but smaller than the number for 1906 by 6,000. He explained that the large figures resulted from the reduction of the term of service from five to three years which, in turn, necessitated the calling of more men to the colors. However, from the point of view of the people's interests, he believed that the demand was excessive. It took the best working strength from the population in a time of economic depression, and the changes involved in the daily routine of the recruits might be reflected adversely on the health of the population. The fact that the government's demands were already excessive was, in

31. *Ibid.*, p. 1,845.

32. *Ibid.*, p. 1,848. At first the duma decided to elect a special committee to consider the bill, but Adzhemov noted that the subcommittee on army affairs of the Budget Committee had the right to review this measure and the duma canceled its first decision. See *Ibid.*, p. 1,846.

33. The debates were twice postponed on April 10, and 12, to enable the committee to review the voluminous statistical materials presented by the government. See *ibid.*, pp. 1,848, 1,915–1,916, 1,995, 1,996, 2,085–2,101; *Riech*, May 11, p. 2; April 14, p. 3. The duma realized from the start that a stormy session awaited it, for at a meeting of opposition fractions at Prince Dolgorukov's, on April 15, the Poles failed to appear, and the entire left declared that they would support a proposal for the rejection of the bill. See *Tovarishch*, April 17, p. 2. The reports of the secret sessions of the Second Duma were published in the same year in *Materialy k stenographicheskim otchetam* by the state press. But since the paging follows that of *Stenog. ot.*, that publication is referred to.

34. In 1899—291,000; 1900—297,000; 1901—308,000; 1903—320,000. In the war years of 1904 and 1905 the quotas rose to 447,000 and 475,000 respectively. See *Stenog. ot.*, I, 2,086.

his opinion, demonstrated by the number called who evaded service.[35] He declared that the population might be relieved if some 200,000 exemptions were abolished.[36] On the other hand, he admitted that these very often included the only productive worker in the family so that in Russia, with its weak economic development, the system could not be immediately abolished. As compared with Europe, he observed that Russia's army of 1,219,003 was apparently huge, but he held that its size was not too great in view of the long frontiers of the empire. Personally, he objected to its proportions, and the Japanese War had convinced him of the advantages of quality over quantity.

But, the reporter complained, not all of this huge army was used primarily for the purpose of defending the fatherland and throne in accordance with the laws on military duty. Some units, for example, were employed as convoy squads (for political prisoners) on the ground that this service was better performed under oath than for hire. Then, there were the gendarme divisions which performed a purely police service. Besides, he pointed out the existence of many non-combatant sections; the host of functionaries and the 53,000 orderlies. He explained that although the government intended to reduce their number to 35,000 the committee believed that the orderly service should be entirely abolished as a vestige of "feudalism." He admitted that sworn duty was cheaper than hired help, but held that popular interests and those of the treasury

35. In 1898—1,500; 1903—3,500; 1904—19,000; 1905—25,000; 1906—21,000. See *ibid.*, p. 2,088.

36. According to the law of January 1, 1874, on universal military service, there were three degrees of exemptions based on family circumstances. In the first category there were placed only sons and grandsons who were the only workers in the family. In the second group there were to be found sons who had brothers younger than eighteen, and in the third, those who immediately followed brothers in service, even if there were other breadwinners in the family. The last two categories were called, in reverse order, if the number of non-exempt recruits was insufficient to fill the quota established for universal service in a given year. The first category was called up only by imperial command. See A. Kornilov, *Modern Russian History,* II, 158–160; N. N. Golovin, *The Russian Army in the World War,* pp. 15–29. *Economic and Social History of the World War, Russian Series,* Vol. 11.

did not coincide in this instance. It would be cheaper for the population to pay taxes (for wages) than to deprive itself of the great productive power which the army absorbed. Considering the police duties of the army, he agreed that a state might rightly use its army to crush rebellion but he saw no justification for employing it in punitive expeditions. Such a task was detrimental to the army itself, for the executioner nowhere inspired the respect which the armed forces demanded.

In summarizing the subcommittee's attitude, he declared that by a majority of four to two it had decided to propose that the duma accept the measure. This majority believed that reduction was impossible, and that all of the reforms desired might be realized. Even the removal of orderlies could not take place immediately for the officers would require a wage increase of 5,000,000 rubles to replace them, and this had not been appropriated. Moreover, the army could not at once be weakened by dropping any of its sections. But, he added, the majority believed that the vote of approval should be accompanied by a formula of passage to the regular order expressing the duma's demands for wide and thorough reforms which would limit the duties of the army to matters pertaining strictly to the defense of the fatherland. Since war had not been replaced by other means of solving clashes of interest between states, the army was vitally necessary and should not be diverted to police duties. But he asserted that demands to refuse the government a single soldier in the current state of international relations was symptomatic of a failure to reckon with reality. He asked the left which had been heckling him whether they would refuse 463,000 recruits if they controlled a duma ministry and were responsible for the safety of the state. Negative cries emanated from the extreme left and Aleksinskii declared that they would create a generally armed populace. Kuzmin-Karavaev doubted that a responsible government could ever adopt that policy and appealed to the duma as a responsible authority to secure the defense of its country.

He was immediately followed by the Minister of War, Rediger.[37] He expressed his sympathy with the demand for reforms, but declared that they were being introduced very gradually and carefully. Furthermore, speed was impossible since insufficient finances retarded the introduction and development of changes. Although he agreed that the size of its non-military divisions should be diminished, he maintained that in no army were they entirely absent for they were a technical necessity. He objected to the classification of orderlies as vestiges of serfdom. He sympathized with the plan to decrease their number, but declared that they could not be entirely abolished since in the outposts of the empire it was impossible to obtain voluntary domestic service except at exorbitant wages. Finally, he agreed with the committee that police duty distracted army divisions from regular military service, but he added that he would be the first to welcome a calmer atmosphere which would allow for the release of all sections for military defense alone.

The Kadets reinforced the committee's arguments and concentrated their attack on the left.[38] They challenged the Socialists to face realities, and maintained that the "extreme" Social-Democrats acted without regard for the needs of the state. For by their refusal to confirm the government's demands for recruits they threatened the security of empire and the prestige of the duma among the people. Moreover, they would allow the government to fix its own quotas annually and thus do grave injury to the cause of popular representation. Furthermore, the Kadets held that as long as the leftist deputies occupied their posts and were at the same time fully aware of the government's right to call up recruits without their consent, they were morally bound to fulfill their obligations as deputies within the narrow limits allowed; they must verify the correctness of the administration's calculations. The duma assumed

37. *Stenog. ot.*, I, 2,101–2,103.
38. See I. V. Gessen's address, *ibid.*, pp. 2,110–2,119, and Kutler's, *ibid.*, pp. 2,138–2,142.

no responsibility for the size of the Russian army, the Kadets maintained, and if the current quotas were rejected the administration would fall back on the figures for 1906 which exceeded the present demand. As a final consideration they urged that rejection of quotas was equivalent to an appeal to refuse recruits.

The only Social-Democratic orator to reply at once was Zurabov who rose to deliver his fateful address.[39] As in the budget debates, he declared, the Social-Democrats were asked to be "practical" because the government could fill all gaps without the duma's consent. But, he asserted, his party could only accept practical considerations if they conformed with its principles. He then reviewed the Marxist attitude toward the army. Modern armies, he maintained, were employed to attain the selfish ends of the ruling classes of the various powers when their interests clashed. But this was contradictory to the best interests of the working masses from which the armies were drawn. Furthermore, the army was used by wealthy elements in each country to ward off the economic attacks of the laboring population. He held that a generally armed people was the best kind of defense against foreign aggression but was feared by the rulers who knew that a standing army would defend their special interests. The new and the old orders, he cried, were at war with each other and the new could not allow the old 400,000 "bayonets" to drive out the duma. The Japanese War had fully demonstrated that the army was not suitable for foreign defense, he asserted amid groans of disgust from the right. It was completely demoralized and could serve only the domestic policies of the government; it could crush uprisings and independent thought and action. The entire education of the soldier was directed to that end. He was taught to repress all opposition to the administration, and by means of an iron,

39. *Ibid.*, pp. 2,160–2,173. Zurabov spoke with a noticeable Armenian accent. He began by asking why the session was closed and was informed by Golovin that his question had nothing to do with the matter under discussion. Moreover, it was explained, according to the Fundamental Laws the president had to comply with a minister's request for a secret session. See *Krasnyi Arkhiv*, XIX, 140.

dispiriting discipline human beings were transformed into insensitive machines, almost entirely without communication with the world outside their barracks. Moreover, the soldier was a slave to his officer, and was underpaid.

Turning to the Kadets, Zurabov maintained that once the duma confirmed the quotas for recruits it would have to shoulder at least a part of the responsibility for the size of the army. The duma, he held, would lose no prestige by refusing to grant recruits. Rather, the people would say that they had not elected the duma to tighten a noose around their necks, snatch their children from them, tear 400,000 Russian citizens from productive work, and equip them for campaigns against the villages in punitive expeditions. Zurabov then launched into a peroration which took the form of a bitter condemnation of the army's activities:

Proceeding from the considerations that the present-day army tears a majority of the masses of the people from productive work and lies as a heavy burden on society, that our autocratic government in taking these social forces, chiefly those who work, directs them against the people itself, acknowledging all that and also that no matter how much is said from these benches (*to the contrary*), in the autocratic state our army will never be fit for the purpose of external defense, that such an army will combat us gloriously and drive you out, sirs, and will suffer defeat in the East.[40]

The right which had long restrained itself under this attack had by now exhausted its patience and filled the chamber with hysterical shouts. They demanded Zurabov's ejection for this "insult" to the army.[41] The speaker, however, reiterated his last words, whereupon Minister of War Rediger left the chamber.[42] The president rapped for silence. He declared that he alone could warn speakers and asked Zurabov not to express himself thus without grounds.

40. *Stenog. ot.*, I, 2,171. The Italics are the author's.
41. *Ibid.*, p. 2,174.
42. *Tovarishch*, April 17, p. 2; *Riech*, April 19, p. 3.

But the right continued its uproar, demanding that Zurabov be expelled under Article 38 of the Duma Statute.
Golovin again called for order and declared that the orator
had undoubtedly been misunderstood and would explain
himself.[43] Zurabov, pale and confused as the rightists
gathered around the tribune with clenched fists, pleaded
that he had spoken only of the army of the Old Régime,
not that of the new "constitutional" era.[44] Golovin added
that there could be no doubt that old Russia was a thing of
the past, that the new Russia had been strengthened, and
that there could likewise be no doubt of the defeat in the
Far East. He forbade further discussion of the matter, but
the right objected strenuously. They announced that they
were leaving since Russia had been insulted, yet the president had demanded no apology from the orator. At that
moment all of the ministers demonstratively left the chamber. The duma was by now in complete disorder and
Golovin called for a recess.[45]

Golovin, thoroughly alarmed, expected immediate dissolution.[46] He made his way to the ministers' pavilion and
there found them conversing excitedly, especially Kokovtsov and Schwanebach. The latter was trying to convince
Rediger, who was comparatively calm, that Zurabov had
insulted him personally, and that the president had been
negligent in not stopping the speaker. Suddenly they
became aware of Golovin's presence and grew silent. The
president sought to calm them by arguing that Zurabov's
words were not essentially insulting. He declared that the
orator was merely guilty of an unfortunate expression;
that he should be requested to renounce his words and thus
expunge any possible "insult." But Schwanebach was
insistent. He maintained that Zurabov had uttered insulting remarks, and that to allow him to speak further would
only invite a repetition of the offensive statements. He

43. *Stenog. ot.*, I, 2,171.
44. *Ibid.*, p. 2,172.
45. *Ibid.*, pp. 2,172, 2,173; *Krasnyi Arkhiv*, XIX, 141.
46. *Krasnyi Arkhiv*, XIX, 141.

heatedly asserted that no matter how radical a Russian might be he would never affront the army; that could be expected only from a representative of the national minorities like the Armenian Zurabov. Golovin then asked for a copy of the *Stenographic Reports* and after carefully perusing the end of Zurabov's speech he concluded that an insult to the army might possibly be discerned.[47]

The president left the indignant ministers and on reaching his office received a telephone call from Stolypin. The premier wanted the story in detail in order that he might report it to the tsar who had been informed of Zurabov's address and had just now called to learn more of the matter. He informed Golovin that the tsar, as supreme chief of the Russian military forces, felt himself and the army insulted, and was displeased that the president of the duma did not consider it necessary to protest against Zurabov's statement. Stolypin added that from the conversation he believed that the tsar would not hesitate to dissolve the duma, and asked Golovin what steps he planned to take. The latter replied with a complete narrative of the events and added that he was sorely grieved that the tsar had been misinformed. He held that although an insult might be found in Zurabov's words, he was certain that the speaker had intended none especially since he was himself an army officer. Even if the army had been insulted he felt that it was unjust to blame the duma and its president since the disturbance caused by the right rendered any control of the assembly impossible, and forced the president to call a recess.[48]

Meanwhile, during the recess, all fractions had met to decide on the stand each would take if Article 38 of the Duma Statute were applied and Zurabov were expelled. Golovin sent out the sergeant at arms to ascertain what the results of the conferences might be. He learned that the Kadets believed that the duma's existence was threatened, and that its only salvation lay in demonstrating that

47. *Ibid.*, pp. 141–142.
48. *Ibid.*, pp. 142.

Zurabov's opinions were not those of the duma. But they regarded the application of Article 38 as a dangerous solution, for the duma might refuse to apply it or do so by a very small majority, thus placing a great number of deputies squarely behind the speech.[49] As on every occasion when the duma was evenly divided the Polish Kolo held the balance of power, and leader Dmovskii's reply was evasive. They did not wish to defy the president, therefore they would not vote against a proposal to' apply Article 38 should he present it. But, in general, they had no desire to vote on the recruit question. Moreover, they could find no insult in Zurabov's speech. They declared that they would give the matter some further consideration. But when the session began they had not yet appeared and Golovin soon learned that they chose to absent themselves.[50]

The president was indeed in a quandary. Suddenly he bethought himself of the more or less pliable elements among the *Narodniki* who wished to avoid complications which might lead to dissolution, but who would not vote for Article 38 since that would appear to be a submission to the government's demands. If their support might be obtained for any action the president should take short of resorting to eviction, Golovin believed that all danger would be averted.[51] Therefore, when the duma assembled he asked Zurabov privately to apologize, and on receiving a categorical refusal he announced that he had carefully studied the *Stenographic Reports* and concluded that Zurabov had, in fact, referred to the army in a manner not permissible in the duma, and therefore deprived him of the right to continue his speech. To demonstrate that a majority of the duma was behind him he proposed that it approve of his actions.[52] Tsereteli immediately arose to declare that the proposal was new, and was in violation of

49. *Ibid.*
50. *Ibid.; Tovarishch*, April 17, p. 2; April 19, p. 3.
51. *Krasnyi Arkhiv*, XIX, 144–145.
52. *Stenog. ot.*, I, 2,173–2,174; Zurabov's letter to *Tovarishch*, May 3, p. 7.

the right of free speech. Cries from all parts of the duma warned him that the president could not be criticized, and Golovin justified his own behavior by arguing that had he not stopped Zurabov for bringing on such serious disorders he might be called to account for not fulfilling his duties. But when Tsereteli referred to these remarks as a "polemic" and was, consequently, ordered to leave the tribune he retired from the hall under protest together with the Social-Democrats and all *Narodnik* groups. The Social-Democrats, he shouted, were forbidden to criticize the autocracy.[53] Amid cheers from the right and center Golovin explained that Tsereteli's action involved a lack of respect for the duma. He then repeated his proposal which was adopted by the rump which remained, and the session was closed.[54] Golovin's tactics had worked too well. Nevertheless, the duma had officially supported the president's action in halting Zurabov and condemning his words.

At about midnight Golovin was visited at his hotel by I. I. Petrunkevich and others of the Kadet central committee. They informed him that they had learned that in governmental circles the duma's decision was not regarded as the end of the matter; that the ministers had decided not to appear in the duma and that Golovin had best find out immediately what the actual state of affairs might be. Accordingly, he telephoned Stolypin who declared that the duma's existence was truly endangered. An hour later Golovin visited him at the Winter Palace. Here he was informed that the tsar had not reached a decision on dissolution and that all would depend on the report which Rediger would make on the following morning. Stolypin advised a visit to the war minister and the adoption of a formula of passage to the regular order expressing the duma's belief in the splendid quality and loyalty of the

53. *Stenog. ot.*, I, 2,174.
54. *Ibid.*, pp. 2,174–2,175, 2,176. *Ukazatel*, pp. 27–33, shows that there were 268 deputies in the combined left and Kolo, and 249 in the remainder of the duma.

army. Golovin then begged the premier to telephone Rediger immediately, to urge him to make a report favorable to the duma, and to advise him that the president would like to see him in the morning before he left for the tsar's residence at Tsarskoe Selo. As a result of Stolypin's efforts a conference was arranged for the following morning between the president of the duma and the minister of war. At this meeting Golovin explained the significance of the duma's decision to Rediger and called his attention to the fact that Zurabov had uttered no actual insult but was guilty of using an unfortunate expression. He pleaded with him to present the matter to the tsar as objectively as possible. Rediger promised to fulfill this request and declared that as far as he was concerned the duma's decision and Golovin's attitude had ended the matter.[55]

The existence of the duma had indeed hung by a thread. On April 17, the council of ministers met and decided that dissolution was inevitable but that the new electoral law then under consideration should first be perfected so that it might be published together with a decree of dissolution. The tsar, who agreed with this procedure, had been deeply stirred by the "Zurabov affair." He believed that the government could no longer tolerate such occurrences unless it was prepared to be swept away by revolution. He informed Stolypin that a few days made little difference, but that he was firm in his desire for dissolution and hoped that it might be brought about as soon as possible.[56]

When the duma met on the morning following the "incident" (April 17) the Social-Democrats resumed the offensive. Kirienko immediately offered a formula of passage to the regular order which summarized the Marxist position as already expressed by Zurabov. The quotas were to be rejected, for an expensive and poorly trained

55. *Krasnyi Arkhiv*, XIX, 145; Stolypin's letter to the tsar, *ibid.*, V, 114. See also Golovin's testimony before the Extraordinary Investigating Committee of the Provisional Government on June 30, 1917. *Padenie tsarskogo rezhima*, V, 374–375.

56. Kokovtsov, *Memoirs*, pp. 181, 187.

army which served only the wealthy and crushed the rest
of the population should not be supported by the people.
By confirming the quotas, the Social-Democrats contended, the duma would be lending its authority and assent
to the purposes for which the army was used and would
give the government grounds for demanding funds for its
upkeep. Finally, the extreme left demanded that the
standing army be entirely liquidated and replaced by a
popular militia with elective officers which would better
serve the popular interests and the cause of peace.[57] But
however the Social-Democrats might explain their pref-
erence for a militia they fully realized that it would be
much easier to overthrow the Old Régime with a universally armed population under popularly chosen officers than to count on revolutionizing the standing
army. For the latter was trained by upper class officers,
and was spiritually dulled by a strict discipline to a point
where it would attack even the people from which it was
drawn. And the Marxists believed, or professed to believe,
that such an army, if well-trained, would be an adequate
defense against foreign invasion.

Kirienko offered a "few" words in explanation of his
proposal.[58] He boldly picked up the threads of Zurabov's
argument—and with approximately the same result. He
proceeded to rub salt in the wounds left in the national
pride by the Japanese War and brought down the frenzied
vituperation of the aroused right on his luckless head.
Roar followed roar of indignation as he criticized the army
for its low educational level, its poor showing in Manchuria, the moral and intellectual weakness of the officer's
corps. Again and again Golovin was forced to restore
order and hold the orator to the matter under consideration in a valiant effort to avoid a repetition of the "Zurabov incident." And finally, when Kirienko heatedly gave
the lie to Rein (Octobrist) for his statement that Jews
made up a great part of those who had evaded service,

57. *Stenog. ot.*, I, 2,185–2,186.
58. *Ibid.*, pp. 2,186–2,196.

the president drove him from the tribune. Golovin had, it is true, warned him twice before, but the suddenness and drastic character of the step following the Zurabov affair aroused a suspicion among the Social-Democrats that he was deporting himself in the manner of a loyal Kadet rather than as an impartial chairman. They believed that he was doing all in his power to avoid any sharp criticism of the government.[59]

Therefore, when Aleksinskii arose to deliver the final Social-Democratic address on the recruits question,[60] he was filled with a righteous wrath and admitted as much. He informed the duma that it would have been difficult to feel otherwise considering the nature of the question, the behavior of the right, and the Zurabov incident. But he promised to restrain his feelings and limit himself to a defense of the Social-Democratic proposal. Nevertheless, he utilized the occasion for a violent attack on the Kadets. The liberal bourgeoisie, he asserted, were quite ready to use the army when their economic interests were at stake. He accused the Russian liberals of urging the employment of the army in the struggle with popular agitation and disorganization of economic life. They were the Judases of the people who would strengthen the hands of an oppressive government. He challenged the Kadet view that refusal to confirm the quotas would have no practical value. On the contrary, the people would have more faith in the duma if it refused to give up their sons. The Kadets feared that the principle of popular representation would suffer if recruits were refused. But, certainly, continual submission to the government would never strengthen the duma. Popular representation was strong only insofar as it championed the people's interests. When it refused soldiers for strike-breaking and village-burning the people would be grateful and would support the duma as their true representatives. The liberals had argued that the

59. *Ibid.*, pp. 2,189, 2,195, 2,196. See *Nakaz*, pp. 41–42, Articles 115–118. The president had complete discretion in stopping an orator.
60. *Stenog. ot.*, I, 2,196–2,211.

duma's refusal to yield recruits would encourage the people to do likewise, and Aleksinskii taunted them for their disavowal of the Vyborg Manifesto.[61] But he saw a ray of hope in the fact that the army was becoming aware of its position; that the soldier was sending instructions and petitions asking for an amelioration of his conditions of service, and demonstrating that he understood that the soldier might never be free in a fettered nation where he was forced to commit fratricide.

The speaker was preparing to close, and his resentment had increased with each interruption by the president. Twice Golovin warned him to stick to the point, and each time (once, amid loud applause) Aleksinskii turned fiercely on him and charged him with attempting to assume the rôle of a preliminary censor. But when he accused the Kadets of confirming the quotas in order to avoid a break with the administration and brought the duma to its feet roaring with approval and indignation, Golovin ordered him to his seat.[62] The Social-Democrats were thoroughly aroused. All three of their speakers on the army had been cut off by the president whom they now regarded as little short of a bourgeois dictator. Aleksinskii tried to continue his speech. Tsereteli questioned the legality of Golovin's actions. But to the accompaniment of shouts of "violence" from the left, the president refused to hear either of them.[63]

Matters began to move more rapidly. Several remaining orators were heard and formulae of passage presented. By a vote of 193 to 129, amid thunderous applause from the right and center, the duma adopted the government's bill.[64] Immediately thereafter, with the Social-Democrats abstaining, the duma voted the committee's formula of passage to the regular order. This statement reminded the minister of war of his promise to introduce reforms which

61. See above, p. 19.
62. *Stenog. ot.*, I, 2,210.
63. *Ibid.*, pp. 2,210–2,211.
64. *Ibid.*, pp. 2,220, 2,227, 2,228, 2,229.

would free the army from non-military duties, reduce the number of orderlies, and revise the system of calling recruits. It also expressed the belief that it was necessary and possible to reduce the army in time of peace by advancing the designated reforms, by abolishing all deficiencies revealed by the last war, and by raising the technical standards of the army.[65]

The business of the secret session was now completed, and Golovin found it necessary only to add a few reassuring words on the matter of Zurabov's speech. He called the incident "sad" in which the "gallant" Russian army had been offended. The army had always shown itself to be self-denying in fulfilling its duties with high discipline and loyalty. These were the true characteristics of the army recognized by all, he declared, and the duma protested against unseemly statements directed against it. The center and right applauded loudly.[66]

But the left had not forgotten Golovin's dictatorial manner in dealing with its spokesmen. At the end of the session they introduced a statement accusing the president of having abused his power to interfere in debates and to stop orators, and thus prevented a complete consideration of the subject under discussion. They declared that this action deprived the president of their confidence and held that the majority of the duma, who had left the hall when his course was to be approved, also shared their views. Accordingly, they proposed that the duma vote immediately on the permissibility of the president's attitude toward orators as revealed lately, and decide whether any person might remain president of the duma who did not have the confidence of a majority of its members.[67] At the following session, on April 29, Dzhaparidze asked the duma to consider the proposal out of the regular order. Golovin, however, ruled that since the matter concerned the president's policies the duma could not consider it and

65. *Ibid.*, p. 2,230.
66. *Ibid.*, p. 2,230.
67. *Ibid.*, pp. 2,285–2,288.

that the proposal could only be added to the *Stenographic Reports*. He stubbornly held his ground over the excited protests of the Social-Democratic leaders, and the duma took no further action on the proposal.[68]

Apparently, the duma had safely rounded a dangerous corner. Actually, however, the course of the debates, especially Zurabov's address, served firmly to convince the administration that a great part of the deputies, perhaps a majority, would never coöperate with it and would use the duma as a platform for agitation against the government. And this incident, and the action of the Kolo, strengthened the conviction that in any future Russian parliament national minorities were not to be allowed a significant voice. Dissolution and a new electoral law diminishing the power of the extreme opposition appeared to the bureaucracy as the only satisfactory solution.[69]

As for the Social-Democratic fraction, in its own opinion, it had acquitted itself gloriously in these debates. And the Bolsheviki felt that the Zurabov incident had com-

68. *Ibid.*, pp. 2,265–2,266. The first session after the Easter recess was held on April 29.

69. For Zurabov himself the situation became exceptionally dangerous. He received numerous threatening letters and challenges to duels. Therefore, to protect him the fraction published a statement assuming the responsibility for his speech. And since the government refused to publish the *Stenographic Reports* of the secret session the fraction published an open letter in *Tovarishch* on May 4, 1907. It told of the futile efforts made to have the reports published and gave the lie to the statements of the official press on the session. It pointed especially to the fact that a majority was absent when the duma voted to uphold Golovin's action in stopping Zurabov. On the previous day *Tovarishch* had published a letter from Zurabov himself containing approximately the same arguments and complaints. He maintained that he had not insulted the army but defended it from that exploitation to which the government had subjected it. He accused Golovin of insincerity and held that the Kadets were not certain that he had insulted the army for they had made no efforts to convince the duma that he had done so. He declared that this scraping of the Kadets before the government was carried on at the expense of the entire population and served only to lower the honor and dignity of the duma which had been won by a long and stubborn struggle involving superhuman efforts and great suffering. See *Riech*, April 19, p. 3; April 22, p. 5; April 26, p. 2; *Tovarishch*, April 21, p. 3; May 1, p. 5; May 3, p. 3; May 4, p. 5. The bulletins of the Information Bureau appeared in the daily press on April 17 and 18. This was a semi-official news agency. See also *Tovarishch*, May 3, p. 2; April 19, p. 2; *Riech*, April 19, p. 3. Another account by the Information Bureau appeared on April 19.

pletely vindicated their point of view. Had the Kadets not taken a stand with the government and the reactionaries while the *Narodnik* groups ranged themselves solidly behind the Social-Democrats? When the attitude of the Marxists threatened a clash with the government and the very existence of the duma, had the Kadet president not conferred with the administration? Had he not arranged a "deal behind the backs of the people" and in the duma silenced all opposition? The events of April 16 and 17, did indeed conspire to make the Social-Democratic fraction more intractable. If they were to follow the dictates of their party it was inevitable that they should assail the army, the chief anti-revolutionary weapon of reaction, with the pent-up hatred of generations. It was inevitable that they should taunt the military for its poor showing in Manchuria regardless of the consequences for the duma. And if the Kadets were to save the duma they had of necessity to restrain the extreme left and thus drive the Mensheviki deeper into the opposition, into the hands of the Bolsheviki. Generally speaking, if governmental circles were hereafter more outspoken in their dislike of the duma, the Social-Democrats were more firmly resolved than ever to employ the duma as a spearhead of open revolution against the domination of the political life of the country by "autocratic-feudal" elements.

XIV

DISSOLUTION

WHEN the deputies had returned from the East-er recess to the Taurida Palace late in April, the attitudes toward the duma of the three contending forces in the liberation movement had become fairly crystallized. Everyone knew by then that the Kadets would consider some "tactical" retreat even from liberalism in order to preserve the duma in its existing form and give it time to take root. It was also obvious that the leaders of the left, the Social-Democrats, were making strenuous efforts in the duma, regardless of its fate, to arouse a population fast losing its revolutionary enthusiasm. As for the government, its animosity toward the duma was common knowledge. There was only the question of how long the Stolypin administration would tolerate it in its current form and whether, if changes were to be made, parliament was to be entirely scrapped or would be allowed to exist in a form more innocuous to the rulers, according to the letter, if not the spirit of the manifesto of October 17, 1905.

And Stolypin's hands, we have seen, were not entirely free. For besides a frontal attack from the entire opposition calling for a responsible ministry, the premier, answerable only to the tsar, had to face pressure from the rear. The tsar himself had become insistent on dissolution, and the reactionary court circle who had his Majesty's ear —Schwanebach, Durnovo, and their ilk—strove for a more pliable legislative body with a highly restricted franchise.[1] As the duma became more assertive, as incident fol-

1. Testimony of Kokovtsov before the Extraordinary Investigating Committee of the Provisional Government in 1917 collected in *Padenie tsarskogo rezhima*, VII, 97–100, 103. (Hereafter only the volume, page, and name of the witness will be noted. Abbreviation will be *Pad. tsarsk. rezh.* See bibliography.) Kryzhanovskii (assistant minister of the interior 1906–1907), *ibid.*, V, 381–382, 389, 417. S. E. Kryzhanovskii, *Vospominaniia*, p. 112.

lowed incident, Stolypin's policy of dealing with the most representative, if most actively oppositional, legislative body in Russian history, became daily more obnoxious to the "ruling spheres," and the premier turned to look to his own fences. The violent criticism from the left, in general, often containing only thinly veiled revolutionary appeals, aroused the government. In particular, the assault on the administration by the entire opposition on the question of the Riga tortures, the frontal attack on the budget, the evasion of an unequivocal condemnation of political murders, the wide differences between the government and the opposition on the agrarian question, and finally, the "Zurabov incident," each, in turn, convinced the administration that this duma was uncontrollable. By the beginning of May, 1907, it fully believed that it could neither hope to dominate nor come to terms with the Second Duma. And since it would not itself submit to popular control and a weak and divided parliament, or make way for a duma ministry, the Stolypin administration, representing itself as a stickler for constitutional form, resorted to measures both legal and unconstitutional to safeguard its continued existence and that of the irresponsible executive established by the constitution of 1905.[2]

The dissolution of the Second Duma, the culminating point of a plan long under consideration by the government, was not in itself an end, but was rather a step in the direction of the greater goal of changing the electoral system. The idea of working such a change arose soon after the dissolution of the First Duma when it was discussed only as an academic question. The council of ministers was, as we know, at that time subjected to great pressure from the nobility and other persons who pointed to the imperfections in the law of December 11, 1905. They noted that it permitted multiple voting, especially

2. Supreme Manifesto dissolving the duma, *Pol. sob. zak.*, XXVII, no. 29,240; Kokovtsov, *Pad. tsarsk. rezh.*, VII, 99; Kryzhanovskii, *ibid.*, V, 416, 417. S. E. Kryzhanovskii, *Vospominaniia*, pp. 107–108.

obnoxious to them as an electoral right of the peasantry.[3]
Among the ministers themselves there were those who
feared that another election under the old law would lead
to the same results thus paralyzing the normal work of
the state.[4]

Yet, in promulgating the new election law the government had of necessity to submit it to the duma before it
could take effect. For if it intended to avoid that procedure by simultaneously publishing the measure as a
decree and dissolving the duma, the administration might
fall back only on Article 87 of the Fundamental Law. But
the constitution explicitly forbade changes in its articles
or those of the electoral law under the authority of Article
87. In other words, neither of these laws could be changed
in an inter-duma period by an emergency measure.

However, it was not until after the composition of the
Second Duma had become clear that Stolypin seriously
considered a change. He had been led by the falsified election reports of the St. Petersburg Telegraphic Agency to
believe that a pliable or coöperative duma might be
obtained under the existing electoral law. Nevertheless, he
was willing to give the duma a fair trial, and restrained
his initial disappointment. But this feeling developed and
turned into downright hostility as the duma showed itself
to be even less tractable than its predecessor.[5] Yet he
arrived at his final decision to change the electoral law
only after much hesitation and long discussions with the
entire cabinet during the winter of 1906-1907.[6] Here he
found two distinct opinions on the matter. Schwanebach,
representing the extreme conservatives, declared for the
necessity of a change which he would publish at the
moment of dissolution. On the other hand, Foreign Minister Izvolskii, somewhat more liberal than his colleagues

3. Kryzhanovskii, *Pad. tsarsk. rezh.*, V, 382, 401; Kokovtsov, *ibid.*, VII, 99;
Kokovtsov, *Memoirs*, p. 165.

4. Kokovtsov, *Memoirs*, p. 165.

5. Kokovtsov, *Pad. tsarsk. rezh.*, VII, 99–101; Kokovtsov, *Memoirs*, p. 165.

6. Kokovtsov, *Memoirs*, p. 166.

and naturally more sensitive to foreign opinion, observed that this move would make a bad impression abroad. Therefore, he opposed dissolution and stood his ground even after Stolypin had become more or less fully converted to Schwanebach's view. But at the end of March, without previous warning, Izvolskii suddenly reversed his stand after receiving a telegram from the Russian ambassador at Lisbon informing him that the Portuguese Cortes had been successfully and easily dissolved.[7]

The new electoral law was written early in May by Assistant Minister of the Interior S. E. Kryzhanovskii. By that time the government had decided on dissolution and was already taking steps to bring it about. The law was immediately adopted by the cabinet with almost no discussion. Following Schwanebach's plan the council decided to issue it at the moment of dissolution and accompany it with a manifesto in order to explain an obvious violation of the constitution as an act of extreme necessity.[8] There was never any doubt in the minds of the ministers that their plan was illegal.[9] But Stolypin feared that should he refuse to change the law, once the duma was dissolved the reactionary circles would put pressure on the tsar to refrain from convoking it for a number of years, or to refuse to recall it at all. Consequently, he considered a change in the electoral law modifying the rules on representation as an absolute necessity if the duma were to be preserved. Moreover, Stolypin was tempted to rationalize his act. He maintained that although a change in the electoral law without the consent of the duma might be essentially illegal, the tsar himself would be formally violating no law in promulgating it for he had taken no oath to support laws issued during his reign. His successor would be the first to do that. Above

7. Kokovtsov, *Pad. tsarsk. rezh.*, VII, 100; Kokovtsov, *Memoirs*, pp. 176–177.

8. Kokovtsov, *Pad. tsarsk. rezh.*, VII, 101, 103; Kryzhanovskii, *ibid.*, V, 381, 417, 425.

9. Kokovtsov, *ibid.*, VII, 102; Kryzhanovskii, *ibid.*, V, 418; Kryzhanovskii, *Vospominaniia*, p. 110.

all, it seemed to him that the tsar had every right to abolish an institution which he himself had founded.[10] But deep in his heart, as usual, Stolypin was "betting on the strong." With the elaboration of a change in the electoral law, the stage was completely set for the final act. And the bureaucratic machine, resorting to old bureaucratic methods, began ponderously to grind a wondrous "cause" for the dissolution of the Second Duma.

Ever since the mutinies at Kronstadt and Sveaborg in the preceding summer, the government had kept a particularly close watch on the movements of the illegal Social-Democratic military organizations through the secret agents of the *Okhrana* or "State Security" department. One such agent was Ekaterina Shornikova.[11] In 1905-1906, at the age of twenty-two she was busily engaged in revolutionary work in the Kazan Social-Democratic organization. When she came to St. Petersburg in 1906, she was arrested at the order of the Kazan Gendarme Administration for having contributed a revolutionary letter to an illegal Social-Revolutionary organ. At police headquarters she was questioned and taken to the *Okhrana* where, after some coaxing, she was prevailed upon to join the secret service. She was then placed directly under the guidance of Lieutenant-Colonel Elenskii who was in charge of agents observing the Social-Democratic Party. She met him almost daily in a "conspirative apartment" and Elenskii, in turn, forwarded her report to A. V. Gerasimov, director of the *Okhrana*. The latter reported directly to Stolypin as minister of the interior.[12]

In the course of her activity she came in contact with Social-Democratic party workers and was invited to join

10. Kokovtsov, *ibid.*, VII, 102; Kryzhanovskii, *ibid.*, V, 381, 417, 418. V. I. Gurko, *Features and Figures of the Past*, pp. 510–511.

11. Shornikova's story is to be found in her testimony to Beletskii, director of the police department, on June 25, 1913. *Pad. tsarsk. rezh.*, V, 94–98; in a letter to the police chief, *ibid.*, III, 456–457; in testimony of Beletskii, *ibid.*, 426–427.

12. Beletskii, *Pad. tsarsk. rezh.*, V, 94–95; Gerasimov (director of *Okhrana*, 1905–1909), *ibid.*, III, 4, 5.

the St. Petersburg organization. This she did with the consent of the *Okhrana* and became an organizer in the Ataman regiment. Elenskii soon pressed her to assume a more responsible post. Therefore, upon being offered the position of secretary of the St. Petersburg Military Organization of the Social-Democratic Party she accepted and proved a valuable source of information. For through her the entire guiding personnel, archives, and activity of the organization were well known at *Okhrana* headquarters.

Through her, again (and through later investigations), the police learned that a meeting had been held on April 23, on Romenskaia, at the initiative of a student of the Polytechnical Institute, Sopotnitskii (Alibei), and one Morozova (Varia). Here Sopotnitskii had reported on the progress of agitational and organizational work in the army.[13] More important, the *Okhrana* learned that the organization had held a second meeting on April 29, in one of the buildings of the Polytechnical Institute attended by Sopotnitskii, Morozova, a student V. S. Voitinskii, the Social-Democratic deputy L. F. Gerus and fourteen soldiers.[14] Gerus questioned the soldiers concerning their daily lives in the army and their attitude toward the duma. He found that they knew and thought little about public affairs. Therefore, the meeting decided to draw up an "instruction" from the army to the Social-Democratic fraction which was to be used as the basis of a bill to be presented to the duma. However, the meeting adjourned prematurely when a false alarm for a police raid caused an immediate evacuation.[15]

An "instruction" was eventually written by Vladimir

13. Beletskii, *ibid.*, V, 95; Gerasimov, *ibid.*, III, 4, 5: Zaitsev's "order," *Stenog. ot.*, II, 1,486.

14. Beletskii, *ibid.*, V, 95; Report of *Okhrana* to Judicial Investigator Zaitsev, *Krasnyi Arkhiv*, XVI, 84–85; V. Voitinskii, *Gody pobied i porazhenii*, II, 201.

15. Report of *Okhrana* to Zaitsev, *Krasnyi Arkhiv*, XVI, 84–85; Indictment of the Social-Democratic fraction of the Second Duma, *Byloe*, no. 14, Popov's testimony on pp. 161–162; Voitinskii, *Gody pobied i porazhenii*, II, 201–202.

Voitinskii[16] on May 3. It was addressed to the Social-Democratic fraction from the army divisions of the St. Petersburg garrison. Its authors explained that they were representatives of that part of the army upon which the government would have to rely immediately to put down any popular uprising resulting from a clash between it and the duma. Therefore, it was the duty of the St. Petersburg organization to tell the soldiers where they should stand, but in this matter they required the aid of the Social-Democratic fraction. The "instruction" then declared that most of the soldiers hardly thought about the duma since it had not concerned itself with their needs, and the few words mentioned were understood by only the "advanced" elements in the army. The organization urged the deputies to correct this situation by saying more about the personal needs and sufferings of the soldiers which were ever present in their minds; of their burdensome work, dull, superfluous studies, prison-like existence, the overbearing attitude of the officers who forced them to do menial service, etc. Further, the "instruction" requested the deputies to draw up a bill safeguarding the soldier's rights while on service, relieving the prison-like atmosphere of their lives, placing them under a general civil court for criminal acts, and under the jurisdiction of their officers only while on duty. It exhorted the deputies to show their interest in the soldiers by appealing to all sections of the army to give them materials on their intimate needs, and by inviting their representatives to the headquarters of the fraction. This they were to do regardless of the attitude of the rest of the duma. And if the government should drive them out as a result of their efforts, the army would rally behind them.[17] On the following day,

16. Voitinskii, *Gody pobied i porazhenii*, II, 203–204. The Okhrana report named his brother I. S. Voitinskii, but at the time of his arrest the police had an order containing only his surname which confused them. Consequently both brothers were taken to the Spasskoi district jail and held for examination. See *Ibid.*, pp. 201–203.

17. *Ibid.*, p. 203. Text in *Krasnyi Arkhiv*, XVI, 78–80.

May 4, Voitinskii gave the script of the "instruction" to Sopotnitskii and on the same evening the committee of the military organization adopted it.[18]

On the following evening, that of Saturday, May 5, eight or ten soldiers were summoned to the apartment of one Solomon Fisher on Fontanka street with the propagandists Sopotnitskii and Shornikova. The latter read the instruction to the soldiers and informed them of a projected visit to the Social-Democratic headquarters. With the soldiers in uniform and mufti they preceded immediately to deputy Ozol's apartment at 92 Nevskii Prospekt, the offices of the Social-Democratic fraction.[19]

On all of these matters, Shornikova had been keeping the *Okhrana* well posted, and this alert body was quick to pounce upon the instruction, when it came to its attention, as proof that the Social-Democratic fraction, or some of its members were participating in an illegal Social-Democratic organization. Here, indeed, the government believed that it had found an excellent means of precipitating the dissolution of the duma. It planned to charge the Social-Democrats with participating in a criminal society, demand their surrender of the duma and upon the expected refusal dissolve parliament.[20] When Stolypin learned of the "instruction" he called for a copy of the document to make certain that it contained the damning evidence.[21] That might have presented great difficulties for Shornikova had not the committee of the military organization asked her to type a copy of the "instruction" since the soldiers could not easily read script. Thereupon the informeress proceeded to make two copies, one of which she gave to Sopotnitskii and the other to Elenskii. She destroyed the original hand-written text in Sopotnitskii's presence.[22]

18. Voitinskii, *Gody pobied i porazhenii*, II, 204; *Stenog. ot.*, II, 1,487.
19. *Krasnyi Arkhiv*, XVI, 85; Beletskii, *Pad. tsarsk. rezh.*, V, 95–96; *Byloe*, no. 14, pp. 141, 144, 145; *Stenog. ot.*, II, 1,488.
20. Kokovtsov, *Memoirs*, p. 184.
21. Gerasimov, *Pad. tsarsk. rezh.*, III, 4, 5, 6.
22. *Ibid.*, p. 8; Beletskii, *ibid.*, V, 95.

The government now believed that it had sufficient information and after obtaining the time of the proposed visit through Shornikova, the *Okhrana* decided to strike at the moment when the soldiers would be at the fraction's headquarters with the "instruction" in the deputies' hands.[23] Accordingly, Lieutenant Colonel Komissarov of the *Okhrana* commissioned a junior clerk, Ksenzenko, officer Gubskii, and the captain of the Litienyi ward to arrest a meeting at 92 Nevskii Prospekt which was to assemble at about 7 P. M., and search all persons and the rooms. If deputies were present they were to be searched only after judicial authorities had been called to the scene. When the military group arrived the police had already set up a watch on the building.[24]

Whether by chance or with purpose, the military group had chosen the time well for their visit, for on Saturday evenings the fraction held its weekly meeting and "open house" for petitioners, correspondents, etc. At about 7.40 P. M. the group arrived and presented themselves to the deputies who, for the most part, had no inkling of its plans.[25] The sailor Arkhipov handed them the "instruction" which they read, and their spokesmen, Ozol, Saltykov, and Lopatkin, informed the visitors that at the moment they could give them no definite reply, but would present the matter to a committee. Ozol then placed the "instruction" in his portfolio. Agitated by the dangerous situation, and perhaps suspecting a trap, the deputies urged the delegates to leave immediately in order to avoid any chance of being arrested in the apartment. Those in civilian dress left by the front entrance while the uniformed men were directed to a passage in the rear.[26]

23. Gerasimov, *ibid.*, III, 4; Komissarov, *ibid.*, p. 152.

24. Ksenzenko's report to the gendarme department, *Krasnyi Arkhiv*, XVI, 80; Report of *Okhrana* to minister of the interior, *ibid.*, p. 82.

25. V. Mandelberg, *Iz perezhitago*, pp. 141–142; *Tovarishch*, May 6, p. 2; Beletskii, *Pad. tsarsk. rezh.*, V, 96; Zurabov, *Vtoraia gosudarstvennaia duma*, p. 84.

26. *Byloe*, no. 14, pp. 154–155, 146; Beletskii, *Pad. tsarsk. rezh.*, V, 96; *Krasnyi Arkhiv*, XVI, 85.

Within the hour the police had burst into the fraction's headquarters. Following their instructions they occupied all rooms and began to search each of the seventy-five persons present, including thirty-five deputies.[27] By the time that Bielanovskii, Lopatkin, Marev, and Prikhodko had been examined, the remaining deputies objected to the violation of their immunity and presented cards to identify themselves. Thereupon the police segregated them in a separate room and returned all that had been taken from the four who had been searched. They called for the assistant prosecutor of the district court and the judicial inspector, and continued their operations on private persons whom they had found in the reception room. This done they began to search the apartment but were immediately opposed by Ozol who maintained that it was his property and was therefore as inviolable as his own person. When the district captain attempted to confiscate some of the written matter lying about, it was snatched from his hands. Therefore, in order to avoid the responsibility for any violence which might result, the captain suspended the search until the judicial authorities should arrive.[28]

After waiting for about two hours the deputies reached the prosecutor of the St. Petersburg Provincial Supreme Court, P. D. Kamyshanskii, and requested his presence at the apartment. He arrived shortly after 11 P. M. close on the heels of the two judicial authorities who had previously been summoned.[29] Kamyshanskii immediately took charge. He glanced at the search warrant, the like of which he had seen hundreds of times before, and maintained that the police were acting entirely within the law on an order of the *Okhrana*. Therefore, he contended, the affair was not within his jurisdiction as prosecutor of an ordinary civil court. It was his opinion that the apart-

27. *Stenog. ot.*, II, 212–213, 203–204.
28. *Krasnyi Arkhiv*, XVI, 81; *Stenog. ot.*, II, 204–207; Mandelberg, *Iz perezhitago*, 141–142.
29. They had attempted to reach the ministers of justice and interior by telephone but failed.

ment, if not the deputies, might be searched. But he was met with a stubborn refusal on the part of the deputies who stood by Ozol. To break the deadlock, at about 1 A.M. Kamyshanskii decided to confer with the minister of justice. He returned in about an hour to inform the deputies that Shcheglovitov and he were of the same opinion. But still the deputies were adamant. At that moment some of them noted that in the *Okhrana* order there was no mention of a "state of protection" under which that body might operate, but simply references to articles of the Criminal Code. This placed the matter within the jurisdiction of civil authorities and made Kamyshanskii master of the situation. He immediately called on the *Okhrana* for those documents which served as grounds for the search, and failing to find a copy of the "instruction" he came to the conclusion that there were no grounds for an investigation and the deputies were allowed to leave.[30]

Thus far, despite all precautions, planning, and informing, the pains taken by the administration had yielded it only added notoriety, for it had found neither the soldiers nor their instruction at the fraction's apartments. However, on May 6, the *Okhrana* arrested everyone known to be connected with the military organization.[31] Several of them were questioned on May 7, and gave information about the organization. Arkhipov, in particular, was talk-

---

30. *Kraznyi Arkhiv*, XVI, 81; *Stenog. ot.*, II, 205–207; V. Mandelberg, *Iz perezhitago*, pp. 142–143; *Tovarishch*, May 9, p. 7; May 6, p. 2; *Riech*, May 6, p. 3; Kamyshanskii's testimony to duma committee, *Krasnyi Arkhiv*, XLIII, 81–83. In the meantime four deputies who had already been examined were allowed to depart earlier. They went directly to Golovin whom they awoke and informed of the proceedings at the fraction's headquarters. Golovin telephoned Stolypin, but the latter refused to interfere. He maintained that the proceedings were perfectly legal if carried out in the presence of judicial authorities. *Riech*, May 8, p. 4 Duma Sup. The non-deputies whose number rose to forty-seven (as all newcomers were held) were subjected to a thorough search and distributed among the district jails to await investigation. *Ibid.* A list of persons held is to be found in *ibid.*, May 12, p. 3, Duma Sup.

31. One Kutyrev somehow eluded the police and Shornikova was forewarned by the department, supplied with funds, and allowed to escape. V. Voitinskii, *Gody pobied i porazhenii*, II, 102–103; *Byloe*, no. 14, p. 164; Beletskii, *Pad. tsarsk. rezh.*, V, 96; Gerasimov, *ibid.*, III, 78; *Krasnyi Arkhiv*, XLIII, 83.

ative. He had been taken to headquarters in an inebriated
state and unburdened himself of all that he knew. Among
other things he revealed that the "instruction" was in the
hands of the Social-Democratic deputies.[32] Consequently,
another raid was staged on Ozol's apartment on May 8,
under the guidance of Judicial Investigator Zaitsev. For
four hours the premises were subjected to a careful search
in the proprietor's absence but the incriminating document was not found and the administration was forced to
rely on the copy produced by Shornikova.[33]

Meanwhile, on the preceding day, May 7, two urgent
interpellations to the ministers of the interior and justice
had been introduced which narrated the events of May 5,
and charged the government with violating Article 15 of
the Duma Statute and Article 16 of the Fundamental
Laws requiring the duma's consent for the arrest of deputies. They asked the ministers if they were aware of the
facts; if they were investigating this violation of the
immunity of deputies; whether or not Kamyshanskii was
being disciplined for supporting the activity of the police,
and what measures were being taken to protect members
of the duma.[34]

Stolypin replied at once.[35] Addressing the duma as
chairman of the council of ministers he declared that the
police had legally entered the apartment where they had
expected to find an illegal meeting of the central committee of a criminal, revolutionary, military organization.
This they could do since St. Petersburg was in a state of
"extraordinary security." He admitted that several deputies had been subjected to personal search, but added that
most of them had refused to submit. No force was applied,

32. Beletskii, *Pad. tsarsk. rezh.*, V, 97; *Byloe*, no. 14, p. 156; *Stenog. ot.*,
II, 1,485–1,486, 1,490; *Krasnyi Arkhiv*, XLIII, 83.
33. *Stenog. ot.*, II, 1,490. Many other materials were gathered including instructions, petitions, letters to the voters, and illegal publications, all of which
played a great part in the activity of the government which followed. *Riech*,
May 9, pp. 2, 7.
34. *Stenog. ot.*, II, 203–207.
35. *Ibid.*, pp. 207–208.

he declared. Evidently referring to the investigation of members of the military organization, he informed the duma that since May 5, the detective department had discovered a connection between the fraction and the revolutionary military society. He further asserted that the police would act in the future as they had in the past. For besides protecting members of the duma they had public safety to look after.

The Social-Democrats defended the urgency of the interpellation. In one of those rare moments when they showed concern for the duma they maintained that its very existence was being threatened. At the very heart of the empire deputies were held at the point of a pistol because officials could not arrive on time. In this manner, they contended, the government might some day detain an entire fraction and thus prevent a quorum from assembling. No greater question faced the duma in their opinion than the dignity of the people's representatives; their freedom and inviolability. For a violation of their rights struck at the very roots of the idea of popular representation as it was understood in Europe. As a final consideration they observed that despite all the indignities to which their fraction had been subjected, Kamyshanskii had found no grounds for an investigation on the night of the search.[36] And the duma, fully aroused by the act and aware of its implications, quickly accepted the interpellation as urgent.[37]

To ensure the adoption of the statement the Social-Democrats offered eye-witness accounts of the search and maintained that if the duma did not check the government at once it would soon be rendered powerless. It would become merely another chancellery. For if allowed to repeat the raid the government might deal with any of its political opponents in the same manner. And since Kamyshanskii had found no cause for a search any deputy might become the victim of lying agents. Any private

36. *Ibid.*, pp. 209–210, 210–211, 211–213.
37. *Ibid.*, pp. 213–214.

home frequented by a number of people might be raided
and all present charged with holding a revolutionary
meeting.[38]

Shcheglovitov, minister of justice, then mounted the
tribune to defend the government.[39] It was true, he
admitted, that the search was made on insufficient
grounds, but that was because the raid was carried out
too late. And the police now had definite evidence that the
illegal society had visited Ozol's apartment. He contended
that the police had acted legally in detaining the deputies
since they proceeded under Article 258 of the Criminal
Code[40] according to which judicial officials had to be
called, and the search carried on if it were of such importance that it could not be postponed. He charged, amid
shouts of "lie," that a joint session of the military organization and the fraction had actually been arranged to
arouse sympathy in the duma for the condition of the
soldiers. The minister maintained that everywhere a
deputy was regarded as inviolable but not the premises
he occupied; these were subject to judicial investigation.
Moreover, he believed that judicial authorities might
search anyone they desired and that inviolability of members of parliament would not suffer thereby.[41] He closed
in a truculent tone, informing the duma that in his opinion
the prosecutor's actions were legal and even though the
duma might regard them otherwise he would refuse to
reply to the interpellation.

The Social-Democrats met the charge of conspiracy
with mingled emotions. They stoutly denied that a meeting

38. *Ibid.*, pp. 214–218, 218–221.
39. *Ibid.*, pp. 221–224.
40. *Svod zakonov rossiiskoi imperii*, XV.
41. He attempted to discredit the Social-Democratic Party by charging that
it had been paid by a shopkeeper for removing a boycott. Ozol explained in an
open letter that the boycott in question had been decreed because the shopkeeper was the first to raise the price of bread and that when it became effective
he pleaded for its removal. This party agreed to do if the store owner would
donate 100 rubles to the unemployed. The receipt for this donation was found
at Ozol's apartment, and was that of the council of unemployed not the fraction's. *Stenog. ot.*, II, 248; *Riech*, May 31, p. 3.

such as the minister described had ever taken place. And Saltykov enumerated all who were likely to be present at the fraction's headquarters on the night of the raid— except the delegation from the military group.[42] The Novgorod peasant Izmailov was full of fear for the future. "I am against anarchy, but I say that after such behavior there will be anarchy in the land. I know the people." And deputy Anikin found cause for mirth in the situation. The government, he declared, acted as if it had committed some deeds which could not be justified by law. Like a monster it tried to hide its ugliness and only succeeded in appearing ridiculous. Saltykov had taken notes on Shcheglovitov's speech and Kamyshanskii's opinion and concluded that the former had attempted to cover the omissions of the latter. He read a summary of an opinion which he declared had been partly written, partly dictated by Kamyshanskii himself. Here the prosecutor had maintained that neither the person nor the property of a deputy would be violated if he were to be searched under a "security" law. He had found nothing illegal in the activities of the police. Saltykov asked that this statement be joined to the interpellation in the record as proof of the prosecutor's illegal stand.[43]

By a vote taken shortly thereafter the duma accepted the interpellation. Lines were being drawn tighter. If the government had already adopted a final attitude toward the duma, the great majority in the Russian parliament was solidly opposed to the Stolypin administration on a vital constitutional issue. The Social-Democrats had argued their case well. Kamyshanskii had made the damaging admission that there were insufficient grounds for the raid and the search for motives which followed aroused the suspicion that the government was seeking a pretext for the arrest of the Social-Democratic fraction. It took little imagination to perceive that the administration had chanced upon a new method of dealing with its

42. *Stenog. ot.*, II, 243–246, 246–250.
43. *Ibid.*, pp. 230–231, 237–238.

political adversaries in the duma. As a matter of fact, the government had not initiated the idea of composing an instruction and presenting it to the fraction. But it had sought to take advantage of the normal constitutional act of presenting a petition to destroy the entire fraction. For although no formal, pre-arranged, joint meeting had taken place, the discovery of the illegal, military organization in the fraction headquarters would have dangerously compromised it. Of these facts and the further plans of the government the Second Duma was not aware, but the very detention of the deputies warned them both of the possible imminence of dissolution and of the serious threat to their liberties and the principles of representative government.

By the end of May the government was ready to strike. On Wednesday, May 30, Stolypin informed the tsar that he would present a demand to the duma on Friday to surrender fifty-five deputies and that he would dissolve it should it refuse to comply. Fifteen deputies considered most culpable would be arrested immediately. He explained that the council had decided that a demand for the arrest of all fifty-five would appear more like an act of political vengeance than a serious judicial accusation. But he believed that all who attempted to hide would be discovered by the police and held for examination. On the following day he sent the tsar, for his signature, a manifesto dissolving the duma. In a note accompanying it Stolypin declared that the new electoral law would be ready for his imperial signature on the next day.[44]

Before the fifty-second session of the duma opened on June 1, Golovin received a request from Stolypin that he be allowed to speak at once on a subject which could not be postponed. Under Article 44 of the Duma Statute he asked that the session be closed to the public.[45] When Golovin announced the premier, the duma seethed with excitement; especially the Social-Democrats who sensed

44. Kokovtsov, *Memoirs*, p. 184; *Krasnyi Arkhiv*, V, 113, 113–114.
45. *Krasnyi Arkhiv*, XLIII, 60.

trouble in the offing. Stolypin then mounted the tribune. With a metallic ring in his voice he informed the duma that the search at Ozol's apartment had revealed the existence of a criminal organization which included several deputies. This state of affairs rendered immediate judicial proceedings necessary. Therefore, he asked the duma to listen to prosecutor Kamyshanskii as he read an "order" of Judicial Investigator Zaitsev for the arrest of a number of its members. Further explanations would be given by the minister of justice. Any dallying with the government's demands, he warned, or failure to satisfy it completely would make it impossible for the administration to guarantee quiet and order in the empire.[46]

Kamyshanskii then arose to read the lengthy "order." It began with a narrative of the events of May 5, and described the documents which had been found. It declared, further, that the provincial prosecutor had gained possession of a copy of the "instruction" and a complete list of the members of the military organization which had written and presented it. Kamyshanskii read the document to the hushed deputies. And still reading from Zaitsev's "order" he informed his listeners that additional important materials had been discovered in the Social-Democratic headquarters on May 8, when a search was conducted for the elusive original of the "instruction." These, he explained, consisted of a copy of the Stockholm Resolutions, letters to party organizations, proclamations, and instructions from local partisan groups.[47]

On the basis of the information derived from this mass of evidence he charged the entire fraction with participation in a criminal society. But he excepted sixteen who had only an advisory vote and could, therefore, not be

46. *Stenog. ot.*, II, 1,481, 1,481–1,482.

47. *Ibid.*, pp. 1,482–1,515. Written May 31, the three letters discussed amnesty, the government's declaration, and the organization of the fraction. And five proclamations were issued stating the party's stand on wages, conditions of railroad workers, unemployment, famine relief, agricultural reform, and the budget. See also Chap. III.

held responsible for its activities.[48] He charged the accused with plotting for the violent overthrow of the established form of government by means of a popular uprising, and the creation of a democratic republic in its stead. For the accomplishment of this end, he declared that the criminal society (the fraction) had entered into relations with the illegal central committee of the Russian Social-Democratic Labor Party and its St. Petersburg committee. Moreover, the society had subordinated itself to the central committee in preparation for a popular uprising. It had directed the activities of local criminal organizations (local Social-Democratic groups) and had sent out circular letters with the intention of inciting the population against the government, military officials, nobles, and landowners. This society had entrusted secret criminal committees with the organization of workers, peasants, and soldiers for the uprising and had itself directly called on these elements to rebel. Then it had entered into relations with secret organizations which aimed to arouse a mutiny in the army. Deputy Gerus had conducted a meeting of a branch of this group, while the society (the fraction) had received instructions from its Vilna and St. Petersburg branches. It had served as a center for the reception of revolutionary demands calling for the convocation of a constituent assembly and the violent establishment of a democratic republic. It was in close contact with secret, illegal committees. It had called on their representatives for instructions and sent out members to agitate among them. Finally, it had in its possession passports for hiding refugees from justice. The order held the entire fraction (with the exceptions noted) guilty of criminal activity, and sixteen deputies were to be investigated immediately and placed under guard. To enable him to

48. These were K. M. Aframovich, A. V. Bodrov, F. I. Gudovich, A. A. Kuznetsov, I. P. Kumelis, A. S. Kupstas, M. M. Murten, A. M. Povilius, V. A. Stashinskii, A. G. Fedorov and Z. Y. Chepovenko. *Stenog. ot.*, II, 1,412. Among those whom he held responsible was N. I. Konshin, who had resigned from the Social-Democratic Party and had joined the Kadets. Compare *Tovarishch*, April 10, p. 2.

fulfill his duty Zaitsev asked the duma for the right to proceed against the accused.[49] The ministry of justice immediately presented identical demands.[50]

The duma was astounded. Orders for the arrest of individual deputies were not new even to the three-month-old duma.[51] But it was amazed by the scope of the demands. And though still incompletely informed on the charges it could perceive an undertone of insincerity. For the "order" accused not individuals of certain political crimes but a whole fraction; even more, a whole party. A precedent had been set and any unlegalized party might be served with broad, general accusations. Moreover, the charges brought against the Social-Democratic Party and its fraction had for years been the common knowledge of the entire Russian nation. It was easy to conclude that the administration had selfish, political aims.

When the duma reassembled, following a recess, Golovin read a proposal which urged the deputies to consider what action they would take on the government's demands.[52] Kadet Teslenko enlarged on the statement.[53] The problem which confronted the duma was serious, and should, of course, be considered at once. But he warned that since the government's demands were not on the agenda the duma was bound by Article 93 of its rules to consider only whether the demands were to be sent to a committee or discussed on the following day.[54] The subject matter of the accusations, he asserted, could not now be discussed. He felt, moreover, that time was needed to study the documents presented. As a precedent, since the duma

49. I. A. Tsereteli, I. V. Kirienko, A. L. Dzhaparidze, V. I. Mitrov, G. A. Aleksinskii, I. P. Ozol, S. N. Saltykov, N. V. Komar, G. I. Bielousov, P. A. Anikin, L. F. Gerus, V. B. Lomtatidze, V. A. Anisimov, V. M. Sierov, A. K. Vinogradov, and I. N. Lopatkin. *Stenog. ot.*, II, 1,510–1,515.

50. At this point Konshin officially noted that he was a member of the Kadet party. *Ibid.*, p. 1,517. See Kuzmin-Karavaev, *ibid.*, pp. 1,523–1,524.

51. See Chapter III on S-D fraction.

52. *Stenog. ot.*, II, 1,517.

53. *Ibid.*, pp. 1,517, 1,518–1.521.

54. *Nakaz*, p. 37. The substance of matters not on the agenda could not be discussed until the following day.

had not yet established an order for handling such matters, he proposed that it create a committee of twenty-two members which was to be elected immediately and bring in its conclusions on the following day.

But others in the duma felt differently and strongly about the government's demands, and Teslenko's statement precipitated a lively debate which continued until after midnight. The extreme right, the Octobrists, and non-partisan right were ranged solidly against the creation of a committee or even prolonged discussion of the matter. Purishkevich and the Octobrist Krupenskii had objected vehemently to the proposal immediately after its introduction.[55] To them the matter was entirely clear from the evidence presented, and Purishkevich went so far as to urge haste in expelling the accused so that the duma might see those sitting in its midst as legislators imprisoned and hanged as was their desert. Russia, the rightists declared, faced not a political but a social revolution as did France in 1871. And they urged the duma to follow the example of the French deputies who had annihilated Socialism with courts-martial. The very existence of the empire was involved, they cried, and this was not a moment to observe "pitiful rules," especially since the article to which Teslenko referred had not yet been adopted. Nor did they feel that it was a moment for thorough discussions; they appealed to the duma's feeling of "patriotism" rather than to its "logic" to settle the fate of the Social-Democrats. Fearing a Kadet-dominated committee which might out-manoeuver Stolypin, exonerate the Marxists, or give them time to escape, the rightists proposed that the fractions meet separately and report to the duma on the following day. Finally, they urged that the duma had no legal or moral right to protract the consideration of the government's demands. For all decisions adopted in a duma where fifty-five offenders against the state sat and voted would be null and void.[56]

55. *Stenog. ot.*, II, 1,518–1,519.
56. *Ibid.*, pp. 1,530–1,532, 1,537–1,540, 1,546, 1,548–1,550.

As was often the case in the Second Duma, the Social-Democrats were at one with their extreme opponents on the right, but for vastly different reasons. They opposed the election of a committee because they feared that such a course might create the impression among the people that the duma was bowing to the government or had not opposed it with sufficient energy. Tsereteli uttered the first word on the matter from the Social-Democratic benches long after the debates had begun.[57] He, too, would not be bound by formalities at this auspicious moment when the very existence of the duma was at stake. And Russia's salvation, he believed, lay in a union of the people with the duma as its mentor. If the Social-Democrats were charged with promoting that union, they would proudly accept the accusation as evidence that their fraction had performed its duty well. If similar moments in the past were to be sought he pointed ironically to the Eighteenth of Brumaire when Napoleon ejected the Five Hundred at the bayonet's point. If the duma should tremble before bayonets, he cried, it might save itself from an attack by the administration, but not from the wrath of the people at the moment when it would hurl the government into the dust. Mandelberg observed that the administration had no need to resort to doubtful material in the hands of doubtful agents. It had but to listen carefully to the campaign speeches of the Social-Democratic candidates for the duma to learn the party's program and aims. He warned the duma that it could not risk a tremendous loss of authority by evicting the only fraction which represented the proletariat. And it could not afford to increase the power of those who regarded the butchery of the Communaires as an example worthy of imitation. It must straightway and unequivocally reject the government's demands.[58] Finally, Dzhaparidze maintained that since the extremely important matter of the partial dissolution of the duma was involved, and since this was the

57. *Ibid.*, pp. 1,535–1,536.
58. *Ibid.*, pp. 1,552–1,554.

government's first step toward regaining its old, absolute authority, the deputies should rebuff the administration at once. Here was no plot hatched by the left, he exclaimed, but by the cabinet to destroy the truly representative body and create a bureaucratic duma, "feudal" in character. Amid loud applause he threatened the government with popular revolution should it dare to expel the deputies.[59]

The remainder of the duma, the center and the *Narodniki*, were ranged more or less solidly behind Teslenko's proposal. The Social-Revolutionaries held that it was unnecessary to create a committee. But realizing the import of the moment and that a political or social revolution might well result from any steps taken, they desired to maintain a united oppositional front to the government. Therefore, they would accept a committee only if it should be chosen quickly and if its decision was to represent the opinion of the entire duma majority.[60]

Berezin and Poznanskii represented the Trudovik point of view which, in general, favored the election of a committee. The former believed that insufficient consideration of a matter as important as that contained in the government's demands would only do harm to the idea of popular representation in Russia. Referring to the extremists he pleaded with the duma to save that principle from a blow which might return to plague those who delivered it, for Russia's only salvation lay in the duma. In all justice he believed that the accused had to be given a chance to defend themselves, even though their views differed from those of the rest of the duma.[61] Poznanskii maintained that Witte had promised that until the new order should be realized old laws would be applied insofar as they did not contradict the October Manifesto. With

59. *Ibid.*, pp. 1,557–1,558.
60. *Ibid.*, pp. 1,532–1,533, 1,540–1,541. The final Social-Revolutionary orator, Rzhekhin, in an attempt to bring the Social-Democrats in line with the rest of the opposition, proposed a compromise whereby the committee would report in two hours. *Ibid.*, pp. 1,558–1,559.
61. *Ibid.*, pp. 1,521–1,523.

that in mind the duma was to decide whether or not the Social-Democrats had acted criminally. If there really was freedom of speech, was propaganda in the villages criminal, he asked. Moreover, if the duma was to expel the accused it should do so only on grounds which would be considered criminal in any country, and not for the purpose of preserving the old order.[62]

But the proposal received the staunchest support from the center and its allied national groups, the Moslems and the Poles.[63] The Democratic-Reformist Kuzmin-Karavaev found both convincing and doubtful material in the "order," but asked that the entire matter be weighed carefully in a committee. He would have this body establish the line between freedom of action allowed the deputies within the duma and outside of it. He demanded concrete charges against individuals not general accusations. And he observed that one error had already been noted in the case of deputy Konshin who was among the accused although he was not a Social-Democrat.[64] He objected to Tseretcli's insinuation that acceptance of the government's plan would be equivalent to a retreat before its bayonets. Each decided according to his conscience, he asserted. Moreover, he noted that besides being charged with establishing an illegal connection between the duma and the people, the Social-Democrats were accused of distributing illegal propaganda among the troops.[65]

The most effective addresses in support of the proposal to create a committee were delivered by the Kadets Rodichev and Kizevetter. The former viewed the session as the most responsible in the history of the duma and could see no danger or delay in carefully considering the government's demands in a committee. He believed that these involved the violation of the duma's rights, and that the question could not be fully considered instantaneously

62. *Ibid.*, 1,533–1,535. The Popular-Socialists held similar views. *Ibid.*, pp. 1,543–1,546.
63. *Ibid.*, pp. 1,535, 1,536–1,537.
64. See above footnotes 48 and 50.
65. *Stenog. ot.*, II, 1,523–1,524, 1,555–1,556.

by merely reading through the lengthy "order." He had listened attentively; had taken marginal notes, but by his conscience he could not be responsible for the opinion he had formed without further investigation. He realized that the accusation had a political significance, and felt that the duma was duty bound to assure itself that in this case motives of "state necessity" had not prevailed over legal principles. The government had no right to demand an immediate decision, he maintained. For the past three months, the Kadets had fought for the establishment of a solid, legal order, and precisely for that reason they now insisted on an impartial examination of the charges as an act of justice, and to forestall any attempt on the part of the government to make use of expulsion as a weapon in its political battle. Violence had to be fought in any quarter whence it arose, and the accused had to be heard. Come what might, he declared, the duma should leave its work with a clear conscience.[66] Kizevetter was more outspoken.[67] Even experienced jurists, accustomed to gathering the essence of indictments as they were rapidly read, would require a more thorough examination of this matter. Personally, he was already able to perceive the government's machinations in the "order." He felt that the duma could draw only one conclusion. But for the sake of thoroughness he would require an examination of the facts in the committee. He agreed with the right that a true conception of the state had to be preserved, but at the same time he believed that the inalienable rights of the duma had to be safeguarded. No matter how much it was hurried, or with what it was threatened, the duma had to defend its constitutional right to direct all matters to a committee for preliminary examination.

When the debates had ended, the duma, with the Social-Democrats and the right abstaining, accepted the Kadet proposal that a committee be created to consider the government's demands, and their suggestion that this body

66. *Ibid.*, pp. 1,526–1,529.
67. *Ibid.*, pp. 1,549–1,551.

return its decision at an evening session on the following day, Saturday, June 2.[68] When the duma assembled after a brief recess A. A. Kuznetsov read a statement signed by Gudovich, Povilius, Kumelis, and Kupstas, all adherents of the Social-Democratic fraction, to the effect that they shared all of the party's views and had participated in all of its activities. Therefore, they desired to share the fate of the regular members of the fraction.[69] Without comment the duma immediately proceeded to elect the committee and established the agenda for the following day. With the announcement of the results of the elections to the committee, the duma adjourned shortly after 12.30 A.M.[70]

Not entirely surprised by the government's demands, the Social-Democrats, like the rest of the opposition, were taken aback by their boldness. To them it appeared that a partial dissolution of the duma was at hand, and the first move toward a restoration of absolutism. Accordingly, the Marxists would reject the administration's demands at once, without creating a committee. But they were in a minority. Although the *Narodniki* deeply sympathized with them they would have a committee consider the accusations made against the Social-Democrats in order to exonerate them. And even though the Kadets and center believed that the charges were fictitious and too general, yet they would examine them to ascertain the facts. Standing, as ever, on legal grounds, they would demonstrate the duma's right to consider matters in a committee even in the face of a demand for instantaneous action by the government, and the threat of dissolution.

68. *Ibid.*, pp. 1,560–1,561. Debates were ended at about 10 P. M. after thirty orators had given up the right to speak. *Ibid.*, pp. 1,559–1,560. With the adoption of the Kadet proposal, Rzhekhin's automatically fell.

69. *Ibid.*, pp. 1,562–1,563.

70. *Ibid.*, pp. 1,563, 1,565–1,566. The special committee consisted of 2 S-R's (Tigranian, Shirskii), 5 Trudoviki (Berezin, Bulat, Karavaev, Kartashev, Saiko), 2 Popular-Socialists (Delarov, Demianov), 7 Kadets (I. V. Gessen, Kizevetter, Kutler, Maklakov, Pergament, Struve, Teslenko), Kuzmin-Karavaev (Democratic-Reform), 2 Cossacks (Arakantsev, Petrovskii), Khan-Khoiskii the Moslem, and Konits and Parchevskii of the Kolo. See *Ukazatel*, p. 43.

They would oppose violation of the law in any quarter.

Although they realized the danger threatening them, the Social-Democrats appeared in the duma in a body on the following morning. In order to consider how they might use most advantageously the time which remained, they agreed with the Populist parties to call a recess at the beginning of the session.[71] Accordingly, after the opening of the fifty-third session of the duma on June 2, the Social-Revolutionary Gorbunov called for a recess to consider matters on which the various fractions had not yet had time to deliberate. The Social-Democrats gathered with the *Narodniki* in the fraction rooms of the Popular-Socialists. Fully aware of the government's intentions, and suspecting that dissolution was but a matter of hours, they unanimously decided to meet the government's *coup d'etat* with extreme measures of their own. They would refuse to confirm the budget and would abolish Stolypin's agrarian laws in the current session. However, they understood that they would have to contend with the rules of the duma whereby only questions on the agenda for the day might be discussed. The first question in order was the local courts bill, and so many deputies had registered to speak on it that there would be no time to discuss any other matter. But the second point on the agenda was a consideration of the manner in which the budget was to be examined. Taking advantage of this situation, the conference decided to propose a change whereby the second topic would be discussed first. This would enable the duma to adopt a passage to the regular order containing a refusal to confirm the budget. Having taken that drastic step, they hoped to convince the duma of the necessity of disregarding rules under extraordinary circumstances, and of annulling all agricultural measures which Stolypin had introduced under Article 87. A committee was chosen to elaborate a formula of passage and edit a statement invalidating the government's agrarian

71. *Ternii bez roz,* pp. 25-26.

measures. Realizing that little could be accomplished without the support of the center, a second committee was selected to confer with the Kadets and the Kolo.[72]

However, the plan met with difficulties from the start. Golovin had either forgotten to ring the bell ending the recess or the assembled leftists had not heard it. And when they failed to appear in their seats Tsereteli rushed to the conference room to inform them that the session had begun and that the bill on local courts was already being discussed. He was followed shortly by Dzhaparidze who brought a categorical refusal from the entire center to participate in the leftist plan. To the very end they would stand on legal grounds and digress not one iota from the duma's rules. The conference was in a quandary. Under the circumstances they decided that it would be best to introduce a proposal to end debates following each address and, should that be rejected, to limit orators to ten minutes. Since the rules allowed a speaker for and against such proposals, each fraction was to name one defense orator who was to speak on dissolution and press for changes in the agenda. The Social-Democrats appointed Tsereteli.[73]

When the duma reassembled the first speaker, Venslavskii (Kolo) spoke on local courts, and as he retired Golovin read a proposal to end debates on this matter.[74] Prince Dolgorukov (Kadet) vehemently objected. The country awaited such practical measures as this, he asserted. Consequently, it should be considered as fully as possible "up to the summer vacation or to that moment when we will be deprived of the physical possibility of working." In this manner the people would understand that the duma strove

72. *Stenog. ot.*, II, 1,573. While the duma session was in progress, the police invaded the homes of many members of the S-D fraction, and searched intensively among their belongings. They took with them a great quantity of books and papers. *Riech*, June 2, 1907, p. 2; *Ternii bez roz*, pp. 21–22. The conference is described in *ibid.*, pp. 26–27, by Mandelberg. See Appendix II, F for discussion of local courts bill.

73. *Ternii bez roz*, p. 28.

74. *Stenog. ot.*, II, 1,574–1,570.

ever to legislate on vital questions. The majority agreed with him and the proposal fell.[75]

Tantsov and Kapustin then addressed the duma on local courts and the latter was followed by a second proposal to end debates. Tsereteli arose to support it.[76] He agreed that under normal circumstances the normal order should be preserved. But he maintained that at the moment not only was the legal order being violated but that the very foundations of the constitution were being attacked. A governmental *coup d'etat* threatened the duma, he asserted amid applause from the left and hoots from the right. Since the government might prevent them from meeting on the morrow by physical force, he beseeched the duma to make use of the rights it had won to realize the political freedom of the people. If the duma adhered to the rules it would miss an opportunity to do as much as possible in the time which remained, and in the face of an assault on the constitution. Consequently, in the name of the Social-Democratic and Populist fractions he proposed to end debates on local courts in order to discuss the budget, the next question on the regular order, and simultaneously to place on the agenda the question of abrogating measures decreed under Article 87. Golovin was quick to protest that the matter was not on the order paper but Tsereteli replied that he would first have the duma consider that which was on the agenda, and then, guided not by formal considerations—by rules—but by considerations of fact, of the good of the people, the duma should inform the population of the grounds for this violence which was being prepared by those plotters on the right.[77]

V. M. Gessen protested in the name of the Kadets.[78] In his opinion, the unusual circumstances of the moment demanded complete self-control on the part of the duma

75. *Ibid.*, pp. 1,579–1,580.

76. *Ibid.*, pp. 1,580–1,585, 1,586–1,591, 1,591–1,593.

77. The president protested that Tsereteli had to present a written proposal which could not be discussed at the current session. *Ibid.*, p. 1,592.

78. *Ibid.*, pp. 1,593–1,594.

and the fulfillment of its duty. The proposal just made
was unconstitutional, for discussion of a question on the
agenda could not be suddenly broken off and replaced by
one unlisted. The Kadets had always tried to remain on
strictly constitutional grounds and, acting within the
law, to use the duma's rights for the good of the people.
At this serious moment, he asserted, they would not forsake these grounds, for they were convinced that the country might be saved only by reinforcing the constitutional
order. The center applauded loudly, and by a vote taken
immediately Tsereteli's proposals were defeated.[79] But
the left persisted and in short order made two more attempts to end the discussion of the local courts bill. Having done nothing for the people to date, they declared,
the Second Duma should utilize the few hours which remained to accomplish something substantial for them.
And the Kadets successfully fought the proposals on
purely constitutional grounds. Fully mobilized, the combined center and right were too strong for the Socialists.[80]

Debates were suddenly interrupted by Kizevetter,
speaking for the committee which since morning had been
examining the charges brought by the government against
the Social-Democrats.[81] He announced that the committee
would not be ready with a report at the beginning of the
session which had been scheduled for that evening. Therefore, he urged the duma to postpone the hearing until
Monday, June 4. Tsereteli immediately grasped the opportunity to move that the evening session be used for a
discussion of those questions which he had already proposed (budget and land laws). "You must place on the
agenda the vital problems of national life . . . in that
moment when the government, in the immortal expression
of Karl Marx 'placed bayonets on the order of the day.' "
The left applauded thunderously. But with the Social-
Democrats abstaining the duma majority adopted Kize-

79. *Ibid.*, pp. 1,594, 1,596.
80. *Ibid.*, pp. 1,599–1,606.
81. *Ibid.*, p. 1,606. See below.

vetter's proposal.[82] And although the left clamored loudly
for a vote on Tsereteli's proposal to consider government
legislation, Golovin refused again to allow a debate since
it was not in order, and the move for an evening session
was defeated. The session was now at an end.[83] Realizing
that in all likelihood they were making their last appearance in the duma, perhaps in public life, the Social-
Democratic deputies made a strenuous effort in this session to demonstrate to the Russian people and the world
that the duma was opposed to the very heart of the administration's policy, its budget and land laws. The fraction
was, indeed, following the dictates of the new party program evolved at London, and in this instance successfully.
For in their last official appearance in the Second Duma
the liberal Kadets and center, fearing for the future of
the representative body, adhered strictly to the law and
were at one with the right in opposing this last attempt
by the Socialist left to utilize the duma as the best revolutionary tribune in the empire.

When the duma assembled on June 2, the special committee which it had appointed to examine the government's demands had been in session for several hours.[84] It
met at 11.40 A.M., elected Kizevetter its chairman and
spent the entire morning considering the order of its work.
It was not until 2.45 P.M. that it began to review Zaitsev's "order" and decided that it must invite Kamyshanskii, through the minister of justice, in order to examine
the original documents in his possession. On the prosecutor's arrival the committee turned to a detailed, critical
analysis of the materials he presented. Kamyshanskii was
forced to admit at once that the edition of the Stockholm
program had been reviewed by the censor and was therefore perfectly legal. One of the high points of the day
was reached when Pergament read an "instruction" of an

82. *Stenog. ot.*, II, 1,606–1,607.
83. *Ibid.*, pp. 1,607–1,608, 1,609, 1,610.
84. The minutes of the meeting are in *Krasnyi Arkhiv*, XLIII, 72–89. See also
Riech, June 3, p. 1, Duma Sup.

army group which had come to the Social-Democratic fraction through the Vilna Organization. He noted that in the "order" Zaitsev had put in quotation marks the words: "to be given to the *Voiennaia Organizatsiia* (Military Organization)." Pergament observed that this was incorrect since the original documents contained only the initials V. O. which might simply mean *Vilenskaia Organizatsiia* (Vilna Organization).[85] The committee then examined three letters published by the fraction and concluded that the purposes discussed therein—the composition of instructions, the sending of messengers, and the creation of unions of non-partisan organizations—were not criminal activities. Moreover, it was noted that the second letter clearly stated that the fraction would realize its aims legally.

At the beginning of the evening session Kuzmin-Karavaev again noted that Konshin had been wrongfully accused and bit by bit, the committee proceeded to break down the formidable mass of evidence against the Social-Democrats. As with the fraction's letters, an examination of the proclamations and the letters on the various matters discussed in the duma revealed nothing illegal. At Teslenko's request for the original of the "instruction" of the St. Petersburg army group, the prosecutor admitted that it had not been found at Ozol's apartment, but that witnesses had established the fact that it had been handed to the fraction.[86] Turning to a "resolution" of the fraction to which Zaitsev had attributed much importance as containing its principal tactics, the committee discovered that only a single handwritten copy existed. As Kuzmin-Karavaev suggested, this might have contained the personal ideas of only one deputy since it bore no signature. When passports found at Ozol's were requested, Kamyshanskii declared that he had no copies with him

85. *Krasnyi Arkhiv*, XLIII, 79.
86. In explanation of his remarks Kamyshanskii told the committee in detail of his part in the search of May 5, and the investigation of the army group which followed on May 7. *Ibid.*, pp. 81–83.

and admitted that it was extremely difficult to prove them false. More material was thus critically examined, and at 11.40 Kamyshanskii departed offering his services on the morrow. After several of its members had impressed the committee with the necessity of disregarding the time element in its search for the truth, the session adjourned at about midnight. Its members were more convinced than ever that the government's accusations had little basis in fact.[87]

By the evening of Saturday June 2, the duma had failed to comply with the government's demands, consequently, according to Stolypin's prearranged plans, its fate was sealed; dissolution was inevitable.[88] The decree and manifesto had been in the tsar's hands since Thursday, May 31, and copies of the former were being printed secretly by the border patrol press.[89] In order to await the arrival of the documents from Tsarskoe Selo with his Majesty's signature the cabinet gathered on Saturday evening at the Elagin Palace. At about 11 P.M. Stolypin was unexpectedly honored with a visit by four Kadet leaders; Bulgakov, Chelnokov, Maklakov, and Struve, the last two being members of the special committee which was then in session. They had come without the knowledge or permission of their party to ascertain the actual state of affairs, and to make a final attempt to avert dissolution should they find that the duma was in reality threatened with it. They asked Stolypin if he intended to investigate all of the fifty-five deputies and the premier replied emphatically in the affirmative. In great detail Maklakov indicated the lack of grounds for accusing the majority of the Social-Democratic deputies on the basis of the documents which Kamyshanskii had presented to the committee. In no case, he asserted, could the duma give them all up. However, it was a late moment for an attempt to move Stolypin to adopt a less drastic course. The premier

87. *Ibid.*, pp. 87–89.
88. *Krasnyi Arkhiv*, V, 113–114; Kokovtsov, *Memoirs*, p. 185.
89. Kokovtsov, *Memoirs*, p. 185.

demanded unconditional submission on the part of the duma; that the Marxists be given up. The government would not retreat.[90]

At about three o'clock Sunday morning the cabinet received the decree and manifesto bearing the tsar's signature.[91] The Supreme Decree called for new elections on September 1, 1907, and the convocation of a new duma on November 1.[92] The Supreme Manifesto accompanying the decree was essentially an indictment of the Second Duma and a justification of the government's policy.[93] The tsar expressed his sorrow that a great part of the duma did not justify the hope that they would work for the good of Russia but had only added to her troubles and encouraged the breakdown of government. In so doing they had prevented the accomplishment of fruitful work in the duma. They did not consider the measures presented by the government, or dallied with them, or rejected them. These persons even went so far as to reject laws punishing those who would praise criminals and create a disturbance in the army, and they evaded a condemnation of murder and violence. Furthermore, they were slow in dealing with the budget and used the right of interpellation as a means of struggle with the government, thereby undermining confidence in it. Finally, a plot was hatched against the state within the duma, and the latter did not immediately fulfill the government's demand that the accused be expelled and given over to justice.

The manifesto then turned to another matter. As a result of imperfections in the electoral law, it declared, the legislative body included many elements which did not express the "true" sentiments of the people. Therefore, leaving intact all of the rights granted by the Manifesto

90. Accounts of the meeting in Kokovtsov, *Memoirs*, pp. 185–186; Kakovtsov, *Pad. tsarsk. rezh.*, VII, 104–106; *Tovarishch*, June 7, p. 3; June 8, p. 2; June 10, p. 5.

91. Kokovtsov, *Memoirs*, pp. 185–186. Kokovtsov, *Pad. tsarsk. rezh.*, VII, 104–105, show how impatient the tsar had become with the duma.

92. *Stenog. ot.*, II, 1,609–1,610; *Pol. sob. zak.*, XXVII, no. 29,241.

93. *Pol. sob. zak.*, XXVII, no. 29,240; *Riech*, June 5, p. 1.

of October 17, and by the Fundamental Laws, the tsar decided to change the electoral law in order to make the duma Russian in spirit. Members of national minorities would not be allowed in such numbers as to enable them to decide purely Russian questions. On the backward frontiers, the suffrage right would be temporarily suspended. These changes, the manifesto explained, could not have been brought about in an "unsatisfactory" duma. Finally, the tsar contended that since he had granted the first electoral law he might replace it under the powers entrusted him by heaven.

The new electoral law was published under a decree issued together with that dissolving the duma.[94] The changes which it made in representation sharpened the class differentiation of the voters and allowed a predominating influence to the wealthier categories, especially the landowners, to the disadvantage of the peasantry. Moreover, it greatly reduced the representation of the racial minorities, while several frontier regions were entirely deprived of seats in the duma. Poland, Siberia, the Caucasus, and Central Asia whose representatives filled the ranks of the opposition, and (with the exception of Poland) those of the Socialist left, were all affected. Poland was now allowed fourteen in place of forty-six deputies, and the remaining border provinces were allotted twenty-five as compared with seventy-five by the law of December 11, 1906. The Iakutsk *oblast* and Central Asiatic regions were entirely cut off (with the exception of one deputy from the Ural Cossack Army). In the frontier provinces with a multi-racial composition, the population was divided into national groups, and the Russians given a disproportionate advantage.

Generally speaking, the population was divided into two categories, the few rich and the many poor, the former receiving representation equal to the latter. The most

94. *Pol. sob. zak.*, XXVII, no. 29,242. See also S. N. Harper, *The New Electoral Law for the Russian Duma.*

important change in this respect concerned the provincial
electoral assemblies where the right held under the old
law by peasants and workers to elect their own deputies
was abrogated. These were now to be elected in plenary
sessions of the provincial assemblies. Since, according to
the new law, the wealthy landowners and burghers were
given a majority in these assemblies, they controlled the
selection of peasant and worker representatives. And
labor was allowed representation only in six provinces. In
dealing with representatives from cities, the law made
significant changes. Seven in place of twenty-six cities
enjoyed separate representation, and in five (St. Petersburg, Moscow, Riga, Kiev, and Odessa) direct elections
were introduced as a new departure. The Polish centers
of Warsaw and Lodz received separate representation,
but elections remained two-staged. In the cities as in the
provinces, voters were divided into the wealthy (industrialists and home-owners) who elected one half of the
city's deputies or electors, and the poor (lower middle
class and workers) who elected the other half. The workers, voting in their curiae, retained the right to elect
their own representatives, but in most cases their representation was diminished by one half. Only in Kiev, Odessa, and Riga was it increased from one to two deputies
each.

Thus, two distinct improvements over the law of 1905
were established. Firstly, direct elections were introduced,
although restricted to only five cities, and secondly, multiple voting was abolished. Though a landowner might
have voting qualifications in several provinces or cities,
he could vote only once. And a peasant might vote either
as a landowner or as a holder of allotment land in the
village commune, but not in both categories. Otherwise,
as compared with its predecessor the law was undoubtedly
a backward step, for it artificially grouped the population
for the purpose of ensuring a preponderance of moderate, if not reactionary, elements in the duma. That it

was illegally promulgated was recognized privately by the administration.[95]

Having made an irrevocable move and published the decree of dissolution, the government took steps on June 3, to prevent, or overcome, any violent reaction which might occur. Guards were thrown around the Taurida Palace, and streets leading to it were occupied by the police. The headquarters of the opposition fractions were placed under strict observation. The Kadet apartments were openly watched by the police; meetings at the Moslem and Popular-Socialist rooms were dispersed and the apartments placed under observation. The police burst into the Trudovik headquarters, searched it thoroughly, and arrested the secretariat of the group. Needless to say, Ozol's rooms were tightly sealed.[96] But the administration's precautions were quite unnecessary. The popular mood had reached the lowest ebb of the post-revolutionary period and received the news that the duma had been dissolved with calmness, almost with indifference. The general atmosphere was rather one of hushed anxiety for the future. St. Petersburg experienced no outbursts. Even the "conscious" workers of the capital merely met, adopted resolutions, and dispersed peaceably. Correspondents from the provinces uniformly reported a similar apathetic reception of the news, and numerous searches by the police.[97]

Now that its hands were freed, the administration immediately sought out the members of the Social-Demo-

95. See above p. 310. See also S. E. Kryzhanovskii, *Vospominaniia*, pp. 107–110.

96. *Riech*, June 5, p. 3; *Tovarishch*, June 5, pp. 3, 4.

97. *Ternii bez roz*, pp. 23, 36; *Tovarishch*, June 3, p. 3; June 5, p. 3; *Riech*, June 5, p. 3. Among the rightists there was universal jubilation. Champagne flowed. The tsar was cheered and toasted along with Stolypin, the rightist deputies, and the future duma as rightists of both the duma and the upper house held a convivial meeting at the Monarchist headquarters. An attempt to decorate the headquarters of the Union of the Russian People attracted a sullen, menacing crowd and the police ordered the removal of the trappings. The tale was uniform in the provinces: parades, music, and public prayer often accompanied by pogromist activities were reported, especially from the southern cities where the Union was strongest. *Riech*, June 5, p. 3.

cratic fraction. Some of these, including Mandelberg, Zurabov, Zhigelev, Komar, and Saltykov had taken steps to conceal themselves. But the majority of those present in St. Petersburg were taken at their lodgings and hustled off to "preliminary detention." [98] Nevertheless, the Marxist deputies were able to compose a counterblast to the Imperial Manifesto and a summary of their attitude toward the late duma in the form of a proclamation.[99] This document exhorted the people to give no credence to the accusations directed against them by the government. Its authors charged the administration with faithlessness in violating the immunity of the Social-Democratic deputies by arresting them and cutting off all protest; with violating the October Manifesto and increasing its own arbitrary power; and with an attempt to prevent the duma from thoroughly examining the budget. They maintained that when the opposition revealed the government's self-interested policy, it feared the rejection of the budget and its foreign obligations and therefore dissolved the duma. The Kadet policy of coöperation with the government, even at the cost of yielding basic rights for a part in legislation had failed entirely, they believed. For the government grew more arrogant and sought to regain its absolute power when it observed that the revolution was on the ebb. The policy of "guarding" the duma only lowered its dignity, they held, and weakened its ties with the population. But the Social-Democrats, fighting for Socialism, had first to win political freedom in order to unite the workers for the final struggle. The Duma was a gain in the fight for freedom. But since it could not defend itself without popular support the Social-Democrats sought to bind the people closely to it by fighting for their needs, informing them of its activities, and welcoming petitions, instructions, etc. The former Social-

98. *Ternii bez roz*, pp. 24, 52; Mandelberg, *Iz perezhitago*, p. 145; Zurabov, *Vtoraia gosudarstvennaia duma*, pp. 86–87; *Riech*, June 5, p. 3; *Tovarishch*, June 5, pp. 3, 4; June 6, p. 3; June 7, p. 3; June 9, p. 3.

99. *Ternii bez roz*, pp. 139–145.

Democratic deputies vehemently denied the charge that they had plotted against the state. For they relied, they asserted, not on conspirative methods but upon an open attack; upon a frank revelation of the class character of the government. Now, as the revolution ebbed, continued the proclamation, the government had avenged its October (1905) defeat. But this unrestrained reaction simply demonstrated that an irreconcilable struggle was the only means of destroying it. For this struggle the former fraction exhorted the population to rally around the Social-Democrats and help them to penetrate even into the Third Duma. Finally, the proclamation called on the people to demand universal, direct, equal, and secret suffrage, and a fully empowered constituent assembly in the face of attempts by the government to dominate the duma. Having paid tribute to the duma as a step forward in the fight for freedom, the Social-Democrats pointed to a constituent assembly as the ultimate goal.

A short time after their arrest on June 5, Kamyshanskii attempted to examine the former Social-Democratic deputies. But they refused to hold any converse with him whatsoever and for half a year languished in the jail of preliminary detention before they were brought to trial, from November 22 to December 1.[100] Moreover, the government decided that its proceedings were to be closed to the public. Political trials had, from time to time, deeply affected Russian public opinion, and the result had never been favorable to the government. Stolypin did not intend to allow these practiced propagandists either to state their case publicly or to use the occasion to denounce his administration.

The indictment handed down against the fraction was a complete repetition of the evidence presented in Zaitsev's "order" to the duma, and the charges made against

100. *Tovarishch*, June 8, p. 3. For a description of the trial see the governmental communique in *Riech*, Dec. 2, p. 3, and newspaper communications in *Riech* and *Tovarishch* from Nov. 23 to Dec. 2.

the fraction on the basis of that material.[101] Under the presidency of Senator Dreier, the court consisted of four senators, two representatives of the nobility, and one each of the burghers and peasants.[102] The entire fraction appeared for trial with the exception of seventeen who had either failed to return from London or had successfully concealed themselves. Along with them the government placed on trial the members of the St. Petersburg military organization and Solomon Fisher, owner of the apartment on Fontanka Street, who was charged with failure to inform the police of the existence of the organization. The accused were represented by a bevy of lawyers including former deputies Pergament, Teslenko, and Adzhemov, and representing some of the finest legal talent in the empire.[103]

When the prisoners were led into the court room they immediately raised a violent protest against the secrecy of the proceedings. And when Sierov and Tsereteli tried to say a few words in an attempt to have the trial opened to the public they were quickly silenced by the president who refused to hear them. His decision was greeted with a further outburst of protest and Dzhaparidze, speaking for the former deputies, declared that they would refuse to remain in the court room. Thereupon the accused released their defense counsel and filed out shouting revolutionary slogans. They were soon followed by their attorneys, seven deputies who had remained, and the military group and their counsel. The indictment was heard only by court officials. The Social-Democrats had, in effect, again boycotted the government.[104]

101. The first part of the indictment is reproduced in *Byloe*, no. 14, 1912, pp. 140–182. The editors had intended to include the remainder in the following issue but that was suppressed. The charges are listed in the government's communique, *Riech*, Dec. 2, p. 3.

102. *Riech*, Nov. 25, p. 2; *Tovarishch*, Nov. 24, p. 3.

103. *Riech*, Nov. 23, p. 2; *Tovarishch*, Nov. 24, p. 3; also government communique in *Riech*, Dec. 2, p. 3.

104. The minutes of the first day of the trial are in *Ternii bez roz*, pp. 146–147; *Riech*, Dec. 2, p. 3. See also *Riech*, Nov. 23, p. 2; Nov. 24, p. 5; *Tovarishch*, Nov. 24, p. 3.

But on the following day, November 23, before the opening of the session Dreier sent the sergeant at arms to the prisoners to ascertain whether any were ready to submit to trial. He returned to inform the court that former deputies Gumenko, Rybalchenko, Kalinin, and Sakhno would appear. These were brought in and, with their attorneys, remained until the end of the trial. But daily attempts were made to have the remaining prisoners brought in.[105]

On November 24, witnesses for both sides were called to the number of sixty-four, and the following three days were spent for the most part in examining documentary evidence consisting of literature and programs seized during the searches and arrests of the accused.[106] Kamyshanskii presented the government's case on November 28. The evidence presented by the government after examining the materials at hand was, in essence, a summary of that presented by Zaitsev to the Second Duma. In the government's opinion this proved that the Social-Democratic fraction according to the resolutions adopted at Stockholm in 1906 was under the strict control of the central committee of the party and was a rallying point for revolutionary forces aiming to overthrow the government and replace it with a democratic republic. According to the prosecution the evidence showed that the fraction had close connections with illegal party organizations, and in its correspondence it was the recipient of hundreds of instructions which were not spontaneous but were copies of models supplied by the fraction. Defense attorneys spoke on November 29. Kalmanovich, Bart, and Tsitron defended the members of the military organization, while Adzhemov, Pergament, and Nazariev, speaking for those deputies who appeared, pointed out the weaknesses in the government's accusations.[107]

105. *Riech,* Dec. 2, p. 3; Nov. 24, p. 5; *Tovarishch,* Nov. 25, p. 2.

106. *Tovarishch,* Nov. 25, p. 2; Nov. 27, p. 5; Nov. 28, p. 2; *Riech,* Nov. 22, p. 4; Nov. 28, p. 3.

107. *Riech,* Nov. 29, p. 3; Nov. 28, p. 3; Dec. 1, p. 4; *Tovarishch,* Nov. 30,

Sentences were passed on December 1. On charges brought against the fraction in the indictment, Zaitsev's "order," and Kamyshanskii's address to the court, Anikin, Anisimov, Dzhaparidze, Lomtatidze, E. A. Petrov, Sierov, Tsereteli, and Chashchin were sentenced to five years at hard labor and loss of rights. The same sentence for four years was meted out to Bielousov, Vagzhanov, Vinogradov, Golovanov, Kirienko, Makharadaze, Mironov, and Iudin. Moreover, Bielanovskii, Vovchinskii, Izmailov, Kalinin, Lopatkin, Nagikh, I. A. Petrov, Prikhodko, Ruban and Fedorov were exiled for an indeterminate term. Ex-deputies Vakhrushev Gubarev, Gumenko, Kandelaki, Katsiashvili, Marev, Rybalehenko, Sakhno, Stepanov, and Fomichev were acquitted. Like sentences were meted out to members of the military group. Cossack Kremenskov was acquitted and Fisher was exiled for an undefined term.[108]

In dismissing their counsel on November 22, the fraction submitted a prepared protest to Dreier through attorney Sokolov. But since the court refused to hear the statement it was published abroad several months later.[109] In this protest the incarcerated deputies attempted to exonerate themselves completely. They would prove, they said, that their activity became a cause for dissolution only when the government itself took illegal steps and violated the Fundamental Laws in an effort to bring about complete restoration. They explained their tactics and their position in the Social-Democratic Party; their subordination to its central committee. They emphatically denied charges of manufacturing and supplying false passports, of distributing illegal literature, of illegal connections with the party's military groups, and finally of conspiracy. Their entire program, they declared, was

p. 6. There are no accounts of the defense speeches available, but they were, in all likelihood, based on the weaknesses discovered by the duma committee investigating the government's charges.

108. *Riech*, Dec. 2, p. 3.

109. The statement is in *Ternii bez roz*, pp. 146, 147–152.

based on the independent activity of the workers striving
for Socialism through the democratic structure. The existence of a single instruction from a military group was
no proof of conspiracy, they contended, for every fraction had received thousands of instructions. There was
not a single document to prove that they were preparing
for an armed uprising—except, perhaps, the Stockholm
resolution. And that was adopted at a moment when the
party felt that a nation-wide upheaval was imminent.
Since then the London Congress had removed armed uprising from its agenda. For the party realized that the
revolutionary wave was receding and that if it should
attempt to organize an uprising artificially it would become liable to charges of plotting. Moreover, the party
would then be guilty of digression from the real Social-
Democratic policy: the political education of the masses
and their organization for struggle. Their bills which
the Social-Democratic deputies knew would never pass
the Imperial Council and the tsar, their reports and
letters to the party and the instructions which they welcomed, all were a part of their effort to educate the population politically so that it would put pressure on the duma
to facilitate its work in defending popular interests.

Finally, the authors maintained that there was nothing
criminal in the activities of their fraction. For all history
demonstrated that historical necessity had to be recognized. Consequently, even though the Social-Democratic
Party would replace one form of government by another,
and planned for a Socialist society, its legality had to be
recognized. Everywhere Socialist parties prepared for a
future clash with the state, if only by propaganda, and
they were not charged with criminal activity. The fact
was, the former deputies maintained, that by law the
government had to recognize the Social-Democratic fraction. But when the state tried to restore autocracy it
openly regarded everything as criminal which ran coun-
ter to its interests, and it placed on trial the most zealous
champions of the new order.

After June 3, the fig leaf of constitutionalism fell and it [the government] stood in all of its despotic nakedness before the land. Now they want to try us. . . . We understand perfectly that not only we are tried—here old, autocratic Russia is trying new Russia straining for freedom. And with complete confidence in the inevitability of the approaching victory of freedom over arbitrariness we say: try us—it is itself tried by history.

Stolypin had played his game successfully to the very end. The "rebellious" duma was gone from the Russian political scene and the premier's position was as strong as ever. The practical bureaucratic mind had utilized a more or less normal incident to bring about the end of legislation on a wide representative basis. Stolypin had guessed shrewdly that the duma, seeing the representative system threatened, could not yield to his demands. A final attack by the left only simplified the justification of a patent violation of the constitution. And although he took all possible precautions, Stolypin was more correct than the duma in evaluating the immediate popular reaction to dissolution. He had, indeed, won the day and had apparently snuffed out the last lingering embers of the Revolution of 1905; he had, it seemed, "pacified" Russia.

XV

CONCLUSION

I T IS a singular characteristic of Russian history that its progress is marked by a series of vital but belated reforms which were of necessity hurriedly carried out and, consequently, with defects that required half a century or more to repair. The Russian people never entirely accommodated themselves to the reforms of Nikon and Peter. And the land changes of 1861 would not have been rectified and completed until the nineteen thirties. The parliamentary reforms of 1905 were no exception to this rule. Inaugurated in the midst of, and as a direct result of, a nation-wide upheaval, the new parliamentary system was grafted, with a few necessary changes, on the old political structure of a country with no parliamentary tradition or experience. The immediate result was universal political uncertainty and instability. Precedents were in the making and the final outcome was dependent on the strength of the various political elements.

It is not surprising, therefore, that the constitutional period of comparative quiet which immediately followed open revolutionary activity, was one of more or less undefined authority. The old executive remained intact along with the old judiciary. But the new legislature—what was to be its share in the government? And whom was it to represent? The Fundamental Law and Duma Statute had apparently defined its powers, and the Electoral Law its content. But the liberals and revolutionaries, the vast majority of the population, were unsatisfied. And, on the other hand, the bureaucracy, able to accommodate itself to the new parliamentary régime, at best, only with great difficulty, was bent on capturing lost territory as the revolution subsided. It sought to regain control over the political machine including the new duma, to lead the representative body by the nose, and exercise tutelage over it. The administration would instruct the duma rather than coöperate with it. Accordingly, Stolypin set up his own ministerial ideal and defined "coöperation" and "revolution" regardless of popular demands. In this spirit the government tried to influence elections, often illegally. And in this spirit it made bold to demand the arrest of deputies for their activities outside of the inviolable Taurida. The Holy Synod even violated that lone sanctuary of political freedom by demanding that priest-deputies abandon the fractions of their choice. The important parliamentary question of the duma's right to invite technically necessary experts the government regarded, in the last analysis, from the point of view of the bureaucratic prefect rather than that of the statesman. The skirmishes with the duma on this point revealed Stolypin as either ignorant of, or fearing, the essence of modern representative government. Stolypin's constitutional phrases were many, his constitutional activity extremely limited. As a result of the government's position there existed in the minds of many neither autocracy nor constitution; that is, a dangerous indefiniteness at the very sources of law and justice. And unless the political structure were clearly defined, the future was likely to witness numerous irritating clashes between the legislative and executive, the bureaucracy and the people.

The immediate upshot of the clash of authorities was a victory for Stolypin, the government. In the familiar patriarchal spirit he would put the duma to test. He would patronize it as long as it would "coöperate" with him—on his own conditions. When he found that the duma would not and could not meet his terms—that its entire concept of parliamentary government and of individual reforms differed widely from his own, Stolypin began to consider a more "agreeable" legislative body. And when at the same time he began to feel that pressure from court circles endangered his own, and, as he maintained, the duma's position, he was determined to dissolve the duma and revise its personnel. Whatever differences there may have been of motive or circumstance, the treatment of the duma, the central representative body, by Stolypin strikingly resembles that of local representation, the *zemstva*, by his predecessors in the interior ministry. Like the *zemstva* the duma was isolated, hindered at each step, fatigued, forbidden necessary implements and materials, and finally threatened with political danger. And the new electoral law which accompanied the dissolution of the Second Duma clearly revealed that whatever his intentions may have been on assuming office, Stolypin would countenance only a very limited form of parliamentary constitutionalism. His class and bureaucratic instincts were at the moment deeper than any aspirations he may have had for the honors of liberal statesmanship. It is impossible for the historian to declare that under the first electoral law parliamentary government in Russia would have developed and sooner or later have resembled the French, British, or American systems. The historical traditions differ widely and the process must necessarily have been a long one. But it is certain that the new electoral law of June 3, only sowed seeds of new dissension. It could only dam vital political currents, not exhaust them.

The duma, we saw, was born of a revolution. And besides the uncertainties of an indefinite political structure, the development of the parliamentary idea along Western European lines was threatened by the revolutionary tradition, the greatest enemy of the Old Régime. For the revolutionaries could not seriously regard a weak parliament which they believed would never develop under tsarism and would, at best, benefit only the small middle class. To them it was a means; a way station on the road to utopia. And should the left gain control over parliament it was highly probable that the government would make short shrift of it. If the revolutionary movement was subsiding during the early constitutional period the revolutionary spirit was much in evidence in the first stages of Russian parliamentary endeavor. It was while more or less successfully combatting this spirit that the duma failed in an effort to frustrate the bureaucratic forces; to hold the government to its October promises.

The spearhead of parliamentary liberalism, the Kadet Party, was central in Russian politics between the government and the revolutionaries. And the Kadets gladly accepted their position as the only one from which they might work a compromise and establish parliamentary government for all time. For this attitude they were widely censured. With later developments in mind it is all too easy to criticize this handful of professional men and scholars, acquainted with western governmental forms, but without a secure foundation in the voting population, and fighting against difficult odds. But in 1907, even though the government was flushed with its victory over revolution, still the promises contained in the October Manifesto were being enacted into law, and there was as much right to foresee the development of truly representative government in Russia as of any other form. There was nothing in the political scene to make a serious digression from the Manifesto inevitable. The changes wrought by the law of June 3, could not positively have been foreseen even though they might have been feared by the liberals and wishfully thought of by the revolutionaries.

The Kadets, on their part, felt that they must and could, in time, acquaint the people and the government with parliamentary methods; that they could get both accustomed to them, and to respect them. But they also realized that the duma was, for the present, in the tragic position of being without means to attain its ends. Therefore, they proclaimed a policy which they called "correct siege" and the revolutionary left regarded as "retreat" and a "betrayal." The liberals understood that the parliamentary method of reform would be a painfully long

process. And they felt that in the course of its development, to survive, the duma would have to accumulate
a tremendous reserve of prestige and moral force in order
to win wide popular support as the basis of its political
strength. The only alternative to that course, they maintained, would be a quixotic, unyielding opposition by
the weak duma to the unified government with all of the
resources of the empire at its disposal. The bolder policy,
they feared, might result in the destruction of the whole
parliamentary structure or at least a vital change which
was likely to make of the duma a sounding board for imperial decrees. In that sense the Kadets regarded their
"retreat" from the more intransigeant stand which they
had assumed in the First Duma as strategic. If they were
now more insistent on restraining revolutionary elements
in the duma; if they were now willing to grant the administration funds and contingents and a significant place
in their "land settlement" organizations it was because
they sought to mollify the government and to demonstrate
their desire to coöperate and reach an understanding.
Besides, they felt that the duma's dignity was involved;
that an inexperienced parliament with an irresponsible,
revolutionary stigma attached to it could hardly expect
to win respect either at home or abroad, should it veto
the budget or refuse to call men to the colors without,
or even with, discussion of the government's proposals.
And it was just these measures which allowed the duma
to use the few significant rights it possessed. Moreover,
the Kadets observed that the numerous reform bills which
they had presented and were ready to support were certainly not symptomatic of retreat.[1] If left to their own
resources and given sufficient control over the duma, that
is, a dependable majority, the success of their tactics was

1. The Kadet fraction presented eleven reform measures including, besides
agrarian reform and the bill on field-courts-martial, projects on the abolition of
the death penalty for political crimes, inviolability of person, elections to the
duma and *zemstva*, working hours for workers and clerks, changes in the duma's
budgetary powers, equality of faith and minority rights, public-works funds,
and abrogation of a number of class laws.

conceivable—even to the point of some agreement on the agrarian question. And the beginnings of true representative government might have been preserved for further development. But the strength and direction of extremist trends, we have often observed, made the chances of success highly problematic.

From our study it is clear that both wings of the duma hampered its legislative activity and considerably weakened its position by assuming a non-parliamentary stand. Neither the right nor the left regarded the representative body as a legislative instrument for enacting political reforms. For both it served outside aims rather than its own purposes. Thus, though working at ultimate cross purposes, the extremes complemented each other in the duma. And the final result of their policies, if successful, was bound to be the same—dissolution.

The revolutionary parties on the left, suffused with hatreds and ideals in their long struggle against autocracy, and bound by social and economic doctrines, found it difficult to separate their ideals from possibilities. On numerous occasions the extreme left failed to face realities and invariably overestimated their strength and their influence among the people. Despite the swift disintegration of the revolutionary movement; despite the lack of a strong revolutionary force, and despite the growing strength of the central government, they ardently and vociferously insisted on far reaching changes in the political, military and economic fields. But their demands found progressively less response among the exhausted and indifferent population and only aroused the government which regarded them as instruments for provocation. Within the duma the numerous, fiery attacks levelled against the government and the center by the Marxists, their proposals to endow parliament with executive functions and send its members all over the empire to organize local investigating committees, their refusal to grant the government money and soldiers, meaningless in the given political atmosphere—all this was grist for the "Black

Hundred" mill; for those who would put an end to all of this upstart parliamentarianism. For the fierce "dissolutionists" on the right, for the reactionaries at court, and for Stolypin, the Social-Democrats offered sufficient pretext for dissolution; and an opportunity to change the electoral law.

But considering their ultimate aims, neither dissolution nor the narrowing of duma representation were particularly harmful to the Social-Democrats. They were not especially interested in representative, parliamentary government, under tsarist rule, they said. And they needed only a few capable orators to carry on an agitational campaign in the duma. This situation would harmonize completely with their party program and was especially congenial to the Bolsheviki who would give duma activity only a secondary place in party tactics. For the liberal idea, however, the outcome could only be disastrous. At the moment when the people, after centuries of absolute rule by autocracy, were at last given a significant voice in the affairs of the state and fairly proportional representation, the game was suddenly lost. The dream of parliamentary progress along democratic, Western European lines vanished. And the government and those conservative forces who alone might now shape legislation were left to deal as they desired with the aims and aspirations of the population.

If the prevalence of undefined authority and the revolutionary tradition helped to destroy the Second Duma and sound the knell of progressive parliamentary development, the duma was placed at a disadvantage in the struggle for existence by the fact that it appeared in a country with no parliamentary tradition. Only a comparatively few lawyers and scholars were at all acquainted with parliamentary government, and were aware of its responsibilities and implications. The bureaucracy, far from acclimating itself to the new structure, wished to subordinate it. And if the Kadets alone in the duma understood the meaning and workings of parliamentary government, it is apparent from the debates that they comprehended the new constitution better than the central government. As for the others, they generally followed either the Kadets or the wing leaders. That one quarter of the duma which consisted of peasants and workers with only the rudiments of learning could hardly have been expected to grasp at once the liberal argument for parliamentary government or the significance of Kadet tactics. They wanted land or work, security, and a less burdensome existence, and they gladly followed anyone who pointed the way to an early fulfillment of their desires. And the leaders on the left, eager to preach from the duma, not only abhorred "bourgeois" legislative activity but hindered it in following tactics which arose from their social and economic doctrines. The right, for its part, recognized the import, for its purposes, of an apparently inept legislature. Working together the extremes prolonged debates and argued incessantly on every minor point of procedure. Debates on the simple question of creating indispensable committees continued for days and even weeks. And despite the adoption of Kadet-inspired rules, the duma sometimes found it difficult to adhere to the matter under consideration and to refrain from discussing the viciousness of the government's policy in general. Only parliamentary inexperience and propagandist aims can explain these futile debates and the repeated presentation of illegal bills. In the turmoil of debates the Kadets had often to repeat the warning that if the duma was to avoid the charge of incompetence and win respect for itself at home and abroad it must legislate fruitfully with the law.

To parliamentary inexperience, in part, and partially to the wavering of the *Narodniki* between legislation and revolution we may attribute the absence of a strong, stable opposition majority which could forge legislation in the face of extreme tactics. In a duma with numerous fractions no group (except, perhaps, the Kolo) seems to have been able or willing to make immediate compromises on secondary matters to gain ultimate ends. And although the Kadets usually had their way, the great body of the peasant deputies was undependable.

Yet, despite the numerous threats to its existence—a hostile, domineering government and provocative wings presenting obstacles which the duma as a whole was too inexperienced to avoid—there were no real grounds for dissolution at the end of May, 1907. The Second Duma was charged on June 3, with being revolutionary and incompetent. But it must be kept in mind that the government classed the entire opposition, including the Kadets, as revolutionary. And in disssolving this most representative parliament in all Russian history, the administration flung defiance at the overwhelming majority of the people. But even if the Social-Revolutionary and Social-Democratic Parties supported thoroughly revolutionary platforms, the Second Duma was not revolutionary in action. On major issues it always followed the Kadet lead. And by a large majority the deputies adopted a set of rules of procedure, written by Kadet President Muromtsev of the First Duma, which managed at crucial moments to frustrate those who would use the duma as an agitational base. The Second Duma was actually more revoutionary in word than in deed.

If not essentially revolutionary, was the duma, then, incompetent? Could it work productively? Considering its duration, difficulties, and inexperience the Second Duma did not come out badly in this respect. Despite the chaos and length of the debates it approached the chief questions (budget, army, land, and famine relief) from a mature point of view. It had forty-two major items on its agenda,[2] and in its evening sessions where the Kadets were in complete control the duma acted with despatch and order more common to western parliaments. Charges that the duma accomplished little legislative work overlooked the intensive activity of the committees. Ten major

2. See *Zak. za.*, table of contents.

bodies controlled by moderate elements—for the most part by the Kadets—worked incessantly to produce measures which sought to ameliorate immeasurably the political, economic, and social plight of the country.[3] It was not the duma's fault that the government ended its existence at the moment when the Budget and Agrarian Committees were ready to report. And the timing of the dissolution aroused suspicions in opposition circles that the government wished to forestall debate and action on these matters. At any rate it is now clear that having failed to find any but indefinite grounds for terminating the existence of the duma, the government had to manufacture a pretext.

But if Stolypin's general aim in dissolving the Second Duma was to stifle the liberation movement he was doomed to failure. For the struggle for greater political freedom which had developed rapidly from the last decade of the nineteenth century now involved too many elementary demands of all classes of the population. And the period of the Second Duma in particular was marked by the culminating development of a consciousness of sharp political and class differentiation which began in 1905 and was to influence deeply the history of the next decade.

And if the immediate aim of the government was to subordinate parliament by so revising the electoral law that its allies in the duma would form an appreciable majority, that purpose, too, was not destined to be fully realized. For as succeeding administrations followed the reactionary court to the right, even Stolypin's mutilated creation and those elements whom the government once implicitly trusted, particularly the great industrialists, refused to follow. And no one forgot the contempt for public opinion and popular interests revealed in the events of June 3, 1907.

3. For a detailed summary of the work of the committees in the Second Duma see P. N. Miliukov, "The Case of the Second Duma," *Contemporary Review*, XCII, 463–464. Also see *Komissii*.

APPENDIX I

A

THE SOCIAL-DEMOCRATIC FRACTION[1]

Bolsheviki	Mensheviki	Mensheviki
Aleksinskii, G. A.	Anikin, P. A.	Lopatkin, I. A.
Anisimov, V. A.	Batashev, P. M.	Makharadze, G. F.
Chashchin, V. A.	Bielanovskii, D. K.	Mandelberg, V. E.
Golovanov, I. F.	Bielousov, G. E.	Mironov, I. E.
Gubarev, I. A.	Dzhaparidze, A. L.	Mitrov, V. I.
Kalinin, A. V.	Dzhugeli, S. M.	Nalivkin, V. P.
Marev, I. L.	Fedorov, G. G.	Nestorov, A. I.
Nagikh, I. N.	Fomichev, M. M.	Ozol, I. P.
Petrov, E. A.	Gerus, L. F.	Piarn, P. G.
Petrov, I. A.	Gumenko, I. A.	Prikhodko, F. G.
Romanov, I. R.	Iudin, I. K.	Ruban, K. A.
Serebriakov, I. G.	Izmailov, P. G.	Rybalchenko, P. M.
Shpagin, A. A.	Kandeliaki, K. P.	Sakhno, V. G.
Sierov, V. M.	Katsiashvili, N. A.	Saltykov, S. N.
Tatarinov, M. S.	Kirienko, I. I.	Stepanov, N. S.
Vagzhanov, A. P.	Komar, N. V.	Tsereteli, I. G.
Vinogradov, A. K.	Kosmodamianskii,	Vakhrushev, V. A.
Zhigelev, N. A.	I. N.	Vovchinskii, M. N.
	Lomtatidze, V. B.	Zurabov, A. G.

Advisory Members
Aframovich, K. M.
Bodrov, A. V.
Chepovenko, Z. I.
Fedorov, A. G.
Gudovich, F. I.
Kumelis, P. I.
Kupstas, A. S.
Kuznetsov, A. A.
Murten, M. M.
Povilius, A. M.
Stashinskii, V. A.

1. See *Protokoly*, pp. 251–252; *Ukazatel*, pp. 27–28. Further information has been received in a letter dated Paris, January 26, 1936, from L. Swatikoff who was a political advisor (expert) to the fraction in the Second Duma.

B

THE NATIONAL SOCIAL-DEMOCRATIC PARTIES.

THE chief national branch of the Social-Democratic Party was the Jewish Bund (The Universal Hebrew Workers' Society). It was composed mainly of Jewish craft workers in the cities of White Russia, the Ukraine, Lithuania, and Poland. The Bund was organized in 1897 and participated in the First Russian Social-Democratic Party Congress at Minsk in 1898. Like the rest of the party it was engaged in a struggle against revisionism and the Zubatov movement. Its influence increased rapidly, especially after the Kishinev Pogrom, as small Jewish artisans saw in it a defense against racial oppression. At the Second Party Congress in 1903, it demanded that it be recognized as the sole representative of the Jewish proletariat in the empire, and withdrew from the pan-Russian party when the congress refused to grant it that status. From 1903 to 1905 the Bund functioned as an independent party. But in 1906 when the Stockholm Congress allowed it to organize branches anywhere in Russia without recognizing it as the sole representative of the Jewish workers, it rejoined the pan-Russian Social-Democratic Party. In the main, it assumed a stand sympathetic to the Mensheviki. In such men as Abramovich, Vinitskii, and Lieber it had able leaders.

The second great branch of the Russian Social-Democratic Party was the Social-Democratic Party of Poland and Lithuania. It was founded in 1893 and stood for a common revolutionary struggle of the Russian and Polish proletariat for the overthrow of tsarism. Under Rosa Luxemburg and Tyshko a central group, the "Worker's Cause," was formed, but was soon destroyed by the *Okhrana*. However, its work was renewed by Felix Dzerzhinskii, who had escaped from exile. The party was invited to attend the Second Congress but refused because it could not give up the slogan of "national self-determination" for the Poles. When it dropped this slogan in 1906 it joined the pan-Russian party at Stockholm.

The two remaining national groups were the Lettish and the Armenian Social-Democratic Parties. The former was established in 1903, and soon won considerable influence among the industrial and agricultural proletariat of the Baltic region. Its leaders were sympathetic to the Mensheviki while the rank and file accepted the Bolshevik viewpoint. The Armenians joined the pan-Russian party at the Fifth Congress (London). Their party was formed during the Revolution of 1905 under the leadership of Shoumian and others. See *Malaia Sovietskaia Entsiklopediia*, I, 421, 891–894; IV, 505–506; VIII, 222–223; N. Popov, *Outline History of the C. P. S. U.*, I, 185.

APPENDIX II

A

THE FAMINE OF 1906

THE famine of 1906, though not as severe as its predecessors in 1891, or at the turn of the century, was due to essentially the same causes: mal-distribution of land, the low cultural level and backward agricultural methods of the majority of the population, and the insufficiency of roads and railroads. To these causes there may be added the lack of reserves from 1905 due to the peasant disturbances. The 1906 harvest of winter crops was $5\frac{1}{5}$ per cent lower than that of 1905 (77,955,300 pud, a pud being 36.11 pounds). After deducting the amount set aside for seed, the total surplus of winter crops for 71 provinces was 7.35 per cent less than the surplus for 1905 and per person was .77 per cent less. (8.35 pud for 1906; and 9.13 pud for 1905). As compared with 1905, the area planted to spring crops was .28 per cent less in 1906 while the harvest of spring crops for 1906 as compared with the average for 1901–1905 was 14.6 per cent less. Potatoes, one of the staple peasant food crops, were 156,323,600 pud less than in 1905, the yield per person being 10.73 in 1905 and 9.32 in 1906.

The general harvests for 1905 and 1906 were as follows in thousands of puds:

	1906	Decrease from 1905
Food grains	2,624,970.3	316,967.2
Potatoes	1,588,684.5	156,323.6
Oats	631,802.5	195,680.7

The figures for the amounts of wheats and cereals stored in the thousands of puds are:

	to January 1, 1907	to January 1, 1906
Wheat	32,259.1	37,961.5
Rye	11,687.6	8,736.2
Barley	9,532.1	7,428.5
Maize	226.6	316.8
Flour	11,705.4	12,602.7

The area which suffered most was the Volga basin with a population of approximately 20,000,000. This region accounted for 60 per cent of all famine-relief expenditures by the state from 1891 to 1908, while the central black-soil provinces accounted for 24 per cent. By the middle of March, 1906, the United Zemstvo organization and the *zemstvo* boards were feeding 250,000 persons in Kazan; in Samara, 179,000; in Saratov, 131,000; in Ufa, 200,000; in Penza, 107,000; in Tambov, 117,000; in Nizhegorod, 87,000; and 100,000 in Simbirsk—1,066,000 persons in all. Moreover, at this time the Red Cross was caring for 209,000 persons, chiefly in Samara. Report of the Famine Relief committee of the Duma, *Stenog. ot.*, I, 1,907, 2,243; A. Suvorin, *Russkii kalendar*, 1908, pp. 175–177; *Bolshaia sovietskaia entsiklopedia*, XIX, 839.

B

UNEMPLOYMENT

In general, it may be noted that there are no complete, official statistics on unemployment for Russia. The data which exist are extremely fragmentary, and are the result of investigations by individuals and trade unions in various cities, and of private investigations. In his work *Isotriia bezrabotitsy v Rossii, 1875–1919* (History of Unemployment in Russia, 1875–1919) L. Kleinbort presents figures based on reports in the periodical press which show that in the first half of 1906 Kharkov had 18,000 unemployed; Tula, 1,000; Tver, 1,500; Poltava, 1,000; Rostov-on-Don, 5,000; Orel, 1,000; Ivanovo-Voznesensk, 1,500; Bielostok, 3,000; while Kazan, Kiev, Batum, Baku, Astrakhan, and the Ural region had 3,000 each. By June, 1906, the St. Petersburg Council of Unemployed had counted 15,776 and with its suburbs, the capital reckoned 30,000 jobless. At the end of the year the Volga provinces were recorded as having 20,000 unemployed, and 10,000 were on the streets in Warsaw. The significance of these figures becomes clearer when it is remembered that according to the official statistics of the factory inspectorate there were 1,683,323 factory workers of both sexes in 1905, and Finn-Enotaevskii puts the figure at 1,894,800 in 1907, in factories employing more than a hundred hands.

See Finn-Enotaevskii, *Sovremmenoe khoziaistvo rossii*, pp. 334,

352–353; *Bolshaia sovietskaia entsiklopediia*, V, 214; Brokhaus i Efron, *Novyi entsiklopedicheskii slovar*, V, 620; A. Suvorin, *Russkii kalendar*, 1909, p. 192.

C

PUBLIC WORKS IN ST. PETERSBURG

PUBLIC works were organized, especially in St. Petersburg, in 1906 as a temporary measure under the pressure of the organized unemployed. In that year the City Duma assigned 500,000 rubles for aid to the unemployed in the form of free kitchens, rentals, the redemption of pledged articles, etc., and created a committee to plan public-works projects which included representatives of the Council of Unemployed. At first many projects were actually realized, the most extensive of which was the construction of earthworks in the Galerny Harbor. The public-works department was awarded many projects which were formerly taken over by private contractors, such as bridge construction work. Until January, 1907, 1,100,000 rubles had been expended on these projects, and 3,450 workers employed. But strenuous opposition was soon offered by the city administration and private contractors, who succeeded in removing 1,500 workers from these projects by the end of 1907. Brokhaus i Efron, *Novyi entsiklopedicheskii slovar*, V, 620.

D

STRIKES

THE official figures of the factory inspectorate department of the ministry of commerce and industry, compiled by V. E. Varzar in *Statistika zabostovok rabochikh na fabrikakh i zavodakh* (Statistics of Strikes of Workers in Factories and Shops), are as follows:

	Number of strikes	Per cent of all factories	Number of workers	Per cent of all workers
1906	6,164	42.2	1,108,406	65.8
1907	3,573	23.8	740,074	41.9

Strikes for purely economic ends were as follows:

	Number of strikes	Per cent of all strikes	Number of workers	Per cent of all strikers
1906	2,545	41.6	457,000	41.7
1907	973	28.0	200,000	27.0

The results of "economic" strikes (in percentages) were:

	Won by workers	Won by employers	Compromises
1906	40.8	25.2	34.0
1907	22.3	45.4	32.3

These figures clearly indicate the stiffening attitude of the employers as the danger of revolution passed away.

See Finn-Enotaevskii, *Sovremmenoe khoziaistvo rossii*, pp. 336–337; Kennard *Russian Year Book*, 1911, pp. 274–275; A. Suvorin, *Russkii kalendar*, 1909, detailed figures for 1905, pp. 202–203.

E

EDUCATION

Two bills introduced by the minister of education were considered by the duma; one on the development of primary education, was introduced on March 12, and the other presented on March 27, on the abolition of the law of April 3, 1892, which forbade teaching in "secret schools," that is, in the native languages, of Lithuania and Poland. In the debates on these measures, the Social-Democrats took no independent stand. In the discussion of the bill on primary education which took place on May 4 and 5, their two orators, Povilius and Mandelberg, spoke as representatives of their respective races, Povilius for the Lithuanians, and Mandelberg for the Jews. The former deplored the persecution of the Lithuanians for teaching their children in their native tongue. Mandelberg attacked the *numerus clausus* for Jews in higher and secondary educational institutions and the restrictions in primary education which drove the children into the "kheder," the small, private religious schools. Here, he maintained, they were maimed, in both body and soul. Public schools, he charged, were developed by the government as nurseries of racial hatred. The bill was taken from the budgetary subcommittee on education to which the duma had sent it, and given to a new Committee on Popular Education. This body was organized on May 28, too late to take even preliminary steps in examining the measure.

On May 21, the Social-Democrats joined in the faint praise which the duma bestowed on the only measure issuing from bureaucratic sources which the opposition regarded as liberal; the abrogation of the law of April 3, 1892. Stashinskii expressed the relief with which the Lithuanians welcomed this act, and the duma quickly adopted the measure by a large majority.

See *Stenog. ot.*, I, 342, 1,157; II, 554–556, 560–563, 567, 902–903, 921–922; *Komissii*, pp. 141–143; *Ukazatel*, p. 41; *Pol. sob., zak.*, XII, no. 8,486.

F

THE LOCAL-COURTS QUESTION

SINCE the consideration of the reform of local justice was in its first stages, and the Social-Democrats had, as yet, taken no part in the general debates, the question is not treated in detail in the text. On March 22, the duma had elected a Committee on the Reform of Local Courts which reported through I. V. Gessen on May 28. It recommended a reform bill whereby the justice of the peace was to be the only legal judge, replacing the *volost* courts, city judges, and the land captains established by the law of July 12, 1889. These judges were to be elected by a majority of the members of local public institutions (*zemstva*, city dumas, etc.,) for three years from among persons over twenty-five years of age who had received an advanced legal education. If such persons could not be found, those over twenty-one years of age who had received a like education might be elected. All elections were to be confirmed by the Ruling Senate.

These judges were to try persons of all classes in civil cases involving moveable objects or real estate valued up to 1,000 rubles. They might try criminal cases not involving limitation or loss of civil status. In considering civil matters the judges might apply local customary law if both sides were agreed to such procedure, and the application of these laws was not forbidden by the imperial civil laws. Matters concerning allotment holdings might be settled according to customary law, but this law might not be applied to non-allotment territory. Finally, the committee recommended that these reforms be introduced into provinces where *zemstva* existed, and into others immediately after the introduction of *zemstva*.

The government had also introduced a measure on March 7, based generally on the same principles but requiring a high property qualification of the judges, and allowing others than those who had received an advanced legal training to hold the posts for as long as six years.

See *Stenog. ot.*, I, 896, 935–937, 1,270; II, 1323–1344, 1372–1401, 1,411–1,434, 1,574–1,591, 1,596–1,604; *Komissii*, pp. 123–238; *Ibid.*, prilozhenie, pp. 551–553; *Ukazatel*, p. 38.

APPENDIX III

A

THE UNITED ZEMSTVO ORGANIZATION

D. N. Shipov, head of the Moscow *Zemstvo* Board, believed, at the outbreak of the war with Japan, that the *zemstva* working together, should be able to provide medical-alimentary aid at the front. Early in 1904, he was instrumental in bringing about an assembly of *zemstvo* representatives in Moscow which created the United *Zemstvo* Organization, in which all *zemstva* were to participate for the relief of the sick and wounded soldiers. Shipov was chosen leader of the movement, and through his initiative field hospitals and canteens were established in Manchuria and Siberia and were placed under the direction of Prince G. E. Lvov. These were nominally under the control of the Red Cross but due to the untiring efforts of Prince Lvov, they achieved a great degree of autonomy. Fourteen *zemstva* legally maintained these establishments with funds which they appropriated for the purpose.

Minister of the Interior Pleve, aroused by these coördinated *zemstvo* activities, decided to put an end to the movement, but Lvov was granted an audience with the tsar and received his public approval of the enterprise. Pleve, however, persisted and forbade all remaining *zemstva* to participate in the Union or even to discuss the movement. He had Shipov removed from the leadership of the organization. But at Pleve's death in July, 1904, these measures were rescinded and all *zemstva* allowed to join the United *Zemstvo* Organization.

After the signing of the Peace of Portsmouth, the field hospitals and canteens were liquidated, but the organization continued to function in famine-relief work, fighting epidemics, providing shelters for peasants who had lost their homes through conflagrations, and in caring for Siberian colonists.

See T. J. Polner, *Russian Local Government During the War and the Union of the Zemstvos*, pp. 53–54; T. J. Polner, *Zhiznennyi put Kniaza Georgiia Evgenievicha Lvova*, pp. 64–90.

B

THE FREE ECONOMIC SOCIETY

THE Free Economic Society was the oldest agricultural organization in the Russian Empire and one of the oldest in Europe. It was founded in 1765 by a group of liberal, educated nobles for the purpose of "disseminating in the empire information beneficial to agriculture and industry." To demonstrate its independence of the government it called itself "free" with the consent of Catherine II. Its activity widened or narrowed according to the policy of the government. Under Paul it was involuntarily inactive for four years, but soon regained its former position under Alexander I. It founded its journal, *Trudy volnago ekonomicheskago obshestva* (Works of the Free Economic Society), established a network of correspondence, and kept in close touch with city and rural administrations. In the course of time it was divided into three general sections and subcommittees for specialized branches of agricultural and statistical work.

In the course of 152 years the society published 280 volumes of *Trudy*, nine other publications, distributed free of charge, millions of copies of books and brochures, including 126 volumes of the committee on literacy (two million copies). It maintained and subsidized agricultural schools and aided progress in many branches by means of exhibitions, competitions, and seed distribution, including the introduction of the potato into Russia.

Its library of 200,000 volumes included the only complete collection of all *zemstvo* publications. It undertook six independent statistical projects, and in 1895 completed a valuable investigation of primary education and literacy under the auspices of its committee on literacy. Because of its energetic, statistical work, the conflicts between this committee and the government were many. Its school in St. Petersburg was suppressed as was the committee itself in 1896 when its funds and publications were confiscated along with the society's history of the committee.

As relations between the government and the progressives became more strained at the beginning of the twentieth century, repression became more active until early in 1900 the government decided to make radical changes in the charter of the society, and temporarily subordinated it to the ministry of agriculture. The society protested by closing all sections thus affected and the new charter, written by a joint committee of government and society representatives, was turned down by the general assembly of the society.

Until 1905, the Free Economic Society was hardly tolerated, and when it gathered, early in 1906, to examine the agricultural question together with members of the First Duma its sessions were closed by the government for the first time in its long history. From then on it continued to exist only in its sections and committees. During the World War it tried to administer the supply of books to Russian war prisoners in Austrian and German camps, but the discovery of revolutionary brochures in their packages (placed there by students) put an end to that activity. The Free Economic Society was dissolved by the Bolsheviki immediately after the November Revolution.

See annual *Otchety o dieistviakh imperatorskago volnago obshestva 1836 po 1916; Istoriia imperatorskago volnago ekonomicheskago obshestva 1796–1865* by A. I. Khodnev; A. N. Beketov, *Istoriia ocherk dieiatelnosti i-go v-go e-go ob-a, 1860–1890; Bolshaia sovietskaia entsiklopediia*, XIII, 51–53; Brokhaus i Efron, *Novyi entsiklopedicheskii slovar*, II, 537–543.

BIBLIOGRAPHICAL NOTE

PRINTED SOURCES

BIBLIOGRAPHICAL

THERE are but two bibliographical compilations which were useful in this study. V. V. Brusianin's *Ukazatel knig i statei o gosudarstvennoi dumie*, Moscow, 1913, is an index of books and articles concerning the activities of the First, Second, and Third Dumas. A. Shilov's *Chto chitat po istorii russkogo revoliutsionnogo dvizheniia*. (What to Read on the History of the Russian Revolutionary Movement), Leningrad, 1922, is, as its subtitle indicates, an index of the most important books, brochures, and articles on all phases of the revolutionary movement. It includes special paragraphs on the Revolution of 1905 and each duma.

GENERAL

THE most valuable, general sources for this investigation are the newspapers *Riech* and *Tovarishch*. *Riech* was the organ of the Kadet Party published by P. N. Miliukov and I. V. Gessen from January, 1906, to the November Revolution in 1917. It is particularly valuable for its special sections. During the electoral period a section was devoted entirely to a description of the course and results of the elections, a detailed summary of which was presented in no. 30 on February 6, 1907. Particularly valuable is the section dedicated to "party life" in which the daily activities of all parties are recorded and party documents are presented in full or are summarized. In the same manner *Riech* presented a daily account of the activities of each fraction while the duma was in session. To cover the activities of the duma it printed a "Duma Supplement" which contained a resumé of all important addresses made in the duma, a description of each session by a special correspondent, a record of the daily activity of the duma committees, and, as noted above, of the activities of each fraction. *Riech* also contained a section on revolutionary acts, the bulletins of the semi-official St. Petersburg Telegraphic Agency and the Information Bureau, and official notices and proclamations. *Tovarishch* was published by E. Kuskova and

S. N. Prokopovich from 1906 to 1910 as a non-partisan Socialist paper. It contained approximately the same information as is presented in *Riech* but had no special duma supplement. It had, however, more detailed information on the activities of the Social-Democratic Party and fraction than the Kadet paper.

Another useful source is the official verbatim report of the proceedings of the Extraordinary Investigating Committee of the Provisional Government, compiled by P. E. Shchegolev and published under the title of *Padenie tsarskogo rezhima* (The Fall of the Tsarist Régime), Leningrad and Moscow, 1924–1927, seven volumes. This committee was established in March, 1917, to investigate higher tsarist officials suspected of "criminal" activities. It examined fifty-nine persons including former ministers, heads of departments, and prominent revolutionary and public figures. The vast amount and variety of evidence given presents an unusually complete picture of Russian public life in the last decades of the Old Régime. This work was published in abridged form in French as *La chute du Régime Tsariste*, Paris, 1927, by J. and L. Polonsky. It contains an interesting historical introduction by B. Maklakov, lawyer and conservative, Kadet member of the Second Duma.

The author has also made wide use of *Krasnyi Arkhiv* (Red Archives), the official journal of the Central Archives of the Russian Socialist Federated Soviet Republic. Publication was begun in 1922 and to date ninety-six volumes have appeared. The material presented concerns, for the most part, modern, Russian, political, diplomatic, and revolutionary history. For this study special use was made of Volumes V, containing Stolypin's correspondence with the tsar; XVI, containing documents pertaining to the dissolution of the Second Duma; XIX, containing the notes of F. A. Golovin; XLIII which has the minutes of the special committee chosen by the duma to investigate the charges brought by the government against the Social-Democratic fraction.

THE DUMA

THE chief source for this work is *Gosudarstvennaia duma. Stenographicheskie otchety* (Imperial Duma. Stenographic Reports) St. Petersburg, 1906–1916, 126 volumes. These are the official verbatim reports of the proceedings of the duma. For this study only the volumes containing the reports of the first two dumas were used; That is, I, Sozyv (First Duma), 1906, 2 vols., and II

Sozyv (Second Duma), 1907, 2 vols. The reports of the secret sessions (28, 29, and 52) were published separately in *Materialy k stenographicheskim otchetam* (Material for the Stenographic Reports), St. Petersburg, 1907. For the volumes on the Second Duma there is an index, *Ukazatel k stenographicheskim otchetam, vtoroi sozyv* (Index to the Stenographic Reports, Second Duma), St. Petersburg, 1907. This contains an index of the occupation, class, age, education, and fraction affiliations of each deputy; an index of the activities of each deputy in the duma, and of each official who had business with the duma (speeches, proposals etc.,); and an index of interpellations. It also contains a directory of the membership of the fractions, and one of the composition of the committees chosen by the duma. Bills presented by the various fractions and groups are to be found in *Gosudarstvennaia dumà, sozyv II. Zakonodatelnyia zaiavleniia vnesennyia na osnovanie st. 55 uchrezhdeniia gosudarstvennoi dumy* (The Second Imperial Duma. Legislative Statements Presented on the Basis of Article 55 of the Duma Statute), St. Petersburg, 1907. Bills presented by the government are included in *Gosudarstvennaia Duma. Vtoroi sozyv. Obzor dieiatelnosti komissii i otdielov, prilozhenie* (Second Imperial Duma. Review of the Activities of the Committees and Sections, Supplement), St. Petersburg, 1907. As the name indicates this volume contains primarily an official account of the activities of the various duma committees. The rules of the duma are to be found in *Materialy po sostavleniiu nakaza gosudarstvennoi dumy* (Materials for the Compilation of the Rules of the Imperial Duma), St. Petersburg, 1907.

LAWS

ALL laws referred to in this study are to be found in *Polnoe sobranie zakonov rossiiskoi imperii. Sobranie tretie.* (Complete Collection of the Laws of the Russian Empire, Third Collection), St. Petersburg, 1885–1916, thirty-four volumes. This is an official collection of laws issued from 1881–1914, arranged chronologically. *Svod zakonov rossiiskoi imperii* (Digest of the Laws of the Russian Empire), St. Petersburg, 1906–1914, sixteen volumes, is a digest of all laws of the empire in force at the time of its publication. In *Modern Constitutions*, Vol. II, Chicago, 1901, W. F. Dodd has included a partial translation of the Fundamental Laws. Another incomplete translation is to be found in *Constitutions of States at War*, Washington, 1919, by H. F.

Wright. In both works, the articles are numbered according to the Complete Collection rather than the Digest as was usual in Russia. The Manifesto of October 17, (October 30, New Style) 1905, is translated in F. A. Golder, *Documents of Russian History*, N. Y. and London, 1927. The electoral law of June 3, 1907, is translated and analyzed by S. N. Harper in *The New Electoral Law for the Russian Empire*, Chicago, 1908.

PARTIES

THE programs and rules of all parties are to be found in V. Ivanovich, *Rossiiskaia partii, soiuzy, i ligi* (Russian Parties, Societies, and Leagues), St. Petersburg, 1906, and in V. V. Vodovozov, *Sbornik programm politicheskikh partii v rossii* (Collection of Programs of Political Parties in Russia), St. Petersburg, 1906. The Kadet platform is presented officially in *Novaia duma, platforma partii narodnoi svobody*, (The New Duma, Platform of the Party of Popular Freedom), St. Petersburg, 1907. The testimony taken by the Extraordinary Investigating Committee which concerned the program and activities of the Union of the Russian People is to be found in *Soiuz russkago naroda* (Union of the Russian People). Moscow, Leningrad, 1929; editor, A. Chernovskii.

THE SOCIAL-DEMOCRATIC PARTY

ALL resolutions adopted by the Social-Democratic Party are to be found in *Vsesoiuznaia kommunisticheskaia partiia (bolshevkov) v resoliutsiakh ee siezdov i konferentsii 1898–1926* (The All-Union Communist Party [Bolshevik] in the Resolutions of its Congresses and Conferences), Moscow, Leningrad, 1927. This is the third edition. The fourth edition was published in 1935 by the Marx-Engels-Lenin Institute under the title *V. K. P. (b) v rezoliutsiakh i resheniakh siezdov, konferentsii i plenumov Tz. K. 1898–1932* (A. C. P. in the Resolutions and Decisions of Congresses, Conferences, and Plenary Sessions of the Central Committee 1898–1932), two vols. Important documents in the history of the Russian Social-Democratic Party including some of the above-mentioned resolutions are collected in *Istoriia R. K. P. (b) v dokumentakh 1883–1916* (History of the Russian Communist Party [Bolshevik] in Documents 1883–1916), Leningrad, 1926, two vols. Its editors are S. M. Levin, V. I. Nevskii, and I. L. Tatarov.

The official (Communist Party) collection of the writings of Lenin is published under the title of *V. I. Lenin, Sobranie sochinenii* (Collection of Works), Moscow. 1921–1925, nineteen vols. A second edition was published in twenty-seven vols., 1927–1930. For this work volumes VII and VIII of the first edition and volume X of the second were used. These are concerned with the period of the first two dumas. Besides the writings of Lenin these collections contain many valuable historical, journalistic, and biographical notes, and resolutions of the Social-Democratic congresses and conferences. *Leninskii sbornik* (Lenin Collection), Moscow, Leningrad, 1924–1936, twenty-nine volumes, contains Lenin's correspondence, memoirs concerning Lenin, and materials pertaining to his literary and political activity. Volume IV containing the outline of the agrarian speech delivered by G. A. Aleksinskii, and volume XII with the fraction letter of March 27 on Stolypin's address were used for this work. V. I. Lenin, *Selected Works*, N. Y., 1935, five volumes, is a translation of some of the writings of the Bolshevik leader. Volume III containing his views on the agrarian problem was used for this study.

The official minutes of the Stockholm (Fourth, or Unification) Congress of the Russian Social-Democratic Party are to be found in *Protokoly obiedinitelnago siezda rossiiskoi sotsialdemokraticheskoi rabochei partii* (Protocols of the Unification Congress of the Russian Social-Democratic Labor Party), Moscow, 1907. The official minutes of the Fifth Congress were published in *Londonskii siezd, polnyi tekst protokolov* (London Congress. Complete Text of the Protocols), Paris, 1909. In 1935, the Marx-Engels Institute in Moscow republished them under the title of *Protokoly piatogo siezda R. S-D. R. P.* (Protocols of the Fifth Congress of the R. S-D. L. P.). Both editions contain detailed statistical material concerning the delegates to the congress and members of the Social-Democratic fraction in the Second Duma (occupation, age, education, repression, soubriquets [in the second edition] etc.,). Reports by Bolshevik leaders, including L. Kamenev, G. Zinoviev, and Lenin, on the congress as a whole, and the various problems discussed, are contained in *Piatyi siezd partii* (The Fifth Party Congress), Moscow, 1923. This volume also includes a statistical article on the delegates and the Social-Democratic deputies by M. Liadov: "Londonskii siezd v tsifrakh" (The London Congress in Figures).

Zhiznennyi put Kniaza G. E. Lvova (The Life of Prince G. E. Lvov), Paris, 1932, is, to be exact, not a memoir but a collection of the correspondence of and facts concerning Prince Lvov by his secretary, T. I. Polner. It contains much information concerning *zemstvo*, *Zemstvo* Union work, and the period of the Revolution of 1905. Similar information is to be found in *Vospominaniia i dumy o perezhitom* (Memoirs and Thoughts on the Past) by D. N. Shipov, Moscow, 1918.

In *Ternii bez roz* (Thorns Without a Rose) there are assembled memoirs of Social-Democratic deputies Dzhaparidze, Gerus, Mandelberg, Mitrov, Nestorov, and Tsereteli on the activities of the Social-Democratic fraction in the Second Duma. It also contains the proclamation of the fraction after the dissolution of the duma and the arrest of many of the Marxist deputies, the fraction's reply to the government's accusations, and the minutes of the first day of the trial of the fraction. G. A. Aleksinskii's article in *Obrazovanie*, no. 4, St. Petersburg, 1908, entitled "Iz perezhitago" (From the Past) contains a description of the fraction's non-parliamentary activities, and an analysis of the many instructions which he received. V. Mandelberg's *Iz perezhitago*, Davos, Switzerland, 1916, gives a vivid picture of his election and many phases of the duma's activity. *Vtoraia gosudarstvennaia duma* (The Second Imperial Duma), St. Petersburg, 1908, by A. G. Zurabov, also describes the proceedings in the duma and explains the "Zurabov incident." V. Voitinskii, author of the fateful instruction of the Social-Democratic military group in St. Petersburg, gives a detailed account of the circumstances surrounding the writing of the "instruction" in *Gody pobied i porazhenii* (Years of Victory and Defeat), Berlin, 1924, two vols.

From the Kadet point of view, A. A. Kizevetter discusses the electoral period and the activities of the duma in *Na rubezhe dvukh stoletii* (On the Boundary of Two Centuries), Prague, 1929. I. V. Gessen presents a lively account of the journalistic background of the period as well as a narrative of the events in the Second Duma in *V dvukh viekakh* (In Two Centuries), vol. XXII of *Arkhiv russkoi revoliutsii* (Archive of the Russian Revolution), Berlin, 1937. Gessen is himself editor of the series. The moderate Kadet position on the duma is best presented by V. A. Maklakov in *Vlast i obshchestvennost na zakatie staroi rossii* (*vospominaniia*) [Authority and Society at the Decline of Old

Russia (Memoirs)], Paris, 1928, three volumes. Here Maklakov, Kadet leader and member of the Second Duma, discusses
his own background, the liberation movement, the Revolution
of 1905, the Kadet party, and the duma as a legislative organ.
His views on the duma are also presented in an article entitled
"Iz proshlago" (From the Past) which appeared in *Sovremennyia
zapiski* (Contemporary Journal), nos. 40–44, 46–48, 50, 51, 53,
54, 56, 58, 60, Paris, 1929–1936. The period of the Second Duma
is discussed from an official standpoint by V. N. Kokovtsov in
Out of My Past, Memoirs of Count Kokovtsov, translated by L.
Matveev, Palo Alto, Calif., 1935. The original Russian edition,
Iz moego proshlago, was published in Paris, in 1933. The official
view is also presented in *The Memoirs of Alexander Izvolsky*,
London, 1920, translated by C. L. Seeger. Two other cabinet
members of the period have written their memoirs. V. I. Gurko,
assistant minister of the interior in 1906–1907, has written an
informative, if prejudiced, narrative of public events during the
first two decades of the present century. This memoir is published in English as *Features and Figures of the Past. Government
and Opinion in the Reign of Nicholas II.*, J. E. Wallace Sterling,
Xenia J. Eudin, H. H. Fisher editors, and L. Matveev, translator,
Stanford University, Calif., London, 1939. *Vospominaniia, iz
bumag S. E. Kryzhanovskago, posliednago gosudarstvennago sekre-
tariia rossiiskoi imperii* (Memoirs, from the Papers of S. E.
Kryzhanovskii, Last State Secretary of the Russian Empire),
Berlin, 1938, is an account of the public record of the assistant
secretary of the interior in 1907 who directed the writing of the
electoral law of June 3, 1907. The tsar's attitude toward the
duma is clearly reflected in his letters to his mother published
by J. Bing as *Letters of Tsar Nicholas and the Empress Marie*,
London, 1938. B. Pares, *My Russian Memoirs*, London, 1931,
presents a factual picture of the period of the first two dumas
from the vantage point of an English correspondent.

REFERENCE WORKS

OF the pre-revolutionary reference works the best known was
Entsiklopedicheskii slovar (Encyclopedic Dictionary), St. Petersburg, 1890–1904, forty-one vols. In 1906, two supplementary
volumes were added. The chief editor of this work is I. E.
Andreevskii. The encyclopedia is commonly known by the name
of its publishers F. A. Brokhaus (Leipzig), and I. A. Efron (St.
Petersburg). The same firm published the *Novyi ontsiklopedi-*

cheskii slovar (New Encyclopedic Dictionary), St. Petersburg, 1912–1916. Of this work only twenty-nine volumes were completed (A—Otto). The house of N. A. Granat published an extensive *Entsiklopedicheskii slovar*, Moscow, 1890–1917, forty volumes. Of special interest for this study is vol. XVII containing brief biographies of all members of the first three dumas. A great wealth of information is to be found in A. Suvorin, *Russkii kalendar* (Russian Calendar), St. Petersburg, 1872–1917, forty-five volumes. This is an almanac containing general and statistical information concerning religion, geography, population, financial affairs, trade, agriculture, means of communication, insurance, and all branches of government and departments of state service in Russia. It also includes a chronicle of both world and Russian events and a necrology containing interesting biographical notes. All statistical materials are derived from official sources which are named. The volumes for 1907, 1908, and 1909 have been used extensively for this work.

The chief reference work published by the Soviet government is *Bolshaia sovietskaia entsiklopediia* (Large Soviet Encyclopedia). Publication of this work was begun in Moscow in 1926 and is as yet unfinished. When complete it will contain sixty-five volumes, but to date there are at hand only vols. I to XXI (A—Dzhut), XXIII (Dode—Evraziia), XXV to XXVII (Zhelezo—Imperializm), and LIX–LXV (Frantsoz—Iaia). O. I. Shmidt is general editor. A draft of the completed work was published as the *Malaia sovietskaia entsiklopediia* (Small Soviet Encyclopedia), Moscow, 1928–1933, ten vols. Its chief editor is N. L. Meshcheriakov. The Pan-Union Society of Political Prisoners and Exiles (*Vsesoiuznoe obshchestvo politicheskikh katorzhan i ssylno-poselentsev*) is now publishing *Dieiateli revoliutsionago dvizhenie v rossii*. (Agents of the Revolutionary Movement in Russia). Publication was begun in 1927 and to date five volumes have been issued. This work contains biographical notes on all important figures in the Russian revolutionary movement. From the earliest period to the end of the eighties of the past century (I–IV) the work is complete. For the Social-Democrats from 1880–1904 it is complete to Gm. (V).

PERIODICALS

FOR contemporary comment on political events, besides *Riech* and *Tovarishch*, noted above, three periodical publications are helpful. *Byloe* (Past) edited by V. L. Burtsev, appeared irregularly in Paris and London from 1901 to 1904, in St. Petersburg in 1907 and 1908, and then from 1917 to 1927. It was dedicated to matters pertaining to the liberation movement and was Populist (*Narodnik*) in temper. A second important Populist publication *Russkoe bogatstvo* (Russian Wealth) appeared in St. Petersburg from 1876 to 1914 when it was closed by the government, and again in 1917 and 1918. It was founded by N. K. Mikhailovskii and after the Revolution of 1905 under V. G. Korolenko it became the organ of the Popular-Socialists and was reckoned as one of the leading politico-literary publications in the country. *Viestnik Evropy* was founded in 1802 by N. M. Karamzin, and appeared regularly during 1866–1914 as a literary and political journal. Of special interest are its articles on "Domestic Affairs" edited by K. K. Arsenev from 1880 to 1912. The journal had no political affiliations, but its point of view was moderately liberal.

SECONDARY MATERIALS

ONLY the most important and helpful secondary works are included here. The list is not exhaustive.

GENERAL

FOR an outline of the events of the Revolution of 1905 up to and including the Second Duma see J. Mavor, *An Economic History of Russia*, II, Book IV, N. Y., 1925. P. N. Miliukov, *Russia and its Crisis*, Chicago, 1906, has presented a general background of the period and has stressed the prevailing political philosophies. Bernard Pares in *Russia and Reform*, London, 1907, gives the political background and events of the First Duma, and of the inter-duma period in the concluding chapters. These have a special value since Pares was then correspondent for the *Spectator* and *Westminster Gazette* in Russia. G. Vernadsky in *A Political and Diplomatic History of Russia*, Boston, 1936, presents a similar account including the period of the Second Duma. D. M. Wallace has presented one of the best works in English on the general social, political, and economic background in *Russia*, N. Y., 1905. Recently Sir Bernard Pares has developed the background for the constitutional era in *The Fall of the Russian Monarchy*, London, 1939.

The agricultural question which played so great a rôle in the duma period is fully discussed by G. Pavlovskii in *Agricultural Russia on the eve of the Revolution*, London, 1930; by G. T.

Robinson in *Rural Russia*, N. Y., 1932, and by A. N. Chelintsev in *Selsko-khoziaistvenaia geografiia rossii* (Agricultural Geography of Russia), Prague, 1924. Each of these works is well supplied with statistical data, especially the last named (Chelintsev). M. S. Miller treats the subject broadly in *The Economic Development of Russia 1905–1914*, London, 1936, in connection with the development of commerce, industry, and finance. An informative work on industrial development which includes much statistical material is A. Finn-Enotaevskii, *Kapitalizm v rossii 1890–1917* (Capitalism in Russia 1890–1917), Moscow, 1925. This is written from a Marxist standpoint.

Special information on the activities and attitudes of peasant and worker during the revolution and first two dumas is to be found in V. Gorn, *Krestianstvo i revoliutsiia* (The Peasantry and Revolution), St. Petersburg, 1907 (?); S. Piontkovskii, *Istoriia rabochego dvizheniia v rossii* (History of the Labor movement in Russia), Leningrad, 1925; A. Shestakov, *Krestianstvo v revoliutsii 1905 goda* (The Peasantry in the Revolution of 1905), Leningrad, 1930, and in a number of articles, the most important of which are D. Koltsov, "Rabochie v 1905–1907 gg." in *Obshchestvennoe dvizhenie v Rossii v nachale xx go veka*, II, Part 1, St. Petersburg, 1910 (See below Secondary Materials, Parties): E. A. Morokhovets, "Krestianskoe dvizhenie 1905–1907 gg. i sotsial-demokratiia" in the Soviet publication *Proletarskaia revoliutsiia* (Proletarian Revolution), nos. 37 to 43, 1925.

Stolypin received special treatment by I. Izgoev in *P. A. Stolypin*, Moscow, 1912. This is a short biography of the premier who had recently been assassinated, and deals mainly with his work as head of the government. In an article in *Viestnik Evropy*, 1912, Part 2, entitled "Iz istoricheskim materialam o pokoinom P. A. Stolypina" (From Historical Material on the Late P. A. Stolypin), P. A. Tverskoi recalled an interview with the premier from notes which he took on the occasion. Since the writer appeared as a correspondent for the Associated Press, Stolypin carefully expounded his position on the most vital problems facing his administration for the benefit of the American public.

The elections to the Second Duma are fully described by A. Smirnov in *Kak proshly vybory vo vtoruiu gosudarstvennuiu dumie* (How Elections to the Second Imperial Duma Resulted), St. Petersburg, 1907. Smirnov was a provincial correspondent for *Riech* and had at hand much material available both to *Riech* and *Tovarishch* which he incorporated into his work. There are no official statistics on elections available. *Riech* presented its compilation of the results in no. 30, 1907. The Menshevik stand in the electoral campaign is ably presented by L. Martov in *Izbiratelniia soglasheniia*, St. Petersburg, 1907.

There has been comparatively little written on the Second Duma, and the only significant works are, properly speaking, contemporary comment. The articles of P. N. Miliukov, Kadet leader, written chiefly for *Riech*, and his lectures on the duma, are collected in *Vtoraia Duma* (Second Duma), St. Petersburg, 1908. Here the electoral period and each question before the duma is discussed from a Kadet point of view, and the Kadet tactics on each question are presented and fully explained. In "The Case of the Second Duma," *Contemporary Review*, XCII, 1907, Miliukov presented a spirited defense of the duma against charges of radicalism and incompetence. *Constitutional Government for Russia*, N. Y., 1908, is an address which Miliukov delivered before the Civic Forum at Carnegie Hall on January 14, 1908 (New Style). Miliukov made the trip from Russia especially for the speech in which he described the Revolution of 1905 to the dissolution of the Second Duma. A. I. Kaminka and V. Nabokov, *Vtoraia gosudarstvennaia duma* (The Second Imperial Duma), St. Petersburg, 1907, and V. Obninskii, *Novy Stroi* (New Structure), Moscow, 1911, are likewise detailed accounts of the events which transpired in the Second Duma as described and analyzed by liberals. Octobrist V. I. Gerie presented the same subject in *Vtoraia gosudarstvennaia duma*, Moscow, 1907. The Bolsheviki K. Nikitin and I. Stepanov analyzed the proceedings in the duma and criticized the Social-Democratic fraction from the Leninist standpoint in *Dieiatelnost vtoroi gosudarstvennoi dumy* (The Activity of the Second Imperial Duma), Moscow, 1907. The activity of the Social-Democratic fraction in the Second Duma is sympathetically presented by M. Mikhailovskii in *Sotsial-Demokraticheskoi fraktsii vo vtoroi gosudarstvennoi dumie*, St. Petersburg, 1907. Photographs of the leading deputies of each fraction are to be found in A. J. Sack, *The Birth of Russian Democracy*, N. Y., 1918, pp. 149–156.

PARTIES

Obshchestvennoe dvizhenie v rossii v nachale XX-ago vieka (Social Movements in Russia at the Beginning of the Twentieth Century), edited by L. Martov, P. Maslov, and A. Potresov, St. Petersburg, 1909–1914, is an extensive and detailed analysis of the social and political movements of the designated period from a Marxist point of view. Of special interest is an article on the "Second Duma" by F. Dan in Vol. II, Part 2. A review of the principles and aims of the Popular-Socialist Party is to be found in *Trudovaia (narodno sotsialisticheskaia) partiia* (Labor [Popular-Socialist] Party), St. Petersburg, 1907, by the Popular-Socialist leader A. V. Pieshekhonov. A hostile but informative analysis of the aims of the Trudovik Party is given by N. P. Vasiliev in *Chto takoe trudoviki?* (What are Trudovki?), St. Petersburg, 1907. The Trudovik T. V. Lokot has presented a clear picture of the position of each party represented in the First Duma in *Politicheskiia partii i gruppy v gosudarstvennoi dumie* (Political Parties and Groups in the Imperial Duma), Moscow, 1907.

The official Bolshevik history of the Social-Democratic Party is to be found in *Bolshaia sovietskaia entsiklopediia*, XI. Another, more detailed, official history of the party was edited by E. Iaroslavskii, namely, *Istoriia V. K. P. (b)*, (History of the Pan-Russian Communist Party [Bolshevik]), Moscow, 1926–1930, four volumes. For the present study volume II is of especial interest, particularly the information given on the military groups by Iaroslavskii who was one of their leaders. N. Popov's *Outline History of the Communist Party of the Soviet Union*, N. Y. 1934, was translated into English under the guidance of A. Fineberg. This is a complete, general history of the party from a rabid Stalinist standpoint. A. I. Spiridovich, a tsarist police official, compiled the factual and critical *Istoriia bolshevizma* (History of Bolshevism), Paris, 1922, from official documents to which he had access before the revolution of 1917. In *Lenin, Red Dictator*, New Haven, 1931, G. Vernadsky had included a general outline of the development and policies of the Social-Democratic Party. The party's agrarian program is explained and defended by N. Valentinov in *Krestianstvo i zemelnaia programma sotsial-demokraticheskoi partii v rossii* (The Peasantry and the Land Program of the Social-Democratic Party in Russia), Moscow, 1906.

ADDITIONAL BIBLIOGRAPHY

A considerable volume of literature directly or indirectly related to duma studies has appeared since the original publication of this work. In areas directly related to the duma period there have been relatively few studies and some significant sources have come to the attention of the author. In the area of party studies there has been, of course, a veritable torrent of materials on the Social-Democrats, particularly on its Bolshevik segment and an increasing interest hás developed in the liberal, conservative and rightist parties. Among the more significant items are both source and secondary materials concerning some of the major figures of the duma period.

A *post mortem* debate on the strengths and weaknesses of the liberal program and policies has engendered a number of important works that would fall within the category of apologetica or, more nearly, memoirs. V. A. Maklakov is represented by his *Pervaiai gosudarstvennaia duma; vospominanlia sovremennika* (The First Imperial Duma; Memoirs of a Contemporary, Paris, 1939. This has been translated by Mary Belkin as *The First State Duma,* Bloomington, Indiana: Indiana University Russian and East European Series, Vol. 30, 1964); *Vtoraia gosudarstvennaia duma; vospominaniia sovremennika* (The Second Imperial Duma; Memoirs of a Contemporary), Paris, 1949 and *Iz vospominaniia* (From Memoirs), New York, 1954. These writings offer the argument that the Kadets blundered in the period when they could have influenced events (that of the first two dumas) by cooperating with the parties to their left and by failing to cooperate with the government. A counterblast justifying Kadet policy is offered by P. N. Miliukov in *Vospominaniia* (Memoirs), N. Y., 1952. V. A. Maklakov's speeches are published in *V. A. Maklakov. Riechi, sudebnyia, dumskiia i publichnyia lektsiia 1904–1926* (V. A. Maklakov, Speeches, Duma and Public Lectures 1904–1926), Paris, 1949.

A considerable bibliography concerning P. A. Stolypin reflects a growing interest in, and appreciation of, the stature of this late statesman of the old regime. His official pronouncements for the period concerned are to be found in *Predsiedatel sovieta ministrov Peter Arkad'evich Stolypin sostavleno E. V.*

386 THE SECOND DUMA

po soobshcheniiam pressa za tri goda (8 Iiul 1906 g - 8 Iiul 1909 g.) (President of the Council of Ministers Peter Arkad-'evich Stolypin Compiled by E. V. from Press Reports for three years [8 July 1906 – 8 July 1909]). A small but consistent flow of memoirs has been appearing since his death. In Vol. I. No. 2 (1912) of the *Russian Review* (London), S. Syromatnikov, the editor of Stolypin's semiofficial organ *Rossiia,* published his "Reminiscences of Stolypin." N. Savitsky wrote an ambitious biographical appraisal of Stolypin in serialized form in *Monde Slave,* IV (1933), pp. 227–263, 360–383; IV (1934), pp. 378–403; II (1935), pp 41–61; I (1936), pp. 340–381. Stolypin's daughter, M. P. Bock, published her personal memoirs in *Vospominaniia o moem otse P. A. Stolypine* (Memoirs About My Father P. A. Stolypin). Leonid I. Strakhovsky, "The Statesmanship of Peter Stolypin: A Reappraisal," *Slavonic And East European Review,* Vol. 37 (June 1959), pp. 348–70 and Alfred Levin, "Peter Arkad'evich Stolypin: A Political Appraisal," *Journal of Modern History,* December, 1965, analyze the constitutionalist aspects of his activity. His migration policy is presented in D. W. Treadgold, *The Great Siberian Migration,* Princeton, 1957.

Samuel N. Harper, *The Russia I Believe In; The Memoirs of Samuel N. Harper, 1902–1941,* Chicago, 1945 and Sir Bernard Pares, *A Wandering Student: The Story of a Purpose,* Syracuse, N. Y., 1948 represent the memoires of leading American and British scholars respectively with heavy emphasis on the duma period.

A significant periodical not mentioned heretofore is the *Russian Review* published in London 1912–14, by Sir Bernard Pares. It contains numerous articles by significant duma figures and experts on Russian affairs and representative speeches given in the duma.

The most considerable interest of historians of the Russian party structure before 1917 has been focused on the Social Democratic Party. Much of it has been a by-product of the study of the Communist Party. Among the more significant works we may note Robert V. Daniels, *A Documentary History of Communism,* New York, 1960; Alfred G. Meyer, *Leninism,* Cambridge, Mass., 1957 and *Communism,* New York, 1960; Leopold H. Haimson, *The Russian Marxists and the Origins of Bolshevism,* Cambridge, Mass., 1955; John Reshetar Jr., *A*

Concise History of the Communist Party of the Soviet Union, New York, 1960; Leonard Schapiro, *The Communist Party of the Soviet Union,* New York, 1960; Donald W. Treadgold, *Lenin and His Rivals,* New York, 1955. The last work includes the socialist and liberal opposition to the Bolsheviks in the nineteenth and twentieth centuries. For biographies of Lenin see Bertram D. Wolfe, *Three Who made a Revolution,* New York, 1948; David Shub, *Lenin: A Biography,* New York, 1948; Louis Fischer, *The Life of Lenin,* N.Y., 1964; Samuel H. Baron, *Plekhanov, The Father of Russian Marxism,* Stanford, California, 1963, reflects both early Social-Democratic development and the career of the Menshevik leader. The more moderate Marxists are treated in Arthur P. Mendel's *Dilemmas of Progress in Tsarist Russia: Legal Marxism and Legal Populism,* Cambridge, Mass., 1961.

For the non-Marxist groups, Franco Venturi's *Roots of Revolution: A History of the Socialist and Populist Movements in Nineteenth Century Russia,* London, 1960, is an encyclopedic study of the ideological development and personalities of the populist movement. Oliver E. Radkey, *The Agrarian Foes of Bolshevism: Promise and Default of the Social Revolutionaries, February to October 1917,* New York, 1963 is the most complete study of the S-R's. Intellectual and institutional approaches to the study of liberalism are represented by George Fischer, *Russian Liberalism: From Gentry to Intelligentsiia,* Cambridge, Mass., 1958 and Jacob Walkin, *The Rise of Democracy in pre-Revolutionary Russia; Political and Social Institutions Under the last Three Tsars,* New York, 1962. The right of the Russian political scene as well as the right of center is a relatively new area of study and is still largely under investigation. The background for modern nationalism in Russia is lucidly presented by Edward C. Thaden, *Conservative Nationalism in Nineteenth-century Russia,* Seattle, Washington, 1964. The rightist parties in the Duma are discussed in Alfred Levin, "The Reactionary Tradition in the Elections to the Third Duma," *Oklahoma State University Arts and Sciences Studies* (Social Studies No. 8, Stillwater, Oklahoma, June, 1962) in Hans Rogger, "The Formation of the Russian Right, 1900 to 1906," *California Slavic Studies,* Vol. III, 1964, pp. 66–94, and "Was There a Russian Fascism," *Journal of Modern History,* December 1964, pp. 398–415.

A number of useful studies directly concerned with the activities of the Second Duma include Pierre Charles, *Le Parlement Russe, son organisation, ses rapports avec l'empereur,* Paris 1910; Alfred Levin, "June 3, 1907: Action and Reaction," in *Essays in Russian History: A Collection Dedicated to George Vernadsky,* Hamden, Conn., 1964. These works are concerned with the legal structure and position of the Duma before and after the promulgation of the electoral law of June 3, 1907. Warren B. Walsh has analyzed the composition of the Second Duma in "The Composition of the Dumas," *Russian Review* (New York and Hanover, New Hampshire), Vol 8, No. 2 (1949), pp. 111–16 and "Political Parties in the Russian Dumas," *Journal of Modern History,* Vol. 22 (1950), pp. 144–50. A number of other significant articles include Paul Miliukov, "The Case of the Second Duma," *Contemporary Review,* Vol. 92 (1907), pp. 457–67; Bernard Pares, "The Second Duma," *Slavonic and East European Review (SEER),* Vol. 2 (1923), pp. 36–55 and "Alexander Guchkov," *SEER,* Vol. 15 (1936), pp. 121–34; Alfred Levin, "The Fifth Social-Democratic Party and the Duma," *Journal of Modern History,* Vol. 11 (1939) pp. 484–508) and "The Shornikova Affair," *American Slavonic and East European Review (ASEER),* Vol. 22, Part 2, (1943) pp. 1–18; Levitsky, S. L., "Legislative Initiative in the Russian Duma," *ASEER,* Vol. 15 (1956), pp. 313–24.

ADDITIONS AND CORRECTIONS
TO TEXT AND FOOTNOTES

p. 4, footnote 6. Add: In the sense that it broadened the base of the City Duma.

p. 10, line 13. "Dr." should read "Professor"

p. 14, footnote 20. Add: This was immediately before the opening of the First Duma.

p. 19, footnote 23. Replace . at end with ; and add: *Pol. sob. zak.*, XXVI, No. 28105.

p. 27, line 10. "Fascism" should read "Naziism" in its tactical, racist, extreme nationalist, anti-liberal and anti-leftist connotations

p. 29, footnote 5. Add: These landowners represented the minority of the zemstvo congress of December, 1905 who opposed the demand for a constituent assembly and favored a duma which would cooperate with the government rather than dictate to it. *Obshchestvennoe dvishenie v Rossii v nachale xx-go veka*, III, pp. 171–175; Shipov, *op. cit.*, pp. 403–404.

p. 41, footnote 24. Add: Although elected first president of the Soviet as a non-partisan, Khrustalev identified himself as a Social-Democrat. After the London Congress in 1907 he left the S-D party. See *Entsiklopedicheskii Slovar Granat*, t. 45–3, pp. 63–64.

p. 75, line 31. "acive" should read "active"

p. 78, line 6. "Dogorukov" should read "Dolgorukov"

p. 78, line 14. "immoral" should read "amoral"

p. 114, footnote 31, line 2. replace "law" with "agricultural science"; line 10. replace . at end of footnote with ; and add: Alfred Levin, "Peter Arkad'evich Stolypin: a Political Appraisal," *Journal of Modern History*, December, 1965.

p. 129, footnote 19, line 2. "cabinet" should read "the proper ministry"

p. 162,   line 8. "1895" should read "1905"

p. 162,   footnote 19. "26,127" should read "26,172"

p. 163,   footnote 24. Add: In the northwestern provinces where he owned extensive holdings, Stolypin observed the peasant enclosure movement and as governor of Grodno and Saratov provinces he had promoted enclosure and zealously argued in its favor in reports to the Crown. N. Savitski, "P. A. Stolypin," *Monde Slave*, 1933, No. 4, pp. 229–234, 244–245; *Krasnyi Arkhiv*, vol. 17, pp. 88–89; Levin, "Peter Arkad'evich Stolypin," *loc. cit.*

p. 190,   footnote 84. Replace . after "Congress" with ; and add: Alfred Levin, "The Fifth Social-Democratic Congress and the Duma," *Journal of Modern History*, December, 1939, pp. 384–508.

p. 211,   footnote 23.   Add: It should be noted that the opposition deeply resented the 1906 loan obtained from French financial circles. See Olga Crisp, "The Russian liberals and the Anglo-French loan to Russia," *Slavonic and East European Review*, Vol. 39, pp. 508–511.

p. 217,   three lines from bottom of page. Delete "42" (indicating footnote No.)

p. 231,   line 5. "Arkadievich" should read "Arkad'evich"

See p. 240,   line 23. The following is a more correct statement on the provisions of the Law of June 3, 1907 concerning the suffrage of national minorities: Polish seats in the duma were reduced from thirty-three to fourteen and in the cities of Warsaw, Lublin and Siedlets and in Vilno and Kovno provinces one deputy was assigned to the Russian population for each city or province. The representation of Asiatic Russia was reduced from forty-four to fifteen and half of the deputies from the area east of Lake Baikal were to be Cossack. The number of deputies in the Transcaucasus was reduced from twenty-nine to ten and the Russian population provided with a deputy for whom the Russian clergy voted even if they had no suffrage qualifications. The "backward" steppe region and Central Asia which lost its representation included several urban centers of over 100,000 population. In the frontier provinces with multiracial composition the population was divided into national curiae (or could be at the governor's discretion) and the Russians given a disproportionate advantage.

p. 262,   line 30. "feudal" should read "landed"

p. 308,   footnote 2. Add: For the history and motivation of the new electoral law see Alfred Levin, "June 3, 1905: Action and Reaction," in Alan D. Ferguson and Alfred Levin, eds., *Essays in Russian History: A Collection Dedicated to George Vernadsky,* pp. 247–255.

p. 311,   footnote 11. Add: See Alfred Levin, "The Shornikova Affair," *American Slavonic* and *East European Review,* XXII (1943), Part 2, pp. 1–18.

p. 331,   footnote 68. Add: See footnote 60.

p. 341,   line 25. Add: An inhibitive factor was added as the non-taxpaying apartment renters were required to register before voting.

p. 357,   first par., last line. "with" should read "within"

p. 358,   line 20. "written" should read "edited"

p. 381,   first par. under GENERAL, line 15. Delete "recently"

p. 381,   next to the last line. "Pavlovskii" should read "Pavlovsky"

p. 382,   line 22. Colon after "Parties" should be a semicolon

INDEX

Abramson, S. G., on temporary meeting place, 108

Academy of Science, representatives of, in Imperial Council, 15

Adamov, at S–D military conference, 281 n

Administration. *See* Government

Adzhemov, M. S., reports on Law of Nov. 6, 1906, 284; on recruits bill, 290 n; counsel for S–D deputies, 345, 346

Afanasev, A. G., on land question, 180 n

Aframovich, K. M., in Agrarian Committee, 183 n; order excepts from arrest, 324 n

Agrarian Committee, in First Duma, 19; S–D's call for, 178; election of, 182–183, 183 n; leftists in, unite, 188–189; activity of, 192–193; functions of, 193; crisis in, 193; evolves reform bill, 199; debates on, 231; report of, 359

Agrarian debates, special days for, 181; endless speechmaking in, 180, 183, 185; loss of interest in, 185–186; closing of, 189–190; effect of, on government, 308

Agrarian depression, effect of, on land economy, 159–160

Agrarian reform, *Zemstvo* Congress demands, 6; in First Duma, 19, 156, 198; of government, 22, 23, 115, 189, 231, 332, 334, 336, 350; in Kadet program, 33; in Trudovik program, 36; in S–D resolutions, 44; S–D's on, 44–45, 85; right on, 119; projects of, 163–173; Trudovik project, 167–168; P–S project, 168–169; S–R project, 169; *Narodnik* projects, 169; Kadet project, 170–171, 190–191; S–D project, 172–173; debates on, 176–192, 358;

N. N. Kutler's project, 178 n; Stolypin on, 187–188; disunion of opposition on, 166, 199; S–D proclamation on, 323 n; agreement on, 355

See also Law of Nov. 9, 1906

Agriculture, stagnation of, in 19th century, 5

Agriculture, Ministry of, controls resettlement, 162; in Kadet land committee, 171; interpellations to, 194–195, 243 n; on resettlement, 195

Aladin, A. F., peasant leader, 18, 61

Aleksinskii, G. A., Bolshevik orator, 71; in fraction committee, 73; at workers' meetings, 80 n; deputy for St. Petersburg, 99; defends election, 99; on fall of ceiling, 108; assails right, 120; on Famine–Relief Committee, 125, 128, 130, 131; on Unemployment Committee, 125, 148–149; gets Trudovik support, 132; in Famine–Relief Committee, 133 n; on unemployment, 145; assails Kadets, 146, 179; secretary of Unemployment Committee, 152; official agrarian orator, 176; on limitation of debates, 181; in Agrarian Committee, 183 n; on land question, 184–185; on Agrarian Committee, 184; on chairman of Agrarian Committee, 192–193; on budget, 209; precipitates uproar, 210 n; on Riga Prison interpellation, 247; on field-courts-martial, 266–267; on recruits bill, 289–290, 302–303; on army, 292; assails Golovin, 303; order for arrest of, 325 n

Alexander I, organizes Imperial Council, 2

Alexander III, russification policy of, 6; restricts minorities, 6

relief bill, 140–141; official agrarian orator, 176; on land question, 189–190; in Budget Committee, 215 n; on real estate tax, 224–225; on Riga Prison interpellation, 246, 247; apartment of, 314; on instruction of military group, 315; on immunity of deputies, 316; order for arrest of, 325 n

Pan-Russian S-D Labor Party Conference, 55–57

Parchevskii, A. I., in Committee on Arrest of S-D's, 331 n

Parliament. See Duma

Parliamentary government, liberals support, 31; lack of tradition of, 356–357

Partisan attacks, public reaction to, 47; S-D resolution on, 47; in press, 276

Party Congress, S-D, relation of, to fraction, 74

Party of Democratic Reform, in duma, 34 n; in First Duma, 67; deputies of, 67

Party of Peaceful Restoration, doctrine of, 34 n; legalization of, 63

Party of Popular Freedom. See Kadet Party

Passage to regular order, formulae of, on government statement, 110, 111, 114, 119, 121, 122; formula of, on famine-relief bill, 140–141; formulae of, on land reform, 189, 192; formula of, on resettlement, 198; formulae of, on Riga Prison interpellation, 253–254; formula of, on Lanchukhti interpellation, 257–258; formula of, on Gershelmann interpellation, 259; formulae of, on army, 292, 300–301, 303–304

Passports, in S-D fraction headquarters, 324, 337–338, 347

Paul I, grants serfs, 177

Pavlov, A. A., meets with Famine-Relief Committee, 133, 135

Pavlov, V., assassination of, 21n

Peasant Land Bank, sells land, 11, 22, 160; reorganization of, 115; regulation of, 160; under Witte, 161;

under Stolypin, 163; in "Project of 104," 167; Budget Committee on 216 n

Peasants, in elections. 8–9, 19, 65, 65 n, 99–100; in Revolution of 1905, 10; in Law of Dec. 11, 1905, 13; class legislation on, 22; demands of, 27; in Union of the Russian People, 28; in Octobrist program, 30; chief concern of Populists, 35; P-S's on, 35; representatives of, 36; in S-R program, 37; S-D's on 44–46, 56, 77, 236; Lenin on, 54; multiple voting of, 61; in First and Second Dumas, 69; in S-D fraction, 70; petitions of, to S-D fraction, 81; delegations of, to S-D fraction, 82; emancipation of, 156; landholdings of, 156–157, 158, 163; landless, 158; low productivity of, 159; in Kadet land committee, 171; restrictions on, 173; in agrarian debates, 180–181, 180 n, 185; Stolypin on, 187; decline in movement of, 233; in army, 279, S-D work among, 324; in Law of June 3, 1907, 340, 341; understanding of constitution by, 357

Pleasant Union, organization of, 6

Penza, crop failures in, 220 n

People's Will, formation of, 35 n; predecessor of S-R party, 37

Peter I, dictum of, on autocracy, 2; subordinates church to state, 2; creates bureaucracy, 3; reforms of, 350

Pereleshin, Dr. D. A., on famine, 126 n

Pergament, O. I., reports on Riga Prison interpellation, 248–250; biographical note, 248 n; reports on bill on praise of crime, 276–277; in Committee on Arrest of S-D's, 331 n, 336–337; counsel for S-D deputies, 345, 346

Peterson, B. L., secretary of Audit Committee, 225

Petitions, to S-D fraction, 81–82, 244; as revolutionary material, 83; to duma, 234; S-D's on, 343

Petrochenko, F. I., on agrarian question, 144, 176 n